Forms of Muslim Children's Spirituality

Studies in Critical Pedagogy, Theology, and Spirituality

Series Editor

James D. Kirylo (*University of South Carolina, USA*)

Editorial Board

Drick Boyd (*Professor Emeritus, Eastern University, USA*)
Nathaniel Bryan (*Miami University, USA*)
Antonia Darder (*Loyola Marymount University, USA*)
Zehavit Gross (*Bar-Ilan University, Israel*)
Peter Mayo (*University of Malta, Malta*)
Peter McLaren (*Chapman University, USA*)
Meir Muller (*University of South Carolina, USA*)

VOLUME 2

The titles published in this series are listed at *brill.com/sctp*

Forms of Muslim Children's Spirituality

A Critical Contribution to the Didactics of Islamic Religious Education Studies

By

Fahimah Ulfat

BRILL

LEIDEN | BOSTON

Originally published as *Die Selbstrelationierung muslimischer Kinder zu Gott* by Ferdinand Schoening in 2017.

Cover illustration: iStock.com/Jorm Sangsorn

All chapters in this book have undergone peer review.

Library of Congress Cataloging-in-Publication Data

Names: Ulfat, Fahimah, author.
Title: Forms of Muslim children's spirituality : a critical contribution to
the didactics of Islamic religious education studies / by Fahimah Ulfat.
Other titles: Selbstrelationierung muslimischer Kinder zu Gott. English
Description: Leiden ; Boston : Brill, 2023. | Series: Studies in critical
pedagogy, theology, and spirituality ; vol. 2 | Includes bibliographical
references (p.) and index. | Translated from German.
Identifiers: LCCN 2022046709 | ISBN 9789004533196 (hardback) | ISBN
9789004533202 (paperback) | ISBN 9789004533219 (ebook)
Subjects: LCSH: Islamic religious education of children--Germany. | God
(Islam) | Faith (Islam) | Muslim children--Religious life--Germany. |
Muslim children--Germany--Anecdotes.
Classification: LCC BP44 .U3813 2023 | DDC 297.7/7083--dc23/eng/20221012
LC record available at https://lccn.loc.gov/2022046709

Typeface for the Latin, Greek, and Cyrillic scripts: "Brill". See and download: brill.com/brill-typeface.

ISSN 2589-9724
ISBN 978-90-04-53319-6 (paperback)
ISBN 978-90-04-53320-2 (hardback)
ISBN 978-90-04-53321-9 (e-book)

Copyright 2023 by Fahimah Ulfat. Published by Koninklijke Brill NV, Leiden, The Netherlands.
Koninklijke Brill NV incorporates the imprints Brill, Brill Nijhoff, Brill Hotei, Brill Schöningh, Brill Fink,
Brill mentis, Vandenhoeck & Ruprecht, Böhlau, V&R unipress and Wageningen Academic.
Koninklijke Brill NV reserves the right to protect this publication against unauthorized use. Requests for
re-use and/or translations must be addressed to Koninklijke Brill NV via brill.com or copyright.com.

This book is printed on acid-free paper and produced in a sustainable manner.

Contents

Acknowledgment   VII
List of Figures   VIII

1   **Introduction**   1
    1   Problem Context   2
    2   Subject of the Study: The Action-Oriented Relevance of Relations to God   9
    3   Methodological Approach   12
    4   Structure of the Study   13

2   **State of Research and Research Question**   15
    1   State of Research in the Field of Children's Conceptions of God   15
    2   Description of the Research Objective   36
    3   Specifying the Research Question   44

3   **Methodological Foundation and Methodological Approach**   47
    1   Methodological Decisions   47
    2   Survey Method: Narrative Interview   51
    3   Interpretation Procedure: Documentary Method   63
    4   Strategy of Generating the Sample   68

4   **Empirical Research Results**   71
    1   Short Portraits of the Interviewed Children in the Sample   71
    2   Development of Typologies in the Present Study: Comparative Analysis and Theoretical Summarization   91
    3   Basic Typology: Forms of Self-Relating   95
    4   Type A: Relating of the Self to God in the Mode of Personalization   98
    5   Type B: Relating of the Self to God in the Mode of Moralization and Orientation towards Tradition   150
    6   Type C: Relating of the Self to Immanent Dimensions in the Mode of Distance from God   199
    7   Summary: Types of Relations to God among Muslim Children   245

5 Discussion of the Research Results 252
- 1 Discussion of the Research Results in the Educational Context 252
- 2 Discussion of the Results in the Theological Context 261
- 3 Reflection on the Results Regarding the Importance of Religious Education 286
- 4 Summary 302

6 Conclusion 311
- 1 Introduction 311
- 2 Praxeological Suggestions 311
- 3 Suggestions for Further Research 313

Appendix: Sample Table 319
References 322
Index 336

Acknowledgment

The copy-editing of this publication has been made possible through the generous support of the Academy for Islam in Research and Society (AIWG) at Frankfurt University.

Figures

1   Cognitive and emotional dimensions of faith in God according to Grom.   3
2   Aspects of religion and exchange processes within religions (Bochinger & Frank, 2013).   4
3   Psychological model of religious experience according to Tamminen (1993, p. 39).   38
4   Kamishibai with props.   61
5   Stages of abstraction for reconstructing the ideal types.   91

CHAPTER 1

Introduction

God is like the Kaaba because the Kaaba is beautiful and God is beautiful.

AMIR (8 years old, 2nd grade)

If God helps me with my exams, isn't that cheating then?

HAMID (8 years old, 2nd grade)

∴

How do children imagine God? What motivates them to construct God in one way or another? Statements by children about God such as the above quotations not only indicate an idea of God, but they also have a much deeper meaning. They indicate a childlike construction of both the world and reality. A closer look at these statements about God reveals that they contain experiences and orientations, which are not visible at first glance. The wish to better understand them has given the impetus to the present study.

In line with this idea, the present study focuses on the question of children's relationships to God respectively to the contents they have learned in their families and social environments as well as in religious education. How do they deal with these contents? What role does God play for them in their daily lives?

The utilized survey and evaluation methods originate from empirical social research. The primary interest of the present study is not the search for metaphysical elements in children, but for empirically verifiable childlike constructions of relations to God. Thus, this study does not assume the anthropological presumption that religiosity is a part of human nature. This becomes decisively clear through the methodical approach as there are no questions asked about God. The interviewed children can bring the idea of God into the conversation on their own initiative or not. They can address the contents that are relevant to their everyday lives and biographies. The postulate of not working with the anthropological presumption mentioned above is also reflected in the results of the study. Consequently, this study neither answers the question of whether there is an anthropological inclination of the human towards God, nor does it claim to answer it. However, the question of whether Muslim children have

© FAHIMAH ULFAT, 2023 | DOI:10.1163/9789004533219_001

concepts of God that are relevant to their actions is indeed answered. Since this study lies in the field of religious education studies (German: *Religionspädagogik*), the question of whether religion is inherent in human beings is addressed from a Muslim-theological perspective in Chapter 5. At its core, the study pursues a fundamentally constructivist approach. Religion is thereby examined as a social construction, omitting the question to what extent the content of this construction is related to reality. Hubert Knoblauch describes this social-scientific approach to religion as "methodological agnosticism".[1]

This study was conducted as part of a dissertation project and was published in German in 2016.

1 Problem Context

Thinking about God is one of the central themes in religious education. The question of children's and adolescents' subjective concepts of faith, which has been barely addressed in Islamic religious education studies up until now, is one of the major challenges that religious educators and teachers face.

1.1 *Explanation of Terms*

Before presenting the various perspectives of research, a terminological clarification is about to take place, since the relevant terms themselves offer a great diversity of further aspects, such as: Faith in God, the image of God, the conception of God, the experience of God, the idea of God, the notion of God, the relationship of God, the concept of God, and the like. This opens up a semantic field which the topic can refer to. The religious psychologist Bernhard Grom distinguishes from a pedagogical-psychological perspective between "cognitive" and "emotional-motivational" dimensions of "faith in God" (Grom, 2000, p. 115). He describes the "cognitive" dimension as an "understanding of God" and the "emotional-motivational" dimension as a "relationship to God". Here, understanding and experiencing are considered to interact with each other.

Figure 1 shows the interaction of the cognitive and emotional-motivational dimensions of faith in God. Grom assumes that religious feelings can have a cognitive component, but the cognitive level can also influence human experience (Grom, 2000, p. 115). This approach helps to fold religious expressions at the functional level into a primary sorting.

Grom refers to Kalevi Tamminen who considers the relationship to God as shaped by experience. The understanding of God, on the other hand, to which he attributes a clearly stronger cognitive load, is shaped by the conception of faith, or more specifically by the conception of God. These conceptions of

INTRODUCTION

FIGURE 1
Cognitive and emotional dimensions of faith in God according to Grom

God are results of a development process from short-lived experiences which nevertheless leave a lasting inner image. Tamminen assumes that experiences remain the "building material" (Tamminen, 1993, p. 40) of conceptions of God and faith even when this image changes. Experiences can be so significant and consistent that they restructure conceptions of faith or even of a person's entire belief system (Tamminen, 1993, pp. 40–41).

In the following, Grom's terminology is used to specify that of this study.

1.2 Thematic Context

Within this context, the question of God and of faith in God is the central theme in religious education. The main question refers to the development of faith in God among children and adolescents. The curricula for Islamic religious education in Germany aim to enable students to critically engage with questions of faith. In doing so, the pupils should approach a responsible, trusting, resilient, grateful, and committed social and ethical attitude.

However, in order to selectively promote a reflected faith in God, a solid knowledge of the development and formation of this faith in God is required. For this purpose, the subjects that are affected by this topic must first be clarified at a meta-level.

Faith in God is located within the realm of religion. Religion, however, cannot be regarded as an individual phenomenon. In religious studies, every religion can be described as a dynamic relationship between "individuals", "community", and a "collection of religious symbols" (Bochinger, 2014, p. 27) (see Figure 2).

In religious studies, the term 'collection of religious symbols' is used for the religious tradition and delimits itself from individual religiosity. Bochinger

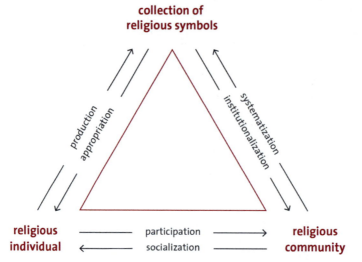

FIGURE 2   Aspects of religion and exchange processes within religions (Bochinger & Frank, 2013)

explains that a collection of religious symbols contains the religious texts, teachings, rites, and customs of a religion that have been passed on, reformulated and partly expanded, abandoned or produced anew over generations. This collection is specific to each religion and is carried by the religious community[2] that consists of religious individuals. These individuals can reinterpret, create anew, reproduce, partially accept or partially reject the religious tradition. The religious community, on the other hand, has the task of systematizing, passing on and interpreting the collection of religious symbols and of socializing future generations. Thus, individuals are socialized by the community in which they simultaneously participate (Bochinger, 2014, pp. 28–32). Bochinger et al. (2009) describe the individual acquisition and adaptation of the collection of religious symbols to one's own lifeworld (German: *Lebenswelt*) as religiosity.

This outline of Bochinger et al. relates to the theoretical concept of the "invisible religion" by Thomas Luckmann (1991) which, in turn, is based on the theory of the "social construction of reality" by Peter L. Berger and Luckmann himself. On the one hand, the theory of "social construction of reality" states that human identity arises through the interrelations between an individual and society and is formed within social processes. On the other hand, identity reacts to the existing social structure by preserving, changing or even reshaping it. Consequently, reality constructs itself in a circular process between society and its acting subjects (Berger & Luckmann, 2013).[3]

On the basis of this thesis, Luckmann has dealt with new social forms of religion. He argues in the context of a differentiated western society. Luckmann

INTRODUCTION

leaves the field of "church sociology" and expands his view to the field of general sociology by focusing on the relationship between the individual and society. Due to fundamental changes within this relationship in modern society, according to his theory, the individual is in a way released from socio-structural determinants into individual autonomy. This is especially evident in the area of religious development. Luckmann defines religion in a functional way, namely through an anthropological function which, in turn, explains the formation of social forms of religion. A person is born into a certain world view (*"Weltansicht"*) which Luckmann calls "socio-historical apriori" (Luckmann, 1991, p. 16) and this world view is internalized in the course of socialization. Thereby, the "world view" is the universal social form which also, and in particular, underlies religion and individual religiosity represents the subjective moulding of this form of world view (Luckmann, 1991, pp. 12–33).

Furthermore, according to Luckmann, the differentiation of knowledge distribution in a society leads, among other things, to specialized institutions administering religion. In Christian denominations, religion is led by a "highly specialized institution" (Luckmann, 1991, p. 18) whose representatives possess expert knowledge that is hardly accessible to laymen anymore. Additionally, the social structure itself is secularized which results in the displacement of religion. This development is the basis for the concept of "invisible religion". The church becomes one institution among many and thus loses its "monopoly of interpretation" (Luckmann, 1991, p. 19). Eventually, the church is just one among many social forms of religion. Thus, a privatization[4] of religion takes place, i.e., religion "finds its ethical basis more and more in the private sphere, especially within the family and its social networks of relationships", and becomes increasingly "wordly in its orientation" (Luckmann, 1991, p. 19). The new social forms of religion are shifting structurally from "primary" institutions to "secondary" institutions and are characterized by a "loss of visibility" at various levels. This means that religion is increasingly dealing with "private" topics while, at the same time, abandoning the conventional form of religious organization. Religion as such is therefore no longer visible as religion in content and in structure (Luckmann, 1991, p. 30).

Is this interpretation of living environments, regarding categories of individualization and privatization of religion, also applicable to Muslims in Germany? Muslims there represent a minority in a culturally and historically Christian shaped environment that particularly influences their religion and religiosity. Moreover, there is no specialized religious institution in Islam like the church in Christianity.

Researchers like Tressat (2011), Karakaşoğlu-Aydın (2000), Klinkhammer (2000), Tietze (2001), Engelbrecht (2011), Gerlach (2006), and many others have carried out studies on the question of individual orientations and forms of Muslim religiosity among adult Muslim migrants. The studies of Gerlach, Tressat, and Tietze are briefly presented here as examples:

Julia Gerlach (2006), for example, interviewed young Muslims who grew up in Germany and show a pronounced religiosity as well as a high degree of social and professional integration. This group is socially engaged in the name of Islam. According to Gerlach, the new youth culture that is developing in Germany and has its origins in the Arab world[5] is just as global and activity oriented as many fundamentalist movements. However, these so-called "pop Muslims" would "adopt western lifestyle" as an "opposition" to fundamentalist movements and, at the same time, "remix" it. According to Gerlach, they are young, deeply religious, and trendy. Furthermore, they have developed their own Islamic etiquette, e.g., in the relationship between the sexes. With their lifestyles, they go beyond conventional limitations (Gerlach, 2006, pp. 7–13). They see no contradiction in being pious believers and active co-designers of a democratic state. They freely follow the rules of Islam without feeling bound to the expectations of the horizon of social references. "Devotion to God" and acting on this principle is at the heart of their attitude (Gerlach, 2006, p. 210).

Michael Tressat (2011) has examined the significance of Muslim religiosity among young migrants in Germany and France,[6] based on biographic-analytical case studies. He comes to the conclusion that the differentiation between self-perception and outside perception plays an important role. Young adolescents who call themselves Muslims consider themselves to be "normal" young people; their origin, culture or religiosity hardly plays a role for them in their daily lives. However, from an outsider's perception they are characterized by Islam and their Muslim religiosity. Tressat's study confirms that a privatization of religiousness is discernible among young people (Tressat, 2011, p. 133).

In young Muslims' confrontation with the outside perception and their own perception, individual forms of Muslim religiosity emerge, which Tressat categorizes as different "patterns of meaning" that are of functional significance. Tressat differentiates between three "meaning patterns of Muslim religiosity in adolescence": a "creative-reflective", a "pragmatic-functional", and a "static-ambivalent" pattern of meaning (Tressat, 2011, pp. 125–127).

The confrontation with the outside perception of their religiosity leads young people to distance themselves both from their parents and from the society in which they live. In this field of tension, their religiosity serves their construction of identity. These case studies document that Muslim religiosity can play an important biographical role for young adolescents. Tressat evaluates religiosity as a "resource" in relation to the "differentiation of one's own design of identity" (Tressat, 2011, p. 133). However, this functional way of identification only requires the confession towards Islam and does not necessarily need to be connected to religious practice. The adolescents integrate religious elements into their design of life in different degrees. The meaning of religiosity, according to Tressat, is not bound to a concrete canon of religious contents, thus ensuring the existence of individualized forms of religiosity. This observed change in practice and meaning has led to a "Muslim way of life, based on individual identities" (Tressat, 2011, p. 133) and is therefore to be understood as a privatization process.

According to Tressat, the more the "process of internalization and individualization" develops, the more religiosity becomes a resource for one's own construction of identity (Tressat, 2011, p. 133). Consequently, processes of individualization and privatization of religion are clearly discernible among Muslim youths as indicated by the case studies. This means that religious elements are used in different ways, depending on biographical processes, the engagement with the inner view, and the "outer" dimension of religiosity (Tressat, 2011, pp. 139–141).

Nikola Tietze (2001) also focuses on forms of Muslim religiosity which she however examines among young men in difficult social, economic, and political situations in Germany and France. She asks about the role of Muslim religiosity in the "social actions" (Tietze, 2001, p. 7) of young Muslims. In doing so, she describes Muslim religiosity as a "mode of subjectification" in modern times. With the concept of subjectification as an indication of modernity, she refers to the sociologist Alain Touraine (1995). In this vein, the subject within modernity is characterized by uniqueness and individual self-determination in connection with cultural values, lifestyle, and community. As Touraine points out, this can be seen in the emergence of new social movements (youth movements, etc.). Tietze explains that subjectification is to be understood as a process "in which, on the one hand, a person distances themselves from their own social experiences and, on the other hand, chooses between different principles of action or combines them" (Tietze, 2001, pp. 7–8). At the same time, she postulates, on the basis of the work "The Structures of the Life-World" (Schütz & Luckmann, 2003), that subjectification is always a social, intersubjective process and takes place within the framework of a living world that provides the concrete context for the intended action (Tietze, 2001, p. 10). She takes up Touraine's sociological considerations of action and explains how religiosity can become a crucial factor in the process of subjectification in certain biographical and social situations. First of all, she assumes that Muslims (especially stigmatized men in large cities in Germany and France) identify themselves with Islamic tradition, although this tradition must be reconstructed in order to give it meaning within the biographical and social situation of an individual. In this way, according to Tietze, a subjective relationship to Islamic tradition emerges. Islam becomes a "subjectification factor" and theological contents are subjectively changed or hierarchized anew (Tietze, 2001, p. 8). Through the process of acquisition of the Islamic way of life, it undergoes changes since it is customized to one's own situation. This subjective process of acquisition is a key point of Tietze's investigation. This means that the various dimensions of religious tradition are emphasized differently by each individual Muslim, creating "a specific dynamic in the construction of individual autonomy and in the particular subjective conception of social action" (Tietze, 2001, p. 9). Tietze documents the individualized identification with Islam by reconstructing four forms of Muslim religiosity among young male adults: (1) Islam as an "extra-social" instance; (2) Islam as a community of remembrance and affiliation to a group; (3) Islam as an ethical code of conduct; (4) Islam as a part of social identity.

The first form indicates an "ethicized" religiosity through which autonomy is acquired and faith becomes an "instruction manual" (Tietze, 2001, p. 157). In the second form, religiosity is "ideologized", thus the affiliation to Islam is emphasized and religious practice acquires a rather "mechanical character" (Tietze, 2001, p. 158). The third form represents an "utopization" of religiosity whereby religious practice represents a challenge for "self-purification". "As a result, religiosity becomes a process of individual perfection" (Tietze, 2001, p. 158). In the fourth form, religiosity is "culturalized" so that it becomes a part of culture and thus creates a sense of cultural affiliation. The practice of religion promotes the "integration into a certain milieu" and has a "subjective function" (Tietze, 2001, p. 159).[7]

The above studies show that these reconstruction and subjectification achievements through which young Muslims acquire Islam and Islamic tradition can be understood as an expression of the challenges of modern times. The similarity of these challenges with those of other religious traditions renders the studies on Muslims compatible with other studies, e.g., on Christian religiosity:

Bochinger, Engelbrecht, and Gebhardt (2009) have provided a differentiated diagnosis of the state of contemporary religious culture in Germany. In a qualitative study on the Christian majority society, Bochinger et al. describe a new ideal type in "late modern" religiosity among general changes in contemporary religious culture. This new ideal type is called "spiritual wanderer". The authors portray the "realities of faith" of members of the two great Christian churches (Bochinger et al., 2009, p. 21) and distinguish precisely between religion, religious institution, clergy, religiosity, and spirituality. Furthermore, and with regard to the "late modern" developments, the authors do not speak about individualization that is to be distinguished from "individualistic religiosity", but – like Tietze – about the "subjectivization" of the religious. This describes a detachment of religiosity from the "objective side" (Bochinger et al., 2009, p. 158) of religion, and thus gives it a "subjective side" (Bochinger et al., 2009,

INTRODUCTION

p. 157). Spiritual wanderers adopt elements from different religious symbolic systems. They reject the dogma and orthodoxy of religion. Therefore, spiritual wanderers use the term "spirituality" which describes an individual religious "personal way" (Bochinger et al., 2009, p. 38). Furthermore, Bochinger et al. recognize both secularization and individualization tendencies in the "late modern" framework conditions of religion (Bochinger et al., 2009, pp. 147–148). In this context, secularization is a necessary prerequisite for the reception of spiritual content. Individualization is based on the idea of "self-empowerment of the religious subject", which states that wanderers only grant themselves "social sovereignty of interpretation over their own spirituality and religiosity" (Bochinger et al., 2009, p. 78).

The case studies of Tressat (2011) and Tietze (2001) as well as the results of Bochinger et al. (2009) show that religious guidelines are adopted individually instead of being implemented one-to-one in one's own lifeworld (*Lebenswelt*). These results are of significance for the present study. Bochinger explains this selection mechanism with the identity-giving function of religiosity. If "components of a religious symbol system are adopted in one's own world in such a manner that they contribute to the identity construction of the person in question" then one could speak of religious identity (Bochinger, 2011, p. 111). Bochinger states this can either be carried out by selective adoption of certain elements of the religious symbolic system and/or by adapting these elements independently to one's own lifeworld and individual needs.

The above studies (except the last one) and other empirical studies mostly refer to young or adult Muslims in Germany in the context of migration and adolescence. However, there are still no empirical studies that refer to Muslim children of primary school age. The question arises whether children also have individual forms of relations to God or whether their relation to God and their religiosity are shaped by their horizon of social reference so that their statements and behavior correspond to the expectations of their social and worldly systems of reference. Social systems of reference are represented by parents, relatives, friends, religious education at school, religious instruction at home, and religious schooling in mosques. This question is examined in the present scientific study.

2 Subject of the Study: The Action-Oriented Relevance of Relations to God

As already mentioned, faith in God has different dimensions. This study focuses on the emotional and motivational dimensions of faith in God and, if applicable, on its cognitive dimension. This is explained in the following.

According to Fritz Oser (1993), the ability to build a relationship to God means to "construct meaning in concrete situations by means of a dynamic relationship exchange with the Divine" (Oser, 1993, p. 1).

Oser assumes that "relationship determinants" which require "psychodynamic activities" play a role in establishing a relation to God. In this way, children "create" God and the child's primary caregivers influence this (Oser, 1993, p. 2). Oser provides a link between stages of development and the emotional dimension in the religious realm by referring to "emotional schemas":

> Emotional schemas allow an immediate, spontaneous, unconscious, effortless and automatically perceived emotional response in given situations; schemas create expectations by filtering and directing attention; they manage the consolidation of episodic memories; they contribute to the generalization of emotional experiences to certain prototypes; if multiple schemas are activated simultaneously, emotional mixes can occur. (Ulrich, 1991, p. 6, quoted in Oser, 1993, p. 3)

Oser regards emotional schemas as religiously relevant. They refer less to the image of God, and more to "the dynamics of the encounter with him which implicitly appears within the respective image of God" (Oser, 1993, p. 3). Oser postulates that transitions to different stages are based on the one hand on the transformation of "structures" (cf. Piaget in Chapter 2, Section 1.1) and on the other on the transformation of emotional schemas. In the question of God, he distinguishes between surface structures and deep structures, thus between a "merely learned God and the real God in the psyche" (Oser, 1993, p. 8).[8] The "learned God" of Oser can be equated with the propositional and learned knowledge of religion. The present study, however, focuses on the 'real God in the psyche' which is reflected in implicit knowledge. Here the emotional dimension has a close and irresolvable connection to implicit knowledge. This is not only in line with Oser's argumentation, but also with the sociological concepts of knowledge which will be used in the following (cf. Chapter 2, Section 2.3 and Chapter 3, Section 3).

Elisabeth Naurath argues similarly, pointing out the cognitive-structuralist theories of development for the development of religiosity and the image of God. She refers to Ana-Maria Rizzuto (1979) who distinquishes like Tamminen (1993), Oser (1993) and Grom (2000) between a rather cognitive idea of God as the "concept of God" and an emotional and motivational dimension as the "image of God" which is based on relationship (Naurath, 2014, p. 20). Constanze Thierfelder (1998) describes Rizzuto's position. She explains that

INTRODUCTION

the formation of the idea of God depends on the "experience-oriented" and not on the "conceptual" idea of God:

> According to Rizzuto, only the experience-oriented idea of God decides between belief and non-belief, since a conceptual idea of God cannot provoke any evidence experience. [...] Rizzuto's interest is predominantly archaeological: She tries to go back beyond piety shaped by church doctrine, and to uncover the idea of God shaped by primary processes. (Thierfelder, 1998, p. 47, quoted in Büttner & Dieterich, 2013, p. 147)

Naurath (2014) concludes that "religious development must be accentuated more strongly than before also in emotional terms" (Naurath, 2014, p. 29).

Therefore, in the center of the present study lies the researching of the emotional and motivational dimension of faith in God in its interrelationship with cognitive dimensions on the empirical basis of children's statements regarding concrete life situations. The question of how this emotional dimension expresses itself in children's utterances remains to be answered. The concept of implicit knowledge, which is outlined below and explained in detail in Chapter 3, is utilized for this very purpose.

Indeed the emotional dimension, i.e., the relationship to God, is an individual phenomenon, but, according to Karl Mannheim (1997), it arises in social practice:

> When bearing himself in an immanently religious manner, the individual believer stands in the same relationship to God, worship, and religion as do the other members of the same cultural community: he possesses these contents in the way of the existential community, a way which is wholly concrete and perspectivistic and which can only be shared conjunctively. (Mannheim, 1997, p. 265)

According to Mannheim, this practice of action is embedded in "atheoretical knowledge" which a human being knows without the need to explain it in "everyday theory" (cited in Nohl, 2012, p. 4). The relationship to God is therefore to be sought in the "atheoretical knowledge" of children that guides their actions, i.e., is implicit and is expressed in their own stories (cf. detailed explanation in Chapter 3).

Research in the field of religious development assumes a complex concept of God among children and adolescents (Tamminen, 1993; Szagun, 2014). The interactive aspect of the complex socialization process is often referred to within that research. Conditions of religious socialization include family and media influences, cultural and social conditions as well as the individual's religiosity in its cognitive and emotional dimensions. A crucial influence on religiosity is attributed to emotional components (Hanisch, 1996, pp. 94–100; Eckerle, 2008, pp. 57–69). Naurath also emphasizes that the development of children's faith in God is overall complex and individual, since influences coming from "socialization (religion, culture, educational background, language ability, gender, etc.) decisively shape religious feelings, thoughts, mindsets, and attitudes" (Naurath, 2014, p. 20).

Like all children, children of Muslims are also born into a "socio-historical a priori" (Luckmann, 1991, p. 16) in the domestic, family, and community sphere which they internalize. However, they are also influenced by the society in which they live and develop their individual religiosity in these diverse environments. In Germany they come into contact with a non-Muslim, culturally and historically Christian, but also secular environment: in kindergarten, school, and among friends. The influence and interaction of these two societal instances of socialization on children is of great scientific interest. The subjective expression of their worldview develops in these fields of influence.

3 Methodological Approach

Based on what has been presented so far, this study aims to use empirical social research methods to reconstruct action-guided orientations of children in relation to their respective constructions of God.

The theoretical research perspective of the present work is based on the reconstructive qualitative social research, which can be traced back to Karl Mannheim (1980, 1997). The approach or survey method used is the narrative interview with narrative theatre as a narrative-generating entry stimulus. Individual interviews are conducted with primary school students of the fourth grade who have completed four years of Islamic religious education and thus have a comprehensive and verifiable propositional knowledge[9] of Islam. In terms of development, they are also able to articulate their thoughts because they are already in the process of religious socialization within the context of religious education in school and possibly in their family contexts. The documentary method is used for evaluation in order to reconstruct the implicit ("atheoretical") knowledge of children (cf. detailed explanation in Chapter 3).

This study uses the terminology of the documentary method to explore children's "implicit" knowledge that guides their actions with regard to their emotional relationship to God. At the beginning of the interview, the children are confronted with a seemingly hopeless situation that has potential parallels to

INTRODUCTION   13

their own experiences. The situation offered provides a powerful incentive to take action. The children are not given any direct encouragement to talk about God or religion during the interview but may do so freely in the defined context. This indirectly collected data on the constructions of God can be interpreted as potentially action-guiding.

4   Structure of the Study

The study is structured as follows: *Chapter 2* reviews the state of research, describes the aims and specifies the research question.

Chapter 3 addresses the methodological decisions and the location of the investigation in qualitative, reconstructive social research. The survey and evaluation methods are described in relation to the research question.

Chapter 4 presents the empirical results. First, an overview of the children from the sample is given in the form of short portraits. Subsequently it is shown how the typical forms of relations to God that are documented in the children's narratives were reconstructed. These relations to God are described in compact form. In the next step, the reconstruction of these various types is explained in detail.

Chapter 5 contains the discussion of the results, which are first contextualized within educational science and then within Islamic theology. The results are then discussed with regard to the importance of religious education more broadly. The reflexive contribution to the didactics of Islamic religious education is presented in *Chapter 6*, in which research directions and recommendations are set out that have resulted from this study.

Arabic technical terms from Islamic contexts are transliterated into Latin script according to the transcription of the German Oriental Society (DMG) by Carl Brockelmann and Hans Wehr with the exception of those terms that are already adopted into German. Text passages from the Qur'an are indicated in brackets and contain two digits separated by a colon. The left digit indicates the number of the chapter (*sura*), the right digit the verse of the chapter. The verses are taken from the transmission of the Qur'an by Ali Quli Qara'i (2005).

Notes

1   "With reference to religion, such a scientific approach thus abstains from a *fideistic definition*, which suspects something that actually exists behind the positively observable phenomenon of religion. It therefore tends towards what can be called *methodological agnosticism*: Scientific studies must mark ultimate truth claims of the statements of their subjects with

brackets. They cannot decide whether there is God, higher beings and a transcendent reality or not, but only whether or not they are considered real by human beings. Within the framework of a science, God thus always appears in (imaginary) quotation marks and transcendence appears as immanence. Religious contents are therefore only given to the extent that they are contents of human consciousness, human action and communication" (Knoblauch, 1999, p. 14).

2 According to Bochinger (2014), a "religious community" encompasses different social levels, such as a small group of Muslims in a neighborhood, a local mosque community or even the community of all Muslims in the world.

3 Klaus Hurrelmann develops his socialization-theoretical concept on the individual as a "productive processor of reality" in a very similar way (Hurrelmann & Bauer, 2015).

4 Privatization is a key concept in the discussion on "invisible religion" (Luckmann, 1991).

5 Gerlach explains that in the late 1990s preachers like the Egyptian Amr Khaled began to spread a friendly and success-oriented message among the Cairo middle class. These preachers did not read the Qur'an as a guide to bomb-making, but sought teachings for a better, more successful life. They described wanting to counteract terror (Gerlach, 2006, p. 10).

6 Biographic-analytical case studies were carried out in Germany and France with two female and two male Muslim adolescents of Maghrebian and Turkish origin.

7 Yasemin Karakaşoğlu-Aydın (2000), who reconstructs different types of religious orientations among Turkish student teachers and pedagogy students in Germany, also comes to the conclusion that a differentiated reflection on religious orientations is necessary. She presents them in detail according to Glock's different dimensions of religiosity (1962) and Geertz's (1987) consideration of "range and intensity".

8 He rejects the position of Carl Gustav Jung who presumes an "anima naturalita religiosa" (Jung, 1940) and instead postulates that positive interpersonal relationships are essential for the establishment of a vivid and emotionally positive relationship to God. If, on the other hand, relationships are negative or disturbed, the emotional schemas cannot transform themselves and thus cannot support the stages (cf. the considerations on the attachment theory in Chapter 2, Section 1.2).

9 Objectifiable information and knowledge.

CHAPTER 2

State of Research and Research Question

1 State of Research in the Field of Children's Conceptions of God

Scientific research on the religious development of Christian children started in 1881 with Granville Stanley Hall who gave lectures presenting studies on the religious imagination of children. Subsequently, research also began in German-speaking countries (Oerter & Montada, 2008, pp. 609–611).

On the one hand, stage models were developed which represent the development of religious judgement, religious consciousness and/or spirituality in the Christian context. They are based on classical models of psychoanalysis and cognitive psychology such as those of Freud, Erikson, Piaget, and Kohlberg. On the other hand, various researchers have more recently begun to empirically investigate the image of God among children, both in denominational (Christian) as well as in non-denominational contexts. The studies deal with various aspects, i.e., with the development of the image of God, with the character, the qualities, and the appearance of God in the perspective of children as well as with the connections between the various aspects of socialization such as the religious orientation of the parents, the educators, and the children's personal image of God (Schori, 2004, pp. 164–165).

In Germany, empirical research on Christian religious education began as early as the 20th century but remained fragmented and was marginalized in the relevant concepts of religious education after WWII. In the context of a general reorientation of Christian religious didactics at the end of the 1960s, Klaus Wegenast (1968) explicitly advocated an "empirical shift in religious education studies" (cited in Bucher, 2000, p. 11). Wegenast called for empirical research in religious education studies as there were many withdrawals from religious education in schools in the 1960s. Through a situation analysis, didactic and methodological suggestions for improvement were to be made. Wegenast's demand was fruitful: didactics and methodology were further developed; the relationship between statements of faith and the reality of the students' lives at school was strengthened, even though empirical research in religious education studies remained marginalized for a longer period.

It was also problematic that empirical studies predominantly surveyed teenagers from the age of 12 and older. Friedrich Schweitzer (2010) writes on this subject:

© FAHIMAH ULFAT, 2023 | DOI:10.1163/9789004533219_002

> The fundamental difficulty in obtaining reliable information about religious development emerges from the fact that one cannot simply ask children about their religiosity. Children can only give limited information about their religiosity. They do not possess the necessary linguistic means and they do not reflect on themselves in such a way that they could describe their religiosity in response to corresponding questions. (Schweitzer, 2010, p. 47)

As a methodical approach, researchers therefore chose painting for younger Christian children, keeping Christian iconography in mind. Letting children draw or paint personal pictures of God became a common approach, as well as the drawing of God and the human being in comparison. This serves to show which characteristics children assign to people and which to God (Pitts, 1977; Bucher, 1994; Hanisch, 1996).

In response to the argument that children have limited language and reflection skills, recent empirical research has extended methodological approaches into other fields (Arnold et al., 1997). For example, the children's own interpretations of their pictures were included (Arnold et al., 1997; Coles, 1992; Klein, 2000). Material collages were also used in connection with conversations (Szagun, 2014), or essays by children and young adolescents about their own conceptions of God were analyzed (Bertenrath, 2011). Oral and written surveys were also carried out in quantitative studies,[1] such as the Shell youth studies (critical: Thonak, 2003). At the same time, qualitative methods were increasingly used in which the statements of children and young adolescents were collected in open interviews and conversations and then analyzed on the basis of current sociological evaluation methods (Coles, 1992; Leyh, 1994; Orth & Hanisch, 1998; Hull, 1997; Flöter, 2006; etc.).

In the following, the religious development models are presented and analyzed in light of recent research on images and conceptions of God among Christian and non-denominational children. Subsequently, the results of the recent empirical research will be examined to determine if they are suitable in terms of contributing to the objective of the present study which is to determine children's relationship to God as implicit knowledge, in order to capture its relevance for the children's lives and daily routines.

1.1 *Piaget's Theory of Cognitive Development*

The earliest models of religious development in the Christian context are based on Jean Piaget's theory of cognitive development. The question regarding the significance of classical stage theories (Oser & Gmünder, 1992; Fowler, 2000) in current research concerning the religious development of faith in

God is further explored below. Firstly, the development of cognitive structures according to Piaget is briefly described, as reference will be made to it afterwards.

According to Piaget's (2003) basic thesis, children construct their own schemas as a combination of individual cognitive achievements in dealing with their physical and social environment. The individual cognitive achievements are connected to create "structures" (Piaget, 2003, p. 48). Children assimilate new elements to these structures. In this way, complex situations can be appropriated by acting or recognizing. This process is called "assimilation". More precisely, assimilation is "the integration of external elements into the developing or already completed structures of an organism" (Piaget, 2003, p. 53). "Every modification of an assimilation plan (or assimilation structure) caused by their assimilated elements" is called "accommodation" (Piaget, 2003, p. 56). Both processes depend on each other and are sub-processes of "adaptation" (Piaget, 2003, p. 56). The relationship between assimilation and accommodation can vary and only "a balance between them characterizes a complete act of intelligence" (Piaget, 2003, p. 57).

Since Piaget presumes that there are structures that are integral to the subject and are being developed, and that this is a gradual process, he concludes that there are stages of development (Piaget, 2003, p. 63):

a.   The sensorimotor period lasts until about the age of one and a half years with a first subperiod in which the subject is centered on their own body (lasting about seven to nine months), followed by a second sub-period in which the plans of practical intelligence are objectified and adapted to the spatial conditions.

b.   The period of imaginative intelligence leads to concrete operations (...) with a first preoperative sub-period (...) that begins at the age of about one and a half to two years with the formation of semiotic processes, such as language and internal images. This is followed by a second sub-period (at about seven to eight years of age), characterized by the beginnings of operational formations in their different concrete forms and with their different types of preservation.

c.   Finally, there is the period of propositional or formal operations. It also begins with a sub-period in which the operations are ordered (11 to 13 years); it is followed by another sub-period which leads to the formation of the general combinatorics and the INCR with its two forms of reversibility (Piaget, 2003, pp. 65–66).

Piaget's structural genetic approach, for example, is the basis for Oser's and Gmünder's theory of the development of religious judgement. They apply this approach which is based on basic biological assumptions to religious concepts (critically: Allolio-Näcke, 2021, pp. 78–103).

Recent developmental psychological studies show that Piaget's results need to be modified in many ways. Especially the question of age development at different stages and its characteristics such as "egocentrism" (the maturity-related inability to take the perspective of others), "animism" (the belief in the vitality of inanimate objects), or "realism" (only that which can be seen is real) are more complex and dependent on their context than stated in Piaget's work. It can be assumed that children have certain competences at a much earlier age than Piaget was ready to accept. Claudia Mähler's (1995) study provides an example of the phenomenon of animism.[2]

Gerhard Büttner (2010) notes that Piaget's assumption that a certain age group corresponds to a certain level of development in all areas of knowledge must be questioned in terms of developmental psychology. The level and complexity of thought operations not only depend on a child's age, but also on their level of knowledge. Büttner gives the example of a 6-year-old chess or dinosaur expert who knows more than a 15-year-old non-expert in this field (Büttner, 2010, p. 210). Based on the assumption that age development is not the only factor that plays a role, but also the knowledge offered and processed, he concludes for the religious sphere that religious education (Büttner calls it "instruction") can convert a "novice" into a religious "expert" and can thus lead to more complex thought operations and differentiated thinking (Büttner, 2010, p. 210). Therefore, Büttner postulates that for every religious topic it is necessary to examine "how the logic of the topic presents itself in the horizon of childlike reception" (Büttner, 2010, p. 211).

Grom (2000) also questions the homogeneity of structures and stages, based on the observation that children think and act preoperatively in one area and operationally in another, concretely in one area and formally in another. From this, Grom concludes that the cognitive structures and stages are not as "cross-divisional homogeneous as Piaget assumes, but to a large extent area-specific" (Grom, 2000, p. 48). Based on her own research, Szagun (2014) also assumes that the unfolding of the cognitive level is domain-specific, i.e., is structured according to (special) areas and does not progress across areas. This means that children correct, expand and systematize their personal concepts of God according to incentives, personal interests and communication spaces.

Furthermore, Grom states that Piaget's theory examines cognitive development in the logical-mathematical and scientific field (Grom, 2000, pp. 42–44). The option of applying his reflections and his sequence of stages to the development of childlike concepts of God and relations to God must at least be subjected to a thorough reflection on the basis of the above considerations.

STATE OF RESEARCH AND RESEARCH QUESTION

1.2 Theories and Empirical Findings on the Development of Childlike Religiosity

The study of childlike religiosity is a broad and multidimensional field that different sciences approach from their own perspectives.

An important and intensely discussed topic in connection with the human relation to God is the theory of attachment. This brings us to the field of developmental psychology. Erik H. Erikson placed the bond between a mother and her child in a "numinous" context (Büttner & Dieterich, 2013, p. 142). Erikson (1976) developed the concept of "basic trust". According to him, this means "to be allowed to rely on the credibility of others and the reliability of oneself" (Erikson, 1976, p. 100). For Erikson, religion has a direct function in developing basic trust as "the faith of the parents that supports trust germinating in the newborn" (Erikson, 1976, p. 100).

Further developmental psychological models such as those of Donald W. Winnicott rest upon the understanding of the mother-child relationship. Based on Winnicott, the English psychoanalyst John Bowlby (1940) then developed "attachment theory" which also focuses on the mother-child relationship.

Attachment theory describes the social developmental steps during infancy with special attention to the mother-child relationship. In contrast to Freud's drive theory, Bowlby assumes a biological connection which is a primary need of the infant to increase its chances of survival as well as an independent motivational system. Bowlby's colleague Mary Ainsworth expanded his theory and developed a test scenario that allowed her to evaluate the degree of a child's bond to their primary caregiver (Büttner & Dieterich, 2013). Recent research investigating the development and effects of bonds on the social and emotional development of children postulates, like Bowlby, that the attachment process appears to have a biological basis. However, it is also dependent on the environment and socio-cultural and familial context (Siegler et al., 2011).

The theory of attachment is also of particular relevance for religious education studies because it focuses on the connections between the formation of an image of God and the relationship to parents and other agents of socialization. Schweitzer (1994) examines the interaction between the parental image and the image of God in a multidimensional way. He refers to comparative psychoanalytical and psycho-empirical research on an international scale that also explores gender differences. Schweitzer concludes that although the image of God arises through "identification" (Schweitzer, 1994, p. 93) with parents there is no one-to-one depiction relationship ("girl-mother-female image of God" or "boy-father-male image of God" (Schweitzer, 1994, p. 93)), since children actively construct their own ideas. This means that maternal and paternal elements "mix in an individually determined relationship" (Schweitzer, 1994, p. 93) and that "traits of the parents that are *actually experienced* and *ideally hoped* for" (Schweitzer, 1994, p. 93) merge into each other. The "role models" prevailing in society and culture and the influence of respective "religious traditions" also play a role in children's individual constructions (Schweitzer, 1994, p. 93).

Büttner and Dieterich (2013) point out that Szagung confirms, in her long-term study from 2006, "the importance of early bonds for establishing a relationship to God". But she also states that it is difficult "to reconstruct an attachment constellation in retrospect" (Büttner & Dieterich, 2013, pp. 153–154). Despite the great relevance of attachment theory, it will not be dealt with in more detail in the further course of the argument of this study since the focus lies on the active processing abilities of children themselves and this research interest requires a specific methodological setting (cf. Chapter 3). An additional survey of the relationships with parents and other agents of socialization would have gone beyond the scope of this methodical setting and would have required a completely different, essentially biographical methodology. The following argumentation focuses on stage theories such as those of Fowler (2000) and Oser and Gmünder (1992).

1.3 *The Stages of Faith in God According to James Fowler*

In 1974, James Fowler developed his stage theory of the development of faith, based on Erikson's development theory and Piaget's theory of cognitive development. He used narrative interviews with children, teenagers and adults (Fowler, 2000, pp. 327–330). Fowler defines faith as something "that concerns us all" (Fowler, 2000, p. 26) or as a "universal characteristic of human life which is similar everywhere" (Fowler, 2000, p. 35). For him, the stages of faith depend on the developmental psychological and cognitive advancement of man:

- Stage 0: Primal undifferentiated faith. Basic trust is formed at this stage (Fowler, 2000, p. 138).
- Stage 1: Intuitive-projective faith. This stage is typical for children aged about 3–7 years. According to Fowler, this is the time when the capacity of imagination develops as the basis for an attitude of faith (Fowler, 2000, pp. 150–151).
- Stage 2: Mythical-literal faith. This stage is typical for children aged 7–12 years. At this point, a child begins to adopt religious contents and rules (Fowler, 2000, pp. 166–167).
- Stage 3: Synthetic-conventional faith. This stage is typical for young adolescents aged 12–18. Faith identity is formed here. The social environment and the reconnection to it is important; therefore faith is described as "conventional" (Fowler, 2000, pp. 191–192).
- Stage 4: Individuative-reflective faith. This stage is typical for early adulthood, but many adults do not reach it. One's own identity and worldview is

distinguished from that of others and an individual position is established (Fowler, 2000, pp. 200–201).

- Stage 5: Conjunctive faith. This stage is common in late adulthood. Here, opposites in thought and experience are united. At this stage, the relativity of one's own faith is recognized in the face of a transcendent reality while one's own faith is maintained (Fowler, 2000, pp. 216–217).
- Stage 6: Universalizing faith. This stage is extremely rare. People who reach this stage "embody and update the spirit of a comprehensive and fulfilled human community" (Fowler, 2000, p. 218).

Fowler's theory is to be commended. However, on the one hand it is pointed out that it is not empirically verifiable. On the other hand, Fowler's attempt to expand Piaget's theory of cognitive development by using the theories of Kohlberg, Selman, and Erikson is questioned. Grom (2000) notes: "The very different approaches that Fowler is trying to put together [...] do not describe homogeneous, coherent structures and hierarchically interdependent stages, but rather different 'styles of faith' and attitudes" (Grom, 2000, p. 64). Nevertheless, Fowler's definition of the term faith is to be appreciated because it emphasizes the importance of one's attitude towards knowledge.

Lars Allolio-Näcke (2021) looks at the stage models from a cultural-psychological perspective and notes that Fowler makes it clear from the very beginning of his work that he assumes an "anthropological anchoring of faith" which enables him to postulate the universality of his model. In doing so, he refers to the Protestant theologians Paul Tillich and H. Richard Niebuhr (Allolio-Näcke, 2021, p. 105). Therefore, Fowler's model should be read from this point of view whenever it is a question of examining the development of children brought up atheistically or with a different faith.

1.4 The Development of Religious Judgement According to Fritz Oser and Paul Gmünder

The theory of the development of religious judgement plays an important role in religious education studies and in religious psychology. The predominant stage model in European discourses is the structural genetic model according to Fritz Oser and Paul Gmünder (1984) which is based on theories of cognitive development (Piaget) and moral development (Kohlberg). The central question in this context is how religious faculty of judgement develops throughout life. This faculty of judgement refers to a person's relationship to an ultimate being that comes into play in critical life situations. In their interviews, Oser and Gmünder used a contingency situation caused by a plane crash as an initial stimulus.[3] They developed a five-stage model of religious judgement (Oser

& Gmünder, 1992). In religious education studies in the Christian context, the results serve as a basis for assessing the level of development of children and for supporting religious development (Oerter & Montada, 2008, pp. 610–611).

- Stage 1: Orientation on absolute heteronomy (Deus ex machina). At this stage, the child assumes that God intervenes actively and directly in the world. "The ultimate being is active, man is passive" (Oser & Gmünder, 1992, p. 81). The feeling of dependence (heteronomy) is predominant here.
- Stage 2: Orientation along 'do ut des' ('I give so that you may give'). At this stage, God is regarded as omnipotent, but can be influenced by religious acts. Misfortune is attributed to the absence of sufficient religious efforts. Moreover, a subjectivity in faith arises (Oser & Gmünder, 1992, p. 84).
- Stage 3: Orientation along absolute autonomy (deism). This stage is characterized by detachment. The human is declared independent in his action, God's influence on man is rejected (Oser & Gmünder, 1992, p. 155).
- Stage 4: Orientation along imparted autonomy and salvation plan. This stage is characterized by reflection. A reconnection of man towards God takes place, but man is free. In his freedom he sees the condition for his connection to God (Oser & Gmünder, 1992, p. 155).
- Stage 5: Orientation along religious intersubjectivity. At this stage, which can only be reached by saints and great thinkers, God manifests himself in intersubjective action, i.e., in encountering others (Oser & Gmünder, 1992, p. 155).

This structural genetic model with its universalistic claim is a subject of controversial discussion because it assumes that the depth structure of religious development is the same for all people regardless of whether or not they belong to a certain religion or religious denomination (universal, transcultural, diachronic, and gender-independent). Furthermore, this model assumes that religious development takes place at the structural level, thus below the linguistic level, and therefore the contents do not affect the structures. This means that "the stages of religious judgement are both 'cognitive structures' and emotionally significant, identity-forming 'deep structures' that develop independently of socialization, language, culture, etc." (Grom, 2000, p. 76). The implicit assumption that, on the one hand, every person is religious and, on the other hand, religion lies within the structure and not within the culture of man is discussed critically by religious psychologists (Grom, 2000, pp. 76–77; as well as Schweitzer, 2010, pp. 134–135, cf. also Chapter 5, Section 2.2).

From a cultural-psychological perspective, Allolio-Näcke criticizes Oser's and Gmünder's stage theory because it surveys religious development based on the way a moral conflict is dealt with. He discusses the "structure-content problem" of this stage model, the universal course of the stages and the

STATE OF RESEARCH AND RESEARCH QUESTION

postulate of the model's universal validity (overview: Allolio-Näcke, 2021, pp. 78–103).

In summary it can be said that the results of Oser and Gmünder are considered as a description of a specific cultural form of religious development and must be interpreted in light of their cultural Christian context (Büttner, 2010). Ernst Nipkow (1988) also refers to this, postulating that the theory of the development of religious judgement follows a "philosophical-theological model of thought that is typical in Protestant and Catholic theology" (Nipkow, 1988, p. 272).

Carl Power (1988) expresses this aspect, also in relation to Fowler, as follows: "Considering the theistic embeddedness of the higher stages, it is probably more appropriate to regard Fowler's and Oser's theories as a description of the *religious development of theists within the Judeo-Christian tradition*" (Power, 1988, p. 115).

The following section presents recent empirical research that critically examines Oser's and Gmünder's stage model. It is also discusses from the perspective of what further suggestions they offer for the present work.

1.5 *Recent Empirical Research on the Concept of God among Christian and Non-Denominational Children*

Researchers such as Anna-Katharina Szagun (2014), Werner Ritter et al. (2006) and Mirjam Zimmermann (2012) also take a critical stance on stage theories.

Szagun, for example, carried out a long-term study on the understanding of God and the relationship to God among children who grew up in a predominantly non-denominational environment (in Rostock) and puts forward the thesis that stage models are unsuitable for religious educational work with children. She states that today's situation of a wide spread "break with tradition" (Szagun & Fiedler, 2008, p. 458) is not compatible with stage theories. The increasing individualization and pluralization of lifeworlds is a further factor. Moreover, stage theories are questionable because the studies were carried out in church contexts (i.e., in firm religious-institutional contexts) of the seventies and eighties, but they claim to be universal and postulate an irreversible sequence of diachronic stages. Szagun's own investigations showed hardly any overlap with the stages 1 and 2 of Oser and Gmünder model (Szagun & Fiedler, 2008, p. 406).

Szagun assumes that children's images of God reflect their lifeworlds and their life experiences. They depend on their "religious homes" (Szagun & Fiedler, 2008, p. 378), family, milieu, and social networks. Therefore, socialization is crucial. Szagun points out that structural genetic processes are integrated into the relations of social contexts and their functions. She states, for example, that loyalty to the family plays a major role. Adults influence children profoundly and sustainably. Children need "emotional permission" (Szagun & Fiedler, 2008, p. 454) in order to develop in a religious way. This means that barriers caused by parents can block their longing for an ultimate being. Szagun therefore recommends a "religious atmosphere" (Szagun & Fiedler, 2008, p. 457) and "protected spaces" of communication (Szagun & Fiedler, 2008, p. 453) that give children the freedom to approach God as well as to distance themselves from him. She states that children are "theologically and philosophically competent and productive subjects" (Szagun & Fiedler, 2008, pp. 458–459). Teachers should therefore assist children in religious education so that they can develop a concept of God which they can bring into line with their life experiences and their world view (Szagun & Fiedler, 2008, p. 453).

Because Szagun works with images and symbols that include a variety of "socialized metaphors" (Szagun & Fiedler, 2008, p. 454), she is aware of the fact that her study may reveal different results in other contexts. However, her study shows clearly that children's intuitions about God are independent of their cognitive level, so she advocates a more serious approach to religious socialization in religious education studies (Szagun & Fiedler, 2008).

Subsequent to Szagun, the present study attempts to explore the level of implicit knowledge of children under the guiding aspect of their relationship to God. Especially among Muslim children, the religious home in the sense of cultural and family-related influence, plays a significant role. A child's tendency to make use of a horizon of social reference in the interview situation must be taken into account. The problem, that children probably articulate statements in order to meet the expectation of the interviewer or of general expectations does exist. Therefore, the present study uses the documentary method of evaluation to determine what is implicitly hidden in the children's utterances and what orientations they have.

Zimmermann (2012), who conducts studies on the thematic complex of "child theology", also supports a "partial relativization of the cognitivist stage theories that follow Piaget" as well as an "appreciation of the individual characteristics of childlike intellectual achievements" (Zimmermann, 2012, p. 400).

Ritter et al. (2006), who examined the topics of sorrow and God from the perspective of children and adolescents state with reference to the stage theories of Oser and Gmünder that the concepts of God postulated in stages 1 and 2 are not bound to any particular age. Ideas concerning the infinity and finiteness of God's power are by no means restricted to childhood. Ritter et al. point out that their results are independent of age, grade, and type of school.

Orth and Hanisch (1998) have used several methods to gain insights into the worlds of faith of 9- to 12-year-old children, such as interviews, conversations, drawings, picture descriptions and essay writing. They focus on the children's everyday reality and strive to fulfil their self-imposed requirement to take the children and their faith seriously. Finally, they concluded that children "do not only receive contents of religious education, but also deal with them in a reflected manner and come to independent interpretations" (Orth & Hanisch, 1998, pp. 7–8).

In their empirical studies with kindergarten children, other researchers have also found stage models to be of little use in pedagogical practice (e.g., Eckerle, 2008). Sandra Eckerle also recommends that the socializational conditions of religious development are taken into account. She comes to the conclusion that even among preschool children there is no universal image of God but diverging priorities and tendencies. There can be no talk of a purely conformist and unreflected faith among children nor of a one-dimensional, mythical, and literal understanding of symbols. Rather, Eckerle confirms that children have a personal image of God that adults must take seriously and get to know.

Christina Schlange (2011) conducted a qualitative study on the development of images of God among children, taking into account their religious socialization. She had students of the third and fourth grades paint a picture of God according to their own imagination. Afterwards, the students were asked to write to a fictitious friend who had never heard of God explaining what they felt he should know about God. The children then completed a questionnaire on their religious socialization in which the thematic complexes of family, community, kindergarten, religious education, and the media as places of learning of religious socialization were examined. The Paul-Dilemma was also a part of the questionnaire (Oser & Gmünder, 1984, cf. Chapter 2, Section 1.4). The aim of her study was to portray the students' ideas of God (the cognitive dimension of faith in God) and to answer the question of whether religious socialization of children has an influence on their ideas of God. In addition, Schlange (2011) tried to use the Paul-Dilemma to find out which stage the children could be assigned to according to the models of Kohlberg, Fowler, and Oser and Gmünder.

The children in Schlange's research represent their propositional knowledge. Their emotional relationship to God does not become clear in their statements. According to Schlange's interpretation, this is due to the children's stage of development or their internalized striving for performance. For example, she noticed among the third graders that a highly religious girl "who attends Sunday school and services every week acquires a broad knowledge of faith content, but [...] cannot yet use it to build a personal, reflected faith" (Schlange, 2011, p. 81). She also notices that another highly religiously socialized child addresses the affection of God towards human beings but does not mention his personal relationship to God and thus merely represents learned faith content. Schlange makes clear that the children's statements do not necessarily correspond with their beliefs "but may meet the presumed expectations of others" (Schlange, 2011, p. 82). In some of the statements and paintings made by children in the fourth grade, Schlange cautiously assumes a personal relevance of the contents and a positive relationship between the children and God, but this cannot be proven (Schlange, 2011, pp. 96–97).

This raises the question of whether similar results can also be found among Muslim children on the basis of the aforementioned survey and evaluation method which does not focus on the children's action guiding orientations, but on their propositional knowledge. The present study aims to remedy this methodological shortcoming and, by means of a suitable survey and evaluation method, not only to record the propositional knowledge of children, but also and above all to reconstruct their implicit, action-guiding knowledge with regard to their relationship to God and its relevance in certain sections of their lifeworlds. Here, the emotional dimension of faith in God is accentuated more intensively.

Stephanie Klein (2000) examined images of God portrayed by girls and has chosen images and conversations as approaches to the religious imagination of children. The girls were between six and twelve years old. She conducted picture interviews with them for three consecutive years. In her empirical analysis, Klein shows that the content of the pictures, the explanations as well as the conversations all points towards the children's religious experiences. The imagination of each child is shaped by biographical experiences. Of importance for the present study is the fact that Klein asked the girls about their personal relationships to God. The girls, however, often reverse the question and deal with God's actions in the world (Klein, 2000, p. 160). According to Klein's interpretation, this means that no personal relationship to God can be reconstructed.

With the survey and evaluation method presented in this study, it should be possible to cross the methodological boundary described by Klein. At the same time, it should also be possible to draw conclusions from the implicit concepts about God, regarding the emotional dimension of the relationship to God in its interactions with the cognitive dimension. However, what is relevant in Klein's study is that the girls frequently had several and often diffuse or even contradictory ideas of God simultaneously. The girls had both personal and nonpersonal ideas about God. They had a differentiated awareness of the problem and were fully aware of the difference between God as an ontological fact and their conception of God. In summary, Klein notes that the religious imaginal world of the girls is diverse, modifiable and can be stimulated spontaneously. Nevertheless, "individual religious concepts, questions, ideas and even images seem to persist over a longer period of time" (Klein, 2000, p. 176).

Numerous studies on the image of God among children have also been carried out in Europe. In 1944, Ernest Harms used drawings to investigate how the image of God develops in children and adolescents from the United States. He distinguished three stages of religious development: fairy tale stage (3–6 year olds), realistic stage (7–12 year olds), individualistic stage (13–18 year olds) (Harms, 1944).

Maare Tamm (1996) has also dealt with this topic. The corresponding study examined the qualitative differences in the concepts of God among children and young people from Sweden as reflected in their drawings. A total of 425 children of both sexes from 9 to 18 years were asked to draw their ideas about the word "God" and comment on them. This resulted in different age- and gender-related categories. It became apparent that the anthropomorphic conception of God decreases with increasing age, but it does not disappear completely. About 8% of the children had no idea about God. More girls than boys considered God as a mystery. More boys than girls regarded God as a male figure (Tamm, 1996).

Among the frequently quoted researchers is Chad W. Nye (1984) who explored the development of the concept of God among 120 children between the age of 5 and 16 from private Protestant and Catholic day schools in the San Diego area. All children took part in an interview in which their answers were categorized and evaluated according to abstractness and concreteness. The results published in 1981 suggest that the children's view of God does not depend on a denomination (Nye & Carlson, 1984).

John Hull (1997) developed the concept of "God-talk with young children", focusing on the subjectivity and self-competence of children when speaking about God. He explored how the religious thinking of British children continues to develop in images and how the religious language ability of children can be promoted.

The effects of religious rules on the moral concepts of Christian and Jewish children in the United States were also examined. Larry Nucci and Elliot Turiel (1993) discovered that children distinguish between moral and non-moral religious rules. Judgements regarding moral issues were justified in terms of justice and solidarity while non-moral issues were justified in terms of their normative character.

Engaging with the Bible, the views on communication with God, and the moral behavior of children were examined in another study by Pamela Ovwigho and Arnold Cole (2010) which involved 1,009 American children aged 8 to 12. It was found that most did not read the Bible regularly but still communicated with God in prayer almost daily. In addition, significant correlations were found between Bible study and moral behavior. An important difference between the children was that the impact on their behavior is the strongest among those who are least subject to parental control and supervision (Ovwigho & Cole, 2010).

Simone de Roos (2006) examined how socialization conditions influence the individual diversity of concepts of God among young children in the Netherlands. In this context, the correspondence hypothesis was used which states that the image of God and the relationship to God among human beings have parallels with their early caregiver-child relationships. This hypothesis was revised to include the religiosity and socialization of the caregivers. These two modes were then used as hypotheses in two studies. The studies showed that children cognitively experience a strong, comforting, and helpful God in their home and school context even if all relationships with their caregiver had been experienced as negative. However, in such an environment they do not build an emotional relationship with a personal God, nor can they experience a personal connection to God (de Roos, 2006).

In the field of religious psychology there are many studies dealing with the concepts of God among children. The psychoanalysts Ana-Maria Rizzuto (1979), Donald W. Winnicott (1973), Charles Rycroft (1968), and others have tried to bridge the gap between psychology and theology in their psychological work. Sandra Eckerle (2001) discussed this aspect in detail in "Gott der Kinder" (Eckerle, 2001, pp. 35–37). In addition, there are numerous studies which examine the effects of parental bonds on the children's concepts of God (cf. Chapter 2, Section 1.2).

For the present research work, the knowledge that the concept of God among children has different dimensions can be applied. From this insight, the methods of questioning and evaluation used here are both justified and sound, since they are suitable for reconstructing the dimension of the children's action-guiding knowledge in relation to their constructions of God.

There are also some interesting studies in the field of pre-school pedagogy which mostly work with children's drawings. The study by Sandra Eckerle should be mentioned here as an example. It investigated the religious socialization of children and found, among other things, that children who were religiously educated at home could relate to the term 'God', and they were able to draw a picture and talk about it. On the other hand, it found an absence of expression among children without religious upbringing (Eckerle, 2001, p. 90).

The current state of research on the religious socialization of adolescent and adult Muslims in Germany is not described in detail here, as the present study is limited to children of primary school age. Overall, the question about God continues to be at the center of most current studies on religious education studies.

Particularly important in connection with the research question of the present empirical study is the sensitivity towards the heterogeneous development processes of children as demanded by Büttner (2010). He postulates

STATE OF RESEARCH AND RESEARCH QUESTION

that children interpret the world in different ways. Their interpretations can be scientific, moral or magical, but social consensus only accepts scientific explanations. The children are expected to follow this "positivistic scientific culture of meaning and interpretation" (Büttner, 2010, p. 211) as they grow up. This basically excludes the traditional-religious interpretation of the world. The demand here is that religious phenomena should be interpreted from the perspective of modern rationality. Therefore, Ronald Goldman (1968) concludes in his study "Religious Thinking from Childhood to Adolescence" that younger children are not capable of an adequate, rational understanding of religious concepts so that only adults can interpret "religious phenomena in the sense of modern rationality" (cited in Büttner, 2010, p. 211).

Büttner points to Anglo-Saxon psychologists (Woolley & Phelps, 2001) who investigate how children abandon their magical patterns of interpretation and choose a different mode of relationship to a higher power. The genuine interpretations that children make are appreciated here instead of being devalued as a lower level of thinking (cited in Büttner, 2010, pp. 211–212).

According to Büttner, the Anglo-Saxon psychologists' approach aims to pick up and develop Piaget's concept of assimilation and accommodation. With the aim of understanding the individual and common constructions of the children expressed in their utterances, Piaget's realization that adolescents perceive the world in ever new patterns serves as an "hermeneutic key" for a constructivist view of children (Büttner, 2010, p. 212).

In summary, the discussion of the recent empirical research on the concept of God among Christian and non-denominational children provides the rationale for the present study to focus on both the cognitive development of children and the stage models for religious development and, in particular on studies that depict the heterogeneous and individual interpretative achievements of children.

In addition, the discussion can provide the impetus for a suitable method of research and evaluation, with the help of which the implicit knowledge of the children that guides their actions can be reconstructed regarding their relationship to God and its relevance to them.

1.6 Research and Comparative Studies on Concepts of God among Christian and Muslim Children and Adolescents

Comparatively, little research has been undertaken on the concepts of God among Christian and Muslim children and adolescents. In the following, some current and particularly relevant studies comparing Christian and Muslim children are described in detail. They will also be assessed in terms of their potential for the present study.

In 2006, Ilse Flöter conducted a qualitative-empirical study on the role of God in the everyday life of ten-year-old children in primary school which also took Muslim children into consideration. Flöter incorporates some suggestions from the instruments of Arnold, Orth and Hanisch (1997) which she develops further.

At first, Flöter critically notes that Arnold et al. (1997) focused on religious education at schools and deliberately chose children from two religious education classes (5th grade) with a socially privileged background (Protestant private schools). The children expressed a consistently positive image of God which, according to Flöter, can probably be attributed to their lifeworld background. Therefore, it is not clear to what extent their socialization influences the positive image of God expressed by all children. On the basis of this criticism, Flöter does not focus on religious education in schools but investigates the question of "the role God plays in the lives of German and Muslim children who live in a plural society that is characterized by secularism and the encounter with Islam or Christianity" (Flöter, 2006, p. 30). For her research she chooses a 3rd and a 4th grade class of a North German primary school in which children from all social and religious backgrounds are represented. Flöter wants to document "religion in the everyday life of children" (Flöter, 2006, p. 31). As with Arnold, Orth and Hanisch, she uses guided interviews while striving to "ask as few direct questions as possible in order to keep the risk of subjective influence as low as possible" (Flöter, 2006, p. 32). To gain access to the religious imagination of ten-year-old children, she uses various methods that offer the children a narrative stimulus (conversations about pictures,[4] personal maps, the "Beppo story",[5] the story of a moral dilemma). Her sample consists of 23 children with Catholic, Protestant, and non-denominational backgrounds who she groups together into the category of "majority children" due to their comparatively homogeneous origins from parental homes not bound to the church (Flöter, 2006, p. 67). She compares them with a group of three children from Evangelically characterized parental homes, four Muslim children, and one Alevi child, that she classifies as having distinct divergent profiles due to their different socialization.

Of particular relevance for the present study is Flöter's distinction between concepts of God and relationships to God. She also raises the question of the influence of the social environment on the formation and development of these ideas (Flöter, 2006, pp. 103–105).

Common to all children in the sample is the fact that God represents an undoubted reality for them (Flöter, 2006, p. 69). With regard to religious socialization, Flöter notes that the "majority children", who hardly experienced any religious socialization at home, construct their own world of faith which she describes as "patchwork religiosity of ten-year-olds" (Flöter, 2006, p. 140) in reference to Keupp's "patchwork identity". Their concepts of religion consist of "set pieces" (Flöter, 2006, p. 140) which they adopt and use from their environment (fairy tales, legends, scientific facts, television, computer games, overheard remarks, books, memories of the Christmas service, and fantasy). Flöter attributes this to "dynamic phases of social change" under the conditions of late modernity described by Keupp (2008, quoted in Flöter, 2006, p. 102). The children receive hardly any answers from their parents to questions concerning religion, so they construct a patchwork religiosity which, however, is colored by Christianity through continuous religious education (Flöter, 2006, p. 140).

With regard to the evangelically influenced children, Flöter notes that they "live in stable cultural frameworks with reliable traditions and a high degree of social control" (Flöter, 2006, p. 140). Social cohesion is ensured through shared religious beliefs and delimitations from others ("non-Christians"). In addition, the children have a high propositional knowledge of the Bible (Flöter, 2006, pp. 140–141).

Muslim children who live in religious households and whose lives are structured by religious orthopraxy are aware of their Muslim identity. They relate their own religion to Christianity, which thus receives a "sharper profiling" (Flöter, 2006, p. 141). Flöter cannot find any syncretistic or exclusionary aspirations among Muslims (Flöter, 2006, p. 141).

With regard to the cognitive dimension, Flöter (2006, pp. 191–192) classifies the children according to the developmental psychological models of Piaget and Fowler. From her results, she concludes that the ideas of God among the "majority children" as well as the Muslim children are "usually positive and free of fear" (Flöter, 2006, p. 233). These two groups regard God as the creator of the world and associate him with help and protection (Flöter, 2006, p. 233), while evangelical children "usually reflect what they have learned and experienced in their religious education" (Flöter, 2006, p. 379). They deny their anthropomorphic images of God since from their point of view "no image of God may be made" (Flöter, 2006, p. 379).

Flöter defines the "idea that God personally intervenes in one's own life" as a "relationship to God" (Flöter, 2006, p. 236). She follows the religious scientist Charles Y. Glock (1962) with her definition of "religious experience" as a dimension of religiosity (Flöter, 2006, p. 242). In her investigation, she therefore interprets the statements of the children as an expression of "religious experience" and states that they "religiously interpret certain affective experiences" (Flöter, 2006, p. 243).

All in all, Flöter finds different intensities of relationships to God among the "majority children" and notes that they have different ways of constructing

God as "protector of people" or "protective companion". She sees this as an affirmation of C. G. Jung's thesis which regards "religion as one of the earliest and most general expressions of the human soul" (Flöter, 2006, p. 265).

With evangelical children, however, it is difficult for Flöter to recognize a relationship to God "because their religious mode of expression is so strongly influenced by upbringing and socialization that it is hardly possible to identify their own contributions" (Flöter, 2006, p. 379).

Flöter notes that Muslim children do not have personal "conversations with God" (Flöter, 2006, p. 371). They mention prayer formulas or "incantations", as Flöter calls them, to which they add their "supplications", especially before school tests (Flöter, 2006, p. 371). She could not determine a "personal, completely private and imaginative relationship to God" (Flöter, 2006, p. 372) and attributes this to the "firmly established dogmatic framework of beliefs and practiced rituals" (Flöter, 2006, p. 373) that does not allow free development.

It is problematic that Flöter is strongly influenced by the views of Ursula Spuler-Stegemann when interpreting the statements of Muslim children and therefore interprets the children's statements in this light. Thus, she is of the opinion that Muslim children would not have access to the "Julia story", designed by her (Flöter, 2006, pp. 60–61) and which deals with charity, because: "It seems to me that this story is not particularly suitable for interviewing Muslim children about a religious connotation of ethical commandments, especially since, according to Ursula Spuler-Stegemann, there is also no explicit commandment for charity in Islam" (Flöter, 2006, p. 375).

Moreover, Flöter classifies the children according to Fowler's stage theory of development of faith, although her diverse results would have given her the opportunity to develop her own typology.

The great merit of Flöter's work is the fact that she also puts the emotional dimension of the children's faith in God at the center of her work. However, due to her methodical approach, she is not aware of the actual relevance of this dimension. Her method, based on Mayring (1983), merely allows her to record the children's explicit statements. But it is also and above all necessary to make the implicit level of the children's statements accessible (cf. Chapter 2, Section 2.3). Another study dealing with Muslim children in Germany, which also draws a comparison with Christian children, was carried out by Halise Kader Zengin (2010). She conducted a study on the development of the concept of God among Muslim children aged 7–12 in Bavaria. She examined Muslim children who participated in religious education at a primary school and a grammar school and compared her results with studies on Muslim children in Turkey. She also compared her results with those of a study on Christian children conducted by John Hull (1997).

As an initial prompt, Zengin (2010) told the children the story of Adam and Eve and asked them to reproduce the meaning of the story in their own drawings. The children's drawings were analyzed and evaluated. She found that some Muslim children were not accustomed to drawing God, and they tried to represent God in a different way. The children brought anthropomorphic ideas of God to paper as well as representations of God as spirit, natural phenomenon or abstract symbol. They also documented the importance they ascribe to God by means of character traits (great, invisible, omnipresent, knowing, seeing, commanding) and additionally depicted God as genderless (Zengin, 2010).

A qualitative study on the ideas of God among Muslim and Protestant students was carried out by Zita Bertenrath (2011), although not with children of primary school age. Bertenrath examined the ideas of God expressed by Muslim and Protestant students from grades 8 to 12 (grammar school and secondary school, Cologne-Bonn area) by using their essays. During religious education classes, the students were asked to write down their personal idea of God. On the basis of this material, Bertenrath analyzed their ideas by means of qualitative content analysis according to Mayring (1983). The aim was to find out to what extent the students include ideas from each other's traditions.

Excerpts from the essays show that Muslim students in particular primarily reproduce propositional knowledge. They show no signs of a personal relationship to God which, however, may not have been examined with regard to Bertenrath's question as it was not of interest to her. Similar to Flöter, Berthenrath's methodical approach leads to a survey of propositional knowledge but does not allow insight into the emotional dimension of the relationship to God.

The empirical work of Adem Aygün, entitled *Religious Socialization and Development of Muslim Youth in Germany and Turkey* (2013), aims to examine the religious development of Muslim youths using the "Faith Development Interview" according to Fowler. This study examined the religious beliefs of 70 Turkish Muslim youths aged 15 to 25 from different types of schools in Turkey and Germany. Their statements were allocated to the six stages of faith according to Fowler.[6] The interviews were evaluated according to the "Criteria of the Manual for Faith Development Research" (Aygün, 2013, p. 75). Aygün creates four types: the traditional, the ideological, the laicistic (secular) and the individual type. He compared the young people from these different types living in Germany and Turkey, with regard to their development of faith (according to Fowler). Since solely insights regarding faith in God are of interest for the present study, only this result is presented here: Aygün states that "the ideas of God expressed by Turkish youths are more diverse than those of their German-Turkish peers" (Aygün, 2013, p. 190). All in all, according to Aygün, the youths' ideas of God remain "conventional and institutional" (Aygün, 2013, p. 190). For them, God is an "instance that determines everything for mankind" and he possesses "a punishing and a rewarding image" (Aygün, 2013, p. 190). In contrast to most of the above-mentioned research, Aygün documents the coexistence of different faith profiles among young people – despite his reference to Fowler. This highlights the need to contrast stage models with type formations.

Further studies deal with the image of God of Muslim youth in German multicultural society within the topic of "migration". The research of Yasemin Karakaşoğlu-Aydın and Ursula Boos-Nünnig (2005) as well as Fred-Ole Sandt (1996) should be mentioned here. In addition, Shell Youth Studies also examined religiosity among young people with and without migration background (Albert et al., 2015). However, this subject area will not be discussed further as the present study focuses on children of primary school age.

A number of works in Europe and Turkey also need to be mentioned. In the Netherlands, for example, Ina ter Avest (2009) carried out a comparative study on the development of the concept of God among native and immigrant children. The students of an interreligious primary school and a Christian primary school were confronted with stories from different religious traditions. The children's concept of God was inductively derived from the material. The results of this comparative research led to the conclusion that students involved in interreligious learning showed explorative behavior towards their own religion and that of others. Their concept of God showed "hybrid" qualities. These students were both rooted in their own tradition and "in motion". On the other hand, the students of the Christian primary school clearly followed their learned Christian framework of interpretation more closely (ter Avest, 2009).

A Swedish meta-study by Tullie Torstenson-Ed (2006) called "Children and God in the Multicultural Society" compares various studies from 1969, 1979, 1987–1990 and 2002 that examine children between the ages of 8 and 12 in Sweden. The research question focuses on the children's concepts of God, changes which occurred within the given time frame and possible connections with developments in society. The results confirm that changes did take place. In 2002, the proportion of children who believe in God was higher than in previous years. Questions about God became comparatively more important in 2002 than before. Also, the faith in God as well as the personal relationship to him seemed to become increasingly widespread (Torstenson-Ed, 2006, p. 33). Torstenson-Ed attributes this to the growing number of children with a migrant background. Especially in multi-ethnic areas and thus also in schools where religious children represent the majority, the interest in religious matters and the dialogue about them increased (Torstenson-Ed, 2006).

Mualla Yıldız and Recep S. Arık (2011) explored how children in Turkey describe their image of God and which impact the children's age has on the

STATE OF RESEARCH AND RESEARCH QUESTION

articulation of their images of God. The sample consisted of 253 randomly selected primary school children aged 8 to 11 from different social backgrounds. The children were asked to write a short essay about their image of God. The essays were analyzed by using content analytical methods. Most children (48.2%) imagine God as the Creator and this concept becomes more wide-spread with age. Many children have anthropomorphic ideas of God, but these decrease with increasing age (50.6% of 9-year-olds, 12.6% of 11-year-olds). Children's knowledge of the difference between God and his creation increases with age (5.5% of 9-year-olds and 38.9% of 11-year-olds). It is important to the children that God neither begat, nor was begotten. Younger children imagine God predominantly as frightening and punishing while older children increasingly imagine God as loving and protective (Yıldız & Arık, 2011).

From Canada, the qualitative study by Ahmad Khizar Zuberi (1988) which deals with the concepts of God of Muslim children is particularly worth mentioning. He assumes that the methodological approach is crucial for researching children's ideas. He emphasizes the importance of the interaction between children and adults and distinguishes between spontaneous and non-spontaneous concepts. In doing so, he refers to Piaget's idea of the child's perception of reality that develops on the basis of mental processes (spontaneous concepts) as well as decisive influences by adults (acquired concepts). Spontaneous concepts are defined as the original childlike reflections about God that are not decisively influenced by adults. Non-spontaneous concepts, on the other hand, are those that are influenced by encounters with adults (Zuberi, 1988).

Zuberi demands that, on a methodological level, researchers must primarily collect children's spontaneous concepts. For this, the child's own perspective as well as her or his expressions and thoughts must be at the center of attention. He conducted a qualitative study with three children aged six, eight, and ten years. The children came from Muslim families with Pakistani, Egyptian, and Bangladeshi backgrounds. He interviewed the children by using some divine attributes (Creator, eternal, omnipresent, omniscient, omnipotent, just, true, real) as a stimulus for conversation. The main goal was to collect the children's own ideas. However, the discussions were not restricted to the named attributes. In addition, structuring and contrasting questions were raised to identify commonalities and differences between the children's statements, e.g., between 'God' and 'spirit'. Furthermore, the children were given cards with terms like God, man, spirit, soul, witch, Adam, angel etc. to sort (e.g., living and non-living, real and non-real etc.). The questions were not standardized (Zuberi, 1988).

The evaluation was carried out by inserting the children's statements into a predefined category system and by constructing separate categories from their statements. Zuberi noted that the data mainly represented the children's non-spontaneous statements. Only a few statements gave insight into their original childlike reflections. He also noted that the children's concepts of God were influenced by adults. Only a few examples of original reflections by the children could be found. His results show that children use different cognitive strategies to develop their concepts of God and to describe or explain God's attributes. One strategy, for example, is the active search for an own hypothesis (e.g., a child explains the omnipresence of God with his greatness and speed) (Zuberi, 1988, p. 39).

It must be critically noted that despite his claim to collect the children's "spontaneous concepts", Zuberi could not access this level. This is ultimately only possible if the children are not given the topic of God, but if they have the space to spontaneously address it themselves. This is the approach of the present study. However, Zuberi's claim to "tickle out" the spontaneous comments of the children remains crucial as it allows the action-guiding dimension of faith in God to be separated from the children's propositional knowledge. This is realized in the present study by reconstructing the children's implicit (action-guiding) knowledge regarding their construction of God and not their own explicit, reflexively available understanding of God.

In summary, the discussion of the comparative studies on the concepts of God by Christian and Muslim children and adolescents, together with research on the concepts of God amongst Muslim children can be used as a starting point for the present study to develop a methodical approach to the level of relationships with God and, thus, to the implicit level of the children's comments.

2 Description of the Research Objective

2.1 *Preliminary Reflections*

As already indicated in the title of this study, the focus of this research interest lies on the self-relating of Muslim children to God (cf. Chapter 4, Section 3) as reflected in their own narrations. In narrative interviews especially developed for this purpose (cf. Chapter 3, Section 2), it becomes clear, how children construct their relationship to God and, above all, which action-guiding orientations these constructions have (cf. Chapter 3, Section 3.1).

As the initially made theoretical considerations and the current state of research suggest, three dimensions are of vital importance for reconstructing self-relating which are firstly named and then described in detail below:

– the children's experiences that are interpreted by them as religious (Tamminen, 1993);

STATE OF RESEARCH AND RESEARCH QUESTION

- the "implicit" knowledge and the "conjunctive experiential space" of children (Mannheim, 1980, 1997);
- the children's "individual systems of relevance" (Nestler, 2000).

At the theoretical level, the interaction between these three dimensions forms the decisive dynamics for the present study. Prior to a more detailed presentation of the different dimensions, this interaction is briefly examined.

In order to adequately grasp the relationship to God, it is necessary, as described, to first include the dimension of experience. According to Tamminen, a child's experiences become 'religious' only when the child interprets her/his experience in the light of her/his emotional relationship to God and her/his cognitive ideas about him. Thus, religious experiences inevitably contain the dimensions of both interpretation and emotion (cf. the detailed explanation of 'religious experience' in Chapter 2, Section 2.2). The interaction of these two dimensions is a precondition for any orientation performance for practical action.

The children do not construct their interpretations out of themselves, but rather derive them from the collective knowledge of their environment. According to Mannheim, these interpretations are part of the collective or "conjunctive" knowledge that "is acquired in the shared lived practice and, at the same time, orientates this practice in a habitualized way" (Bohnsack, 2003, p. 137). This means that in order to grasp the relationship to God, the dimension of the collective or "conjunctive experiential space" (Mannheim, 1980, p. 214) plays a crucial role (cf. the detailed explanation of the "conjunctive experiential space" in Chapter 2, Section 2.3). At the same time, a second dimension is crucial for grasping of the relationship to God which is the individual "system of relevance" (Nestler, 2000, p. 151). In this dimension, the children subjectify the interpretations of the conjunctive experiential space according to their individual relevance, which do not merge into the conjunctive experiential space, but are to be regarded as an independent factor in relation to it (cf. the detailed explanation of the "system of relevance" in Chapter 2, Section 2.4). The individual system of relevance, in turn, affects the level of experience that touches the entire personality of the individual.

In the following, the just theoretically generated framework is explained in detail.

2.2   *The Children's Experiences That Are Interpreted by Them as Religious*
In the field of religious development of children and adolescents, Kalevi Tamminen (1993) has investigated the question of whether children have religious experiences from a religious-psychological perspective and, if so, what kind of experiences they have. Based on existing research, in particular the works of

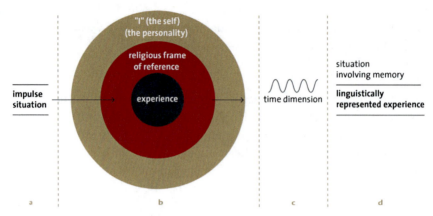

FIGURE 3   Psychological model of religious experience according to Tamminen (1993, p. 39)

Rodney Stark and Charles Y. Glock, Tamminen defines: "Religious experience is an experience with which a feeling of dependence on or connection to God/the divine and the transcendent is linked" (Tamminen, 1993, p. 36).

Tamminen states that a child's experiences only become "religious" when the child interprets these experiences in the light of her/his emotional relationship to God and her/his cognitive ideas about God. Experience, however, involves two dimensions, that of recognition and that of emotion so that through experience the whole personality of an individual is affected. Tamminen made a sketch of religious experience and its psychological origin which helps to clarify and understand the phenomenon (see Figure 3). The figure shows that

a. Any experience results from a situation or prompt that may be an outer or inner event.
b. Within the 'I', the 'experience' is interpreted in a religious frame of reference. This means that the meaning of an experience depends on a person's religious upbringing in a particular tradition, past experiences, and religious beliefs. Depending on the frame of reference, inner or outer situations are interpreted differently. Thereby, the respective image of God is an essential element of an inner religious frame of reference. According to Tamminen, every religious experience thus entails a certain interpretation of reality.
c. The experience expressed dates back in time.
d. In a situation involving memory, the experience is presented linguistically. This means that the output is not the experience itself but rather its linguistic explanation which may change over time, both in terms of content and assessment. Consequently, the linguistic comment about a past experience always reflects the religious attitudes of the interviewee at the time of the survey (Tamminen, 1993, pp. 39–40).

STATE OF RESEARCH AND RESEARCH QUESTION

Tamminen is aware that experience as a psychological process cannot be divided into its individual components. In his model, however, he refers to the verbalization of experience that the individual interprets in a religious way, i.e., as her/his experience of God. He also points out that religious tradition and teaching influence how a subject interprets something experienced and realized. This means that religious tradition does influence the way events are perceived. The religious frame of reference is thus the basis of memory itself (Tamminen, 1993).

According to the empirical findings of Tamminen, it is possible to experience God's presence, closeness, and guidance in difficult situations or when feeling lonely as well as in explicitly religious situations (e.g., funerals, church attendance), i.e., to interpret the situation as a state of being close to or guided by God. Tamminen asked students which situations they would identify as suitable for experiencing God's nearness. In addition, he asked the children and young adolescents to tell him about situations they interpreted as experiences of God's presence. There was a considerable difference between the students' assessments of situations and their reports about actual experienced situations. He attributes this to the fact that the assessments are more based on what has been learned while the reports are based on what had actually been experienced (Tamminen, 1993, pp. 49–50).

According to Tamminen, situations of loneliness, emergencies (especially escaping from danger), questions of morality, religious practice, school, and, in a few cases, situations of joy are suitable for primary school children to be interpreted through religion (Tamminen, 1993, pp. 54–60). Stories about God's guidance and protection are usually told with regard to situations of external threats and difficulties. Furthermore, God's guidance plays a role in moral decisions as well as in moments of success (after trials), happy coincidence, inner strength, and courage. The fact that religious experiences are often associated with negative incidents does not mean that they cause fear and anxiety, but rather that they may induce feelings of safety, security, comfort, relief, and encouragement. Tamminen notes that younger children, due to their cognitive development, describe concrete events when they talk about their religious experiences. In the narrations about the experiences of nearness to God, the children concentrate more on emergency situations, while they rarely associate everyday situations with God (Tamminen, 1993, pp. 63–67). Also essential is Tamminen's observation that the religious experiences of most of the children and adolescents correlate with their religious and communal activities as well as with the experiences of their parents.

In her Rostock study, Szagun also observed that children think of God in negatively connotated moments, i.e., in situations of fear, sadness, insecurity,

40   CHAPTER 2

and anger. Children associate a close relationship to God with these situations of discomfort, insecurity, and fear, and they also pray most frequently in situations of inner or outer distress (Szagun, 2014). This aspect is considered in the survey and evaluation (cf. Chapter 3).

2.3   The "Implicit" Knowledge of Children – Shared Experience in the Social Sphere

The idea of implicit knowledge in children used in this study is based on the sociological model of the construction of knowledge according to Mannheim as explained in his book *Structures of Thinking* (in German: Mannheim, 1980, in English: 1997). Mannheim assumes that the knowledge of humans can always only be reconstructed in relation to their social and cultural living spaces which he calls "conjunctive experiential spaces".

According to Mannheim, the basis of a conjunctive experiential space is first and foremost a special kind of existential relationship between people and their counterparts, which forms the basis for a specific kind of cognition. Mannheim distinguishes this cognition from objectified natural scientific cognition. In his posthumously published treatise, he writes "that every act of knowledge is a specific kind of existential relation to the object and founds a specific communion, a specific unity between subject and object" (Mannheim, 1997, p. 187). This means that one only becomes conscious of oneself through an "existential contact" towards a "vis-à-vis" (*"Gegenüber"*) (Mannheim, 1997, p. 187). Mannheim (1980) calls this a "brief fusion of duality into unity" (Mannheim, 1980, p. 206), and he calls this particular type of cognition "contagion". A contagion can occur between subject and object as well as between two subjects:

> Contagion is a kind of existential relatedness, a specific union with the object. We believe that the same phenomenon of contagion is before us when, for example, there wals into our room a strange person whom wie have never seen before, who hast not yet spoken a word but from whose physiognomy and bearing, from whose gestures and movements wie nevertheless take in hins whole being in a destict way and all at once. In the true sense of the word we 'taste' the distictive properties of his soul. (Mannheim, 1997, p. 189)

Mannheim (1997) states that this spiritual contact creates an "existential relationship" which forms the ground for "every subsequent communication and every experience of him" (Mannheim, 1997, p. 189). Thus he concludes that each act of cognition creates a specific commonality with the other because it emerges in an "existential relationship" to the other. This existential relationship has its own special "coloring" to every human being and is continuously

STATE OF RESEARCH AND RESEARCH QUESTION 41

transformed, which means that it is a "living relationship" (Mannheim, 1980, p. 211) for those who participate in it. In the first contagion of two people – and before any form of address and "conceptual formulation" (Mannheim, 1980, p. 211) has occurred – there is a certain kind of perception, namely knowledge of the other in cognition, that is concrete enough so that both can orient themselves and react accordingly.

Mannheim (1997) calls this "conjunctive knowledge" (Mannheim, 1997, p. 192) which he describes as necessarily perspectivistic, i.e., it is bound to theoretical locations:

> If the object of my knowledge is a person, then [...] – the perspectivistic image (the side of his psychic self theat is turned toward me) – is transferable from my knowledge to his on the basis of the existential relationship in which we stand, just as conversely he can convey to me his knowledge of me. (Mannheim, 1997, p. 192)

In this way, Mannheim makes it evident that the "self-knowledge" of an individual is only possible in "social existence" (Mannheim, 1997, p. 192). This kind of knowledge, however, only applies to those who enter into existential relationships, and thus it only has a "conjunctive validity" (Mannheim, 1997, p. 193) and not a general one. In contrast to general cognition, conjunctive cognition is therefore perspectivistic and tied to a particular experiential space. If a third person joins two people, they create a "conjunctive experiential space". The conjunction is a "dynamic nexus" connecting them, meaning it provides a framework for the connectedness between people. "The living relationship is the basis of every subsequent conjunctive experience" (Mannheim, 1997, p. 194). Experiences can therefore only be passed on to the members of the experiential space.

According to Mannheim, a "unification and extension of the experiential space" (Mannheim, 1997, p. 195) is only possible through language. He distinguishes between "conjunctive meaning of a word" and "supra-conjunctive meaning of a word" (Mannheim, 1997, p. 196) and explains this using the example of a community. In a "conjunctively community", terminologies gain a certain "distinctive conjunctively determined meaning" that only those who share the experiential space will understand. For other communities, a particular word is a general term (Mannheim, 1997, p. 197).[7] A "community of experience" can expand into a "cultural community" and, according to Mannheim (1980), this is the "most comprehensive expansion" of a conjunctive community of experience (Mannheim, 1980, p. 226).

Thus, conjunctive experiential spaces can also consist of experiential communities or cultural communities. Mannheim describes this as "collective conjunctive experiential spaces" (Mannheim, 1997, p. 229). He points out that the community with its conjunctive experiential space and its language existed prior to one's becoming aware of oneself as an individual. The "basic stages of thinking" are influenced by the community's field of experience: "In this experiential field there are what may be called prescribed courses of obligatory experiences, in which all the important events of the community are 'ritualized' and 'magically' stereotyped (Mannheim, 1997, p. 206). In addition, Mannheim postulates that "the basic form for conveying things that have happened is the narration, behind which the narrator stands" (Mannheim, 1997, p. 192).

In relation to the present study, this means that a religious community (here the Muslim one) also represents a conjunctive experiential space. The structures of thought and the frames of orientation of the individual are to a certain extent influenced by collective religious beliefs. The members of this experiential space possess conjunctive knowledge.

This conjunctive knowledge and the orientations which are based on a conjunctive experiential space are not easily explicable conceptually and theoretically. Mannheim describes conjunctive knowledge that is intuitively available as "atheoretical", because it is not explicitly present. The atheoretical and action-guiding knowledge is, as explained above, acquired and experienced in social practice. In other words, a child who is raised in a Muslim family and/or community and grows into it acquires the ritual prayer, the positions in prayer, the Muslim-theological idea of God and other knowledge in social practice which is based on similar actions and experience.

The action-guiding knowledge of Muslim children is thus tied to individual experiences when it comes to their construction of God. However, it emerges within a specific social practice which, in turn, is embedded in a conjunctive experiential space.

In this study, it is not the general knowledge about God among Muslim children that is of interest, but their conjunctive, atheoretical, action-guiding knowledge which is closely linked to the specific social practice of their lifeworld and milieu, and also to their religion.

Based on Mannheim, Ralf Bohnsack (2009) has developed a praxeological sociology of knowledge that uses the documentary method in order to reconstruct implicit, atheoretical, conjunctive knowledge which is habitually anchored. This evaluation method, which was also used in the present study, is explained in more detail in Chapter 3, Section 3. After describing the aspects of conjunctive knowledge, the following section focuses on the "individual system of relevance".

2.4   *Children's Systems of Relevance – Children's Own Theories*
Recent research in the field of empirical assessment of religiosity as well as on the question of the development of religiosity among children and adolescents

strongly adresses the methodological weaknesses of older research. They focus more on the children's relevancies and less on the researchers' relevancies (Ritter et al., 2006).

Erich Nestler coins the term "system of relevance" in relation to Schütz (Schütz & Luckmann, 2003). He defines it as "the individual or group-specific modification of a reference system", meaning specifically the religious reference system. Nestler continues: "The system of relevance of an individual or a group describes the significance (valence, value, hierarchy) of the elements of the reference system" (Nestler, 2000, p. 151).

In the following, the focus lies on the individual system of relevance. According to Nestler, it is determined both by personality-specific conditions as well as socializational conditions. Individual systems of relevance include cognitive, emotional, and action-guiding aspects. Nestler assumes that in relation to religion, all aspects are always present, but one of them (cognitive, emotional or action guiding) is in the foreground.

He therefore assumes that the system of relevance of an individual serves as a "motor of reception and adaptation" (Nestler, 2000, p. 152). For the present study, this means that children actively seek their access to religion through their individual systems of relevance and, accordingly, can also adopt individual positions. (The individual access of children to religion becomes evident in numerous passages of the material; cf. Chapter 4.)

In order to meet the requirement of focusing on the individual meanings and constructions by children as outlined above, survey methods must be used that give the interviewed children the opportunity to articulate themselves, both explicitly and implicitly. Group discussions, individual interviews, and narrative interviews are suitable for this purpose. In open interview procedures, interviewees are stimulated to talk about a topic with the help of conversational or narrative prompts. Narrations or dilemma stories are usually used to initiate conversations. Key points are then sought in the interviews which are used to reconstruct the relevancies of the participants.

With its concept of the individual system of relevance, Nestler offers an alternative to structural genetic theories to tackle the reconstruction of the development of religious thought anew. He thereby changes the analytical perspective and foregrounds the individual constructive achievement. The child who, from a structural genetic perspective, was primarily regarded as the recipient of its environment's religious input has now become the focus of research interest with its individual, active processing performance. This shift in focus finds expression in the concept of a children's theology which derives from the child as the constructor of their own reality and receives strong influences from the field of philosophy of children. This concept is based on the subjectivity and self-competence of children. According to Kuld (2001), the image of the child has changed to the effect that children are regarded as "subjects of independent religious thought and not as objects of instruction" (Kuld, 2001, p. 8). Children's theology found its way into religious education studies mainly through the Catholic religious pedagogue Anton A. Bucher with his plea for "Erste Naivität" ("first naivety") (1989). He also assumes that children construct a religiously qualified reality. Fritz Oser and Helmut Reich (1990), Konrad Fikenscher (1995), Gottfried Orth and Helmut Hanisch (1998), as well as others, support the program of an independent children's theology, whereby the level of knowledge on this subject has expanded considerably to this day (Bucher, 2008). A more concrete definition of children's theology was provided by Friedrich Schweitzer (2003). He raises awareness for a distinction between religious thinking and a children's theology which is about reflecting on religious thinking. Schweitzer presents the following three dimensions of child theology:

- theology by children as the children's own theological reflection;
- theology with children as religious-pedagogical practice of theological questioning and answering together with children;
- theology for children as education by theology, starting beyond the mere deduction from academic theology. (Schweitzer, 2003, p. 18)

If the child and their subjective constructional achievements are placed at the center of empirical religious education studies, a number of new theoretical challenges emerge which have been incorporated into the present study. Thus, special emphasis is placed on the action-guiding relevance of the construction of God among Muslim children in concrete situations (for empirical examples cf. Chapter 4). In the course of interpreting the narrative interviews of the children, their individual relevancies are reconstructed.

With regard to children's systems of relevance, it is important within the framework of the present study to create access to children's experienced reality of life. It must be left to the children whether or not to bring God or Islamic patterns of interpretation into the conversation.

3 Specifying the Research Question

The three dimensions of experience, conjunctive experiential space, and the individual system of relevance described above are now considered to formulate and specify the research question.

On the basis of the previous findings, it becomes clear that the emotional dimension of the children's relationship to God cannot be deduced from their propositional knowledge of God. To reconstruct the relationship of children to God, the researcher must relate to their lifeworld and make their own emotions and relevancies the starting point. The knowledge of God is a knowledge anchored in actions, since children experience God in the interactive use of language, i.e., through imitation and active participation in family and social life (conjunctive experiential space). The experience, as well as knowledge of God, also depends on the experiencing subject, here the child. The lifeworld, as a place where individuals find meaning and ascribe it to their experiences, contains the practical, implicit knowledge acquired through the course of socialization. Therefore, children's knowledge of God, and especially his relevance, can only be found in their everyday knowledge, i.e., in implicit, atheoretic knowledge, that is expressed linguistically in their own narration.

Consequently, the research question is: What action-oriented relevance does the construction of God have for Muslim children?

The goal here is to use empirical social research methods to reconstruct children's experiences with God and their orientations for action which were developed in the context of conjunctive experiential spaces through the course of socialization and subjectivized through their own individual systems of relevance. The results of the study will then be discussed in terms of the influence of Islamic religious education on the religious education of children.

Notes

1 The classical approaches of Gordon W. Allport, Charles Y. Glock, Rodney Stark and others can be used as paradigmatic studies in the field of quantitative social-scientific research on religiosity. Stefan Huber combined some approaches into a synthesis. His "constructional-psychological model for measuring religiosity" contains four core postulates.

Huber describes his first postulate with the help of "religious glasses" which are used here for the sake of simplicity:
- "A person is always religious when they put on their 'religious glasses' in a way and perceive reality through these glasses. On the basis of this perception they make experiences and develop perspectives for action". Thus, human experience and behavior is directed by "internal representations of one's environment", i.e. by "personal constructs" (Huber, 2004, pp. 80–81).
- "The more often a person puts on their 'religious glasses', the more religious they are". Hence, the „centrality of the religious construct system" depends on the strength of its "experience- and behavior-navigating influence" (Huber, 2004, p. 81).
- "It is not enough to ask how often someone puts on 'religious glasses'; it is also necessary to ask how these glasses are tinted". Not only is the centrality of religiosity examined here, but also its concrete content (Huber, 2004, p. 81). Religious experience and behavior can be measured by considering them as a "function of centrality and the content of personal construct systems" (Huber, 2004, p. 81).

2 According to Piaget, animism is a form of precausal thinking. In this phase of development, the child animates inanimate objects. In her research, Mähler concludes that animism is not a lack of knowledge. In her experiments, Mähler confirms the hypothesis that "animistic thinking is to be understood as an expression of imaginative activity, as a change of consciousness to the level of the unreal" (Mähler, 1995, p. 198). In particular, she notes that "the occurrence and interpretation of animistic thought depends very much on the survey method" (Mähler, 1995, p. 200).

In the context of Piaget's work and the research based on it, the structural genetic research on the development of children's and young people's world view and idea of God by Reto Luzius Fetz, Karl Helmut Reich and Peter Valentin (1992) should be mentioned here as examples for similar studies. These researchers examined the "artificialism" postulated by Piaget as a childlike pattern of interpretation and development towards a reflective approach to such a pattern of interpretation in adolescence. In the case of religiously educated children, an unreflected, artificial understanding of creation was found, that goes hand in hand with anthropomorphic ideas of God. In addition, the emergence and dissolution of this pattern of interpretation and its development in stages have been documented (more in: Fetz et al., 1992).

3 Paul-Dilemma: Paul, a young doctor, is on a plane. He wants to marry his girlfriend Pauline. The plane crashes. Paul takes a vow that in case he survives the crash he will go to the Third World to spend his life in the service of development aid. He does survive, and his girlfriend tells him that she will not accompany him to any developing country. He is also offered a good job shortly afterwards. How does Paul decide what to do (Oser & Gmünder, 1992).

4 Flöter says that children cannot really express their idea of God in a drawing. Her investigation, like other investigations, has shown that children aged 9–11 years usually still paint anthropomorphic images of God whereby the symbolic level is also partly relevant. However, Flöter uses these paintings as an occasion for conversation in order to find out what qualities the children associate with God (Flöter, 2006, p. 60).

5 The story of "Beppo" by Barbara Imgrund is about an eight-year-old boy who has many siblings. Whilst on a hill, he releases a balloon with a letter to the beloved God in which he asks for bedclothes for a soon to be born sibling. After four days a parcel with bedclothes arrives. Beppo rushes to the hill and thanks God.

6 Here the question arises whether Fowler's stage theory, which is based on Christian anthropology and is relevant for a specific environment, is appropriate to classify Muslim youths coming from a completely different context (cf. Chapter 2, Section 1.3).

7 In a conjunctive experiential space, the members can understand each other directly because they share common experiences. As soon as no conjunctive experiential space is given and one wants to communicate their own conjunctive experience with those who are not taking part in it, the meaning of the activity must be explained theoretically. Here, Mannheim speaks of "communicative" knowledge, which is necessary for communication beyond conjunctive experiential spaces (Nohl, 2012).

CHAPTER 3

Methodological Foundation and Methodological Approach

1 Methodological Decisions

In the context of this research study, the action-guiding orientations of Muslim children will be examined with regard to the relevance of their construction of God. The methodological approach is described in detail in the following, beginning with a brief comment on childhood studies.

After the paradigm shift in childhood research at the beginning of the 1980s, children have been regarded as "social actors and constructors of their own reality" who are able to provide information about themselves and their environment (Bamler et al., 2010, p. 74). This approach is based on a different view of childhood and youth as independent stages of life that are no longer just a preparatory period for adulthood. Socialization-theoretical approaches consider child development to be a "self-forming process" in which children "co-construct" (Bamler et al., 2010, p. 74). This means that the individual constructions of children receive meaning only in interdependency and interaction with others through which they "(re)construct" impressions, thoughts and experiences in mutual communication (Bamler et al., 2010, p. 75). Childhood is seen as a "socially constructed world of its own" in which children and adults participate. This perspective on childhood as "a way of life that is partly designed by children themselves [...] draws attention to the orienting and action-guiding thinking and feeling of children, to their world theories and their concrete actions" (Hülst, 2012, p. 53). As a result, the children's lifeworld and their own "coping strategies, perceptions, and orientations" become the focus of attention. Children are regarded as "productive processors of reality" (Hurrelmann & Bauer, 2015), as capable of acting, and thus as active and autonomous subjects (Bamler et al., 2010, p. 61).

This has consequences for the methodological focus of research work. According to this understanding of childlike construction processes, childhood studies primarily use qualitative, reconstructive research methods, since they offer adequate access to the lifeworld of children (Bamler et al., 2010, pp. 85–87).

In the following, the positioning of the present study in qualitative social research is substantiated, making concrete references to the research question.

© FAHIMAH ULFAT, 2023 | DOI:10.1163/9789004533219_003

According to Uwe Flick (2011), qualitative research is a relatively open method that pursues the approach of a "theory development grounded in the subject matter" (Flick, 2011, p. 124). A limited number of participants are examined. The theory is developed and established inductively from the analysis of the subject matter. In this research approach, the research subjects have priority over theoretical assumptions, since theoretical assumptions are reconstructed from empirical material. Thus, the "principle of openness" is established which ensures that the researcher does not miss out on the discovery of the "actually new" (Flick, 2011, p. 125). Qualitative research therefore has no fixed idea of the investigated subject matter, but, according to Flick, is open to the "unknown in the seemingly familiar" (Flick et al., 2005, p. 17). It aims at "describing lifeworlds 'from within', from the point of view of the acting individuals" by taking into account the subjective and social constructions of the subjects (Flick et al., 2005, p. 14).

As far as guiding theories are concerned, qualitative methods generally show a high affinity to interactionist approaches and to approaches of sociology of knowledge that are also commonly applied for their theoretical foundation. Thus, according to Berger and Luckmann, social reality results from constantly occurring social construction processes (Berger & Luckmann, 2013). Social reality is thus a "result of meanings and contexts produced jointly in social interaction" (Flick et al., 2005, p. 20). People act on the basis of these shared meanings by modifying them in response to interpretations made by others. Accordingly, qualitative research concentrates on these social production processes and attempts to reconstruct people's subjective interpretations from their internal perspective (Flick et al., 2005).

Cornelia Helfferich (2011) explains that only in a "communication relationship" does a researcher have the possibility to gain access to the "system of meaning" of their interviewee (Helfferich, 2011, p. 79). The "systems of relevance and constructions of reality" of the interviewer and the interviewee are integrated into the "communication situation", even if only one of them is talking. Interviews are therefore "communicative and social acts", i.e., "co-productions" of the interview partners in which meaning is produced "interactively and intersubjectively" (Helfferich, 2011, p. 80). This form of "co-production" also includes the intentions and interpretations of the interviewer and the interviewee as well as their relationship to each other. These dimensions must therefore be fully included in the interpretation (Helfferich, 2011, pp. 79–80). Hence the communicative character of qualitative research becomes apparent.

The relationship of children to God and their action-guiding, implicit knowledge of God is a complex research subject which requires a method that is sufficiently open to do justice to this complexity as well as to include the diversity of everyday contexts.

METHODOLOGICAL FOUNDATION AND METHODOLOGICAL APPROACH   49

The indirect access necessary here, i.e., the (only presumed) detour via the children's everyday knowledge, can only be realized qualitatively. A quantitative approach based on a questionnaire that can merely check pre-formulated items does not allow an assessment of the actual everyday relevance of the answers. By using an indirect, qualitative method, the diversity of the perspectives of the interviewed children can be recorded and their individual systems of relevance can be represented in their own logic. It is precisely the relationship to God that is the result of subjectivizing the interpretations of conjunctive experiential spaces on the basis of individual systems of relevance. It is therefore necessary to describe interrelations in the context of the individual case and also to explain them on this basis (cf. Chapter 4, Section 1).

Friederike Heinzel (2012) points out that qualitative childhood research which claims to adopt children's perspectives and reconstruct children's reality from their point of view, presents considerable methodological and theoretical challenges. One cannot automatically "speak of describing 'the children's perspective' just because the investigated are given a chance to speak" (Heinzel, 2012, p. 24). Researchers, for example, have certain ideas about childhood that vary according to cultural, historical, and personal experiences. These ideas are reflected in their research interests, but also in their expectations of the results. Consequently, research approaches into the perspective of children are likewise "written perspectively" (Heinzel, 2012, p. 24). This must be considered when evaluating the data.

Bamler et al. (2010) also highlight the fact that perspectivity in social science research requires a method that is open to children's constructions and their perception of reality. Moreover, gender, age, and cultural as well as social characteristics must also be taken into account in the sample.

The interrelation between the three outlined dimensions of experience, conjunctive experiential space, and children's individual system of relevance requires an open research approach. The narrative interview used in this study gives the children the opportunity to share their experiences and interpretations within the framework of their own system of relevance.

In the following, the position of the present study in the field of reconstructive social research is explained and concrete references to the research question are made.

Ralf Bohnsack (2010b) explains that reconstructive methods are open approaches, "leaving the structuring of the communication within the framework of the topic relevant to the investigation as far as possible to those who are the subject of research so that they can develop their system of relevance and their communicative control system" (Bohnsack, 2010b, p. 21). He goes on to say that this openness creates a greater "possibility of control", in the sense that interviewees are given the opportunity to develop a topic within their own system of relevance. They themselves can make clear what is relevant for them. Regarding the present study, this means that a direct and close questioning about God would aim at objectifiable information and knowledge (propositional knowledge). However, it would not clarify whether this knowledge actually has any relevance for action. Direct questioning by no means says anything with certainty about whether faith in God really plays a role in any domain of the children's world. From a methodological point of view, when using such a method of questioning it cannot be ruled out with certainty that particularly children of primary school age only express what they have been told by adults. There is always the possibility that children will interpret the interview situation as an examination scenario and therefore will provide the 'correct' answers as expected from them. Consequently, it is only through open methods that children can express their own meanings and thoughts in relation to the topic of God.

The researcher is also monitored to ensure that no inappropriate meanings are "projected" into the statements of the interviewees (Bohnsack, 2010b, p. 21). The "context" (Bohnsack, 2010b, p. 21) is of particular importance here because only "in the overall context of a narrative" can the statements of the interviewees be adequately understood. Bohnsack calls the differentiation between the systems of relevance of the interviewees and those of the researchers "methodically controlled understanding of others" (Bohnsack, 2010b, p. 21). This is based on two methodological principles: the "principle of openness" (the structuring of the research topic by the subjects has priority) and the "principle of communication" (the communicative regulatory system of the subjects becomes effective) (Bohnsack, 2010b, pp. 21–22).

The methodology of the reconstructive method is based on "second-degree constructions": These are "constructions of those constructions which are formed by the actors in the social field" (Schütz, 1971, p. 6, quoted in Bohnsack, 2010b, p. 23). According to Bohnsack, this "everyday action" is directed by an action plan (Bohnsack, 2010b, p. 23). The researcher's task is to comprehend this action plan. However, by using the example of driving to one' s workplace, Bohnsack shows that this everyday action is "inaccessible to mere observation" (Bohnsack, 2010b, p. 23). The driver intending to drive to his workplace has a plan in mind which his actions are based on. It is therefore not enough that the researcher observes the driver. The researcher must know the driver's action plan or make assumptions about it in order to understand what he is observing. "Everyday experience is symbolically structured and consists of symbolic constructions, even in the area of routine actions, pre-theoretical or – as Mannheim states – atheoretic, unreflected actions. From the viewpoint of

METHODOLOGICAL FOUNDATION AND METHODOLOGICAL APPROACH 51

scientific construction, those of everyday life are first degree constructions. The social scientist must first *reconstruct* the methods implied in them – before he himself constructs and develops methods" (Bohnsack, 2010b, p. 24). In order to reconstruct the constructions of the individuals examined, they must be given the opportunity to express themselves linguistically.

Thus a change from an "observation of the first order to an observation of the second order" takes place (Vogd, 2010, p. 124). Werner Vogd explains that an observation of first order corresponds to a "common sense understanding" (Vogd, 2010, p. 126). The observation of the second order then refers to the "endowment with meaning", i.e., to the "framework" in which a topic is dealt with (Vogd, 2010, p. 126). Bohnsack (2010a) calls this "praxeological type formation" (Bohnsack, 2010a, p. 298). He makes clear that type formations of common sense represent only one level of reality.

> The other level is that of the *practical, habitual* production of reality. The central point here is not the action plan and the intended meaning, but the modus operandi, the generative formula which, as practical knowledge of action, underlies the production of practice as a whole. (Bohnsack, 2010a, p. 298)

2 Survey Method: Narrative Interview

2.1 *Preliminary Considerations*

Qualitative methods use various forms of interviews in order to gain access to individual worlds of experience through the openness that can be realized by them. In the present research study, the narrative interview is used for the survey.

According to Fritz Schütze (1976), narratives about one's own experiences emerge because the narrator becomes entangled in a "triple tight spot of narration" (*"dreifacher Zugzwang des Erzählens"*) as soon as he has begun the narrative. He finds himself in a *"Gestaltschließungszwang"* (a narrative once begun is told to the end), in a *"Kondensierungszwang"* (the narrative only contains what is important for understanding the storyline) and in a *"Detaillierungszwang"* (necessary background information and correlations are provided for comprehension) (Schütze, 1976, p. 225). The narrative interview provides data that other forms of questioning cannot provide; firstly due to the dynamics of the narrative's independence outlined above, secondly because of the fact that people's knowledge of their lives is implicitly available in the narrative, and thirdly by assuming a correspondence between the narrative and the experience narrated: "In the narrative-retrospective processing of experience, it is reported in principle how the narrator as the acting human experienced biographical events (whether actions or natural events)" (Schütze, 1976, p. 197). Schütze additionally assumes that in impromptu stories, narrators are "driven" to speak about events they would not mention in normal conversations due to "guilt or shame" (Schütze, 1976, p. 255). This means that narratives possess their own dynamics that go beyond the narrator.

In narrative interviews, the question should be as open as possible

> so that the interviewees structure the communication by themselves to a great extent and, thus, also have the opportunity to document whether they are interested in the question at all, whether it has a place in their lifeworld – one may also use the term: system of relevance – and if so, under which aspect it gains importance for them. (Bohnsack, 2010b, p. 20)

A narrative interview is usually started with a narrative invitation that is "formulated so broadly and so specifically [...] that it addresses the intended area of experience as a stage of life" (Flick, 2011, p. 229).

2.2 *Characteristics of Interviews with Children*

The methodology of qualitative interviews with adults is well researched scientifically. However, these methods cannot simply be applied to children. Although, according to Burkhard Fuhs (2012), interviews with children had been already conducted successfully in numerous studies, fundamental reservations do exist as such interviews require careful planning as well as a methodological foundation. Fuhs refers to Petermann and Windmann (1993) who argue that interviews with children depend on many factors, including the children's stage of development, their expectations, their previous experiences, their motivation, the interviewer's behavior, the premises, the social environment, and the interview process. However, they and also other researchers point out that a child-appropriate survey makes obtaining personal disclosures from the child possible (Fuhs, 2012, p. 90). In the following the possibilities and limitations of the narrative interview with children are discussed and the relation to the present study is established.

Fuhs explains that the "communicative abilities" of children play an important role in the use of open interviews. The development of childlike forms of expression evolves from "non-verbal communication" (gestures) to "linguistic communication". Children can thus express their "subjective world" differently at different ages and developmental stages (Fuhs, 2012, pp. 87–88).

Thomas Trautmann (2010) summarizes the "degree of expected qualities of answers" according to age groups (Trautmann, 2010, p. 46). He describes how a first grader at primary school age

> has a firm awareness of themselves. The pupil is able to distinguish between their own feelings and those of others and to differentiate between reality and illusion. Language is used correctly to a large extent and complex stories can be told. Although the children still reflect little on what they say, this does not affect successful communication, especially as most children can already lie consciously. In middle primary school age, children have complex patterns of thought and behavior as well as metacognition ability. The child reflects on their own thoughts – a phenomenon just as inestimable for interviews as correcting oneself while speaking. The now 'functioning' mental reversal of action and the multi-dimensionality of approaches will also exponentially increase the quality of interviews. (Trautmann, 2010, p. 46)

Trautmann describes further stages but these are not relevant for the following argumentation since the children interviewed in the present study are only of middle primary school age.

Trautmann mentions another characteristic, namely the "quality of mental representations", that is developed through one's own experiences or/and narratives by others (Trautmann, 2010, p. 60). According to Hülst (2012), mental representations are schematic structures of knowledge that – like "templates of spiritual orientation [...] – automatically and unconsciously control the course of information processing by directing attention" (Hülst, 2012, p. 62). Trautmann states that schoolchildren aged seven or older, unlike preschool children, can distinguish between their own experiences and what others tell them. Since language is a basic medium for communicating thoughts and feelings, Trautmann suggests that interviews as a survey method in research only be used after school enrollment (Trautmann, 2010, p. 62). Fuhs, on the other hand, points out that qualitative interview methods that are combined with playful activities can be used successfully in the pre-primary sector and he refers to Paus-Haase who used qualitative interviews in kindergarten (Fuhs, 2012, p. 85).

Each interview is based on updating memories. Fuhs refers to the work of Schneider and Büttner who describe that the strength of memory increases most at primary school age and that even kindergarten children can remember "autobiographical experiences" quite accurately over a longer period of time (Fuhs, 2012, p. 89).

Trautmann points out that younger children will try to show socially desirable behavior in the interview. However, he also states that despite their socially desirable behavior, children nevertheless have a "partially personal canon of perception" and that their still developing "perceptual organization" is already very individual (Trautmann, 2010, p. 54). The "preservation of information" is achieved through "regular recalls" which build up "mental representations" in the brain (Trautmann, 2010, p. 54). The actual memory process in school children is described as a stable process that is less often subject to "deceptions of perception". Individual "fantasy lies" (Trautmann, 2010, p. 55) may appear, but the temporal localization of what has been experienced becomes increasingly precise, the emotional memory increasingly long-lived.

Distortions in the memory process may occur "when attention is directed" (e.g., when the interviewer intervenes during the narrative and directs attention to other elements), "when the situation is overstrained during the event" (e.g., when the environment is distracting or the expectations imposed on the child are too high), "when the child is traumatically involved in a certain event", when a "memory culture" in the family is neglected, etc. (Trautmann, 2010, pp. 56–58). Children can also reveal several "levels of communication" in an interview, e.g., by speaking as the carefree child as well as "through the mouth" of an adult (usually parent) (Trautmann, 2010, p. 58). Hence, when interpreting the interviews, special attention must be paid to distinguish these levels.

2.3 Relationship between Interviewer and Children in the Concrete Implementation and Concrete Research Setting

Interview situations are always "artificial" situations. Common problems in conducting narrative interviews are the role expectations of the interview partner to each other as well as expectations regarding the situation.

Helfferich (2011) explains that not only the unfamiliarity of the field, but also the tension between closeness and unfamiliarity in the interview situation is a principle of qualitative research. Both partners react reciprocally to each other and assess each other. Closeness and unfamiliarity have an "emotional" and a "cognitive" dimension. Closeness can be described emotionally as "trust" between the two interview partners and, on the cognitive level, as "familiarity" if there is a common "background of experience, knowledge, and interpretation" (Helfferich, 2011, p. 120). In an interview situation, "trust" can also emerge from "familiarity". But these two dimensions do not necessarily have to coincide. The relationship of the interview partners can also be characterized by "distance", and yet "trusting communication" can develop if the interviewee feels that the interviewer is somebody who can understand her/him. Helfferich emphasizes that the interviewer is the "social horizon" (Helfferich, 2011, p. 120) towards which one speaks. This means that a shared experiential

METHODOLOGICAL FOUNDATION AND METHODOLOGICAL APPROACH 55

space facilitates the access to the interviewees and increases their willingness to participate (Helfferich, 2011, pp. 119–120).

Also in the present research study, the question has been asked from the outset as to how Muslim students would react to an interviewer from their experiential space as well as to a recognizably religious survey setting. For this reason, the concrete setting is presented here:

The interviewer can be recognized as a Muslim by her headscarf. She introduced herself to the children in the respective schools during religious education in order to find volunteers for her project. The children were given the general information that the interviewer is a researcher from the university who is interested in children's thinking. To understand how children think, she wants to play with them. This play will involve telling stories.

The children asked questions about the university and the activities there. The interviewer explained the different research fields at university and talked about the play Kamishibai (cf. Chapter 3, Section 2.4). Religion was not mentioned in the setting. The interviewer was only identified as a Muslim by her headscarf. Apart from that, Islam and being a Muslim were not discussed any further. It can be assumed that the interviewer's headscarf is taken for granted by the Muslim children.

The children's questions showed that they were mainly interested in the play. Children who wanted to participate in the play were given a letter for their parents with information about the project, a privacy statement, and a request for their consent. The letter informed the parents that both the children and the parents could cancel participation at any time and that participation had no impact on school performance assessments. Then the interviewer bade farewell to the children and waited for the responses from their parents. After receiving the consent forms, the interviews were performed during the religious education period, but in a different room.

This setting was intended to control expressions that were oriented towards social expectations. It can be assumed that the presence of a woman wearing a headscarf was not experienced as specifically religious by the Muslim children interviewed. It became apparent that this setting provided the children with a framework in which they could use religious terms in their own language (Turkish, Arabic, Persian) without having to fear that the interviewer would not be able to understand them or even perceive their statements to be strange, as the common experiential space facilitated communication with the children. This means that the setting established a form of religious normality that was familiar to the children without the topic of religion dominating.

According to Mannheim, since concepts and thoughts are existential in nature, it is consistent with the theoretical considerations of the present study that the person interviewing the children also belongs to their conjunctive experiential space in order to be able to understand the conjunctively rooted concepts in their context of meaning. If the interviewee is afraid that the interviewer may not understand them, important information may be withheld. In this case, the children would only tell the interviewer, as a member of another conjunctive experiential space, what they think the interviewer wants to hear or is able to understand. However, if the interviewee can assume that the interviewer understands their cultural or religious thinking, acting, and feeling, little or no shyness will exist. The familiarity that existed between the interviewer and the Muslim children allowed the children to talk freely and easily about their family and religious lives, also using religious terms from their mother tongue.

The evaluation method allowed the identification and description of those expressions used by the children that were oriented towards social expectations. This required continuous reflection on the interviewer's part during the interviews as well as during their analysis.

According to Heinzel, "generational orders" (Heinzel, 2012, p. 25) are formed between children and adults in the interview situation which can be described as a "hierarchical situation" between "unequal partners" (Heinzel, 2012, p. 27). This unequal situation influences the roles of the conversation partners as well as the course of the conversation, despite the aspiration to have open communication (Heinzel, 2012, p. 27). The interviews carried out in the present study also took place on the premises of the respective school. Accordingly, it was possible that the children might interpret the interview as an educational situation. Fuhs points out that it is precisely this "generational order" that can lead to the fact that researchers with pedagogical competence (e.g., teachers and pedagogues) have a certain image of childhood and are trained in a particular way to deal with children, which can lead to their not perceiving the individual lifeworlds of the children (Fuhs, 2012, p. 91).

For the present study, this means that the interviewer, who is also pedagogically trained, must abandon her "professional self-image" and her "pedagogical action and communication strategies" in order to encounter the foreign in the familiar. Hülst describes this as "problematizing one's own understanding" (Hülst, 2012, p. 71).

The "generational structure" that children are accustomed to when dealing with adults had to be constantly reflected in the present study. According to Heinzel, the role behavior of the interviewer has a supportive and positive effect (Heinzel, 2012, p. 29). For this reason, Fuhs (2012) always considers research with children to be also methodological research, since methodological procedures and the associated requirements are tested, discussed, adapted, and newly developed (Fuhs, 2012, p. 93). Also in the present study, a specifically

METHODOLOGICAL FOUNDATION AND METHODOLOGICAL APPROACH 57

developed method was used for the narrative-generating input stimulus to generate narratives (cf. Chapter 3, Section 2.4).

Fuhs emphasizes that this "generational order" must remain committed to a "value-oriented, advocacy perspective" that has to be oriented towards "human rights and the UN Convention on the Rights of the Child" (Fuhs, 2012, p. 83). Therefore, the fundamental focus on the protection of children's personal rights was taken into consideration as follows:

- Data protection regulations: Since students of the Muslim faith participating in Islamic religious education were interviewed, the survey was conducted at state schools. An application for permission to conduct a survey in state schools was submitted. The application included declarations of consent by the parents, which were voluntary and had to be submitted in writing, information on the anonymization of the transcripts, the deletion requirement for the recordings, names, addresses, and telephone numbers as well as declarations regarding the employees' obligation to observe data security. The application was approved.
- All data were anonymized and masked to protect the children.
- Superordinate ethical principles were on the one hand the "informed consent" of the narrators, on the other hand the "non-infringement" of the narrators.
- These principles also include the imperatives for openness, acceptance, empathy, and tolerance for the children's experiences and attitudes (Fuhs, 2012, p. 83).

In addition to role expectations, content-related expectations also exist which, according to Trautmann (2010), may cause uncertainty as the children cannot assess what is expected by the interviewer in terms of content. They do not know what the interviewer wants to hear and may be confused. It may happen that children provide socially desirable answers in order to satisfy the interviewer. Moreover, it is also possible that the interview becomes a one-sided questioning situation that only generates monosyllabic answers. These problems also had to be reflected in the evaluation of the interviews.

For all these reasons, the questioning technique is of utmost importance. In particular, the interviewer should not be tempted to suggest answer patterns to the child or ask the next question too quickly. Waiting patiently for further narratives proves to be fruitful in most cases. Nevertheless, it might be difficult to lure the children out of their comfort zone for reasons such as insecurity or rejection (Trautmann, 2010).

Flick (2011) explains that in interviews an empathetic attitude on the part of the interviewer is of particular importance. The interviewer's role must be characterized by "active listening", "signalling of interest", "non-verbal-appreciative communication", the absence of "interventions", and by "maintaining the relationship with the interviewees" (Flick, 2011, p. 235). The narration is stimulated by a precise and unambiguous narrative prompt and maintained by the aforementioned attitude (Flick, 2011). This applies in particular to interviews with children.

2.4 The Narrative-Generating Initial Stimulus of the Present Study

In order to encourage the children to narrate, the author chose Kamishibai (a Japanese form of narrative theatre) as a "motivational episode" (Trautmann, 2010, p. 75). The methodological decision for Kamishibai was made on the basis of previous experience from concrete teaching situations.

Various props are part of the external sequence of this narrative theatre. The author first procured a wooden frame. The frame is constructed like a theatre stage and has openings at the top as well as on the sides so that sequences of pictures can be inserted which are then gradually removed during the story. The stage can be closed with two wooden doors. The author created a child-oriented story (see below) as well as two stage sets matching the story; she also had a carpenter make small wooden figures (male and female, adult and child figures) to support the narrative.

This provided the children with an additional setting that was familiar to them and gave them the opportunity to become actively involved in creative activities. They were recipients only at the beginning because after the stimulus was provided by the interviewer, the 'direction' of playing was left to them. This was initialized by handing over the wooden figures to the children. The modified Kamishibai thus matches the form of a puppetry interview but offers the child the opportunity to take on the role of an active designer due to the special setting of stage and puppets.

The attractiveness of the modified Kamishibai lies in the mixture of verbal prompts and a stylized stage which has the character of a children's stage. The child is offered the setting of the theater in order to slip into the role of the active designer more easily. In narratives or films, the child remains the recipient. The creation of a space in which the child can take over the 'direction' and thus switches from being a passive recipient to an active designer is the added value of the modified Kamishibai. The wooden figures were added to the Kamishibai in order to facilitate this change of perspective.

It was found that the children show an increased willingness to actively respond to this. The aim was first and foremost to hide the presence of the interviewer as a person. The story told as the narrative-generating stimulus was thus not directly offered to the child by the interviewer but was communicated through the medium of the narrative theatre. This allowed the children to leave the educational situation behind. Additionally, they were initially given time to relax at the beginning of the interview, as theatre acting was the focus and the interviewer began telling the story. After the end, a subtle transition into the conversation was possible as the focus was not immediately directed on the children themselves. By asking the children to slip into the role of the play's characters, a highly specific and, as it turned out, extraordinarily fruitful incentive was created that enabled the children to start narrating.

Kamishibai stimulates "childlike play" which, according to Rolf Oerter (1996), represents a "typical means of coping with life" in the form of a "meaningful activity" (Oerter, 1996, p. 27). According to Oerter, a child has no "knowledge and experience" to "realistically process experiences and wishes" and therefore uses the possibility to "assimilate" and "accommodate experiences and observations" in play (Oerter, 1996, p. 27). For Oerter, play is a "universal trait of human development" and a "central processing mechanism of human development". It is a "form of coping with existence in the world" (Oerter, 1996, p. 28).

As explained in Chapter 2, Section 2.2, Tamminen (1993) and Szagun (2014) noted that children tend to focus on emergency situations when reporting experiences of closeness to God. This means that in order to grasp children's action-guiding knowledge in relation to their construction of God, emergency situations are particularly suitable. Therefore, the hypothetically threatening scenario created by the author herself aims at putting children in a situation of inner or outer discomfort in which thinking of God as well as praying to God can be activated and the children may have easier access to the situation and to talking about it. The situation in the story is close to everyday life.

Since direct questions about God are presumed to evoke predominantly propositional knowledge that cannot be assessed for its relevance for action, the subject of God was not included in the narrative prompts. Thus, the children are not given a narrative that addresses God. They are free to make their own choices and are not encouraged to include religious elements in their narratives.

"Atheoretical knowledge" (cf. Chapter 2, Section 2.3) depends on a concrete context of action. For this reason, the children were offered a concrete context of action within the narrative-generating input stimulus to which they could respond with reference to their own experiences.

This approach should not be confused with the "dilemma method" in which a narrative basis is presented that raises decision-making problems and for which the interviewees should develop and justify a procedure based on moral judgements (Trautmann, 2010).[1]

The narrative theatre, as well as the way the author approached the children, proved to be very effective as the children were made to feel comfortable and this was an important condition for their openness and accessibility. Thus they were interested in the topics and communicated with the interviewer, as similarly insisted by Bamler et al. (2010).

The following story, which the narrative theatre was based on, offers an authorial narrative prompt with insights into the thoughts of the actors. The narrator is all-knowing because s/he can also express the internal perspectives of the people involved. This gives the maximum possible choice of whether or not to slip into a role. The story leads to an existential point which the children then playfully can relate to their own experiences.

Narrative-generating input stimulus:

> *Ali's class teacher likes him very much. When he raises his hand, she smiles and picks him right away. She often praises him for his good answers. Ali is diligent and always does his homework. He is friendly and greets all students and teachers. He helps his classmates and does not argue with them.*
>
> *But some of the students in his class are jealous of him and envy him. They're trying to figure out a way to bug him. Esad has an idea.*
>
> *"How about we just lock him up in the old hut? We'll leave him in the lurch for a while".*
>
> *Everybody thinks it's a great idea. "Yes, that's what we're gonna do!"*
>
> *The next day after school, four classmates catch him on the way home. They drag him to the old hut near the path and push him in. Esad has brought a padlock and locks the door.*
>
> *The hut has no windows. It is dark inside. Ali is scared. He knocks and calls for help. Nobody comes by. Nobody can hear him. He doesn't have a cell phone with him ...* (Author's text)

Then the child was asked to continue the story. The narrative prompt went something like: "*Now it's your turn to continue narrating*".

The interviewed child had the opportunity to take up the situation completely independently of themselves and to continue the storyline using their imagination. Similar to a "puppet interview" (Trautmann, 2010, p. 76), the child can also drift to a purely imaginary level in Kamishibai, and their statements then lose reference to their own reality. Hence, after the narrative theatre, conversation and narrative stimuli were used, which first revisited the performed situation and then slowly transferred to the level of the child's experiences. These stimuli allowed access to the child's '(experienced) reality of life' and thus to their individual system of relevance. For the reasons given above, the author consistently avoided mentioning God or Islamic theological terms, since it was to be left to the children themselves whether or not to bring God

FIGURE 4   Kamishibai with props

or Islamic patterns of interpretation into the conversation. Thus the narrative interview does not allow for questions that would evoke predetermined or desirable answers. The only stimuli used are those that inspire the generation of further narrations.

For the sake of the quality of the data, it was particularly important that the interviewed child was not disturbed during their narration by the interviewer's questions, instructions or "evaluative interventions". Reinforcing prompting should help the interviewed child to continue their narrative as long as possible (Flick, 2011, p. 230). Non-verbal reactions such as nodding, communicative posture, and interested body language also contributed to keep the narrative flowing (Bamler et al., 2010).

The interviewed children usually indicated the end of the narrative with a "coda" (Flick, 2011, p. 230), e.g., with the phrase "and I don't know what happens next".

This was followed by a "narrative part with questions" (Flick, 2011, p. 230) in which the author initially set immanent and later exmanent question stimuli. The latter serve primarily to complete initially unexplained narrative approaches and, through renewed narrative stimuli, to immerse the child deeper into the story. Afterwards, stimuli were provided in order to narrate their own biographical experiences. In the final "accounting phase" (Flick, 2011, p. 230), the children were asked questions about theoretical explanations of what had happened and what had been narrated. The subject of God was brought into the conversation if it had not already been introduced by the children themselves. In this part of the interview, more abstract questions were asked, directed at the levels of "description and argumentation" (Flick, 2011, p. 230).

All the stimuli in the interview were used to determine where knowledge becomes relevant for action. Of research interest were questions such as: Where is religious knowledge used? Which knowledge is applied in everyday situations? Which is applied habitually? Through the narrative context, the children led the author into areas in which God becomes relevant to everyday life. The children were encouraged to narrate situations in which they start to reflect and have to deal with situations in which their construction of God has potential relevance. Linguistically, an attempt was made to remain at the children's level of thought and language.

Specific to the present study is that on the one hand narrations were initiated, but on the other hand speaking about God was only stimulated in the explicit part of the interview. This reveals the quality and extent of Muslim children's ability to speak about God.

2.5 Final Remarks

One might think that the scope of children's narrations is not particularly broad. Nevertheless, this study found that the children's ability to reflect and remember in addition to their linguistic abilities resulted in narrations that contained considerable biographical elements. This is also supported by Fuhs who points out that interviews with children can be successfully used as an established method in school and childhood research (Fuhs, 2012, p. 85).

The narrative interview is very suitable for research approaches in the present category, whereby the strategy of case selection also depends on the method used (gradual selection of cases according to the concept of "theoretical sampling" (Glaser & Strauss, 2010, pp. 61–63; cf. Chapter 3, Section 4). The method also determines the interpretation procedure, which is explained below (cf. Chapter 3, Section 3).

In qualitative childhood research, the issue of appropriate analysis and evaluation of children's statements is discussed in detail. Hülst explains that "understanding" as a social science method in the context of childhood sociological questions focuses on two objects of knowledge: "understanding what children are saying in their statements (understanding the meaning), and understanding what their statements (from the respective subject-specific perspective) signify (understanding interpretation)" (Hülst, 2012, p. 54). The documentary method focuses particularly on this distinction so that it is especially suitable for the evaluation of children's statements in the context of this study's research interest.

The combination of the two approaches, "narrative interview" and "documentary method", has already been methodologically reflected by Arndt-Michael Nohl, hence the reference to his remarks in this study (Nohl, 2005).

3   Interpretation Procedure: Documentary Method

The documentary method is based on the sociological model of the construction of knowledge according to Karl Mannheim who, in the 1920s, developed a theoretical and methodological approach to implicit, action-guiding or, according to Mannheim, "atheoretical" knowledge.

Mannheim developed his approach based on his understanding that not only is the content of what is being said is important, but so is its context (Vogd, 2010). The theory on which the documentary method is based thus goes beyond the common-sense typifications that examine social reality. The documentary method, which was further developed by Ralf Bohnsack, goes one step further and asks how this reality is created (Nohl, 2012, p. 45).

Vogd argues that the documentary method shows a similarity to Bourdieu's sociological research, since both are based on a praxeological sociology of knowledge, which states that "the distinctions that guide action are usually not consciously, but rather pre-reflexively woven into the practice of the individual actors" (Vogd, 2010, p. 125), i.e., in the tradition of Bourdieu, they are usually habitually embodied.

This "pre-reflexive" knowledge is thus "intuitive" and action-guiding (Bohnsack, 2009, p. 298). Mannheim illustrates this by using the example of tying a knot. The action of tying is based on knowledge that is implicit and difficult to explain. The habitualization of this practice is the product of a "modus operandi" (Bohnsack, 2010a, p. 299). In other words, this "modus operandi" describes the habitus on which the practice is based. The habitus is woven into the practice, so it is based on implicit knowledge and the actors themselves are usually not aware of it. This practice can be analyzed through "the empirical reconstruction of metaphorical representations, narratives, and descriptions of the actions of the actors, thus through the reconstruction of their own *mental* images" (Bohnsack, 2010a, p. 299). "The documentary method in essence takes on the function of *making implicit knowledge explicit*" (Bohnsack, 2009, p. 324).

By means of the documentary interpretation of interviews, not only "perspectives and *orientations*, but also the *experiences* from which the orientations emerged" are reconstructed (Nohl, 2012, p. 1). In the present study, children talk about their own experiences, starting from a seemingly hopeless situation, presented and narrated in a scenic and playful way. The evaluation focuses on the orienting and action-guiding knowledge of the children in relation to their construction of God. The method thus serves to reconstruct the children's practical experiences with 'God' and gives insight into their action orientations. These orientations can be documented in the narrated practice. The method thus opens an "access to the practice of action" (Nohl, 2012, p. 2). Therefore, the relationship to God is to be reconstructed through the habitus on which the practice of action is based on ("modus operandi"), namely at the level of implicit knowledge. The explication of children's atheoretical knowledge about God is the objective of documentary interpretation.

3.1   *Empirical Approach: The Question Concerning What and How*

In reconstructing people's experiences and orientations, Mannheim makes a distinction between two levels of meaning. Nohl explains these two levels of meaning in relation to the documentary method.

According to Mannheim, an experiential report contains both a literal, explicit, "immanent meaning" as well as a "documentary meaning" (Nohl, 2012, p. 2). The immanent meaning can in turn be divided into a subjectively intended "intentional meaning of expression" (the narrator's intentions and motives) and an "object meaning" (general meaning of a textual content or an action) (Nohl, 2012, p. 2).

Bohnsack points out that the subjectively intended meaning or the actor's motive can, according to Schütz, only be reconstructed once the actor's "concept" or "communicative intention" is known (Bohnsack, 1993, p. 520). Since this study does not aim to reconstruct the subjectively intended meaning of the children's statements or their "intention to communicate" (Bohnsack, 1993, p. 520), this aspect is not discussed any further here.

The object meaning refers to the "object" of communication. The documentary meaning, however, can be made accessible by "explication of the context(-knowledge)". Bohnsack (1993) defines context as the experiential space of an individual (biography) or of a collective (milieu, generation, epoch) from which orientation can be derived. This contextual and experiential, "atheoretical" knowledge is "conceptually and theoretically explicated" with the help of the documentary method (Bohnsack, 1993, pp. 520–521).

In research practice, at the level of the immanent meaning (object meaning), a "phrasing interpretation" is carried out, whereby a "(re)formulation" of

METHODOLOGICAL FOUNDATION AND METHODOLOGICAL APPROACH   65

what is literally communicated takes place. This concerns the question "what". The transcribed statements are divided thematically into main and sub-topics and structured according to subjects. This step corresponds to a "first-order observation" (Bohnsack, 2009, p. 325).

In the second step, a "reflective interpretation" of the documentary meaning is performed in research practice. The question of "how" is addressed here. Thus, a change from a first-order observation to a second-order observation occurs. Consequently, documentary meaning "reconstructs the described experience as a document of orientation" by investigating the question of "*how* the text and the action reported within it are constructed". It is therefore a matter "of the 'orientation framework' in which a problem is dealt with" (Nohl, 2012, p. 2).

In reflective interpretation, a sequence analysis is performed. Bohnsack and Nohl explain that "the (implicit) regularity which is to be explored or explicated [constitutes itself] in the relation of the (empirically observable) statement and the (empirically observable) reaction" (Bohnsack & Nohl, 2013, p. 325). For this purpose, the interviews are examined for "*similarities*, more precisely for homologous, functionally equivalent reactions, i.e., reactions belonging to the same category" (Bohnsack & Nohl, 2013, p. 326). This step requires a "comparison horizon" (Bohnsack & Nohl, 2013, p. 326). This means that a comparative analysis is carried out in which "contrasting" reactions are compared in the form of a "case comparison" (Bohnsack & Nohl, 2013, p. 326). The objective is to analyze comparatively how the same topic is dealt with in other interviews within a different framework of orientation. In this step, "the *scope* that is decisive for the treatment of the topic is made discernible" (Bohnsack, 2010b, p. 34). In other words, it is examined how another interviewee sets the course in dealing with the same or a similar topic.

This case comparison should be carried out at an early stage. It is used for controlling the "blind spot" that mirrors "the interpreter's attachments (*Seins-verbundenheit*)" (Bohnsack & Nohl, 2013, p. 326). This means that a methodical control of the researcher's perspective and attachment to a position ("*Stand-ortgebundenheit*") is achieved in order for him to not represent the central interpretation matrix for evaluating the interviews, but rather the interviews are analyzed in a contrastive case comparison. In addition, the interpretations are validated communicatively in the context of a research workshop that also controls the "blind spot" of the interpreter by means of "intersubjective verifi-ability" (Helfferich, 2011, p. 156).

In the present study, the reflective interpretation is used to reconstruct the children's atheoretical, action-guiding knowledge about God. This knowledge, which is implicit, is made explicit by the interpreter through reflective interpretation. The question is about the frame of orientation in which the children contextualize their experience of God. Since the children's orientations implicitly contained in the narrations which are relevant for the research question are brought into an explicit form through interpretation, there is no danger that those descriptions of God that they have heard and learned from their parents, teachers, friends, and other caregivers are included.

Consequently, it is possible to assess the meaning of statements "within the specific experiential space in their milieu-specific or also individual case-specific particularity" (Bohnsack, 2003, p. 43).

3.2 Type Formation

Aglaja Przyborski and Monika Wohlrab-Sahr (2014) explain that type formation is a matter of "generalization" of contexts and structures that can be inferred from the examined cases. The documentary method developed as an evaluation process its specific solutions for the generalization of the findings. "The question of generalization is always connected with the development of theory and is based on case comparisons and/or on the systematic use of contrast horizons" (Przyborski & Wohlrab-Sahr, 2014, p. 359).

Ralf Bohnsack has reformulated the central quality criteria of standardized procedures (reliability, validity, and generalizability) in the context of reconstructive methodology. He points out "that in methodological terms, the key to generalization lies in the formation of ideal types, and that in terms of research practice, the grounded theory (Glaser & Strauss, 1967), with its strategies of comparative analysis and theoretical sampling, offers a suitable approach" (Bohnsack, 2005, p. 76).

Max Weber (1988) has described the ideal type as something that portrays a pattern of reality in an ideal-typical, but not in a specific form: The ideal image "is gained by the one-sided emphasis of one or some points of view and by the combination of an abundance of diffuse and discrete, here more, there less, sometimes non-existent individual phenomena, which fit in with those unilaterally emphasized points of view, to form a unified body of thought. In its conceptual purity, this thought image cannot be found empirically anywhere in reality; it is a utopia" (Weber, 1988, p. 191). In practical research terms, this means that certain single facets can be omitted or exaggerated in order to outline certain aspects. The construction of ideal types, therefore, represents an intensification of individual characteristics. A type is thus a mental construction and not an exact image of reality.

Against this backdrop, two models of type formation were developed: the case-analogical and the ideal-typical type formation. In the case-analogical type formation, the case specific observations match the type to a large extent, i.e., the type formation occurs parallel to the case structure. However, in an ideal-typical type formation "fundamentally different types or typologies, i.e., different dimensions or 'experiential spaces', must be determined in the case based on comparative analysis [...] and their 'superimpositions' must be reconstructed empirically" (Bohnsack, 2005, p. 76). This means that the type is no longer identical to the case and the case is therefore only recorded as "aspect-like" or "type-like", depending on the dimensions of the case that are recorded on the basis of the comparisons (Bohnsack, 2005, p. 77). Iris Nentwig-Gesemann (2007) explains that a "multidimensionality of type formation and typology" is given if not each case is assigned to a type, but the typologies represent a composition of several cases (Nentwig-Gesemann, 2007, p. 290).

Hence type formation depends on the researcher's practical research decisions, i.e., which aspects of the case are to be documented and which dimensions – and thus which points are to be summarized and abstracted. Due to the maximum and minimum contrasts, reconstructions do suggest a certain form of type formation. However, within this framework which emerges from the empirical material, the researcher chooses where to focus on, depending on the research question, and which working categories are the central points of summarization.

Furthermore, there are two levels in "praxeological type formation" which examines *how* social reality is produced on the basis of similar contexts of experience and experiential knowledge (conjunctive experiential spaces): the level of "genesis of meaning" and the level of "sociogenesis" (Nentwig-Gesemann, 2007, p. 278).

Nentwig-Gesemann shows that the "generation and specification of types" occurs at the level of genesis of meaning (Nentwig-Gesemann, 2007, p. 292) which differs in terms of orientation and practice of action. For this purpose, "minimum and maximum contrasts", which represent the "patterns" of a case, are worked out in the "cross-case" and "case-internal" comparison. This means that the individual cases are "broken down" into their different experiential spaces. The patterns are summarized and "abstracted". The typologies that are subsequently formed represent a composition of individual dimensions from several individual cases (Nentwig-Gesemann, 2007, p. 279).

According to Nentwig-Gesemann, the question "which orientation patterns are typical in which existential context of experience" (Nentwig-Gesemann, 2007, p. 279) is investigated at the level of sociogenesis. This means that the "social genesis of differences" is reconstructed (Nentwig-Gesemann, 2007, p. 284).

At the level of genesis of meaning, type formation – with reference to the present research question – only asks about typical forms of relations to God. It is therefore a matter of summarizing different patterns. Type formation at this level presents a spectrum of variations of different forms of relations to God. Sociogenesis asks where these different forms of relations to God come from, whether they can be related to aspects such as gender, age/generation, institutional affinity, cultural background, and the like. In the present research work, genesis of meaning is pursued, but no sociogenic types are created. Although milieu, age/generation, gender, language, migration background, level of achievement, and religious socialization are parameters of the study, the social genesis of the various experiential spaces is not reconstructed. In the present work, implicit forms of knowledge are reconstructed which allow typecasting the various relations of the self to God. They are not unrelated to the social dimensions of gender, religious socialization, milieu, etc., but they cannot be clearly assigned to these parameters in their complexity. Therefore, this research work does not link back orientation to social dimension.

4　Strategy of Generating the Sample

Helfferich (2011) explains that the strategy used for collecting samples affects the validity of the results, i.e., the intended coverage of the results is achieved by the generation of the sample. The validity of the research results is based on their "generalizability". In contrast to quantitative research, which derives its generalizability from the "criterion of representativeness" (the structure of the sample must correspond to the structure of the population), "generalizations of interpretations of qualitative interviews aim at the reconstruction of typical patterns" (Helfferich, 2011, p. 172). This means that the "criterion of representativeness" is replaced by the "criterion of inner representation" (Helfferich, 2011, p. 173). This is achieved "if, on the one hand, the center of the field is well represented in the sample and, on the other hand, the differing representatives have been sufficiently included in the sample" (Merkens, 1997, p. 100, cited in Helfferich, 2011, p. 173). Helfferich recommends a three-stage procedure in order to be able to assess generalizability:

a.　A detailed and precise definition of the group (Helfferich, 2011, p. 174). For the present study, Muslim students were selected from various primary schools who had taken part in Islamic religious education and/or religious schooling in mosques and who were thus accustomed to religious semantics. Children from the 4th grade were chosen because they had finished elementary school education and therefore completed a curriculum (contrast cases: Eljan [3rd grade], Olivia and Paiman [5th grade]). Their vocabulary and language skills were suitable for participating in narrative interviews. As contrasting cases, students who had not yet completed primary school (Eljan [3rd grade]) as well as students who had not participated in Islamic religious education at school (Olivia and Qamar) were selected.

b. Obtaining a "wide variety" within the group (Helfferich, 2011, p. 174).

In the present study, girls and boys were interviewed. It was assured that the children attended different primary schools and had different religious teachers. The children came from various cultural and linguistic backgrounds. Since children who had taken part in Islamic religious education were selected for this study, a religious socialization was assumed. The children were of Muslim faith and their parents had consciously enrolled them in denominational Islamic religious education. With the help of a background questionnaire, a basic assessment of the family structure, the religious environment, and the religious schooling in the mosque and community was carried out in order to ensure the participation of children from families with a wide range of religious reference points. For this purpose, the children themselves were surveyed (at the end of the interview), as were the teachers. The assessment of the religious background allowed the inclusion of children whose families belonged to different religious and mystical groups within Islam, reflecting the inner heterogeneity of Islam. Thus, the sample shows a wide variety of cases.

c. A "narrowing of the group definition and thus a limitation of validity" (Helfferich, 2011, p. 174).

After the interviews had been carried out, a further check was made to see which "constellations" were not included in the sample in order to re-examine the "scope" (Helfferich, 2011, p. 174). The sample was limited to formally religious children and does not include all possible groups of children. According to Flick, the most effective strategy for obtaining samples in narrative interviews is a gradual selection of cases according to the concept of "theoretical sampling" (Flick, 2011, p. 237). This allows for the principle of "formation of opposite horizons" according to Bohnsack (2010b, p. 38) by gradually including "contrasting extremes into the sample" (Helfferich, 2011, p. 174). For example, an interview with a girl of Turkish background from a more religiously liberal parental home can be compared with an interview with a boy of Arabic background from a more religiously traditional family or with a boy of German background from a religiously more mystically oriented family. This large variation of cases and the contrasting juxtaposition of the cases give their respective characteristics and commonalities a contour and allow patterns of orientation to be recognized. Whether the results are generalizable can be tested in qualitative research according to the principle of "saturation"

(Helfferich, 2011, p. 174). This means that interviews are conducted until no more new information is obtained through new interviews so that the "acquisition of knowledge" is "saturated" (Helfferich, 2011, p. 175). In the present study, such saturation was achieved after 15 interviews.

Note

1   The problem with the dilemma method is that it may mainly evaluate "progress in logical competence, critical faculties, and knowledge of the laws of nature, both in childhood and adolescence, and thereafter a religiously based universal humanity" (Grom, 2000, p. 73). With regard to the research of Oser and Gmünder (1992), Grom further states that the dilemma method only covers a part of religious thinking and experiencing, namely that which is addressed in the dilemmas and subsequent questions. In addition, he points out that by thematizing God as well as being committed to him in the Paul-Dilemma and the subsequent catalogue of questions will evoke exactly those answers that can be assigned to the stages 1 and 2. Grom also points out that the situations in the dilemmas were not close to everyday life, but artificial.

CHAPTER 4

Empirical Research Results

1 Short Portraits of the Interviewed Children in the Sample

The following short portraits describe the different cases and, furthermore, summarize the cases with regard to the research question.

The descriptions are divided into thematic paragraphs. In the first paragraph, objective sample criteria are set out and thus the respective cases are outlined descriptively. In the second paragraph, the topics covered in the interview are briefly presented. From the third paragraph onwards, a classification into type formation is carried out by means of case summarization. A description of the frame of orientation follows which is specified by the exploration of the mode of speech of the respective child in the dimensions perspectivity,[1] ethics,[2] and temporality[3] (cf. the detailed description of the dimensions in Chapter 4, Section 2). Finally, a summary of the child's self-relating to God and a description of her/his religious reference is given.

The names of the interviewed children, places, and other people were anonymized, pseudonymized and, if necessary, masked to protect the children. For intuitive support and facilitation for the reader, the anonymized names are chosen according to the migration backgrounds.

1.1 Betül

Betül is a 10-year-old girl with a Turkish migration background who attends the 4th grade of a primary school in a German city. She says that she has participated in Islamic religious education at primary school since the 1st grade, she does not attend any additional lessons at the mosque, and she will go to secondary school in the future. Her linguistic performance shows deficits in grammar and syntax. Betül's parents are divorced. Both the mother and the grandmother are mentioned in the interview as being important for her religious socialization. In the interview, Betül is communicative and responsive to the narrative.

At the end of the Ali narrative, Betül presents five variations of the further course of the story in the form of a medial dramaturgy. Her different narrative threads are interwoven, but no connection to biographical elements becomes evident. Betül often talks about punishment in her storylines. In the interview, prayers also play an important role as well as the question of when and how prayers – which, however, are formal rather than situated in her lifeworld – are

© FAHIMAH ULFAT, 2023 | DOI:10.1163/9789004533219_004

used. In Betül's narrative threads about Ali, the adult role is connoted with restriction and sanction. In addition, a negative connotation of masculinity becomes apparent. In her biographical narratives on the subject of 'wish fulfilment', the topics of bedtime, grades in school, and the desire to go to grammar school are activated.

In the context of contrastive, reconstructive analysis, it becomes clear that Betül's narrations during the interview document an orientation towards the religiously expected as well as towards tradition. A general responsiveness to religious questions as well as accessibility to transcendence-related interpretations of the world and the self become clear during the interview.

From the interpretation of the data, it can be concluded that Betül's mode of speech regarding God is morally coded and dichotomizing in the dimension of perspectivity. She furthermore constructs a concrete relation to God under an aspect relevant to her life, namely to her school career and to her wish to attend grammar school. Here it becomes apparent that she sees God in the function of an almighty leader of the world (omnipotent perspective) with whom she enters into a relationship when she has a wish. Hence, she places her aspirations in a God perspective, i.e. she attributes what happens in her life to God. By doing so, she subsequently justifies that God has not fulfilled some of her wishes, for example her wish to attend grammar school.

This affirmative and intentional reference is indicated in the interview by a 'do ut des' context[4] (cf. Chapter 2, Section 1.4). This means that a purposive rationality becomes visible in Betül's comments which is expressed in the fact that for her God is not only the transcendent authority who decides immutably but she herself has an influence on God's decision to do something good for her. She does not deal with the relevance of the divine in general, rather this relevance goes only as far as her own interests. Betül's interaction with God is therefore purposively rational, childlike-egocentric[5] and rooted in magical thinking.

The interpretation of the interview shows in the dimension of ethics that Betül frames moral considerations religiously. She does not clearly differentiate between fantasy and reality, i.e., between the inner and outer world. In the context of comparative analysis, her narrations represent an interest in interpersonal relationships and social ties which she also connotes religiously. She shows an individual responsiveness to religious questions in the interview.

In the dimension of temporality, Betül's narrations demonstrate that she deals with everyday life topics in the here and now. There is a childlike-egocentric and temporary occupation with religious elements that are more likely to be located in her fantasy world.

In the course of the contrastive analysis, it was found that Betül has propositional knowledge about religious practice which she applies without request. In summary, it can be seen that for Betül the line between her and

EMPIRICAL RESEARCH RESULTS

God is smooth due to pragmatic-magical reasons. The material illustrates that her childlike-egocentric relation to God is not abstract but experiential and shaped by pragmatism and situativity, i.e., God plays a role for her in certain situations and, thus, is temporarily, magically, and pragmatically activated. In her speech mode, social markers which are shaped by cultural space and language become recognizable. In her narrations, a reference to tradition is evident. An effort to deal with the divine becomes clear. In summary, it can be concluded from the interpretation of the interview that Betül represents a relating of the self to God in the mode of moralization and orientation towards tradition as well as a positive religious reference.

1.2 *Canan*

Canan is a 10-year-old girl with a Turkish migration background who attends the 4th grade of a primary school in a German city. She explains that she has been attending Islamic religious education in primary school since the 1st grade, she is not participating in any mosque classes, and will go to secondary school in the future. Her linguistic performance shows deficits in grammar and syntax, whereby she speaks gender-appropriately. Canan reports that her parents practice their faith. During the interview, it becomes apparent that meaning is assigned to family and religious education in the process of religious socialization. Canan appears to be reserved and cautious in the interview situation.

At the end of the Ali narrative, Canan offers a variation by continuing the opening narrative through integrating parents and teachers from her own life as relevant people. In this context, the topics of verses for protection, paradise, and hell are addressed. She tells two stories from her own lifeworld, and in doing so she goes far back in her memory.

In the context of contrastive, reconstructive analysis, it becomes clear that Canan's narrations during the interview document an orientation towards the religiously expected as well as towards tradition, but the analysis shows that religious interpretations do not play an action-guiding role. The interview does not reveal any individual responsiveness to religious questions.

In the dimension of perspectivity, a morally coded, dichotomizing God perspective appears on the explicit level in the sense that God has a protective function for 'good' people. She talks about verses for protection in the interview that help against fear; she also speaks about the confession of faith which is seen as the key to *ǧanna* (paradise), about *ǧanna* and *ǧahannam* (paradise and hell), good and bad people, punishment and protection. The narrative structure of the interview shows that Canan makes no connection between her religious knowledge and her everyday life. The interview is characterized by an intense question-answer mode because she keeps saying "I don't know what happens next". It can be interpretatively assumed from the narrative structure that the subject of the interview has little biographical relevance for Canan. Her personal construction of God appears purposively rational and egocentric.

In the dimension of ethics it can be seen that Canan frames moral considerations religiously. It shows that she clearly differentiates between fantasy and reality and thus makes a clear distinction between the inner and outer world.

In the dimension of temporality, the occupation with religious elements is oriented towards the past, both childlike-egocentric as well as situational, and only happens when asked in the interview situation. Canan, like Mesut (see below), connects past events with God in retrospect.

In the context of contrastive, reconstructive analysis it was possible to determine that Canan includes a religious setting when asked and has textbook knowledge that she can contribute and explain; the analysis also shows that she does not establish any real-life references to her religious knowledge. Her propositional knowledge reflected in her linguistic phrases and response strategies reveals the social markers that are shaped by cultural space and language. However, religious patterns of interpretation are not action-guiding in her biographical narrating. In summary, it can be concluded from the interpretation of the interview that Canan represents a relating of the self to God in the mode of moralization and orientation towards tradition as well as a passive religious reference.

1.3   *Dilara*

Dilara is a 10-year-old girl with a Turkish migration background who attends the 4th grade of a primary school in a German town. She explains that she has been attending Islamic religious education in primary school since the 2nd grade, does regularly participate in mosque lessons, and will go to an intermediate secondary school in the future. Her linguistic performance shows a competent use of correctly structured sentences appropriate to the respective context. Dilara also shows a strong educational commitment. The interview reveals that meaning is assigned to her parents – especially her mother – in the process of religious socialization. Dilara presents herself as relaxed, open-minded, and in a positive mood during the interview.

At the end of the Ali narrative, Dilara offers five different variations for the opening narrative's further course which have a clear narrative structure and always end harmoniously. These variations are characterized by positive thinking and sociability. In some variations, she herself brings God into the storyline in connection with guardian angels. In the course of that she uses comforting language. The central topics Dilara addresses in the interview are questions of human behavior as well as changes in behavior which she locates within

EMPIRICAL RESEARCH RESULTS

human potential and responsibility. Ethical and moral values play an essential role, especially with regard to charitable donations, helping, sharing, and comforting. From her own lifeworld, she refers to the subject of friendship in the context of interpersonal and social phenomena. This topic is also assessed morally and religiously by her.

The interpretation of the interview shows that faith has a positive meaning for Dilara and gives her a sense of security. Within the framework of contrastive, reconstructive analysis, it becomes clear that Dilara's narrations in the context of the interview represent a fundamental responsiveness to transcendence-related world- and self-interpretations, a positive religious reference as well as an active reference to religious practice and to God.

In the dimension of perspectivity, the material shows an immanent and intuitive relation to God on the implicit level. The perspective is also characterized by an omnipresent perspective of God who offers comfort and security in situations of fear and distress. In addition, Dilara's perspective on people, which is particularly characterized by personal initiative and responsibility as well as self-confidence, is revealed in the interview. It can be seen that Dilara constructs the relation to God on an abstract level by linking the perspective of taking initiative and responsibility to the help of God and the guardian angel, but she distinguishes between the levels of divine power and human power.

From the interpretation of the interview it can be concluded in the dimension of ethics that Dilara combines moral evaluations with religious contents and addresses religion in the context of moral considerations. Social activities such as donations, social connections, and interpersonal relations are framed religiously. In this respect, it is evident that Dilara deals with God and religious elements in a contextual way and at a moral level.

In the dimension of temporality, the material illustrates Dilara's connection to the present in relation to topics relevant to life which she deals with in the here and now.

She relates religious elements provided by herself to the present and the hereafter. From the interpretation of the interview it can be concluded that Dilara's narrations illustrate a context-related relevance to religious matters and to God for her personal life. Therefore, Dilara represents a relating of the self to God in the mode of personalization (individual relationship) as well as an active and positive religious reference.

1.4 *Eljan*

Eljan is a 9-year-old boy with a Serbian migrant background in the 3rd grade of a primary school in a German town. He reports that he has been participating in Islamic religious education since the 1st grade, but does not go to mosque lessons. His pronunciation and grammar and syntax deficits are evident in his linguistic performance. He states that his parents are divorced and that he does not know his father. Eljan mentions his two older brothers, the eldest of whom functions as a role model for him. He says that he often has quarrels with the younger one. In the interview, it becomes apparent that his eldest brother and his grandparents are regarded as important in the process of religious socialization. Eljan appears uneasy and restless in the interview.

At the end of the Ali narrative, Eljan offers a short variation of the continuation of the opening narrative in which he brings the story to a pragmatic solution. From his own experience he describes an incident in which he had been choked by his classmates. Happiness, a prayer carpet, a driving licence, tests at school, quarrels with his brother, aspirations, and his grandparents have a central position in the interview.

In the context of contrastive, reconstructive analysis, it becomes clear that Eljan's stories in the course of the interview show an affirmative reference to religious practice. The interpretation of the interview reveals that Eljan's interest in the practice of prayer is based on an instrumental intention, in the sense that he wants to achieve something by praying. He addresses the subject of prayer alone, without being asked. His narrations document a magical and fatalistic approach to religion, apparent in his connecting God and happiness; he believes that God only helps him if he is fortunate.

The material shows an omnipotent perspective of God on the implicit level in the dimension of ethics; here, Eljan places his aspirations in a God perspective. The interview also shows that he does not attribute any influence of himself (e.g. on dictations). There is no active role of the individual as with Dilara. His personal construction of God presents itself as magical, purposively rational, and childlike-egocentric.

Regarding the dimension of ethics, it can be concluded from the interview that Eljan does not associate moral evaluations with religious content. There is no decentration in his mode of speech at the level of ethics. The comparative analysis shows that topics relevant to life are dealt with in the context of interpersonal relations and social connections. However, they are not religiously framed.

In the dimension of temporality, Eljan's connectedness to present relevant lifeworld issues which he deals with in the here and now becomes apparent; his narrations are close to reality. In this respect, it is evident that Eljan deals with religious elements in relation to himself in a temporal, magical, and situational way.

The analysis shows that God has a certain relevance for Eljan, but does not represent a stable factor. From the interpretation of the interview it can be

EMPIRICAL RESEARCH RESULTS 77

generally concluded that Eljan's narrations document a childlike-egocentric and situational relevance to religious matters for his own life. Eljan represents a relating of the self to God in the mode of moralization and tradition as well as an affirmative and magical religious reference.

1.5 *Filiz*

Filiz is a 9-year-old girl with a Turkish migrant background who attends the 4th grade of a primary school in a German city. She says that she has been participating in Islamic religious education since the 1st grade, attends mosque lessons on an irregular basis and will go to grammar school in the future. Her linguistic performance testifies to a competent use of correctly structured sentences according to the respective context. Filiz also has a strong commitment to education. She reports that her father does not practice religion because of his work and her mother does not always participate in religious practice because of her little sister. In the interview, Filiz is talkative and a reflective listener.

Following the Ali narrative, Filiz offers a variation of the further course of the opening narrative in which she introduces generalized knowledge from her childlike environment as a solution strategy and resolves the situation in a harmonizing way. The fire brigade is repeatedly addressed as a source of help. Filiz initially remains within the narrative structure and context of the input stimulus. From the moment she integrates aspects of her own life into the narration, the narrative structure is opened up. Friendship and playing together are central in her storyline. The topics of gratitude towards God, punishment, paradise, hell as well as transmitted stories about the writing angels (the accompanying angels who write down the words, deeds, and thoughts of every human being; cf. Qur'an 43:80) and prophet Muhammad are also dealt within the interview.

In the context of contrastive, reconstructive analysis, it can be seen that Filiz's narrations in the context of the interview document an orientation towards the religiously expected and towards tradition, but no significant references to everyday life are made. Her fundamental responsiveness to religious questions as well as a accessibility to transcendence-related world- and self-interpretations become clear during the interview.

In the dimension of perspectivity, a morally coded, dichotomizing God perspective appears on the explicit level. This reference is indicated in the interview by a 'do ut des' context (cf. Chapter 2, Section 1.4). Filiz does not bring religious content into the interview herself, but on request. She knows traditional religious narratives that she reproduces. However, it could be reconstructed that she has an aesthetic understanding of the narratives which she reproduces in the form of aestheticized stories. Her personal construction of God manifests itself as purposively rational and childlike-egocentric.

In the dimension of ethics, the interview shows that Filiz also links moral actions with religious content. Within the framework of comparative analysis, her narrations reveal an interest in interpersonal relations and social ties which she, however, does not frame religiously.

Within the dimension of temporality, Filiz's narrations demonstrate that she lives in the here and now and keeps an intellectual distance to religion and to God. Accordingly, an aesthetic, situational, and temporary occupation with religious elements does exist that only emerges when addressed in the interview situation.

Within the context of contrastive, reconstructive analysis, it was possible to show that Filiz possesses propositional knowledge in relation to traditional narratives, but a passive and aestheticized reference to them is evident. In her mode of speech, the social markers which are influenced by cultural space and language become visible. From the interpretation of the interview, it can be concluded that her narrations reflect relevant references to tradition. Filiz represents a relating of the self to God in the mode of moralization and orientation towards tradition as well as an aestheticized religious reference.

1.6   *Gökmen*

Gökmen is a 10-year-old boy with a Turkish migration background who attends the 4th grade of a primary school in a German town. He reports that he has been attending Islamic religious education in primary school since the 1st grade, he also attends in mosque lessons regularly and will attend secondary school in the future. His linguistic performance shows deficits in grammar and syntax. Gökmen's religious socialization primarily results from religious education at school and in the mosque. He reports that his parents practice their faith; no further information about his religious socialization in the family is available. In the interview situation, Gökmen initially appears hesitant and insecure. Over the course of the interview, however, he becomes more relaxed.

At the end of the Ali narrative, Gökmen presents a variation of the further course of the initial story, whereby it has no clear narrative structure. His conflict resolution strategy consists of a "tit for tat" tactic in which the victim is also punished. From his own life, he speaks about his grandmother who died of a heart attack and about a past event in the pool when he almost choked. During the interview, Gökmen also talks about his friends and their shared activities.

In the context of contrastive, reconstructive analysis, it becomes obvious that Gökmen's narrations in the context of the interview do not document any

EMPIRICAL RESEARCH RESULTS

action guiding reference to religious interpretations, to God, or to religious practice. The interpretation of the interview shows that Gökmen mentions his religious knowledge and God as elements of a referenced religion of his own accord. On a concrete level, a reference to his lifeworld becomes discernible but his statements show that this reference is made on the basis of an orientation towards the socially expected and is not subjectively oriented. Thus, the interview indicates that he has learned which situations require a religious language and that he can meet this social requirement. No fundamental accessibility to transcendence-related world- and self-interpretations becomes apparent during the interview.

In the dimension of perspectivity, a differentiation between fantasy and reality appears on the explicit level with Gökmen placing God in the realm of fantasy. Regarding this differentiation, the analysis shows that Gökmen accepts the phenomenon of death without questioning it which is in maximum contrast to Qamar and Hagen (see below). In this respect, his statements demonstrate an anthropocentric position and a materialistic argumentation, in the sense that he explains the world and its processes without mental or immaterial elements. Therefore, death is not questioned and interpreted immanently.

In the dimension of ethics, no positive or negative utterances with normative potential could be reconstructed for Gökmen. The comparative analysis shows that topics relevant for life are dealt with in the context of interpersonal relations and social connections. However, they are not framed religiously.

With regard to these lifeworld relevant topics, Gökmen's narrations in the dimension of temporality show that he remains in the here and now. In this respect, the interview shows neither a selective nor a continuous preoccupation with religious questions.

The analysis demonstrates that Gökmen regards God as an ontic fact in the world and thus positions himself in the mode of distance from God. God is only formally described as an existence, but is not filled with any content. It can be concluded from the interpretation of the interview that Gökmen's reference to tradition or religion is schematic and standardized.

1.7 *Hagen*

Hagen is a 10-year-old boy in the 4th grade of a primary school in a German city who has no migration background, i.e. his parents are both native Germans. He reports that he has been attending Islamic religious education in primary school since the 4th grade, that he participates irregularly in lessons at the mosque and that he will go to grammar school in the future. His linguistic performance demonstrates a competent use of correctly structured sentences according to the respective context. Hagen also has a strong commitment to education. In the interview, he reports that his family converted to Islam about a year ago. He has two younger siblings. The interview shows that his parents are assigned meaning in the process of religious socialization. Hagen is balanced and calm, talkative and a reflective listener during the interview situation.

Following the Ali narrative, Hagen offers an extensive and diverse variation for the introductory narrative's further storyline in which he constructs a self-organized and self-sufficient life in nature, activating the themes of animate and inanimate nature, healthy lifestyle, religious rituals as well as interpersonal and social relations. In the interview, his closeness to nature, his curiosity for the transcendence-related world- and self-interpretations and his individual responsiveness to religious questions become apparent.

The interpretation of the interview shows that Hagen identifies himself with his parents' natural and religiously oriented way of life and that he accepts it. In the context of contrastive, reconstructive analysis it becomes clear that Hagen's narrations document a positive attitude towards religiosity as well as an active reference to religious practice and to God.

In the dimension of perspectivity, Hagen shows an immanent, intuitive relation to God on the implicit level, and on the explicit level an abstract perspective towards God as well as an intellectual, reflected examination of the themes of life, death, and life after death.

Comparative analysis demonstrates in the dimension of ethics that Hagen's narrations indicate his interest in interpersonal relations and social connections. They are not religiously framed. This reflects his ethical convictions and his understanding of norms which are characterized by a strong need for harmonization and are not framed religiously. In his mode of speech, a decentration (abandonment of the egocentric world view) is evident.

In the dimension of temporality, the material reveals Hagen's connectedness to present day life issues which he deals with in the here and now; an intuitive introduction of religious elements is also evident. In addition, an engagement with religious elements related to the hereafter becomes apparent.

From the interpretation of the interview, it can be concluded that Hagen represents a relating of the self to God in the mode of personalization and an intuitive, active, and positive religious reference.

1.8   *Jurislav*

Jurislav is a 9-year-old boy who attends the 4th grade of a primary school in a German city and probably has a Serbian migration background. He says he has been attending Islamic religious education in primary school since 1st grade, does not additionally attend mosque lessons, and will go to an intermediate

EMPIRICAL RESEARCH RESULTS

secondary school in the future. His linguistic performance shows adequate linguistic and grammatical knowledge. The interview reveals that his mother is assigned meaning in the process of religious socialization. At the beginning of the interview, Jurislav is sceptical and has concerns about meeting the interviewer's expectations. Later on, however, he opens up and even talks – as he himself says – about his "most embarrassing" moments.

At the end of the Ali narrative, Jurislav continues the introductory story with two short variations without a clear narrative structure in which he immediately integrates the topic of prayer. His conflict resolution strategy is that the damaged party apologizes to the damaging one. From his own lifeworld, he talks about two events that are embarrassing to him. He reaches far back in his memory and recalls that he stole something and got caught. The second embarrassing incident is that he once fell into a rubbish dump at a folk festival which was very unpleasant for him. Furthermore, the themes of desire, fear, and prayer as religious practice are treated in the interview.

In the context of contrastive, reconstructive analysis, it becomes apparent that Jurislav's narrations in the context of the interview document an orientation towards the religiously expected and towards tradition, but no significant everyday life references are made. His narrations show a general accessibility to transcendental world- and self-interpretations.

In the dimension of perspectivity, Jurislav's perspective of God, which is characterized by an omnipotent approach and in which he places his aspirations in a God perspective, appears on the explicit level. The interpretation of the interview shows that Jurislav himself brings religious practice but not God into the narrative, rather the technique of achieving something through prayer. The contrastive, reconstructive analysis clearly reveals that Jurislav, as well as Eljan, regard praying as an action to solve problems. In this respect, an instrumental, childlike-egocentric intention can be documented in his statements. In contrast to Eljan, Jurislav also sees himself as having an influence on events by introducing boxing as a pragmatic problem-solving strategy. His narrations document a childlike-egocentric understanding of religion in which things can be achieved through prayer while he also has worldly instruments at hand. From the interpretation of the data, it can be concluded that Jurislav's perspective on God is dichotomizing, magical, and purposefully rational.

In the dimension of ethics, a childlike-egocentric way of thinking is also evident in the sense that Jurislav does not adopt the perspective of others and does not abstract from himself. He does not frame moral considerations religiously.

In the dimension of temporality, Jurislav's connectedness to the present becomes clear in the data material. He deals with topics relevant to everyday life in the here and now and his narrations are close to reality. In this respect, it is evident that he deals with religious elements situatively, temporarily, and pragmatically on a childlike-egocentric level.

Within the framework of contrastive, reconstructive analysis it was possible to demonstrate that Jurislav's narrations document a childlike-egocentric and pragmatic relevance to religious practice for his own life. It shows that he represents a relating of the self to God in the mode of moralization and orientation towards tradition as well as a childlike-egocentric reference to religion.

1.9 *Kaltrina*

Kaltrina is a 9-year-old girl with an Albanian migrant background in the 4th grade of a primary school in a German city. She says that she has been attending Islamic religious education in primary school since the 1st grade, she is not attending lessons at the mosque and will go to an intermediate secondary school or grammar school in the future. Her linguistic performance demonstrates a competent use of correct sentences consistent with the context. Kaltrina also shows a strong educational commitment. In the interview, she presents herself as bright and agile. No information on her religious socialization in the family is available.

Of all the children interviewed, Kaltrina tells the most precise and best thought-out story. In her narrations, it becomes clear that she is linguistically fluent and has a strong capacity for reflection, since she listens to herself while narrating, distances herself from her own narrative, and reflects on it. Like Gökmen and Navid (see below), Kaltrina clearly differentiates between fantasy and reality. People, interpersonal relationships as well as social ties play an essential role in her narrations. She further develops the Ali story, adds new characters, creates a new name for Esad (Jonathan), removes Jonathan as Ali's best friend, and replaces him with a girl. It becomes clear that the gender aspect is important to her. She adds a girl to the story who directs the storyline. Kaltrina creates meta-narratives and side strands. Repeatedly she puts herself in the position of Ali or his parents and reports how they would feel in the given situation. She asks herself questions about Ali's character and has doubts regarding his exemplariness. In between she talks about her own experiences, especially with her family, that have no connection to the Ali narrative.

The interpretation of the data shows that Kaltrina does not address God, religion or transcendence-related questions of her own accord. She mentions the recitation of verses as protection in connection with overcoming fear and relates the topic of religious confession to her aunt's husband, who she says is not a Muslim. In the context of contrastive, reconstructive analysis it becomes apparent that Kaltrina's narrations during the interview show no action-guiding reference to religious interpretations, to God or to religious practice. A

EMPIRICAL RESEARCH RESULTS

fundamental responsiveness to religious questions can be seen on a superficial and cultural-spatial level with regard to her uncle who, according to her own statements, is German but not a Muslim.

In the dimension of perspectivity it becomes apparent on the explicit level that God has a protective function for Kaltrina that is expressed in a childlike belief in encouragement with regard to dealing with her fear. Her personal construction of God manifests as purposively rational and childlike-egocentric.

In the dimension of ethics, comparative analysis shows that Kaltrina deals with life-relevant issues within the framework of interpersonal relations and social ties. However, they are not framed religiously. On this level, she expresses her ethical convictions and her understanding of norms which she does not frame religiously, but rather expresses them on a principal level whereby her mode of speech shows a decentration (abandonment of the egocentric world view) as well as gender sensitivity.

In the dimension of temporality, the material shows that in the course of her narrations Kaltrina remains in the here and now with regard to topics relevant to life. Thus, the child's connectedness to the present is evident. In this respect, the interview does not reveal any selective or continuous preoccupation with religious questions. There is also no fundamental accessibility to transcendental world- and self-interpretations.

The analysis shows that overall Kaltrina regards God as an ontic fact in the world, i.e. that she relates herself in a mode that is remote from God. Similar to Gökmen, this engagement does not require content, since God is only formally described as existence, but is not filled with content. In addition, a weak, pragmatic religious reference is evident which is oriented towards tradition and culture.

1.10   Leyla

Leyla is a 9-year-old girl with a Turkish migration background who attends the 4th grade of a primary school in a German town. She reports that she has been going to mosque lessons irregularly for 2–3 years, that she has been participating in Islamic religious education since the 1st grade, and that she will go to grammar school in the future. Her linguistic performance demonstrates a competent use of correctly structured sentences consistent with the context. Leyla also shows a strong educational commitment. She reports that her family practises religion, especially her mother who teaches children in a mosque as a Hoca (teacher of religious education), and that she sometimes assists her in doing so. The interview demonstrates that her mother is assigned meaning in the process of religious socialization. Leyla seems bright and sensitive in the interview situation.

At the end of the Ali narrative, Leyla continues the introductory narrative with a short and pragmatic variation, focusing on the topics of friendship, behavior (well-behaved, helpful), school performance, and transitioning to a secondary school. In her biographical narratives, she addresses prayer and supplication as well as the question of the effect of prayers in relation to the topic of fear. These prayers are situated in the context of everyday life. Leyla mentions God and religious practice on her own when speaking about her reaction to the death of her cousin. It becomes clear that she recognizes the value of life in the face of this event. Her narrations are characterized by strong harmonization and solicity.

In the context of contrastive, reconstructive analysis, Leyla's narrations during the interview document an active reference to religious practice and to God. In her narrations, an understanding of religion is manifest that implies a religiously performance-oriented attitude, e.g., in her understanding of the ritual prayer. However, the prayer of supplication also plays an essential role in her interaction with God.

In the dimension of perspectivity, Leyla's data material on the implicit level indicates a turning to God due to an existential need in connection with the death of her cousin. Through this, Leyla has become aware of the finiteness of life. An immanent and intuitive relation to God becomes evident. In this respect, however, there are also signs of subtle uncertainties as it becomes apparent that Leyla cannot reconcile suffering, death, and religion; here, she reaches her existential limit. This is reflected in her falling silent ("then I would be sad, would pray more, would plea to Allah, and when it then still wouldn't work, then Allah would maybe want it so and because of that [about that?] I would say nothing anymore. nothing anymore"). In the dimension of perspectivity, a dichotomizing perspective on God and thinking in a 'do ut des' context (cf. Chapter 2, Section 1.4) is manifest at an explicit level.

In the dimension of ethics, Leyla frames her own social actions religiously. Her understanding of religious norms shows childlike-egocentric traits. Her longing for harmonization as well as her interest in interpersonal and social relations can also be seen at this level.

In the dimension of temporality, Leyla's material demonstrates her connectedness to the present in relation to topics relevant to everyday life which she explores in the here and now. In her narrations, an intuitive, hereafter-related interest in religious elements is also evident, based on her experience with her cousin's death.

From the interpretation of the interview, it can be concluded that Leyla's narrations document a context-related relevance to the religious and to God for her own life. It shows that Leyla relations herself to God in the mode of personalization as well as an active and intuitive religious reference.

EMPIRICAL RESEARCH RESULTS

1.11 *Mesut*

Mesut is a 10-year-old boy with a Turkish migration background who attends the 4th grade of a primary school in a German town. He reports that he has been participating in Islamic religious education since the 1st grade, has been attending mosque lessons for a year, and will go to secondary school in the future. His linguistic performance shows deficits in grammar and syntax. In the interview situation, Mesut appears as a warm-hearted and friendly boy who likes sports. His narrations are characterized by a high degree of harmonization and a caring attitude. There is no information available on his religious socialization in the family.

At the end of the Ali narrative, Mesut continues the opening narrative by quickly solving Ali's situation through one variation and then begins to fabulate a long story with "soap" characters. A connection to biographical elements becomes clear in so far as he actualizes sports activities, family, and friends from his lifeworld. In his biographical narratives, he actualizes his brother, his friends, and their common activities. Mesut also talks about a real-life fearful situation, a car accident, in which his entire family was at risk.

Mesut's narrations document his strong need for harmonization as well as his caring attitude. His statements are socially anchored. The interpretation of the interview shows that Mesut, similar to Canan, associates the car accident with God in retrospect, using the expression "thanks be to God" as a statement of emphasis. In the context of contrastive, reconstructive analysis, it becomes clear that Mesut's narrations do not contain any action-guiding reference to religious interpretative content or to God. In his case, no fundamental accessibility to transcendence-related world- and self-interpretations is evident.

Within the dimension of perspectivity, it becomes manifest on the explicit level that Mesut sees God in the function of an all-powerful leader whereby he subsequently places non-plausible, life-relevant events into a God perspective. The data material shows that he receives religious patterns of interpretation in a purely passive way. His personal construction of God appears purposefully rational and childlike-egocentric.

In the dimension of ethics, no positive or negative statements with normative potential could be reconstructed. The comparative analysis shows that Mesut deals with topics relevant for life within the framework of interpersonal relationships and social ties. His mode of speech is decentralized and harmonizing. In his narrations, fantasy and reality become blurred with neither fantasy nor reality being framed by religion.

In the dimension of temporality, Mesut remains in the here and now in his narrations with regard to interpersonal and social relations. The child's connectedness to the present becomes clear during the interview. In this respect, the interview does not reveal any selective or continuous concern with religious issues.

The analysis shows that Mesut regards God as an ontic fact in the world, i.e., that he positions himself at a distance from God. Like Gökmen and Kaltrina, this relating does not require content, since God is only formally described as existence. In addition, he shows a weak religious reference.

1.12   *Navid*

Navid is a 10-year-old boy with an Iraqi migrant background in the 4th grade of a primary school in a German town. He reports that he has participated in Islamic religious education since the 1st grade, does not attend mosque lessons, and will go to grammar school in the future. He has a strong educational commitment and reports that he is mathematically and scientifically gifted. His linguistic performance shows a competent use of correctly structured sentences appropriate to the respective context. He says that his parents were originally from Iraq, whereas his mother also speaks Persian. Unlike the other children in this study, they are Shiite Muslims as are Qamar and Paiman. Regarding his religious socialization in the family, he says that his family does not practice religion. Navid speaks about himself and his family openly without being asked. He reports that his older brother is autistic and that he also has a little sister. He is communicative, reflective, and talkative in the interview situation.

At the end of the Ali narrative, Navid continues the opening narrative and resolves the situation of Ali in a down-to-earth and pragmatic way. He then reinvents the family of Ali by integrating into the storyline his own family circumstances as he would like them to be. In his biographical narratives, he actualizes his older brother and his autism which seems to have had an impact on him. His statements document a distance to his brother. Topics like monster films, monster fantasies, and fireworks are also addressed in the interview. Like Gökmen and Kaltrina, Navid clearly separates fantasy from reality. His narrations are close to reality; he himself locates his monster fantasies within his imaginary world.

In the framework of contrastive, reconstructive analysis, Navid's narrations in the interview do not document any action-guiding reference to religious interpretations, to God or to religious practice. There is also no fundamental accessibility to transcendental world- and self-interpretations.

In the dimension of perspectivity, no relation to God can be reconstructed also for the explicit level due to a lack of information.

In the dimension of ethics, no positive or negative statements with normative potential could be reconstructed from the interview. The comparative

EMPIRICAL RESEARCH RESULTS

analysis shows that he deals with topics relevant to everyday life within the framework of interpersonal and social ties that are not framed religiously. His mode of speech indicates an anthropocentric way of thinking.

In the dimension of temporality, the material demonstrates that Navid remains in the here and now in his narrations with regard to everyday topics. The interview thus reveals the child's connectedness to the present. In this respect, the interview shows neither a selective nor a continuing concern with religious questions.

Altogether, the analysis shows that although Navid himself addresses the topic of fasting and knows its practice, he does so within the framework of eating habits and weight loss. Navid knows various methods to help himself in situations of distress, but no religious coping strategies or patterns of interpretation could be reconstructed. The interpretation of the interview shows that his patterns of world- and self-interpretation are not related to transcendence, but are rather rational, pragmatic, and related to this world. In summary, Navid shows neither an active nor a passive reception of religious patterns of interpretation. Therefore, a relevant reference to tradition or to God could not be reconstructed in the material. From the interpretation of the interview it can be concluded that Navid positions himself at a distance from God.

1.13   *Olivia*

Olivia is a 9-year-old girl who will soon be 10 years old. This means that although she is of the same age as the other interviewed children, she has already completed primary school. Olivia, like Hagen, has no migration background, her parents are both native Germans. She says that she did not attend Islamic religious education at school because it was not offered and that she will go to the 5th grade of an intermediate secondary school in a German metropolitan region after the upcoming summer holidays. Her linguistic performance demonstrates a competent use of correctly structured sentences appropriate to the respective context. Olivia's father explains that the family belongs to a mystical school of Islam and that Olivia has irregular Islamic lessons at home and in the order. Olivia comes from a well-off family and has two older sisters. The interview shows that her parents are assigned meaning in the process of religious socialization. In the interview situation, Olivia shows herself hesitant and reserved.

At the end of the Ali narrative, Olivia continues the storyline with a variation of the opening narrative, resolving the situation of Ali in a down-to-earth and pragmatic way. She actualizes the subjects of friendship and interpersonal relations in her biographical narratives. In the interview, she also deals with ethical topics.

In the context of contrastive, reconstructive analysis, it shows that Olivia's narrations in the context of the interview do not reveal any action-guiding reference to religious interpretations, to God or to religious practice. She herself mentions the religious practice of prayer, but talks about God only when asked. A basic responsiveness to religious questions as well as an accessibility to transcendental world- and self-interpretations becomes clear in the interview.

In the dimension of perspectivity, it can be seen on the explicit level that Olivia, like Dilara, connects God and guardian angels with each other and attributes a protective function to them. She attributes a kind of medical effect to the religious practice of praying which is used in case of need. In addition, her statements regarding ethical questions reflect a karma idea ("and I think ... so if one does something bad, then it also comes back again"). This idea of every action having a consequence is not framed religiously.

In the dimension of ethics, the comparative analysis shows that Olivia deals with topics relevant for everyday life in the context of interpersonal relations and social ties which are not religiously framed by her. On this level, she expresses her ethical beliefs and her understanding of norms which she does not frame religiously, but rather expresses on a principal level. A decentration (abandonment of the egocentric world view) becomes apparent in her mode of speech.

In the dimension of temporality, the data material documents that Olivia remains in the here and now in her narrations on topics relevant to everyday life. The child's connectedness to the present becomes visible here. In this respect, the interview does not reveal any selective or continuous concern with religious issues.

The comparative analysis shows that Olivia, like Gökmen, Kaltrina, and Navid, regards God as an ontic fact in the world, i.e., that she represents a relating of the self in the mode of distance from God. In addition, she shows a religious reference that is oriented towards tradition.

1.14   *Paiman*

Paiman is a 10-year-old boy with an Iraqi migration background attending the 5th grade of a comprehensive school in a German metropolitan region. Although Paiman is at the age of the other children interviewed, he is already attending lower secondary education. He reports that he had participated in Islamic religious education throughout his primary school years and has been going to Islamic lessons in his Shiite community for one year. His linguistic performance demonstrates a competent use of correctly structured sentences appropriate to the respective context. Paiman shows a strong educational commitment. His mother teaches Islamic religious education in the same

EMPIRICAL RESEARCH RESULTS

community. Unlike the other children of this research study, Paiman and his family are Shiite Muslims like Navid and Qamar. The interview shows that his mother is assigned meaning in the process of religious socialization. During the interview, Paiman appears bright and initially suspicious and jittery. In the further process, his restlessness and excitement subsides, and he opens up.

At the end of the Ali narrative, he continues the storyline with a variation of the opening narrative by using stories from television. In doing so, he himself introduces paradise into the storyline without establishing any biographical reference to it. In his biographical narrative, his fear, which he calls a "hard fear", as well as the solution strategies he uses to overcome it do play a major role. He locates the origin of his fear in his brain and speaks of his brain as "it". With the help of this mental construction it becomes clear that he can differentiate between himself and his brain and thus can distance himself from his fear.

In the context of contrastive, reconstructive analysis, it can be seen that Paiman's narrations in the context of the interview document an action-guiding reference to religious practice and to God. Thus, a general accessibility to transcendental world- and self-interpretations is evident.

In the dimension of perspectivity, it can be concluded on the implicit level that religious practice is a way for Paiman to overcome his fear. Contrastive analysis reveals that he developed a quasi-magical, childlike-egocentric understanding of religion like Eljan and Jurislav. He uses verses from the Qur'an as a remedy against his real fear. His statements document – in maximum contrast to Jurislav and Eljan – that this solution strategy is existential for him due to his distress. Hence, there is a reference to religious practice. Paiman also mentions God, whereby an ambivalent relation to God is apparent. In the dimension of perspectivity, it can be seen on the explicit level that Paiman's construction of God is characterized by an omnipresent perspective and a protective function.

From the interpretation of the interview, it can be concluded in the dimension of ethics that Paiman combines moral evaluations with religious content and frames social activities religiously.

In the dimension of temporality, the data material demonstrates Paiman's connectedness to the present. He deals with everyday life topics in the here and now. In this respect, it becomes clear that he deals with God and religious elements in an incidental manner as well as fundamentally within the framework of his fear problem.

From the interpretation of the interview, it can be concluded that Paiman's narrations document an incidental relevance to the religious and to God for his own life. Paiman represents a relating of the self to God in the mode of personalization as well as an existential and purposively rational relation to religious practice.

1.15 Qamar

Qamar is a 10-year-old girl with an Afghan migration background who attends the 4th grade of a primary school in a German metropolitan region. She reports that she participates in ethics classes in primary school as no Islamic religious education is offered and that she has been attending Islamic classes in her Shiite community regularly for four years. She will probably go to grammar school. Her linguistic performance demonstrates a competent use of correctly structured sentences appropriate to the respective context. A strong educational commitment is evident. The interview shows that her parents are assigned meaning in the process of religious socialization. Qamar is bright, reflective, and polite in the interview. Right at the beginning, she explains the religious meaning of her name.

Qamar, like Kaltrina, continues the story of Ali with a long variation of the introductory narrative. In her storyline, she shows the courage to let him die. Inspired by that, she starts reflecting on death. After being asked directly about God, she incorporates God into the story as an actor. Within contrasting comparison, Betül, Filiz, Kaltrina, and Qamar converge on being imaginative and liking to live and act in their imaginations. In the interview, life has the role of a test and death is the salvation from this test.

In the context of contrastive, reconstructive analysis, Qamar's narrations in the context of the interview document an orientation towards the religiously expected and towards tradition, but no significant everyday life references are made here. An individual responsiveness to religious questions as well as a fundamental accessibility to transcendental world- and self-interpretations can be seen in the interview.

In the dimension of perspectivity, the material shows Qamar's perspective of God at the explicit level which becomes clear in the context of the themes of dying and death. The interpretation of the interview shows that death is a relevant topic for Qamar. She treats the subject of life as a test and death as salvation within the framework of a dichotomous and morally coded God perspective. In her narrations, thinking is documented in a "do ut des" context (cf. Chapter 2, Section 1.4) and has a justification function. The contrastive, reconstructive analysis reveals that Qamar takes up God as a subject and integrates God into the Ali narrative as an actor; but it also shows that God has no relevance in her own biography. Her personal construction of God appears purposively rational and childlike-egocentric.

In the dimension of ethics, it can be concluded from the interpretation of the interview that Qamar frames moral considerations religiously. Within the framework of comparative analysis, her narrations reveal an interest in interpersonal and social ties which she also frames religiously.

In the dimension of temporality, Qamar's material shows a relatedness to the hereafter, which she deals with actively and reflexively. In this respect, the interview shows that she deals with religious elements on an occasion related and intellectual basis.

The contrastive, reconstructive analysis demonstrates that Qamar presents her propositional knowledge in relation to religion and God which, however, is highly morally charged. She does not establish any real-life references to her knowledge.

In her mode of speech, the social markers which are influenced by cultural space and language become apparent. It can be concluded from the interpretation of the interview that Qamar's narrations show a relatedness to tradition. Qamar represents a relating of the self to God in the mode of moralization and orientation towards tradition as well as an active and positive religious reference.

2 Development of Typologies in the Present Study: Comparative Analysis and Theoretical Summarization

After the short portraits, the following section explains the steps by which the ideal types that represent the core result of this study were reconstructed from the data material. These steps lead in several stages of abstraction from the concrete material to increasingly summarized categories.

Figure 5 presents these stages of abstraction which then will be explained in detail.[6]

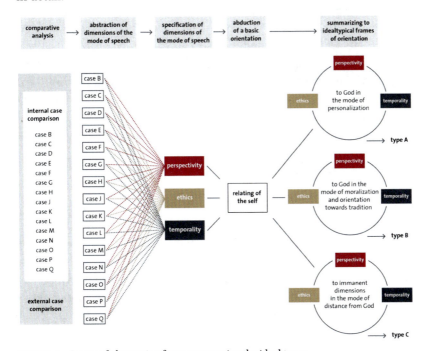

FIGURE 5   Stages of abstraction for reconstructing the ideal types

To understand the illustration, it is important to note that the temporal sequence of the interpretation is not outlined, but the different stages of abstraction, whereby the degree of abstraction increases to the right.

Stage 1: Comparative analysis

At the level of comparative analysis, the cases are compared internally (comparison of different sequences of a single case) as well as across cases (comparison of sequences of different cases). The first categories are formed from clearly prominent topics that can be worked out in the interviews using minimum and maximum "comparative horizons" (cf. Chapter 3, Section 3.1 and Section 3.2).

Stage 2: Abstraction of dimensions of the mode of speech

On the basis of these comparative horizons, work categories are developed that are crucial to the research topic. This requires a detailed explanation: As already mentioned (cf. Chapter 2, Section 3), the central research interest of the present study is to reconstruct the action-guiding orientation of the relating of the self to God among children. In order to reconstruct the implicit, action-guiding knowledge of children, the evaluation focuses on their mode of speech, i.e., *how* children speak about God and to God and *how* they possibly relate themselves to God. In the second stage of abstraction, the children's mode of speech is abstracted into dimensions called *perspectivity*, *ethics*, and *temporality*. These dimensions represent modes of speaking that can be identified in the interview material as relevant and typical modes of how children speak to and about God. The modes of speech help to reconstruct the relations to God by reconstructing the *how* of the relation to God from the three dimensions of the *how* of speaking. This approach is intended to ensure that the children's propositional knowledge about God is not equated with their relation to God and that their relation to God is not reconstructed from their propositional knowledge. The modes of speech are described in detail below.

Stage 3: Specification of dimensions of the mode of speech

PERSPECTIVITY (mode of speaking with and about God)

The dimension of perspectivity describes the way in which God, the relationship to God, and, if applicable, the talking to and about God is presented by the children in the interviews.

Here, two forms of knowledge can be identified that are described in the terminology of the documentary method as explicit "communicative-theoretical knowledge" and "implicit atheoretical-conjunctive knowledge" (Nohl, 2012, p. 45). Implicit knowledge always comes to the fore when the children themselves

EMPIRICAL RESEARCH RESULTS

mention the subject of God or their relationship to God during the interview in the context of a habitus on which their practice of action is based without having received any prompts in terms of content or language from the interviewer. The explicit level describes the children's speaking about God and their relationship to God as soon as they have taken up or just assume the interviewer's prompts in content or language.

It becomes apparent that the implicit level is always created by the children from their own lifeworld and is referred back to it. When children construct God on the implicit level, they do so on the basis of interpretations derived from their lifeworld knowledge.

The dimension of perspectivity can be differentiated with regard to reflexivity or adoption of perspective (awareness and distance from oneself).

ETHICS (*mode of speaking about normativity*)
The dimension of ethics describes the way in which morality, divine commandments, and everyday ethics are presented by the children in the interviews. The term 'normativity' is not chosen here, since the term 'ethics' is intended to express the question of attitude, i.e., the level of principles relevant for the child's individual lifestyle as opposed to a collectively conceived term of normativity.

Here, how the children express their ethical beliefs, their understanding of norms, and their subjective ethics, for example by formulating regular indicative sentences or normative demands, is analyzed.

The speech mode of ethics shows to what extent children adopt their values and norms from their environment or horizon of social reference. It is possible to assess the differentiations they make as well as the role this horizon of social reference plays therein. This corresponds with specific forms of perspectivity and temporality.

The dimension of ethics can be differentiated with regard to decentration (abandonment of the egocentric world view). It also becomes apparent to what extent these statements follow ethical maxims of conviction or responsibility according to Weber.[7]

TEMPORALITY (*mode of speaking about time, immanence, and transcendence*)
The dimension of temporality describes the way in which questions of temporality, of this world, and the hereafter – in other words, the dimensions 'time' and 'eternity' – are presented by the children in the interviews.

Temporality correlates with other relevant cognitive abilities such as the ability to abandon the perspective of the ego. The children's expressions also document that they have different memories. Some of them remain in the here and now in their narrations, others go far back in their horizons of experience, and others deal with topics related to the hereafter.

The mode of temporality also shows whether the children deal with religious elements and God only occasionally or continuously.

Interrelations between these three modes

In all cases, specific forms of perspectivity correspond with specific forms of temporality and ethics.

Even at this level of abstraction, typical patterns of relating between the three dimensions can be seen. The *stages of abstraction* are the criteria for evaluating the modes of speech.

Stage 4: Abduction of a basic orientation

At a further level of abstraction, a meta dimension as a *basic orientation* across all cases was discovered during the abductive process from the three dimensions which is crucial for answering the research question.

The analysis of the sample showed that the children construct their relation to God, to themselves, and to their environment in different ways. This means that all cases show that in this construction process relatings are made 'implicitly according to the documentary method. The basic orientation that can thus be derived from the material is called *relating of the self*.

Stage 5: Summarizing to ideal-typical frames of orientation

The material shows three different types of relating, i.e., three different *frames of orientation*, each forming a type. In two of them God is included in the relating, in the third one the children exclusively mention immanent dimensions (values, happiness, relationships, friends, material objects, etc.).

The orientation frameworks are composed multidimensionally from the three dimensions of perspectivity, ethics, and temporality which in their interplay specifically describe the patterns of the three modes or types of relating (cf. Chapter 4, Section 4, 5, 6). The resulting typologies are characterized by specific modes of relating of the self.

The following *types of relating of the self* could be reconstructed:
– relating of the self to God in the mode of personalization (type A);
– relating of the self to God in the mode of moralization and orientation towards tradition (type B);
– relating of the self to immanent dimensions in the mode of distance from God (type C).

An overview of the interpretations illustrates that type formation is no longer practicable on the basis of the cases, but results from the "dimensional ties" of the cases' multidimensionality (Weber, 1988; cf. Chapter 3, Section 3.2) that has been elaborated by means of the selected comparisons. Thus, there are strong links between the cases and the reconstructed patterns. Consequently, an ideal-typical construction is carried out. In the abductive phase of type formation, the type is thus contoured by ideal-typical constructions so that the pattern appears as a homologous, logical pattern and thus can also be distinguished from other patterns.

Every ideal-typical construction is to be understood as a shell in which different facets can be found. Type formation is thus ultimately the output of reconstructive research, i.e., type formation provides a systematic answer to the research question in a summarized form.

The form of 'type formation according to genesis of sense' (cf. Chapter 3, Section 3.2) that is used here gives an answer to the question of different typical forms of relations to God among children.

How these types of self-relating become action-guiding for the respective children is described in the following section.

3   Basic Typology: Forms of Self-Relating

The central part of the present empirical study begins with the reconstruction of implicit relations to God that become apparent in the action-guiding knowledge of the interviewed Muslim pupils. For this purpose, the children's constructions of meaning and the underlying orientations in relation to their construction of God are developed. Thus, different types of relations to God appear as implicit forms of knowledge that can be seen in the reconstruction of the social practice of the actors.

The relating of the self to God is documented in this social practice. The different forms of references to God are now presented on an empirically substantiated basis that are missing in the discourse about faith in God among children in general and Muslim children in particular.

The following types could be reconstructed from the material:

Type A: Relating of the Self to God in the Mode of Personalization
At the level of sense-genetic type formation, it was possible to reconstruct those children who have been associated with this type of 'relating of the self to God in the mode of personalization' speaking of a personal construction of God. The perspective from which they construct God shows a closeness to God based on experience. God is experienced in the mode of a 'you' whose existence is unquestioned. Social-worldly, interpersonal, and transcendental phenomena are addressed with a high degree of abstraction and relations to

God are created. In this context, it can be seen that religious or transcendence-related self- and world-interpretations play a role for action in certain situations, but that immanent self- and world-interpretations are also included. Here, in Weber's sense, responsible-ethical attitudes dominate which can be explained by religion. The core responsible-ethical aspect that is reflected in the narrations of this type consists of performing duties and responsibilities towards other people so that others and oneself may feel well. Some of the children give religious reasons for this and some do not. Religious patterns of interpretation thus represent a part of the overall interpretation of life. An individual discussion of the interpretation of the world and the human being from a Muslim perspective is evident by the thematization of the dimension of the invisible. A variety of emotional relationships to God exist within the type, ranging from positive to ambivalent relationships. Ambivalent relations to God also have a great significance in the life and daily routine of the children. The type of relating of the self to God in the mode of personalization shows the desired as well as the actual relationship to God. In maximum contrast to the moralizing and tradition-compliant self-relating type, this type does not primarily use the reward-penalty system (cf. Chapter 4, Section 4).

Type B: Relating of the Self to God in the Mode of Moralization and Orientation towards Tradition
The type 'relating of the self to God in the mode of moralization and orientation towards tradition' is characterized by the children speaking in the mode of orientation towards social expectations or towards tradition by adopting a social norm. Here, the orientation towards tradition shows itself in a moralizing, dichotomizing God perspective. It shows that the children switch between an understanding of God as a fact and as a social norm. They address God in the dimensions and categories that the learned tradition offers them. In addition, there is no implicit action-guiding relation to God or to religious content. In Weber's sense, a conviction-ethical attitude is dominant. A purposively rational relation to God becomes visible in this type, in the sense that a religious effort must be made in order to influence the ultimate being. God is assigned the role of the Creator of a reward-penalty system, so this type focuses on the system but not on the entity that created it. At the explicit level, this type is characterized by the fact that the children know traditional religious narratives and can communicate a minimum level of religious knowledge from which they draw their religious patterns of interpretation. Their response strategies are shaped by Islamic-religious linguistic markers. It is evident that the connection made to religion in many aspects represents a mirror of social desirability whose unifying element is moralizing dichotomization. The preoccupation with religious elements takes place

EMPIRICAL RESEARCH RESULTS

with reference to the past, is selective and without biographical stability. In summary, the reconstructive contrastive analysis shows that in most of the cases the declarative knowledge of the children and their own practice of action does not emerge congruently in the material (cf. Chapter 4, Section 5).

Type C: Relating of the Self to Immanent Dimensions in the Mode of Distance from God
In this type of 'relating of the self to immanent dimensions in the mode of distance from God', God exists peripherally as an element of social reality. Here, children speak in a mode that is detached from personal references. This frame of orientation is characterized by the absence of a relation to God, to religion or to transcendence-related questions as well as by an orientation to the present and a focus on interpersonal interactions and references. Interpersonal and social phenomena are primarily perceived from a responsible-ethical perspective. The expressions are socially anchored. There is no highly moral behavior that is actualized and could be described in Weber's sense as ethics of conviction. Topics with normative potential – in maximum contrast to the other two types – are not framed religiously. The empty space where the relationship to God could manifest itself is filled with immanent world- and self-interpretations. The declarative knowledge about God is hardly ever presented in this type, although the children of this type have also learned some things about God and religion. Accordingly, and in maximum contrast to the other two types, it becomes apparent that the response strategies of the relating of the self in the mode of distance from God do not show any social, cultural, and religious markers that are linguistically influenced by Islamic religious phrases. It can be seen in the material that this type makes a clear distinction between fantasy and reality. God is usually located in the imaginary realm (cf. Chapter 4, Section 6).

In the following, the ideal types that have been developed successively through comparative analysis and theoretical summarization are described abstractly. The patterns of the respective types are then presented in their facets as these are the common denominators for the formation of the ideal types. It should be noted that in this formation of ideal types, individual aspects can appear in all of them. Hence, types are not mutually exclusive on the basis of their profiles. The patterns of the types are taken up for structuring of the following subsection and are represented exemplarily by different transcript excerpts from the cases. These patterns organize the subsections and thus become the classification perspective.

In the further course of this study, the terms personal relationship, moral relationship as well as God-distant relationship will be used as linguistic simplifications.

98 CHAPTER 4

The transcription is based on Hoffmann-Riem (1984), the detailed transcription rules are presented in the Appendix of this work.

4 Type A: Relating of the Self to God in the Mode of Personalization

In the following, the ideal type, 'Relating of the Self to God in the Mode of Personalization' is described. This has successively emerged through comparative analysis and theoretical summarization.

The respective central orientations of the children are reconstructed on the basis of selected passages from the interviews. These passages are characterized either by focal metaphors or by interactive sequences that refer to the epistemological interest of the study.

The respective patterns of the types are described in detail in the subsections (first in brief descriptions and then in detail). Thereby, the dimensions of the speech modes perspectivity, ethics, and temporality serve to represent the respective patterns. We begin with the dimension of perspectivity, which documents the children's active turning to faith in God. This is followed by the dimension of ethics, which shows the normative perspective of the children, which has responsibility-ethical and conviction-ethical features. Finally, the dimension of temporality is presented, which illustrates the reflection of transcendence.

4.1 *Brief Description of the Type*

4.1.1 Perspectivity: Active Turn to Faith in God

The dimension of perspectivity plays an essential role in reconstructing a relation to God. Here it becomes evident that the children themselves bring God into the narrative and weave God into it at a high level of abstraction. The perspective from which they construct God reveals a closeness to God based on experience.

By assessing the mode of speech with regard to reflexivity or adoption of perspective (consciousness of, as well as distance from oneself), a high degree of abstraction becomes apparent in the material. This means that a phenomenon is viewed not only from one but from various perspectives and that the perspective of others is adopted; in other words: the children abstract from themselves. The horizon of perception is accordingly de-centered or socially centered. Here, a maximum contrast to moral relationship that shows a mostly dichotomous horizon of perception is emerging.

The mode of perspectivity reveals the role that children ascribe to God in their statements (tendency to adopt perspective). The role assigned to God in the interview situation is that of a 'you'. The emotional aspect of the relation

EMPIRICAL RESEARCH RESULTS 99

dominates here. This shows that God is part of a socially defined everyday reality. God is conceptualized as a person who is part of the lifeworld. Hence, a distinction is made between the power of God and the power of man.

In general, a personalizing reference in different ways based on experience is evident. This reference, to some extent, underlies action, depending on the respective type of reference. The types of reference that could be reconstructed are either based on an existential need or on an active devotion to faith. The narrations document the fact that the children feel addressed as a person in their everyday lives, i.e., that they integrate faith into their lifeworld. This demonstrates a personal construction of God with individual traits and is characterized by a positive image of God. This type shows an overall positive religiousness and an active orientation towards a religious way of life.

4.1.2   Ethics: Norms between Ethics of Responsibility and Ethics of Conviction

In the dimension of ethics, this type addresses social-worldly, interpersonal, and hereafter-related phenomena within a high degree of abstraction and makes relations to God.

Social-worldly and interpersonal issues are addressed in the context of responsibility, as can be seen in the harmonizing conflict resolution strategy, the concept of friendship as well as the statements on educational commitment. The topic of responsibility is primarily perceived from a responsible-ethical perspective in Weber's sense. In this context, an accessibility to transcendental as well as to immanent or anthropological world- and self-interpretations becomes apparent. Religious interpretations play an action-guiding role in many situations, including biographically important ones. Religious patterns of interpretation therefore do not appear as a separate pattern of interpretation rather as a part of the overall interpretation of life.

4.1.3   Temporality: Reflection of Transcendence

In the dimension of temporality, this type displays an orientation towards the hereafter. In maximum contrast to moral relationship, which reduces the question of the hereafter to the problem of reaching it (entry into paradise through good behavior), this type deals emotionally and cognitively with the character of events after death. In addition, it intensively deals with the question of God on the explicit level. The material is characterized by curiosity and thirst for knowledge. God is being reflected upon.

All in all, this type shows an individual engagement with the interpretation of the world and the human being from an Islamic perspective, whereby the dimension of the invisible is addressed by this type here (cf. Chapter 5, Section 2).

4.2 *Perspectivity: Active Turning to Faith in God*

The active turning to faith in God in the dimension of perspectivity shows itself in two facets: from a positive perspective and out of need. The reconstruction begins with a presentation of the aspect that children who are assigned to this type ideally turn to faith and the practice of faith from a positive perspective.

4.2.1 Active Turning to Faith in God from a Positive Perspective

The personalizing relation to God shows itself in its specific form within this pattern in such a way, that during the interviews children embed God and religious practice into their narrations on their own initiative. This embedding also has a positive connotation.

Dilara immediately starts the continuation of the narration of the opening stimulus with a relation to God. In terms of narrative perspective, she provides different perspectives in the five variations she offers. In the first variation of her story, she starts to narrate from the outside in, with a direct relation to God (25–32):

Description of the text passage: Opening passage – Continuation of the Story of Ali – Text type differentiation: Narration

> Dilara: /Uhm/ it could be, that Allah /uh/ helps him and makes light in the hut /uhm/ and then a man can come and listen how he screams to shout for help and after that maybe he can come and try him well to bring him out of there and Allah makes Light in there so that he knows that Allah is beside him and helps him and /uhm/ maybe it could be that an angel comes and well the guardian angel gives him a good feeling and that something good is going to happen now and something good is going to happen when the guardian angel is here yes ((laughs)) ( )?

The second variation shows a change of perspective and role. Dilara refers to the side actors, views the story from her own perspective and adds dialogical sequences (34–42):

Description of the text passage: Opening passage – Continuation of the Story of Ali – Text type differentiation: Narration

> Dilara: /uhm/ it could be that now the kids well get some kind of a bad feeling and say come we will get him out and then /uh/ they talk it over and they say ok /uh/ and after that they get him maybe out of there and say /

EMPIRICAL RESEARCH RESULTS

uhm/ could you give us tutoring that we also as good as you are Sorry that we did it and after that they don't do it anymore and then they all learn together and then they are good as well .. yes and then the teacher is also proud that they so good // well that they are so good friends and learnt well together ((laughs)) yes that's (it)? Yeah/uhm/ and further I don't know .. it could

In the third variation, Dilara narrates again from an outside perspective and offers a new possibility for Ali's rescue (42–46):

Description of the text passage: Opening passage – Continuation of the Story of Ali – Text type differentiation: Narration

Dilara: ((laughs)) yeah that's (it)? yeah /uhm/ and further I don't know .. it could be /uhm/ that now /uh/ children come when they go also the same way maybe from the school and then also /uh/ hear how he's screaming in there and then /uh/ maybe find something so that they can open the look yeah and then they could maybe save him from in there

In the fourth variation, Dilara continues the change of perspective and role. She now refers to the main actor, views the story from Ali's' perspective, and introduces dialogical sequences. Here, variation two of the story reappears. In the situation addressed here, there is great potential for conflict but no conflict at all occurs. Dilara does not feel the tension that is created by the conflict situation but aims to resolve the tension. This shows that she continuously wants to bring the situation to a harmonious end (48–55):

Description of the text passage: Opening passage – Continuation of the Story of Ali – Text type differentiation: Narration

Dilara: Yeah.. and Ali /uhm/ goes to m...... // well goes /uhm/ maybe to the boys and says /uhm/ it wasn't nice that you did it I was very lonely and sad and then /uhm/ the.... It could also be that the boys say we are sorry that we did it we were jealous of you and after that they could learn together do something go to school and they could play together and so on /uhm/ it could be that they are very good friends and don't fight anymore ((laughs)) yeah.. further I can't tell

102   CHAPTER 4

In the fifth variation Ali helps himself. Furthermore, Dilara includes Allah and the guardian angel again (58–82):

Description of the text passage: Opening passage – Continuation of the Story of Ali – Text type differentiation: Narration

> Dilara: /uhm/ maybe /uhm/ something is /uh/ well some kind of lock door on the ground maybe he can open it and through this well go down there and find a way with which he can get out of there or he simply digs with his hand and /uhm/ Allah helps him doing it and it could be that Allah gives him a good feeling so that he's not lonely because Allah is beside him and the guardian angel /uhm/ and the guardian angel can always stay with him then he gives a feeling that he's beside him and that he shouldn't be afraid because surely /uh/ something good is going to happen then /uh/ the guardian angel can say /uh/ well give some kind of feeling someone's coming soon or someone hears you they are coming soon or other things that make him less lonely shouldn't make him sad and after that surely something good is going to happen.. yeah.. and the boys are surely sad as well that they did it they surely have a feeling that they well that that well they will notice that it /uh/ was bad and they /uhm/ could think about it again if they should free him and then /uhm/ so that /uh/ he well isn't as sad they could talk it over and after that come back and get him out and say that they are sorry that they did it and (then)? They could befriend each other yeah.. and then.. well in any case Allah for sure helps them and the guardian angel is with him as well Allah helps him as well /uhm/ Allah is always with him and helps the humans and the guardian angel he is always with him and protects him yeah that's why he's called guardian angel /uh/ well he protects the kid so that nothing happens to it and maybe the lock breaks in parts or something happens with the door /uh/ and then he can go out.. yeah.. ((laughs)) further I don't know

In the minimal case comparison to Betül, Dilara narrates how she has different versions of the story. In the maximum comparison to her, however, a different mode is chosen. Dilara finishes telling a story, laughs, relaxes, and tells a new variation of the story. Betül, on the other hand, loses herself in the narration, it becomes more and more dramatic, up to the death of the main protagonist. Dilara has a clear narrative structure; she varies, but always concludes in a harmonizing way. She looks at the story from the outside perspective as well as from the perspectives of the side and main actors. She introduces dialogic sequences

EMPIRICAL RESEARCH RESULTS

in her narrations. Therefore, in terms of reflexivity or perspective-adoption in the different variations she offers, her speech mode shows a high level of abstraction.

Here, the perspectivity and reflexivity with a high level of abstraction shows a minimal contrast to Betül, Hagen, Kaltrina, and Qamar. In the construction of her different variations, Dilara follows the urge to reach a good and harmonious resolution of the situation. She works to unravel the mystery, heal the damage, resolve the conflict, and to resolve the situation harmoniously at the end. No variation of her stories has a negative ending in contrast to Betül, Mesut, and Qamar, who end their stories with the death of the protagonist. The harmonizing conflict resolution strategy is also evident in Hagen, Filiz, Mesut, Leyla, Navid, and Kaltrina.

The opening passage already shows how Dilara relates the theme of being imprisoned perspectively in relation to God and the role she ascribes to him. In the first variation of her narrative, she introduces God by herself. She begins the continuation of the narrative of the opening stimulus directly with a relation to God. She relates that it may be that God "helps him [the boy] and makes light in the hut". Two interpretations suggest themselves here, namely that Dilara is speaking of light in the physical sense or of the symbol of 'light' metaphorically.

This implies, that Dilara continues a theological tradition at the beginning of her narration. However, she localizes and objectifies the motive of Light ("Allah makes Light in there"), in such a way that it should be assumed that she is not moving on a symbolic level of interpretation. To bring light into the dark and localize it, points to a childlike Imagination. (concrete-operational stage of development).

Ali, who is in the hut, is supposed to get a feeling of hope, of not being lost and of trust through this idea or conception of light.

Moreover, she reinforces this feeling of security by introducing a guardian angel into the scenario. After God has made light, that is God's nearness has been felt by Ali, a man comes who hears Ali's cries for help and his scream and tries to free him. The significant other in this case is actually an 'other', that is, not a central figure from the child's lifeworld in maximum contrast to Canan, who chooses real people from her lifeworld as the central protagonists of her narrative.

Dilara speaks of a feeling that brings with it an inkling that something good is about to happen. Dilara's ability to deal with the theme of light in relation to the description of feeling indicates a high capacity for abstraction. Dilara's narrative seems to have the character of a prophet's story. There are some features of symbolism in her narrative that are found in the Joseph story: One feature is that she tells of the light that God makes in the hut. In the Qur'anic version of the Joseph story, Joseph as a child is thrown into darkness. This darkness completely envelops him and triggers his inner vision in terms of light, as his gaze is blocked. His gaze turns inward, and the light is symbolic not only of hope but also of seeing and knowing.

In Dilara's narration, another theme emerges, that is the motif of hope at the emotional level, as Dilara brings in Ali's feeling "that something good will happen". On top of the immanent inquiry stimulus to Ali's feelings in the hut, she still brings in the digging, which can be called the 'Hagarite motif' in the Muslim narrative tradition (125–133):

Description of the text passage: Immanent stimulus to Ali's feelings in the hut – Text type differentiation: Narration

> Dilara: Yes ... so there is in there it can be that if he looks for something or digs something also something good comes from it maybe he can find a way to go out of it for example in front of the door if it is earth he can dig quite a lot and after that in front of the door it can also dig then and after that comes ( )? so inside you can also do things that also help to maybe find water somewhere or a piece of bread somewhere in the corner or something and after that it can /uh/ so he doesn't need to be afraid because Allah is with him and the guardian angel nothing can happen to him when Allah is there ....

When Hagar, Abraham's wife, is left in the desert with her son, she starts digging and water gushes out of the ground. Dilara talks about Ali digging and something good coming out of it. It is possible that Dilara knows this story, is connecting to it, and is trying to interpret it against the background of her own thinking. It is striking that Dilara always uses the term guardian angel in connection with Allah. This combination is also evident in Olivia (193–196):

Description of the text passage: Exmanent stimulus to a story about God – Text type differentiation: Narration

> Olivia: /uhm/ ... /uhm/ so I often think about when . something almost happened to me but only almost . and it didn't happen but . very . almost happened . so to speak my . guardian angels saved me from it and also Allah . that it didn't happen to me ...

EMPIRICAL RESEARCH RESULTS   105

In the Sunni and Shiite traditions, the belief in a personal guardian angel is not established. Perhaps this comes from a mystical tradition or is based on a syncretism that comes from contacts with esoteric forms. Dilara concludes her different variations with a laugh. It could be reconstructed that this laughter indicates that the good and positive solution is a personal satisfaction and relief for Dilara herself. The laughter here is a sign of relaxation and the good outcome of the story. In the fifth variation of her story, a peculiarity in the language appears. Dilara uses a comforting language. The metaphorical density of the sequence indicates that this form of consolation is narratively saturated with experience. In this passage, Dilara demonstrates how to comfort on a linguistic level, weaving God and the guardian angel into her narration (58–82):

Description of the text passage: Opening passage – Continuation of Ali's story – Text type differentiation: Narration

Dilara: /Uhm/ maybe /Uhm/ is something /Uh/ so a lock door on the floor maybe he can open it and so by going under there and finding a way to get out or he just digs with his hand and /uh/ Allah helps him with that and it can also be that Allah gives him a good feeling that he is not lonely because Allah is next to him and the guardian angel /uhm/ and the guardian angel can always stay with him then he gives a feeling that he is next to him and that he should not be afraid because surely /uh/ something good will happen then /uh/ the guardian angel can say /uh/ so give such a feeling someone is coming or someone hears you they are coming soon or other things that should not make him so lonely should not make him sad and after that surely something good will happen .. yes ... and the boys are certainly also sad that they did it, they certainly also have such a feeling that they then realize that it was /uh/ bad and /uhm/ can think again whether they will free him and afterwards /uhm/ so that /uh/ he is not so sad, they can discuss it and then come back and get him out and apologize that they did it and (afterwards)? Can they make friends yes ... and further ... so in any case Allah helps him for sure and the guardian angel is also with him Allah helps him too /uhm/ Allah is always with him he helps the people and the guardian angel is always with him and protects him yes that's why he is called guardian angel /uh/ so he protects the child so that nothing happens to him and maybe the lock breaks down or something happens to the door /uh/ and after that he can go out. Yes ... ((laughs)) further I don't know any more ...

Dilara constructs an abstract relation to God. She brings up social-worldly and interpersonal phenomena with a high degree of abstraction and thereby establishes relations to God. The role she assigns to God and the guardian angels as a 'you' also shows her tendency to adopt perspective. In Dilara's case, it is evident overall that she views a phenomenon not only from one perspective, but from different perspectives, and that she adopts the perspective of others, that is that she abstracts from herself. Her perceptual horizon and her thinking are therefore decentered. Case-immanent comparison reveals that the first variation of Dilara's story, which follows tradition, is more experientially abstract and formulaic. The fifth variation, however, is full of her own experience.

Dilara has an experience of comfort and links it to something numinous. Accordingly, Dilara shows a personalizing, positive reference that is linked to experience. Her stories are interwoven with God and end harmoniously. Because this perspective may be experience-saturated, it does not occur to Dilara to find a variation that receives a negative outcome. Because Dilara has a saturated experience of comfort that she associates with God, it is only logical that this is given in any severe situation, so there is no reason for a negative outcome.

From line 75 ("so in any case Allah helps him for sure and the guardian angel is also with him Allah helps him ...") Dilara comes out of the narrative, goes into explanation mode and argues. In terms of narrative theory, this indicates that the saturation of experience decreases here. With regard to her construction of God, Dilara connects the perspective that one must become active oneself and can get oneself out of a difficult situation with the help of Allah and the guardian angel (58–68):

Description of the text passage: Opening passage – Continuation of Ali's story – Text type differentiation: Narration

Dilara: /uhm/ maybe /uhm/ something is /uh/ so a lock door on the ground maybe he can open it and go under it and find a way to get out or he just digs with his hand and /uhm/ Allah helps him with that and it can also be that Allah gives him a good feeling that he is not lonely because Allah is next to him and the guardian angel /uhm/ and the guardian angel can always stay with him then he gives a feeling that he is next to him and that he should not be afraid because surely /uh/ something good happens then /uh/ the guardian angel can say /uh/ so give such a feeling someone is coming or someone hears you they are coming soon or other things that should not make him so lonely should not make him sad and after that surely something good happens .. yes.

EMPIRICAL RESEARCH RESULTS 107

The meaning of this connection is shown in the fact that Dilara distinguishes between God's power of action and man's power of action. In her narrative, there is a passivity in the role of God, and an activity in the role of the acting human being. She keeps the two levels of divine and human agency apart. Possibly, a homology between the role of God and the role of the teacher is revealed here, which Dilara introduces in the second variation of her story (34–42):

Description of the text passage: Opening passage – Continuation of Ali's story – Text type differentiation: Narration

> Dilara: /Uhm/ it can also be that now the children get such a bad feeling and say come on we'll get him out again and then /uh/ they discuss it and say ok /uh/ and then they get him maybe out and say /uhm/ can you tutor us so that we are also as good as you are sorry that we did it and then they don't do it any more and after that they all learn together then they are also good … yes and after that the teacher is also proud that they so good // so that they are such good friends and have learned well together ((laughs)) yes that (was it)? yes /uhm/ and further I don't know … it can be

A homology is revealed in the sense that the teacher is satisfied with the children's behavior, just as God is satisfied with people's 'good' behavior. The teacher is also given a more passive role in Dilara's narrative in maximum contrast to that of Betül and Canan.

In Betül's case, the teacher is given a punitive role and in Canan's case, she is given an active role as a seeker of Ali. In Dilara's case, she is proud of the children's good behavior and learning performance. The teacher sees the results and is satisfied with what is happening, but she has not intervened in it herself. The children have positively changed their behavior themselves and are active. The teacher thus looks down from above and is given a passive role. The homology lies in the fact that Dilara does not relate the behavior and its changes to the influence of a higher person or a numinous force but locates it in the children's own agency and responsibility. This reading is condensed through further passages in which Dilara brings in God, repeatedly addressing the agency and responsibility of humans and separating the levels of God and humans (116–133):

Description of the text passage: Opening passage – Immanent inquiry stimulus on the story of Ali – Text type differentiation: Narration

> I: Tell me about Ali's feelings in the hut.
>
> Dilara: He is surely sad that his friends did something like that he is lonely in there he is lonely in there he is afraid but /uhm/ he surely knows that Allah is with him and the guardian angel so he shouldn't be afraid but he is surely sad his heart is surely broken and he is very lonely in there and maybe nobody can hear him and stay in there he can cry he can be sad in any case he has to find a way inside /uhm/ so he can go out as well
>
> I: Yes
>
> Dilara: Yes ... so in there it can be that if he is looking for something or digging something also something good comes out of it maybe he can find a way to go out of it for example in front of the door if it is earth he can dig a lot and after that in front of the door it can also dig then and after that comes ( )? Out so inside you can also do things that also help to it maybe you find water somewhere or a piece of bread somewhere in the corner or so and after that it can /uh/ so there he does not need to be afraid because Allah is with him and the guardian angel nothing can happen to him if Allah is there ....

Dilara attributes to Allah and the guardian angel the role of givers of a good feeling so that the one who is in distress does not have to be afraid. However, a way out or a solution to his problem must be sought by the person themselves. It can be seen in the material that Dilara assigns an emotional support function to these numinous effect powers, but she sees the responsibility for action with herself or with the person. With regard to the agency of humans, it is clear from Dilara's mode of speech that she adopts a normative perspective (104–115):

Description of the text passage: Immanent inquiry stimulus on Ali's story – Text type differentiation: Narration, description

> Dilara: Yes but if they don't study then it doesn't work you always have to study you have to work you have to study so that you are so smart and so good in school and so you always have to work you can't just sit at home and just watch TV so you always have to if it's even ten or five minutes you always have to study for school so that you are good /uhm/ you can also go to a tutor or a teacher and ask them to help read books /uh/ not just watch TV all day at home so /uh/ take a book read or do math so that you are also

EMPIRICAL RESEARCH RESULTS 109

> so good so that you get good grades you can't just sit around lazily you have to study no matter what even five minutes is enough for that if you study you are also so smart yes .. ( )?

Here Dilara emphasizes independent and self-responsible learning, which she distinguishes from watching television. In this way, she expresses what good action and correct behavior mean to her. Other passages clarify her image of humanity (147–166 and 183–185):

Description of the text passage: Immanent inquiry stimulus on Ali's feelings in the hut – Text type differentiation: Narration, description

> Dilara: He mustn't give up in any case if he gives up it's bad he has to try something he has to do something so in any case he has to try it so that he can also believe he has to be able to believe in himself and he mustn't be afraid first he has to try and then not give up so that he doesn't just leave it like that and sit there and do nothing he has to find a way that he goes out so /uhm/ for example he can also do things like that ( )? So digging or something and in any case he must not give up he must try it so if you try something it is also good if you are for example now in there and do nothing then it is bad because maybe there is a way that you can go out there or you find something good in any case you have to do it so that /uh/ you are also sure you have to be sure so he has to be able to believe in himself /uhm/ for sure so maybe he will find something in there that it will help. so that you can open the door if you /uhm/ don't try anything then you can't do anything so break open the door or something you have to try something that it opens you can't just sit and cry so you have to do something you have to find a way you can't just quickly give up for example you only dig /uh/ for five minutes and give up you can't just give up you have to try it

Description of the text passage: Immanent inquiry stimulus on Ali's thoughts in the hut – Text type differentiation: Narration, description

> Dilara: now something good is happening so you mustn't quickly think bad things are happening to me now always /uh/ think positive not negative you must always so think good

Here, too, the overemphasis and weighting of learning reveals a homology to the opening narrative. Here, Dilara treats the entire theme of learning within the framework of active self-direction of events by the learner. In Dilara's narrations, the individual is given a role that is characterized in a particular way by activities and the assumption of responsibility. From line 147, Dilara operates with the term "believe". Here, she does not apply the motif of faith to God, but to the human being, who must believe in himself. God, on the other hand, is there to help by making one feel good and being happy about people's 'good' behavior.

This reading is condensed by the maximum contrast with Betül, who places her aspirations, such as wanting to get into grammar school, in a God perspective rather than seeing them as her own responsibility (285–292):

Description of the text passage: Own desires and experiences – Text type differentiation: Narration, description

> Betül: and I once said to him no I say it several times to Allah if you think that Gymnasium or Haupt or Gymmi uh the Gymnasium Haupt or Real is the best for me put me where you just want where I am just secured what I where I just under quite good for me I said then I just came to Haupt and then I have I was not angry at all I said Allah has Allah has decided that I said to him what is best for me and then Haupt is best for me and then I just went to Haupt now I go to Haupt

Dilara deals with religious-ethical topics such as donating in the context of helping and taking responsibility. Her statements show a normative potential that contains elements of responsibility ethics and ethics of convictions. Moreover, there are also elements of a do-become interpretation (328–333 and 346–357):

Description of the text passage: Exmanent inquiry stimulus on bad deeds – Text type differentiation: Narration

> Dilara: you do that and at the Feast of Sacrifice that's also good if you /uh/ sacrifice an animal a cow or something and then /uh/ donate half of the cow to the others so that they also have something to eat or give half of your money to the others so that they are also happy in Ramadan or at the Feast of Sacrifice so that they also have something to eat or so that they can also buy something with the money so that's always good if you do that

EMPIRICAL RESEARCH RESULTS

> Dilara: And after that when you donate it's very good there are a lot of good deeds from Allah and if you don't do it it's a bad deed so when you yell at someone and say no go away and go to someone else that's my money that's well a bad deed because you have to donate you have to donate if you're rich /uhm/ half of your money to the poor in the five pillars it's because of the poor tax and you have to donate that would be good for the poor people and for you because you /uhm/ give something to someone and make them happy and you also get good deeds when you do it but if you don't it's bad for you because you get the bad deeds from Allah and if you also don't do it /uh/ it's also bad for the po ... poor people because after that they have no food no drink no money with that

Dilara takes the responsibility for the needy out of her religious attitude. It can be seen that she socially connotes the religious act of donating by referring to the fact that it makes the recipients happy. Again, she addresses the secular and transcendent levels on an explicit level and describes the positive and negative consequences on both levels.

In the context of the reconstructive analysis, Dilara's narratives reveal a close, action-guiding reference to a God who is relevant to her lifeworld, which is documented in her implicit action-guiding knowledge. In addition, her narrations document a self-responsible position of the human being.

Hagen is similar to Dilara in terms of his profile. In his continuation of Ali's narrative, he offers only one, but a very long variation that initially assumes a reality. He quickly resolves Ali's situation by first presenting Ali's own attempts to get out of the hut and then addressing the search by his parents, who eventually find him. He thus brings the parents directly into play as significant others, describing Ali's joy (63–70):

Description of the text passage: Opening passage – Continuation of Ali's story – Text type differentiation: Narration

> Hagen: came or so ... and /uhm/ ... then in any case they also searched in the forest and so and then /uhm/ also the parents and so and then they saw the hut and /uhm/ have him /uhm/ have looked inside whether there is someone there and have opened the lock and yes and then he was in any case certainly fully happy that he /uhm/ is outside again because it was very creepy and so because it was definitely creepy for him because it was dark and he felt lonely ... yes and then he was in any case very happy and fell into his parents' arms.

Following the resolution of the confinement situation, the minimal contrast with Dilara and Filiz shows that Hagen tries to overcome the negative motive of action by letting Ali help the children to make them accept Ali. He changes the group dynamic and turns the adversaries into friends who help each other and improve their performances. In the process, considerable educational effort is evident. In minimal contrast to Dilara and Filiz, he also transforms the forest into a positive place where the children camp together. He also brings the girls into the story, who are among the four jealous children in Ali's narrative and constructs their own tent for them. The gender theme reveals a minimal contrast with Kaltrina, who deliberately brings a girl into the story. Kaltrina and Hagen are the only children who incorporate girls into their story.[8] Inspired by camping, campfires, and barbecues in his own story, Hagen begins to tell a fantasy story (95–103). Here, a parallel to Paiman emerges, who also incorporates elements into the story, but draws from the cinematic realm.

Description of the text passage: Opening passage – Continuation of Ali's story – Text type differentiation: Narration

> Hagen: Batteries empty they forgot to put them in and then /uhm/ they tried somehow to find their way home again and then they got lost ... /uhm/ Ali had however // was quite clever and louder /uhm/ secretly threw stones on like thicker stones on the ground and then they always tried to find the stones and then at some point they were out of the forest and after that // they also have // an owl also then scared them because they thought it was a gh was a ghost (4) and then /uhm/ they were in any case happy again and /uhm/ said we'll do that more often now . then they moved on.

The place of fear, "hut", is also turned around positively, in that the children construct a realm of their own out of this hut (129–152):

Description of the text passage: Opening passage – Continuation of Ali's story – Text type differentiation: Narration

> Hagen: they made something great they went to the forest again to this hut to think ... to the hut there and made something great out of the hut they built in windows like with wood an and made the door good again with nails and a hammer and /uhm/ have built a lock with like a key and /uhm/ they also built a lot of windows on top of it they like like further built it up

EMPIRICAL RESEARCH RESULTS

> with stones so that it looked like a tower and there in the tower on top there were beds inside to sleep in when one was tired because there he could then sleep inside then nothing could happen and also a lot of animals went in and and wanted to see what was inside and then they were allowed to go in everywhere ... yes (5) and then /uhm/ they also built a roof so that it didn't really rain inside and they like also built there a garden like with their own things like tomatoes and cucumbers and pumpkins and /uhm/ raspberries strawberries and wild strawberries and blueberries and then they always ate from it there they made their own things from it and also /uhm/ planted mushrooms . and then they have they have learned almost all the tree species by heart .. instead of /uhm/ like playing around with cell phones and stuff and then . and then they discovered lots of new animal species and stuff .. and . and then they have they have built something extra for the animals and /uhm/ then /uhm/ Ali ha had not paid attention and accidentally sat on a hedgehog ((smiling)) and then there was a cat// he just wrote Aaaah and yeees and then /uhm/ . he has again these /uhm/ what's it called .. these /uhm/ mmm in any case these pointed thingies

It becomes apparent that Hagen is completely immersed in the story. His narrative reveals his own relevancies which he brings up, such as his educational orientation ("and then they learned almost all the tree species by heart ... instead of /uhm/ like playing around with cell phones and stuff"), his closeness to nature, his understanding of friendship, his love for animals, and his knowledge of the different kinds of fruits and vegetables (154–160):

Description of the text passage: Opening passage – Continuation of Ali's story – Text type differentiation: Narration

> Hagen: Exactly the spines were pulled out yes and then .. the hedgehog left and /uhm/ they did a lot of things for the animals in any case even more and then they also /uhm/ discovered poisonous things fly agaric and tuber leaf mushrooms and then they also found truffles .. on like trees . and /uhm/ they gave them to a wild boar because they also like truffles very much . and then /uhm/ . in any case they were in there for a long time and slept there.

In further sequences, Hagen explains that the protagonists of his own narration grow fruit and vegetables, but do not want to earn money from this, but rather to live from the produce themselves (191–195):

Description of the text passage: Opening passage – Continuation of Ali's story –
Text type differentiation: Narration

> Hagen: then uh they all lived in there in the forest ... yes ... and then /uhm/ they made like a huge field full of tomatoes and plants like gigantically big with that they would have had they would have been rich if they had sold them but they didn't want that they wanted to have that themselves didn't want to get rich with . then they also like

This is strongly reminiscent of the romantic-idealistic exaltation of a subsistence economy lifestyle cultivated in green-alternative circles since the turn of the 20th century (Kerbs, 1998). This distinct way of life is reflected in Hagen's story. His narrations show in these metaphorically dense passages that he may be actualizing these experiences from his lifeworld. The fact that he has the children create an organic farm as a utopia shows that he knows and identifies with this way of life. His narrations reflect a conscious and nature-loving way of life. In his narrations, Hagen brings in ritual prayer (195–203):

Description of the text passage: Opening passage – Continuation of Ali's story –
Text type differentiation: Narration

> Hagen: they didn't want to get rich with . then they also built like a prayer tower and and have have made like a small room where /uhm/ where you can pray (inside)? and always when prayer time was /uhm/ he has he has /uhm/ called adaan[9] and /uhm/ and then all have come to pray and have prayed and water they had also with like there was like a small pond there were also frogs and like in it yes and then they have lived in there and and have taught themselves everything like have practiced because the parents could do you know already the whole and like with math and stuff like that .. yes and then they knew their way around the forest really well and then they lived there

Hagen contextualizes in his story all the requirements for prayer, such as place of prayer (prayer tower, small room), time of prayer, call to prayer ($\bar{a}\underline{d}\bar{a}n$), and water (small pond) for ritual purification. Here it is clear that he perceives ritual prayer in its entirety and incorporates it within the context of his story. However, in maximum contrast to Leyla, it is evident that Hagen does not thematize prayer under a religious, convictional ethics, or ethic-of-responsibility

EMPIRICAL RESEARCH RESULTS 115

maxim. He connects the religious elements in his life with nature and animals, which play an essential role for him, and throughout his narration he sketches the idea of living in harmony with nature and religion. Hagen addresses prayer in one other place in his story (218–224):

Description of the text passage: Opening passage – Continuation of Ali's story – Text type differentiation: Narration

> Hagen: pretty likes and then they have ea the all have eaten something always they have also cooked chili … /uhm/ m have put tofu in it and /uhm/ with like corn they have also put in and also rice with very hot pepperonis peppero peppers and /uhm/ they have eaten that and /uhm/ and then their mouths ha have burned like really badly and there they had to drink quite a lot of milk and eat bread … and then /uhm/ was already night and then they also did their night prayer and then slept and the

Hagen's attitude toward prayer is evident in that he brings it into his narrations as a habitualized ritual, making it clear that prayer is a natural part of his way of life. In minimal contrast to Dilara, an active orientation in religious lifestyle is evident. On the explicit level, Hagen expresses his conception of God (388–391):

Description of the text passage: Exmanent inquiry stimulus on his own thoughts about God – Text type differentiation: Description

> Hagen: I think you certainly feel safe or .. because he you know created us .. you have to imagine him quite nice . because if you imagine him nice then he also is nice . but if you imagine him evil then well he also is evil for you (7) yes (5)

Hagen is the only child who assumes that God is like how a human being imagines him to be. This positive conception of God is also evident in Dilara, who relates her concept of positive thinking to her ideas of God and a guardian angel in an immanent stimulus to Ali's thoughts in the hut (174–185):

Description of the text passage: Immanent inquiry stimulus on Ali's thoughts in the hut – Text type differentiation: Narration

> Dilara: and certainly thinks bad things he must not think bad things or something bad will you know also happen he must always think good and not negative always think positive so that something so you are sure that something good will happen he must think so he must consider what he can do and he he surely also thinks that Allah is with him and is ..... it is also like that and the guardian angel is there nothing can you know happen to him he must always think well and not so badly oh me /uh/ I will surely die soon something bad will surely happen to me maybe nothing bad will happen maybe something good will happen now so one must not think so quickly bad things always happen to me now /uh/ think positively not negatively one must always contemplate well

In minimal contrast the case of Hagen and Dilara makes clear that they have a positive, emotionally reinforcing relationship to their religiosity. In Dilara's case, this is connected with a reflective attitude of thinking positively and also forming a positive image of God. Both make virtually no reference to a reward-punishment concept. In maximum contrast to Paiman and Leyla, it can be seen that Hagen and Dilara actively turn to faith and do not practice it out of necessity, as will be detailed below. Faith has a positive connotation, and a positively oriented religiosity is evident.

Hence, in the case of Dilara and Hagen, it is evident that the Muslim way of life and the worldview is something positive with which they identify.

4.2.1.1 *Summary*

In the dimension of perspectivity, the children of this type show that God is brought into the narrative by themselves, without being asked. The children address God and religious practice in metaphorically dense passages. They construct the relation to God on an abstract level, showing a high awareness and distance from themselves. They establish the reference to more abstract spheres by bringing up social-worldly and interpersonal phenomena with a high degree of abstraction, making references to God. With these children it is recognizable that they view a phenomenon not only from one, but from different perspectives and adopt the perspective of others, i.e., the abstract from themselves. Their narrations document an action-guiding reference to a God who is part of their socially defined everyday world.

4.2.2 Active Turning to Faith in God out of Need

The following facet of active turning to faith in God is characterized by the fact that it emerged out of an existential need resulting from experiences.

EMPIRICAL RESEARCH RESULTS

Leyla does not introduce God in the continuation of Ali's story. She offers a variation on the continuation of Ali's story. Leyla's mode of speech shows a high level of abstraction in minimal contrast to Dilara and Hagen in terms of reflexivity and perspective taking. In response to the exmanent stimulus about her fear, Leyla addresses her fear of losing a family member or someone she likes, adding that she had lost her cousin. Leyla talks about the death of her cousin, which affected her greatly. She brings God in on her own here as she tells of her reaction to her cousin's death. She was so upset by her death that in her helplessness she spoke to God as the one who can prevent such an event from happening again in her family. In this emergency situation, Leyla automatically turns to God. She draws on a religious imprint that she has experienced in the course of her socialization. In the corresponding passage, the mode of speaking with and about God is revealed with regard to the dimension of perspectivity (174–191):

Description of the text passage: Own experiences – Text type differentiation: Narration, description

I: hmm (5) and /uhm/ . are you sometimes afraid

Leyla: so I'm sometimes afraid of dark or when I can't breathe or I'm afraid that I'll get asthma or . that I'll lose my parents maybe or my brother or someone I like very much . like my cousin she died and I don't want anyone to die again either (14)

I: tell me more about it

Leyla: ... so ... my cousin she was 17 or 16 /uhm/ . she // so she wanted to cross the street it was green but she was run over by a coach . was very sad I cried . so I told then Allah that never something like that should happen also not to my parents or relatives or someone I like very much and that's why I now usually find someone nice before he dies or something like that (15)

I: ((asking)) you said this to Allah

Leyla: yes I opened my hands said that never something like this should happen made dua[10] I also told my mother that she should also // so make dua maybe that there is an effect or something like that (5) and since then I also always pray I make namaz[11] I just do it

The form of direct address to God shows in the dimension of perspectivity that Leyla puts herself in the place of a counterpart (here God) and assumes that he is listening to her. At the same time, her attempt to come to terms with death is also immanent and can be interpreted in an inner-worldly way, in the sense that she has come to know the value of life through the death of her cousin. These two strategies are not mutually exclusive.

Leyla recounts how she opened her hands and said a supplication when she learned of her cousin's death. This experience is apparently still so recent or salient that Leyla recalls her hand gesture. In the greatest distress, she said a supplication (*du'ā'*). It is possible that this religious act became so habitualized in her that she was able to fall back on it automatically and used the supplication as relief from the situation. She also asked her mother to say a supplication because her own prayer was not sufficient for her. However, she is not sure if these supplications are sufficient and have an effect. Therefore, she has also been performing the ritual prayer (*namaz*) since the incident. She performs this prayer in the hope that something so terrible will never happen again. Particularly striking is the statement "that's why I usually find someone nice now before they die now". The frame in which she thematizes the entire passage is marked by accomplishments. Leyla makes to avert catastrophe. This religious, achievement-oriented attitude is particularly evident in her statement that she "finds someone nice before they die".[12]

Leyla shows an orientation towards 'relative autonomy', the second stage of the development of religious judgment according to Oser and Gmüder (do ut des = I give so you may give (cf. Chapter 2, Section 1.4)). This stage is characterized by the fact that the ultimate is still seen as omnipotent, but man can act on the ultimate.

Leyla is quite aware that the terrible can happen again. Here she shows a silencing (202–207):

Description of the text passage: Own experiences – Text type differentiation: Narration, description

> I: ((questioning)) and if that happens after all
>
> Leyla: then I would be sad would pray more would ask Allah and if it still wouldn't work then maybe Allah would want it that way and that's why [about that?] I wouldn't say anything anymore. nothing anymore. So but you would still pray because you you know also just want to go to paradise . yes (30)

Leyla is aware that the effect of prayer does not necessarily have to be realized, that her wishes are not necessarily fulfilled. This awareness and the surrender

EMPIRICAL RESEARCH RESULTS

to God's will are also shown in minimal contrast with Betül when she discusses her wishes and hopes (285–292):

Description of the text passage: Own desires and experiences – Text type differentiation: Narration, description

> Betül: and I once said to him no I say it several times to Allah if you think that Gymnasium or Haupt or Gymmi uh the Gymnasium Haupt or Real is the best for me put me where you just want where I am just secured what I where I just under is quite good for me I said then I just came to Haupt and then I was I not angry at all I said Allah has Allah has decided I said to him what is best for me for and then Haupt is best for me and then I just went to Haupt I go now to Haupt

Betül's view of God shows that for her God has the function of an omnipotent guide (omnipotence perspective), with whom she enters into a relationship when she has a wish. At this explicit level, the interview reveals that she places her aspirations and hopes in a God perspective. What happens in her life is attributed to God. She uses this to justify, after the fact, that God did not fulfill certain desires of hers, such as the desire to get into grammar school (*Gymnasium*). Here it becomes clear that Betül introduces a topic that has a biographical relevance for her.

In Leyla's case, it becomes apparent that she closely links and thematizes her relationship to God with the death of her cousin. Thus, it becomes clear that her relation to God in the interview situation is biographically connected with this emergency situation.

The emotional relationship aspect dominates here. It becomes apparent that God is part of a socially defined everyday reality and is conceived as a You who listens to her. It becomes clear that ritual prayer also plays a role for Leyla. The role of ritual prayer for her is to ward off disasters from herself and others and to be protected. Leyla also prays for her mother and for her brother to go to paradise. She uses prayer here for to protect her family (decentering)[13] (193–198):

Description of the text passage: Own experiences – Text type differentiation: Description

> Leyla: so . that my dua comes true and that Allah also likes me . that I can also come to cennet to paradise or I also pray sometimes for my mother so tell Allah that my mother also comes to paradise and not to hell because I would be very sad or my brother that he should also pray . because he prays very little but that he should pray much more so that he can come to paradise.

In minimal contrast to Dilara and Betül, Leyla abstractly constructs the relation to God under an aspect that is relevant to her life. She brings up interpersonal phenomena with a high degree of abstraction and thereby establishes relations to God. It is evident in her expressions that she has decided to find someone nice because she has become aware of the finite nature of life, and it is important for her to like a person before he or she dies. The role she ascribes to God in her utterances is also a mode of perspectivity, and a tendency to take on perspective is evident. The form of direct address to God also relates to the dimension of perspectivity, since she puts herself in God's place, or at least assumes that he is listening. The role assigned to God is that of being a You. It becomes apparent that Leyla abstracts from herself and her horizon of perception and her thinking are decentered.

Within the framework of the comparative analysis, it becomes apparent that Leyla, in the context of the death of a family member, has a saturated experience with God. Religious interpretive content thus plays a role for her in certain situations, for she establishes a connection between distress and religious interpretive content. In Paiman's case too, his mode of speech in the continuation of the story of Ali in the dimension of perspectivity, shows a high level of abstraction.

Paiman's narration in the continuation of the narrative is modeled on dramatic scenes that have the characteristics of television movies. He constructs Ali as an active and dominant person who directs his own narrative. A man is introduced as a significant other who helps Ali, and Ali himself tells him how to free himself (81–89):

Description of the text passage: Opening passage – Continuation of Ali's story – Text type differentiation: Narration

> Paiman: after a few hours a man came by and heard him .. he went to this old hut .. and asked // is someone in there // so little Ali says // yes help can you get me out // said the old man // yeah sure but the door is locked
>
> I: mhm
>
> Paiman: Ali said // yes try to break it with a stone // he took a stone and broke it // then when he opened it Ali was inside .. Ali went out and thanked the man for helping him ... done

The entire following storyline is dominated by Ali. Paiman leaves the context of school and stages a police search operation, giving Ali a kind of heroic character who helps the police in their search (124–141):

EMPIRICAL RESEARCH RESULTS

Description of the text passage: Opening passage – Continuation of Ali's story – Text type differentiation: Narration

> Paiman: the teacher said // I agree with Ali because he doesn't want to do something like that why do you do it // they didn't have an answer for that they got a reprimand // the children were so angry that they left school during the lessons // they hardly wanted to stay in class anymore
>
> I: mhm
>
> Paiman: there is Ali // the teacher said // where are the other children // the teacher only now noticed that they were not there ... he sent Ali to the secretary's office and asked if they were there and the mother said // they are not with me // and with all four children // they ran away somewhere I think .. I think we have to call the police // said Ali .. then the secretary quickly called the police and asked Ali what like happened and why they ran away // they ran away because they got a reprimand .. they just wanted to annoy me and I told the teacher that's why they got a reprimand // that's what Ali said and the policeman said // can you come with us we'll look for the kids we don't know what they look like

Paiman's narration takes on a medial character. In maximum contrast to Hagen, it is evident here that Hagen incorporates elements he has experienced himself, while Paiman possibly draws his inspiration from television. He dramatizes the situation to provide a stage for the main actor and then brings the situation to a harmonious end. In minimal contrast to Dilara and Leyla, Paiman's speech mode also shows a high level of abstraction in the dimension of perspectivity. Biographically, he actualizes his little brother in the story. He describes Ali's character as helpful, and he attributes the function of a savior to him. In connection with Ali's function as a savior, Paiman thematizes religion by portraying paradise as an otherworldly focus of life that can be achieved through positive deeds:

Description of the text passage: Immanent inquiry stimulus on Ali – Text type differentiation: Description

> Paiman: there the parents were already angry have given him already things and tips if he can still improve ... for the environment.
>
> I: ((asking)) hm

> Paiman: for the world just because it also needs help
>
> I: mhm ... does that bring something
>
> Paiman: so there ... when he dies you know // and when he dies he could go to paradise and that would be very nice for him because paradise is the most beautiful thing there is ... yes ... that's why he wants you know to do good things ...
>
> I: mhm
>
> Paiman: hm yes
>
> I: mhm ... ok ... hm ... so he would then go to paradise
>
> Paiman: yes ... not to hell

In response to the stimulus to talk about Ali, Paiman talks in detail about Ali's helpfulness and his avoidance of trouble with others. Paiman emphasizes Ali's responsible ethical actions related to the welfare of others (parents, teacher, and friends). At this level, he sharpens his description by addressing "bettering oneself for the environment" from an ethical perspective and then turning to death. Here it becomes apparent that Paiman, in minimal contrast to Betül, Canan, and Filiz, addresses paradise and hell in the context of good and bad behavior, that is, in a 'do ut des' context (cf. Chapter 2, Section 1.4). In response to the immanent inquiry stimulus for Ali's feelings, Paiman addresses Ali's "hard gigantic fear" and in this context also God (252–264):

Description of the text passage: Immanent inquiry stimulus on Ali's feelings in the hut – Text type differentiation: Narration

> I: mhm (7) tell me .. about Ali's feelings in the hut .. when he was locked up.
>
> Paiman: when he was in the hut he had really hard .. gigantic fear but .. a little bit at night he thought that he also needed help to get out – after all he can't stay inside forever .. he screamed until a gentleman came but // and he didn't have any worries or no big fear because he already .. because it was already an hour so he got used to the fact that he can stay in the night .. and maybe he also felt like God was with him .. so he doesn't have to be afraid

EMPIRICAL RESEARCH RESULTS

> I: hm ... ((asking)) felt
>
> Paiman: so I don't mean felt either now but he knows that God is **always** with him so he doesn't have to have hard fear

Paiman uses the phrase "hard fear" several times in the interview. This composition is unusual in German. Also in his native language, Arabic, this composition is not common either. With the word fear, one uses either *kabīr* (big) or *katīr* (a lot), neither of which translates as 'hard'.

Paiman mentions that Ali may have felt that God was with him. When the interviewer says the word "felt" back to him, he corrects himself. It turns out that he reformulates feeling God, which is a more transcendent interpretive pattern, into knowing God, which is a more anthropological interpretive pattern. God's proximity as a defense against fear is also shown in the minimal contrast by Betül, Kaltrina, and Dilara. Betül and Kaltrina, however, in the maximum contrast with Dilara and Paiman, he makes no action-guiding description of God. As shown below, both immanent and transcendent strategies are evident that the children thematize: Paiman also uses the expression "hard fear" as a fixed phrase in the context of his own fear (449–453):

Description of the text passage: Own experiences – Text type differentiation: Description

> I: mhm (6) what helps you in such a situation?
>
> Paiman: so I always say verses /uhm/ so that I don't have to get like hard fear .. I just say verses that I know // all the ones that I almost know I always say so that I don't get any hard fear like Ali ...

In minimal contrast to Betül, Canan, Filiz, Jurislav, and Kaltrina, Paiman introduces the "verses" (the protective verses)[14] in response to the exmanent stimulus for his anxiety management strategy, whereby the maximum contrast shows that in contrast to Paiman, there is no action-guiding reference to the verses for these children (459–495):

Description of the text passage: Own experiences – Text type differentiation: Narration, Description

I: mhm (14) tell me about the situation where you were afraid the last time.

Paiman: that night I still had .. there I had nightmares .. well I was scared //
I had to go to my parents and ask them what I could do // they told me that
I () didn't help me because I was still

I: what did they

Paiman: they said that I should say verses // I just said that it somehow did
nothing then I just had to sleep with my parents

I: mhm ...

Paiman: when I was still small like five six seven eight years old

I: ((asking)) didn't bring you anything

Paiman: no, I just had hard fear so somehow the verses did nothing that
I had to stay with my parents .. as if I had a connection then against the /
uh/ that I had to against the ... /uh/ against the fear I can .. (dare?) when I ..
when my parents are around

I: mhm

Paiman: so when I sleep with them when I am with them and so on

I: hmm (19) what helps you when you are afraid?

Paiman: so ... saying verses that brings the most actually .. but I was still small
then I could almost none only two .. that's why they didn't bring me anything
// now I can say eight nine ten and they will definitely bring me something if
I // recite so many verses that will definitely bring me if I'm scared

I: then what's the use

Paiman: that brings you no more fear if you sleep or somewhere where it's
dark there is no fear // before I sleep I say all the verses .. so that you don't
have fear and don't have to be afraid all the time you could say every day so
that you // get a little afraid but not hard fear as before so I always recite it
and then I have /uhm/ I lose more and more of the fear then .. I'm hardly
afraid anymore yes

EMPIRICAL RESEARCH RESULTS

Paiman speaks of his fears in relation to nightmares. His parents advised him to recite the verses, which did nothing for him. He talks about how the closeness to his parents gives him the courage to stand against his "hard" fear.

Here it becomes clear how important his parents are to him. He speaks of a connection to them. His fears seem big and real to him. He speaks of them very authentically in metaphorically dense passages, which is in maximum contrast to the other interviews. Paiman is revealed to be afraid and he finds that the remedy for his fears, the verses, does not always work. This indicates a quasi-magical understanding in minimal contrast to Jurislav and Betül, for whom, according to childish, magical thinking, prayer and supplication are a quasi-magical action to solve problems, a technique to achieve something. They all explain the non-effectiveness of the verses by a mistake made on their part. Paiman provides a self-theory for his fears. In doing so, he differentiates between himself and his brain and speaks of his brain in the third person. He may have developed or adapted this idea (518–524):

Description of the text passage: Own experiences – Text type differentiation: Description

> I: mhm (7) tell me a story about you and God.
>
> Paiman: so ... /uhm/ I don't know now any .. don't know exactly what to say ... so .. I then always have the feeling when I am afraid that .. I always say that God is with me so that I am not afraid and so that my brain also understands it and not to get afraid and then I can walk around freely in the night and not be afraid ... hm yes (6) I'm done

Paiman's differentiation between himself and his brain functions as a relief, as he describes. By dealing with his anxiety in this way, he actively deals with his "hard" fear (525–531):

Description of the text passage: Own experiences – Text type differentiation: Description

> I: does your brain understand God
>
> Paiman: so he only understands it when I say it .. so .. he doesn't understand that he is with me so that's it right now ... only when I say it he gets it and

> then sometimes it stays and then after a few days it goes away again and then I always have to say it but it always brings me when I say God .. God should be with me I say // then it brings me something most of the time (5)

This shows that Paiman has fears that he fights with the verses. However, this approach does not always work. Therefore, he tries to convince his brain that God is with him. The fact that he differentiates between his brain and himself enables him to distance himself from his fears. His self-theory of differentiating between himself and his brain represents an immanent interpretation of his problem.

Here Paiman thematizes faith as an achievement because he has experienced that the will to believe, that is, to mentally perceive God as a reality, takes away his fears. Though when Paiman fails to convince his brain of this, he seeks an immanent solution strategy, as is shown in the next section. The struggle to overcome fear does not show up in the maximum contrast in Hagen and Dilara. In their case, on the contrary, an instinctive security is revealed.

It suggests that Paiman separates between understanding and emotion altogether (540–545):

Description of the text passage: Own experiences – Text type differentiation: Description

> Paiman: so there I'm almost hardly afraid anymore ... there I still need the verses with it and then I'm no longer afraid at all ...
>
> I: and if your brain doesn't understand that
>
> Paiman: then I say the verses and if that doesn't help either I try to find someone and he should somehow // keep me close to him.

Paiman's intrinsic solution strategy for combating his fears also includes an immanent strategy, namely the search for closeness. He seeks the closeness of other people because he has experienced that this helps him.

The thesis that Paiman distinguishes between understanding and feeling is condensed by the stimulus of whether Paiman can feel God (571–582):

Description of the text passage: Own experiences – Text type differentiation: Description

EMPIRICAL RESEARCH RESULTS

I: can you feel what he is like

Paiman: I can't feel that right now but .. I // in my thoughts I feel something a little .. well like not quite but like I feel a little that he is with me .. there is something with me .. but in any case he is always with me .. no but somebody .. nobody .. somebody // nobody has the feeling that he is with us ...

I: mhm ... nobody has the feeling that he is with us

Paiman: (...) barely nobody exactly ... but I ... like I think that you // nobody can feel it but he is with us ... he is with everybody but you just don't have it // so you don't have the feeling because you can't touch him or make out with him or do anything with him so there you don't know for sure

Paiman thinks about the gap between what he wants to believe and what he feels. His strategy is to convince his brain to believe. It turns out that he is not afraid if he succeeds in putting himself in a believing attitude. But he does not always succeed, which he explains with the immanent concept that his brain does not always cooperate. Regarding the question of faith, there is confirmation that Paiman oscillates between transcendence-related and immanent or anthropological interpretations of the world and the self. The framework in which he addresses feeling and understanding shows that for him to feel God means closeness and thus coping with his anxiety. Therefore, he speaks of trying to convince his mind of this.

In summary, Paiman's experience shows that the desire to believe is central to him. His experience is that he loses his fear when he succeeds in believing. The crucial thing is the longing for a relationship with God in order to be able to use the function of faith as a way of coping with contingency. The longing is ultimately directed towards an emotional relationship with God because closeness is important for Paiman. In his case, there is no magical answer in maximum contrast to Jurlislav and Eljan. For Jurlislav and Eljan, it is about reciting the protective verses in the sense of a magic spell in order to achieve something with it. Paiman, on the other hand, can imagine God as a counterpart. The strategy of convincing oneself of the effect of the protective verses is also evident in Kaltrina's narrative (501–506):

Description of the text passage: Exmanent inquiry stimulus on coping with fears – Text type differentiation: Description

> Kaltrina: Myeah .. I always say my verses then I believe but I also always believe in it and then I'm no longer afraid even at night I also always say that after sleeping before sleeping (4) I'm not so afraid with Allah with me I'm not so afraid .. but if I don't believe in it then I'm afraid ( ) (14) that's a nice chain

Kaltrina remarks that she wants to convince herself to believe in the effect of the protective verses: "But if I don't believe in it then I'm afraid". Here, a minimal contrast with Jurlislav and Eljan is evident in the appearance of magical elements of thought, which are mixed with other elements in Paiman's description. What the four children have in common is the use of the protective verses. However, Jurlislav and Eljan attribute the non-effect of the recitation of the verses to the fact that they themselves have done something wrong, while Kaltrina and Paiman reflect on their faith and assume that their fear results from their own non-belief in the protective verses. Thus, two strategies emerge here: One is the attitude of faith, and the other is a correct application of the protective verses.

It turns out that the children do use this transcendence-related solution strategy against their fears, but they are aware that this protective effect is unavailable. When Paiman's transcendent solution strategies do not help, he looks for an immanent solution to his anxiety: proximity to people.

It proves to be the case that this strategy helps him to distance himself from his fears and to externalize his problem to some extent. In the thematization of the levels of feeling and understanding, i.e., the relationship to God and the concept of God, his ability to reflect becomes clear. It becomes apparent that in his case the cognitive and the emotional or motivational dimension of belief in God are two parameters that interact with each other.

Overall, Paiman combines two solution strategies to reduce his anxiety: a transcendence-related strategy, namely belief in the impact of the verses, and an intrinsic, anthropological strategy, namely seeking closeness to other people. Both strategies are existential for Paiman.

The distinction between an immanent and a transcendent solution strategy against his fears is also evident for Jurislav (340–359):

Description of the text passage: Exmanent inquiry stimulus on coping with fears – Text type differentiation: Description

> I: Mhm (22) is there then something that helps you when you are afraid ...
>
> Jurislav: (first of all?) .. Prayer .. and then just not do anything (5) so as .. say el-Nas el-Felek.

EMPIRICAL RESEARCH RESULTS

> I: Mhm (5).
>
> Jurislav: Nas supports you // protects you from creatures .. and al-Felek ..
> protects you from ... /uhm/ spaces ...
>
> I: Mhm ..
>
> Jurislav: From such .. Rooms .. something /uhm/ (7) and that's it // or just
> put on boxing gloves and .. anyone who gets in my way I box him ...

The minimal comparison shows that Jurislav uses the protective verses
(*an-Nās* and *al-Falaq*) against his fear, and also uses boxing as an immanent
solution. In this sense of separation between immanence and transcendence,
it has already been shown above that Dilara distinguishes between the agency
of man and the agency of the divine.

In the minimal case comparison, it is clear that this type uses both levels
(immanence and transcendence), but at the same time makes a clear separation between these two dimensions. Here, a maximum contrast to the type of
God-distant relationship, which only presents immanent solution strategies
for coping with anxiety (cf. Chapter 4, Section 6), becomes apparent.

Since Paiman does not name the cause of his fear, it cannot be determined.
In any case, he tries to deal with his fear and to find both immanent and transcendent solution strategies. He typically experiences fear at night, because
then he is alone without the proximity of people.

The following passage condenses the thesis that Paiman actively turns to
God out of his distress (546–550):

*Description of the text passage: Own experiences – Text type differentiation:
Description*

> I: mhm (11) do you know another story about God
>
> Paiman: /uhm/ so not like exactly .. I only know that you can't see him and
> so on .. that he created us so that he can also see whether if .. that we believe
> in him because he created us .. yes .. and I also believe in God so that I don't
> have to be afraid (4)

Paiman thematizes the creation of man as a believer. He expresses a theological assumption here and makes a connection to himself. His belief in God is

based on his fear. It is revealed in this passage that he needs faith in God in order not to have to be afraid. Overall, Paiman shows a strong aspect of functionalizing the God-relationship to reduce fear.

In summary, Paiman brings God into the narrative himself. It is evident from the analysis that belief in God and the protective verses are a way for him to cope with his anxiety. This is existential for him. Therefore, he has a relationship with religious practice and with God.

It is documented in his expressions that he would like to feel God, whereas he is convinced that this is not possible. Therefore, he tries to convince his brain about God. His relation to God seems to have been born out of necessity and represents an independent approach. Paiman is not concerned with otherworldly notions of paradise and hell, but with believing in God as a contingency coping strategy. For Paiman, the attempt to believe is manifested in acquiring the right attitude. Whether or not he acquires this attitude, he determines from his reaction to fear.

Here, overall, a search and turning toward a you and a desire to believe is evident. It is crucial that no successful God-relationship is shown here. Rather, it is about a desired God-relationship, that is, a longing for a God-relationship. Thus, the meaning of the God-relationship is also shown in the failure to succeed.

4.2.2.1   *Summary*

The facet of the type of personal relationship presented above is characterized by an active turning to faith and to God out of need. The relevance of God is evident in this type because of the children's lifeworld experiences. The central aspect of the type of personal relationship is the search for or the attempt to turn to the transcendent You, in maximum contrast to the type of moral relationship. Because with the latter, a purpose-rational relationship to God becomes clear in the sense that a religious achievement must be produced, in order to be able to have an effect on the ultimate ('do ut des'). God is seen as the creator of a reward-punishment system, with the type focusing on the system but not on the greatness that created the system (cf. Chapter 4, Section 5). Achievements are also made by the children of the personal relationship type. However, they interpret these performances anthropologically. Thus, they perform achievements which they regard as God-ordained because they see them as good for themselves. For them, it is a matter of acquiring the right attitude.

Within the framework of the contrastive, comparative analysis, it becomes clear that religious interpretive content plays a role in acting in existential situations. At the same time, this type shows that a distinction is made between transcendence-related and immanent or anthropological interpretations of the world and the self, and that both levels are applied situationally. Religious

EMPIRICAL RESEARCH RESULTS

interpretation patterns thus represent a part of the overall interpretation of life.

From an anthropological perspective, the type of personal relationship is not about the successful relationship with God, but about the desired relationship with God. From a theological perspective, the God-relationship is shown to have meaning even when not successful.

4.3 Ethics: Norms between Ethics of Responsibility and Ethics of Attitude

In the dimension of ethics, the normative ideas of the children in relation to the themes of 'helping' and 'consideration' are evident. These themes are continually updated in the interviews, with references made to religion. In maximum contrast to the God-distant relationship, it becomes apparent that normative ideas are also shaped by religion and that moral ideas are connected with religious elements. In Weberian terms, social actions are perceived from both a convictional-ethical perspective and a responsibility-ethical perspective, with the responsibility-ethical perspective dominating.

The reconstruction shall begin with the presentation of the normative perspective of the children, who are ideally assigned to this type, a form of responsibility ethics prevails.

4.3.1 Responsibility-Ethical Traits

In the dimension of ethics, Dilara actualizes helping in relation to donating and in doing so engages with God and religion. In the second variation of Ali's story, which Dilara tells, changes of perspective and role become apparent. She refers to the secondary actors and views the story from their perspective. Dialogic sequences occur. Dilara puts herself in the shoes of the other children (Esad and his friends) without being prompted. Overall, this sequence is experiential because there is a high metaphorical density here (34–42):

Description of the text passage: Opening passage – Continuation of Ali's story – Text type differentiation: Narration

Dilara: /Uhm/ it can also be that now the children get such a bad feeling and say come on we'll go get him out again and then /uh/ they discuss it and say ok /uh/ and after that they maybe take him out and say /uhm/ can you give us tutoring so that we are also as good as you are sorry that we did it and after that they don't do it anymore and after that they all learn together then they are also good .. yes and after that the teacher is also proud that they are so good // so that they are such good friends and have learned well together ((laughs)) yes that (was it)? yes /uhm/ and further I don't know .. it can be

132   CHAPTER 4

Through the input stimulus, the perspective of envy is introduced as an action motive, which has negative connotations. Dilara averts this negative perspective by changing the action motive. She focuses on sharing and lets the other children demand tutoring from Ali in order to improve their own performance. After this demand, she makes the children apologize. Thus, they are supposed to overcome their envy by transforming this into a positive motive, namely the demand for tutoring. This conflict resolution strategy of Dilara's shows her idea of how to overcome a bad feeling like envy by offering a sequence of motives for action. In Dilara's case, the normative level shows how a negative perspective can be turned positive. Her normative perspective consists of a threefold morality: 1) One should not feel envy. 2) One should do something (here: learn) so that one does not feel envy. 3) The one who gives rise to envy must do something so that others do not feel envy. This perspective is condensed by passages that illustrate Dilara's educational effort and are also linked to issues of morality (89–115):

Description of the text passage: Immanent inquiry stimulus on Ali – Text type differentiation: Narration

I: Mhm tell me about Ali

Dilara: Anyway he doesn't show off he's a good kid he just studies then he's a // so smart and so nice he's surely also because he studies he's also so good at school if the other kids don't study then they can't be so good either but if the /uh/ other kids study then they're also as good as Ali and maybe /uh/ because Ali is so good they can go to him and ask if the kids can get tutoring from him... yes and after that they can be like Ali.. yes... it can also be that they /uh/ like go and say can we have tutoring from you and after that if he agrees they can go to Ali and /uhm/ study together and after that they can do something together in school and after that they can also be like Ali so smart so nice and after that they don't have to be jealous if the others are also studying then they are also as smart as Ali

I: Mhm

Dilara: Yes but if they don't study then it doesn't work you always have to study you have to work you have to study so that you are so smart and so good in school and so you always have to work you can't just sit at home and just watch TV so you always have to even if it's ten or five minutes you always have to study for school so that you are good /uhm/ you can also go to a tutor or to a teacher and ask her to help read books /uh/ at home not

EMPIRICAL RESEARCH RESULTS

just watch TV all day so /uh/ take a book read or do math so that they are also so good so that they get good grades you can't just sit around so lazy you have to study in any case even five minutes are enough for that if you study you are also so smart yes ( )?

In response to the stimulus to talk about Ali, Dilara discusses Ali's educational efforts, which distinguish him from the other children and trigger their envy. In the second paragraph, Dilara formulates regular sentences in the indicative, which reveal her convictions of norms. In addition, Dilara further sharpens the value of sharing knowledge by focusing on studying together with others and passing on knowledge. This reveals a minimal contrast to Kaltrina, who also addresses sharing knowledge (111–125):

Description of the text passage: Opening passage – Continuation of Ali's story – Text type differentiation: Narration

Kaltrina: that's not so bad that you have such bad grades oh I always have such bad grades I will never be like you everyone is different and my parents are also not always happy about it but Ali said come we'll study a bit and then you'll be better we'll talk to your teacher // and then onathan wiped his tears and pulled himself together again they went to the classroom they read something in HSU read something learned in math did some exercises but then the teacher and the other kids came back in and there was a test and when they got the grades back Ali got a B and Jonathan got an A and Jonathan said yes finally I got a good grade good that we are friends and then the next day Ali wasn't so mad at Jonathan he was happy that he finally had a best friend he was so good that he didn't have so many friends and Ali and Jonathan were best friends until then(4) are there other pictures

In the continuation of Ali's story, Kaltrina constructs Ali as the one who is studying with Jonathan (formerly Esad, renamed Jonathan by her) so that he can do better in school. Kaltrina also averts the negative perspective of envy by focusing on educational effort and studying together.

The theme of high educational effort is also evident in Leyla's narrative (72-. 81):

Description of the text passage: Opening passage – Continuation of Ali's story – Text type differentiation: Narration

> Leyla: then . then everyone was good again and then they became friends and met every day and played . yes . and . did homework together ... and . they played romped outside . and sometimes they also had toys with them and played together always . they never fought and /uhm/ they then became best friends . always paid to the teachers atten // paid attention to the teachers always in the rehearsals and . in the fifth grade so in the fourth grade, they were all able to go to grammar school if they wanted to (10) and . now I can't think of anything else.

After the negative situation is resolved, Leyla talks about the children's friendship in a longer passage. Leyla now also operates in her child's lifeworld and updates her own experiences in a minimal case comparison to Filiz. Although she weaves in the school context, her focus here is not on being 'good', but on achievement. Leyla reports on the friendship of Filiz. They do homework together and play outside. They don't fight anymore, and they listen to the teachers during class. They get good grades, and all get into grammar school. In Leyla's case, it is clear that, like in Dilara's and Hagen's, the focus is on education. Leyla describes herself as a very good student. The good grades and grammar school are in the foreground for her and are updated in the interview. As with Filiz, Leyla does not put Ali above the other children. The focus is on 'doing things together' and 'friendship'. An egalitarian friendship-relationship is evident here. With Dilara and Hagen, on the other hand, Ali takes a superior position, from which he then helps them overcome jealousy (79–85).

Description of the text passage: Opening passage – Continuation of Ali's story – Text type differentiation: Narration

> Hagen: never got angry again and so (15) joo and then /uhm/ ... /uhm/ Ali also taught the children good things so that they would never be so cheeky again and so and /uhm/ then they made a group seating arrangement that (means)? like a group table ((points to the group tables in the class)) and /uhm/ then they all sat there together . and helped each other .. and then that wa was the best class (satisfied) .. yes (4) and then they all went to grammar school (satisfied) (5)

In minimal contrast to Dilara, Hagen, Filiz, Mesut, Navid, and Kaltrina, Leyla also has a need for harmonization. Overall, the pattern of this type in the dimension of ethics shows a strong emphasis on learning and thus an intense educational effort. In the context of the contrastive comparison, a minimal

EMPIRICAL RESEARCH RESULTS

contrast emerges between Dilara, Filiz, Hagen, Kaltrina, Leyla, Mesut, and Navid, who prioritize studying together with others.

Dilara and Kaltrina, in turn, have another minimal contrast in that they refine shared studying into sharing knowledge. The conflict resolution strategy of this type is characterized by responsibility ethics. In the maximum contrast to the type of moral relationship, it is evident that these children place little emphasis on punishment, but that their focus is primarily on restoring harmonious relationships (the children should talk, play, and learn with each other again).

In Hagen's case, his subjective ethics and understanding of norms appears in connection with the treatment of animals, which he updates repeatedly throughout the interview. Continuing Ali's story, Hagen constructs an ecological farm in the forest, the place where the negative event took place, which he now transforms into an absolutely positive and harmonious place. This transformation of the negative perspective into a positive one is shown in the minimal contrast to Filiz. In his construction of the yard, Hagen includes animals, which he constructs not as food or food-givers for humans, but as equal creatures in need of human protection (146–149 and 182–184):

Description of the text passage: Opening passage – Continuation of Ali's story – Text type differentiation: Narration

Hagen: play and then . and then they discovered lots of new kinds of animals and so ... and . and then they built something extra for the animals and /uhm/ then /uhm/ Ali wa wasn't paying attention and accidentally sat on a hedgehog (smiling) and then there was a

Hagen: they always did so /uhm/ .. so the hunters were allowed to shoot animals then they had to were allowed to do nothing more in the forest because that also you know hurts the animals . yes and then . the forest was like their home (5) and then the

Hagen is interested in animals, and his narrations show his compassion and attention in dealing with them. In his ecological yard, which he constructs narratively in the interview, animals live with humans not as farm animals, but as creatures. A connection on the religious level emerges as he addresses the Prophet Muhammad's affection for animals.

In his curiosity about animals, Hagen brings in the Prophet Muhammad and tells of a hadith,[15] in which the Prophet makes a statement about camels in the form of a joke. In doing so, Hagen reflects on the fact that there is truth in it as well (289–298):

Description of the text passage: own experiences – text type differentiation: Description

> Hagen: /uhm/ .. I also think a lot about .. Allah and so (5) and yes (6) and I also like to listen to stories about Mohammed and and stuff like that .. and he always made like a joke . but he always just like made just jokes that are also true and so ... for example that he once / a man once said to him /uhm/ I let / let me please climb on a camel then Mohammed said yes I let you climb on a baby camel and then he said I can't climb on a baby camel .. and then he said I can't climb on a baby camel then it would collapse and then he said every camel is the baby of another camel .. yes .. and in any case I like to

In his responsible-ethical perspective, Hagen relies on the prophet. In his narrations, basic attitudes of self and world are indicated, which become apparent in the context of dealing with animals. These are characterized by kindness, compassion, and curiosity toward animals. It is evident in his narratives that he brings the Prophet Muhammad into his narrations precisely because of this component, as he values his interaction with animals. Hagen is the only child who reflects on the Prophet Muhammad. His narration suggests that the prophet has the character of a role model for him. He orients himself to the prophet here because his attitude makes sense to him. Possibly this has to do with his religious socialization as a convert.

Olivia also addresses her environmental awareness with regard to animals. Like Hagen, she shows a high awareness of environmental and animal protection. She thematizes man's responsibility for the earth and constructs man as the one who acts on behalf of God on earth.[16] After Olivia thematizes the fact that God cares for all living things on earth, the conversation turns to man's actions. Olivia addresses the issues of animal welfare, environmental protection, and equality in response to this stimulus (404–433):

Description of the text passage: Exmanent inquiry stimulus on the importance of God and man's task – Text type differentiation: Narration

> Olivia: he can also . somehow protect the animals and protect the world from . any smoke poisoning for example or something.
>
> I: mhm
>
> Olivia: you just have to somehow also do that the earth is protected so . yes . not so much . somehow // also don't let any garbage just be thrown

EMPIRICAL RESEARCH RESULTS

around so // it was Allah who made the earth so to speak and then . we also have to treat it well

I: mhm

Olivia: for that . yes

I: ((asking)) so we are responsible for the earth

Olivia: yes also

I: and what else

Olivia: like what else ..

I: uhm you have just said also so what else

Olivia: so we are allowed to // we are also somehow for the animals // we are also not allowed to eat too much meat

I: mhm

Olivia: so that not so many die /uhm/ animals have to die

I: mhm

Olivia: yes (8) that must just . treat every living being equally well . so that it is not now for example . the dogs better off than the cats or the other way round

I: mhm

Olivia: but all must be treated equally well .. that is actually also so with the people that they must also be treated equally well . not somehow the browns are bad and the whites are good

I: mhm

Olivia: So they are both equally good just because they look different doesn't mean that they are different at heart.

In minimal contrast to Hagen, Olivia also shows a high awareness of justice and equality among living beings, which she explicitly expresses. Hagen and Olivia make no distinction between animals and humans. Olivia is concerned with questions of social justice, which she develops from a religiously based thought ("Allah made the earth, so to speak and then . we have to treat it well") and relates to humans and animals. In the case of Hagen and Olivia, it becomes apparent that the reference point of their statements regarding their moral ideas is the effect of the action, i.e., a responsibility-ethical perspective.

Dilara also shows a similar way of thinking when, as already described, she refers to the secondary actors in her second variation of the continuation of Ali's story and views the story from their perspective. The responsible ethical perspective of the children of this type is also evident with regard to social justice issues.

4.3.1.1 *Summary*

It is clear from the mode of speech of the children of this type in the dimension of ethics that their morality is primarily characterized by a responsible-ethical perspective. In doing so, they also establish a reference to the religious level, whereby it becomes apparent in their narrations that the reference point of their motivation for action is not solely the religious morality of the action, but also the desired, morally justified success of their action, namely: overcoming envy, making friends, bringing the situation to a harmonious end, and their attitude towards animals and people. In the dimension of ethics, this type exhibits a decentering (abandonment of the egocentric worldview).

4.3.2 Convictional-Ethical Traits

Furthermore, the mode of speech of the children of this type in the dimension of ethics shows that their normative perspective is also characterized by convictional-ethical components. In the narrative about herself, Dilara actualizes social processes that take place between herself and her friends. She remains within her lifeworld reference. In response to the stimulus to tell a story about herself, Dilara begins to address the situation between herself and her friend, which is complex due to the involvement of another friend. In her narrative, it becomes apparent that she and the other girl are fighting over the friend's favor. This constellation repeatedly leads to the exclusion of one of the girls. Dilara tries to prevent this exclusion by reacting in a conciliatory and yielding way (217–240):

Description of the text passage: Own experiences – Text type differentiation: Narration

EMPIRICAL RESEARCH RESULTS

> Dilara: Yes.. we also thought like this // so I thought that she so that /uhm/ my friend likes her girlfriend more than me afterwards /uhm/ my girlfriend said to me /uhm/ my girlfriend doesn't like you that you are so jealous although I wasn't jealous and afterwards I said to her I'm not jealous I just want that all the three of us can play together and after that /uhm/ I said I'm not jealous I just want you to spend time with me because you both play so often for example you take my girlfriend away you both always play and when she whispers or says something to me you think we say something about you I said she said but do you really not talk about me? I said yes of course you are my girlfriend I said and after that /uhm/ was once so she got a rabbit so my girlfriend and after that /uhm/ I was allowed to pet her and so on and after that my girlfriend the girlfriend came and said let her go that is not yours my girlfriend said you are not allowed to touch her even though she didn't say it so she just wants that all that she my girlfriend should only play with her only be with her and after that /uhm/ I said but she didn't say anything like that she said don't touch her anyway she is sleeping and after that she always touches it she always carries it and after that // so she just wants it to be with her that only she has it /uhm/ and not that I do it after that I said I am sorry that I did that it was not good of me could ..... we make up again she said ok that day the three of us played a lot yes

In her narrative Dilara reflects on the events that happen between her friends and her. It is evident from her mode of speech that she has no distance from these incidents. She introduces self-theoretical, argumentative interventions, while morally judging the actions of her friends. In the continuation of her narrative, Dilara combines her subjective ethics with religious elements.

Dilara talks a lot about the social processes between her, her friend, and her friend's friend. Talking about others or excluding others is seemingly a social process, which in her experience is continuously repeated and which she updates twice here. It can be seen that she deals with these processes and tries to keep a grip on the situations between her and the other two girls. In the following, she addresses the slander. Her friend's friend tried to gossip with Dilara about the friend. Dilara says that she did not join the conversation, but recommended that the girl talks to her friend about the problem and they work it out together (242–256):

Description of the text passage: Own experiences – Text type differentiation: Narration, description

> Dilara: And further one day /uh/ so I was with my friend the friend played together and afterwards she told me so my friend the friend told me I don't like my friend she she thinks wow I'm beautiful I'm great they argue about me then I said no don't think like that there /uh/ about it /uh/ if you have a problem with her please don't talk to me and talk to /uh/ her yourself so you both can work it out because I'm really not so /uhm/ that I talk about others so that's not good so if you have a problem /uh/ talk to her I said then she said but still I don't like her she's /uh/ she thinks she's a star now and we would fight about her and then I said ok you think like that but /uh/ then I said it can be that she does so but surely it's not like that because after that I said she said yes ok and after that I said so please go to her and talk to her yourself so you can solve the problem too .. yes

Here it can be seen that Dilara does not want to speak negatively about the other friend in her absence out of a responsible-ethical maxim. She does not participate in the conversation and recommends that the girl should seek the conversation with her friend. In doing so, she distinguishes herself from this type of conversation or from such a character who talks about others by describing herself as different: "I'm really not so /uhm/ that I talk about others like that it's not good". She tries to dissuade the girl from thinking negatively about the friend: "then I said no don't think like that there /uh/ about it". Her ethical decision is based on morality: "that is not good". The question is, to which criterion of morality she orients herself and which moral attitude is the basis of its motivation for action. This is made clear in the following passage (268–282):

Description of the text passage: Own experiences – Text type differentiation: Narration, description

> Dilara: Well, you always have to so you are allowed to talk about others but not bad and like mean things only good and nice things about them.
>
> I: Mhm
>
> Dilara: Yes
>
> I: And what happens if you talk badly

EMPIRICAL RESEARCH RESULTS

141

> Dilara: So that /uh/ I think as like that you /uh/ get bad deeds about it and that it is very bad is very mean and is very evil and that you get bad deeds also maybe about it because others are nice and ( )? But if you /uh/ think /uh/ yes she is bitchy and is as /uh/ if she would be famous now but you should not think like that maybe she is also like that she /eh/ is just so smart so nice and so pretty and after that maybe some say look she sucks up to everyone but that can also be like that she wants to talk to someone and wants to play with someone and maybe wants to find another friend so that is not good when you talk about others that is then a bad deed

Dilara specifies talking about others by differentiating between 'good' and 'bad' speech. In her vehement rejection, she mixes ethics of attitude with ethics of responsibility and, moreover, represents a "do ut des" context[17] (cf. Chapter 2, Section 1.4). That is, bad talk entails bad consequences. She contextualizes the 'bad talk' with religion by calling the consequence a 'bad deed'. She puts herself in the place of the person who is being bad-mouthed and feels empathy for that person, who she believes is excluded by the bad-mouthing. It is documented in her narrations that the frame in which Dilara addresses the whole issue with the two friends concerns being excluded from the group, which she actualizes from her own lifeworld and wants to counteract.[18]

Another social act that is treated under convictional-ethical maxims is donating. Dilara actualizes this through the theme of 'good' and 'bad' actions in the religious sense. She mentions "sevab" (*ṭawāb*[19]) and "*günah*"[20] in the topic of donation in the context of the month of Ramadan. It is possible that this contextualization occurs because the interview was conducted during Ramadan. Through the stimulus of talking about bad deeds, Dilara has used this term herself in connection with defamation, and went on to bring up lying and not helping (315–333):

Description of the text passage: Exmanent inquiry stimulus on the topic of 'bad deeds' – Text type differentiation: Description

> Dilara: Günah is something in Turkish means bad deed and in Arabic that means bad deeds and in Turkish and in Arabic there's also sevab that's /uh/ good deeds that people do good things /uhm/ good deeds are doing something good not doing something bad not lying /uh/ always helping other people for example someone comes and asks can you tutor me and you say no study on your own you can do that then that's not good to say that so then so if it's even ten minutes you just have to help for example poor people who are cleaning cars or so they want money but the others don't give or /uhm/

for example a man is there there is no money is no house there you just have to donate in Ramadan there you also have to donate because /uhm/ there you have to give some of your half of the money or half of your food to the poor people to the other people so it is a good deed that is also a good deed what you do there and at the Feast of Sacrifice that is also good if you /uh/ sacrifice an animal a cow or something like that and then /uh/ donate half of the cow to the others so that they have something to eat or give half of your money to the others so that they are happy during Ramadan or the Feast of Sacrifice so that they also have something to eat or so that they can buy something with the money so that is always good if you do that

On the level of regularity, Dilara's statements on principles such as "you simply have to help" or "you simply have to donate" are evident. Her statements document her motivation for donating, which has both convictional-ethical and responsibility-ethical features. It becomes clear that Dilara strives to perceive responsibility for other people out of a religious ethos. The way religion is lived in Dilara's family is reflected in her narrations. Donations take place in a religiously framed context.

Dilara makes an explicit connection between her actions and religious contexts. This reading is condensed by other passages in which Dilara evaluates social actions under an accepting one's fate context, such as the dealings of food. It becomes clear that in this respect, too, her expressions of the ethical show a religious context for her motivation to act (391–404):

Description of the text passage: Exmanent inquiry stimulus on their own actions – Text type differentiation: Description

Dilara: So when I see poor people on TV they make such an advertisement so that we donate then I always think // for example my mother always makes food and we don't like it but we see on TV that poor people don't have food but we don't like the food that my mother makes and afterwards /uh/ I just think I don't care I just eat it because the poor people also have no food and no drink because they also have to survive very hard /uh/ there and we don't like the food what my mother makes so I have to eat it because /uhm/ just other people have no food but we have food and we don't like the food for example /uh/ with the poor people they have no food and no drink and they have to survive but can we if we don't like food and say that's disgusting we don't like it then Allah can make it take away all our food that we can also become poor all at once and that's why you always have to think /uh/ there are poor people outside

EMPIRICAL RESEARCH RESULTS

Leyla also updates the topics of helping, supporting, and taking responsibility throughout the interview. Her narrative shows that the reference point of her actions lies in a convictional-ethical perspective. Even in the continuation of the opening narrative, Leyla shows an urge to harmonize and resolve the conflict well. She only tells one variation of the story by directly introducing a significant other who frees Ali from the hut. She adopts the auctorial[21] narrative structure of the opening stimulus and wants to bring the story to a harmonious resolution (42–49):

Description of the text passage: Opening passage – Continuation of Ali's story – Text type differentiation: Narration

Leyla: (4) there comes a man now he hears that Ali needs help and he is a . /uh/ . what do you call it ... so he usually builds something he wanted to go to someone else to build and he had heard his // help from Ali and had his hammer with him and had broken /uh/ his lock with the hammer and opened it . then Ali could come again he thanked him and went on home and the two of them then talked and talked until they had to leave again .. that was it (8) and . End (26)

In the continuation of the story, Leyla also narrates from the perspective of the four children, from that of the teacher, and from that of Ali. She lets the protagonists speak through direct speech. In terms of narrative theory, a decentering takes place here. Therefore, in Leyla's case, her mode of speech in the dimension of perspectivity and ethics also shows a high level of abstraction in minimal contrast to Dilara.

Leyla narrates from Ali's perspective in the following sequence. He asks the children about their motive for action (61–68):

Description of the text passage: Opening passage – Continuation of Ali's story – Text type differentiation: Narration

Leyla: to the four people // why did you do such a thing to me so why did you do it / no we don't tell the truth / I tell it but Ali we are jealous because you are always the best and when you report then the teacher always picks you first . you could // then Ali says // you could be as good as me that would be good then you would always be /uh/ taken first // /uhm/ then they all went to their house . and the next day they were all good and were allowed to sit together again (sniff).

It can be seen that Leyla, in minimal contrast to Hagen and Olivia, quickly brings the story to a harmonious end. In Leyla's minimal contrast to Dilara, a moralizing behavior is shown, which is repeatedly updated in the interview. In the lines above (61–68), the role of the teacher reveals the moral construction of a 'do ut des' context (cf. Chapter 2, Section 1.4) in the sense that the one who behaves better is preferred. In this construction, the teacher is seen as having a protective role (56–60):

Description of the text passage: Opening passage – Continuation of Ali's story – Text type differentiation: Narration

> Leyla: they went into the classroom … The teacher saw that they were still fighting and she said // Ali, don't go to those boys, they might do something bad to you and that's why I'll place you somewhere else // then the boys were allowed to sit there in fours /uh/ sit in fours at the back and Ali was allowed to sit there at the front . and that's how he was saved

Leyla tells the story from the teacher's perspective. She does not punish here. She sees that the children are "still" arguing and intervenes. Crucial is that the teacher recognizes the children's intentions and wants to protect Ali by separating him from the four children. The teacher is given a dominant role here, in maximum contrast to the interviews with Betül, Dilara, and Filiz, though this role is not to punish but to protect. Leyla constructs the teacher's actions in the form of a 'do ut des' context, so that the student who behaves well is protected. The following sequence condenses this thesis (112–118):

Description of the text passage: Immanent inquiry stimulus on the other children – Text type differentiation: Narration

> Leyla: maybe the others thought that Ali was gone or . or maybe they wondered where Ali was . and maybe one child asked the four and the four lied . could also be .. and yes . and then they lied that they didn't know maybe even the teacher asked because the teacher asked because the teacher is also worried about // like her best student . could also be or they lied that they don't know

The teacher is worried about her "best" student. Again, Leyla reinforces her construction that one can work one's way into the teacher's emotional caring by behaving well. The reference point of her actions exhibits a convictional-ethical

EMPIRICAL RESEARCH RESULTS   145

perspective and elements of a 'do ut des' context, but this does not have religious connotations here.

4.3.2.1 Summary

Overall, the expressions of the children of this type in the dimension of ethics also show elements of convictional-ethical thinking and elements of thinking in an accepting one's fate context. These are embedded in a religious ethos.

The comparative analysis makes it clear that this type perceives social actions from both a religious-convictional-ethical perspective and a responsibility-ethical perspective. The reference point of the motivation for action is not solely the religious morality of the action, but also the desired and morally justified success of the action. These results are reflected in the findings under Chapter 4, Section 4.2, where it became clear that this type makes both immanent and transcendence-related interpretations of the world and the self.

4.3.3 Temporality: Reflection of Transcendence

In the analyses below, the narrations of the children of the personal relationship type reveal an orientation of the hereafter and a reflection of transcendence in the dimension of temporality. The children assigned to this type deal extensively and explicitly with what happens after death and express their ideas about the afterlife. Hagen and Qamar deal explicitly with what happens in the grave and after death. In both of their narratives, as well as in Paiman's, curiosity and a thirst for knowledge concerning the afterlife are evident. Hagen says that he thinks a lot about God and also likes to hear stories of Muhammad. He imagines the phase after death as a new, exciting stage of life (340–344):

Description of the text passage: Exmanent inquiry stimulus on his own thoughts – Text type differentiation: Explanation

> Hagen: ... /uhm/ ye ah I often think well .. often well always .. how it . well what then happens after that .. when you are dead because you are you know not dead because you are in the grave and wait until well the world ends ... yes .. and yes . and what happens there and stuff like that and (5) yes .. what animal species there might be and such ... I think of course also

In Qamar's case, curiosity about the topic of death is evident in the 'tingling' in her stomach (314–321):

Description of the text passage: Exmanent inquiry stimulus on her own thoughts about death – Text type differentiation: Explanation

Qamar: but I can't say that death is something happy and .. if I now imagine that I am dead what could I then think about it so .. I still think it's great .. to go up and feel what it's like but I can't come back again ..

I: mhm

Qamar: exactly that is that when you want to say // I'd rather not or I'd like // so .. when I talk about death then my stomach does get a bit tingly ..

In the context of comparative analysis, death for Hagen and Qamar, in maximum contrast to Gökmen (cf. Chapter 4, Section 6.2), does not represent a non-existence in the perceivable world, but a transition to a next life. Hagen explicates that the dead person is not dead but is in a waiting state in the grave.[22] Hagen deals with the interpretation of the world and man individually from his view of Islam. In doing so, he deals with the non-visible World (370–383):

Description of the text passage: Exmanent inquiry stimulus on the topic of death – Text type differentiation: Description

Hagen: Oh well .. ok .. /uhm/ .. yes .. that one is just not really dead yet just in the grave because one just waits until just the world ends .. because /uhm/ . /uhm/ .. I don't know what this angel's name is / he blows through like a horn . and .. then people just fall down because they've done a lot of good deeds . and they've done bad deeds and stuff like that they just experience everything . and so do the others .. and .. then there are tidal waves and stuff . yeah . and ... in any case, there'll be another . two angels and they ask you like questions . who do you believe in and something like that (5) yes and then in any case there is a window to paradise or to hell (10) /uhm/ .. death / there is then still the angel of death who does . your / it's / I don't know more I think the soul or so pull out and then just t a k e i t up to Allah ... yes well to the Day of Judgement (4) myeah (5)

Hagen thematizes the traditional conception of the events in the grave and the traditional events on the Last Day. His propositional knowledge in this regard is very high. He uses specific traditional terms such as "horn", "flood waves", "angel of death" and "Judgment Day".

The framework in which he addresses the events shows that he has absorbed this information out of curiosity and relates it to his own lifeworld, namely his

EMPIRICAL RESEARCH RESULTS 147

great interest in nature and animals. Overall, the dimension of temporality in Hagen shows a differentiation and an afterlife reference, which are also visible in Qamar. Qamar thematizes an emotional curiosity by addressing the feelings she herself experiences, such as her 'tingling' in her stomach. She is concerned with what life after death feels like (323–330):

Description of the text passage: Exmanent inquiry stimulus on her own thoughts about death – Text type differentiation: Description

> Qamar: so you kind of feel sad and at the same time a little .. surprised or a little . that you have to say // what's happening there // so it's something where you can't find an answer ... you can say you feel sad you can say you feel happy when you're dead but there's no fixed explanation for it .. so .. mainly when I talk about death then it's kind of tingling for me and I'm .. just not afraid but it's kind of like // what's happening there .. is it something bad .. to become dead .. so how does it feel there ...

Qamar's expressions show her fascination with life after death, whereby it becomes clear that she focuses on the emotional dimension of this topic, in maximum contrast to Hagen, who does not address this dimension and deals with life after death more cognitively. In Qamar's case, a fascination with the ambivalence of life after death is evident, which she addresses in sophisticated, emotional language. In maximum contrast to the tendency of most of the other children in the sample to resolve ambivalence, Qamar shows no effort in this direction. It almost seems as if she perceives this ambivalence as something stimulating to a certain extent.

In minimal contrast to Hagen, death does not mean the end of human existence for Qamar either, and she comes to terms with the non-visible world (337–346):

Description of the text passage: Exmanent inquiry stimulus on her own thoughts about death – Text type differentiation: Description

> Qamar: there's no fixed explanation for it or no explanation because if you're dead then you know the dead can't come back and say // oh I experienced that and it was really great // so ... death is for me also a happy word for those who had a bad disease and then finally got rid of it . but death is for me also a sad thing because when someone is dead then . then you are very

148   CHAPTER 4

> sad well very much // we had already really many attacks of death ... here's also really many ... and / uhm / mostly you have to cry then so you get tears . because the one you really love is now gone

Within the emotional dimension, Qamar puts herself in the position of the person who is released from an illness through death, but also in the position of the bereaved who mourn the dead. Her distance from herself in the mode of perspectivity continues in her thinking about life after death.

Moreover, Qamar's narratives document that death represents for her a redemption from the trial of life (348–351):

Description of the text passage: Exmanent inquiry stimulus on her own thoughts about death – Text type differentiation: Description

> Qamar: so ... you already feel for him a bit // yes you have made it you are over with the test // but you still feel a bit ... you are so alone you stand there alone and the one is just gone and yes so it is something so happy and sad

Qamar connotes this redemption positively with the term happiness. The dead person has made it and is over the trial, she argues. In the interview situation, she does not express a concrete idea of what happens to the person after death. Hagen, on the other hand, comes to talk about God from the idea of the Last Judgment and locates the soul of the dead person with God. Here he expresses his thoughts about God. He speaks in the interview of the angels[23] taking the soul of man to God (380–383). In response to the stimulus of how one feels with God, Hagen addresses his idea of God (388–391):

Description of the text passage: Exmanent inquiry stimulus on his own thoughts about God – Text type differentiation: Description

> Hagen: I think you certainly feel safe or ... because he created us you know ... you have to imagine him quite nice . because if you imagine him nice then he is nice . but if you imagine him evil well then he is also evil for you (7) yes (5)

Hagen is the only child who assumes that God is as man imagines him.[24] Here the dimension of temporality reveals his ability to reflect. He extends his tendency to adopt perspective to his image of God in relation to the afterlife. In

EMPIRICAL RESEARCH RESULTS   149

this regard, his thinking exhibits abstract and individualized traits. Paiman thinks about God in his own way. In his case, an orientation towards the hereafter is also evident in the dimension of temporality. In addition to the concept of the afterlife, he also has an element of prophecy, which belongs to the core of religion (554–570):

Description of the text passage: Exmanent inquiry stimulus on God – Text type differentiation: Explanation

> I: and ... tell me more about God
>
> Paiman: so about God I know a few names .. actually none actually only the one and ... I believe in him I pray for him .. I do everything whe when he wants something from me if I ... if he ... so ... if like the prophet // that he comes to me like a prophet as if I were a prophet and tells me what I should do then I just do it .. because he is you know my God he created me and I also have to do what my father tells me that is like .. so he is like my father
>
> I: mhm (6) and he tells you
>
> Paiman: so I don't know exactly that but ... I dream that I // that if it happens ... that something like that happens and I would be very happy if something like that really happens ... at least then I can .. see for the first time in my life
>
> I: mhm (5) how is he then?
>
> Paiman: I don't know now either because I've never been // I'm not you know dead yet but when I'm dead then I'll really know ...

Paiman compares God with a father and puts himself in the position of the prophets. He dreams of being in the position of a prophet to see God. Paiman is intensely concerned with the question of God and is seized by curiosity and a thirst for knowledge. On the one hand, his statements about God can be interpreted as an implicit longing for God that connected to the afterlife; on the other hand, the statements could also be interpreted as a desire to overcome inner doubts. These interpretations need not be mutually exclusive. For Paiman, his own existence is dependent on the existence of God (583–586):

Description of the text passage: Exmanent inquiry stimulus on God – Text type differentiation: Explanation

> I: mhm (7) and if he were not there.
>
> Paiman: if he wasn't there we wouldn't be alive either .. then we wouldn't even be here now .. so everything would be nothing ... there would be even no earth there nothing would have existed actually

In Paiman's utterances there is a principle accessibility for transcendence-related world and self interpretations and his personal belief construction, in the sense that for him God is the one who takes care of his creation in every respect, is revealed in minimal contrast to Olivia.[25]

4.3.3.1 *Summary*

The relating of the self to God reconstructed with this type can be described as a closeness to God, insofar as the interviewees exhibit a personalization that goes hand in hand with the notion of care. At the same time, their understanding of time exhibits a differentiation that states an outlasting of the subject after death, which is also partially problematized. This type deals with the non-visible world behind the visible world and shows an accessibility for transcendence-related interpretations of the world and the self. In this respect, in the narrations of the interviewees of this type, one can speak of a beyond-orientation in the mode of temporality. It can be seen that the interviewees make an effort to explain the world with the help of religion, thereby relating life and death, happiness and suffering, and man and community to one another. In maximum contrast to the type of moral relationship, this type does not ostensibly use the reward-punishment concept. The positive relation to God does not exclude doubts about faith, which are also addressed. The point is not that these children are sure of their relationship with God, but that they talk about and interpret it as something positive. They not only believe in God, but they trust him or want to trust him. The definitions of this group may be the desire to have a positive relationship with God.

5 Type B: Relating of the Self to God in the Mode of Moralization and Orientation towards Tradition

In the following, the ideal type 'relating of the self to God in the mode of moralization and tradition orientation' is described. This has successively emerged through comparative analysis and theoretical condensation. The respective central orientations of the children are reconstructed on the basis of selected passages from the interviews. These passages are characterized either by focal

EMPIRICAL RESEARCH RESULTS 151

metaphors or by interactive sequences that serve the epistemological interest of the study.

The respective patterns of type are described in detail in the subsections (first in brief form, then in detail). Thereby, the dimensions of the speech modes, perspectivity, ethics, and temporality serve to represent the respective patterns. We begin with the dimension of perspectivity, which illustrates a moralizing relationship to God. This is followed by the dimension of ethics, which shows the normative perspective of the children and which is characterized by a convictional-ethical, dichotomizing moralization. Finally, the dimension of temporality is presented, which documents God's remoteness from life without biographical reference.

5.1 Brief Description of Type B

5.1.1 Perspectivity: Moralizing Relation to God

This pattern characteristically shares a moral dichotomization in the mindsets of the children. The world is interpreted in binary terms through moralizing basic assumptions, i.e. – according to Weber – in a convictional-ethical way. In the children's construction, religion is primarily associated with morality, namely dichotomizing morality. With regard to the correspondence between worldview and the construction of God, the material shows that God is prospectively unfolded by the children from a dichotomous, moralizing point of view and integrated into their lifeworld. God steps back behind dichotomizing moral concepts.

Although the children see God as the epitome of morality and as the center of the value system, the dichotomous value system or the dichotomous horizon of perception is predominant for them and God is subordinate and peripheral to this horizon which is in maximum contrast to the personal relationship type.

The dichotomous division into good and evil or reward and punishment reveals a childlike-egocentric way of thinking, insofar as the children locate themselves and others on the side of the good, as long as they show an attitude and way of life that conforms to tradition. Good and evil are always addressed in connection with the idea of hell and paradise (reward and punishment). This results in a quasi purposively rational relation to God, connected with the idea of a 'do ut des' context linked to the dichotomous division into good and evil. In the 'do ut des' relation to God, one deals with God, meaning that a traditionally compliant attitude and way of life is regarded as a pledge of one's hope for a place in paradise. The role assigned to God in the interview situation is that of an almighty ultimate being who can be influenced through religious achievements.

In maximum contrast to the personal relationship type where God is an emotional reference point whom one feels connected with, the children of the moral relationship type always update the described patterns of reward

152 CHAPTER 4

and punishment or of 'do ut des' in their orientation towards God. A more far-reaching relation to God on the implicit level cannot be found in the material. For this reason, the following section goes directly to the explicit level.

5.1.2 Ethics: Convictional-Ethical, Dichotomizing Moralization

A reconstruction of how the children's available knowledge about God and religion is presented is carried out at the explicit level. Here it can be seen that God is constructed as an element of their social system of reference. In this respect, the children's remarks are oriented towards tradition and the social system of reference.

This pattern is characterized by the children knowing about traditional religious narratives and by their being able to reproduce a minimum of religious knowledge from which they get their religious patterns of interpretation. Their response strategies are shaped by Islamic-religious linguistic markers. With regard to the traditional stories, little emotional closeness and, at least for some children, an intellectual distance can be discerned. It turns out that the connection made to religion is in many aspects a mirror of social desirability and that moralizing dichotomization is the unifying element.

In summary, the reconstructive, contrastive analysis shows that in most cases the declarative knowledge of the children and their own practice of action do not appear congruently in the material. For the children, the religious information provided to them by the cultural reference system is part of the horizon of expectation in the religious treatment of life situations (explicit level) which is also reflected in the dimension of ethics. However, religious information does not contribute to the development of an independent, individual relation to God (implicit level). Thus, the implicit and explicit level represent a religious-pedagogical tension (cf. Chapter 5, Section 3.3).

5.1.3 Temporality: God's Distance from Life without Biographical Reference

When the children of this type make a connection between biographical experiences and God and/or religious contents, they almost always only do so when asked or retrospectively. When being asked about events in which God has played a role in their lives, it becomes recognizable that the children have difficulties actualizing biographical memories which they can interpret religiously for themselves as well as for the interviewer. Their statements document that their religious patterns of interpretation are merely reproduced. Behind these interpretations of experiences which are told in relation to God, no connection can be reconstructed between a relation to God and elements of the children's own biography. Thus, this pattern in the dimension of temporality

EMPIRICAL RESEARCH RESULTS

is characterized by the fact that the preoccupation with religious elements, which takes place only when asked about, is related to the past, selective, and without biographical stability. The reconstruction shows that in certain social situations the children can refer to traditional matters, i.e., what they have heard and learned is reproduced for the sake of social expectation, but not because they expect something substantial for themselves from religion beyond tradition. Because the handed down knowledge is subsequently theoretically dealt with in relation to various problems, the narrations take on an argumentative character in many passages.

5.2 *Perspectivity: Moralizing Relation to God*

In the following analyses, sequences are discussed in which the relationship between God and the dichotomizing morality presented becomes clear. It becomes clear that God takes a step back behind dichotomizing moral concepts in the narrations of the type of moral relationship.

The moralizing God-relationship in the dimension of perspectivity shows itself through three facets: firstly, through a moralizing God-relationship in dichotomizing value constructions, secondly, through moralizing talk of God as a social marker of belonging, and thirdly, as moralizing talk of God without demonstrable relevance to action.

The reconstruction begins with the presentation of the aspect that the children who are ideally assigned to this type show a moralizing relationship to God in dichotomizing value constructions.

5.2.1 Moralizing Relationship to God in Dichotomizing Value Constructions

The specific formation of this pattern is shown by the fact that in the interview situation, God is constructed out of a dichotomous horizon of perception, which in turn is assigned a dichotomizing role. In the following, sequences about morally dichotomizing ways of thinking are presented first.

In minimal contrast to Dilara, Betül also gives five variations of the continuation of Ali's story. In maximum contrast to Dilara, who weaves biographical elements into her narratives, Betül, however, shapes her stories in the form of a media dramaturgy (short cuts, changes of sequence and character, etc.). The different narrative strands are interwoven and further fabricated in a very creative way (change of perspective). It can be detected that Betül's stories do not conceal any personal experience, i.e., no connection to biographical elements could be reconstructed. Betül not only invents variations of the possible actions, but also deals with the different characters, lets them speak, and shows their motives. In the process, her mode of speech exhibits a high degree of abstraction in the dimension of reflexivity.

Dichotomous relationships are documented in her narrations. Betül's portrayal of Ali's character, which she initially adopts from the stimulus as positive, abruptly turns into the complete opposite (76–80):

Description of the text passage: Opening passage – Continuation of Ali's story – Text type differentiation: Narration

> Betül: ... and ... the child was still so nice but then all of a sudden something happened to the child he has now become completely mean they don't know why and the mum said why is my child like this and like that and then the child completely meant as because he was hanging out with the other bad boys then he has become completely mean then he has always hit children and like that

The dichotomous division into good and evil is also evident in the construction of Ali's parents, with the father being assigned the role of evil and the mother the role of good (87–96):

Description of the text passage: Opening passage – Continuation of Ali's story – Text type differentiation: Narration

> Betül: the Mum scolded him like that and everything and then the child came to his senses again and then the mum called the dad and said to the son if you don't /uhm/ (draw) like that again? and so I'll take you to your dad and the son doesn't want to go to the dad and then she said I'll call dad now and then he came and then he wanted to take him with him and then he said no no ok I'll do better and then his mum said I'll give you another week and then he said ok and then he took advantage of that and then he had he got a bit better again then /uhm/ ... he just had everyone he apologized to everyone now he /uhm/ gave everyone presents he said

Jurislav also displays this moralizing, dichotomous way of thinking. He tells of his theft, but clearly does not want to be portrayed as a liar (161–169):

Description of the text passage: Own experiences – text type differentiation: Narration

EMPIRICAL RESEARCH RESULTS

Jurislav: I once stole

I: Mhm....

Jurislav: And then .. the police came .. but actually I didn't know that ..
// I was at a shop like ***

I: Mhm

Jurislav: There I looked at the shoes

I: Hm

Jurislav: I was there with my friend xxx .. and .. I think he put shoes in my bag.

Jurislav describes how his friend shoved the shoes into the bag without his knowledge and that he then walked through the security barriers and triggered the alarm in the process. When they searched his bag, they found the shoes in his bag and called the police. He was then taken home and got into a lot of trouble from his parents. Jurislav talks about his fear in this situation and how his legs were shaking. He describes how he freaked out in the situation and beat up his friend who was in fourth grade. He was so angry that he almost broke the arm of the owner of the shop.

In response to the stimulus about his thoughts in this situation (231–240), it becomes apparent that he separates between good and evil and wants to be on the good side:

Description of the text passage: Exmanent inquiry stimulus on one's own thoughts during the experience of theft – Text type differentiation: Narration, description

Jurislav: /Uhm/ .. then I .. thought about that .../uhm/ (8) that they would let me go free

I: Mhm ..

Jurislav: That they believed me // but no they didn't and said I was a liar

> I: Mhm (7)
>
> Jurislav: They can't know that either by the fact that they uhm ... knows ...
>
> I: Mhm
>
> Jurislav: That I am not a liar

Jurislav, who says that he "freaked out" in the theft situation and almost "broke the arm" of the shop owner, does not evaluate his own actions but the fact that he was viewed as a liar. He judges his own actions pragmatically and does not portray himself ambivalently. Here a tension becomes clear between his actions, which show a clear aggressiveness, and his desire not to be considered a liar. The accusation of lying hits him hard. He is the focus of the judgement between good or well-behaved and evil.

This need to be on the good side is also evident in Canan's description (164–174):

Description of the text passage: Exmanent inquiry stimulus on own actions – Text type differentiation: Description

> Canan: mm ... (24) well I'm also so good at school AND /uhm/ always do my homework ... AND if I don't UNDERSTAND something ((voice goes up)) then I ask and if I want to say something I raise MY hand ((voice goes up)) and don't call in ... AND /uhm/ ... for example if someone from our class is talking then I don't interrupt and do maybe if it's wrong /uhm/ is wrong I don't call in wrong ... /uhm/ or right .. otherwise I don't know any more ...
>
> I: And at home
>
> Canan: And at home I sometimes help my MOM ((voice goes up)) and also do my homework at HOME ((voice goes up)) ... /uhm/ (20) otherwise there's nothing (9)

It turns out that the children who are ideally assigned to this type, place themselves on the side of the good, but judge others dichotomously.

The types of personal and God-distant relationship are in maximum contrast to this. Playing and studying together is important to them. The contrast is that it is not important to be good, but to solve conflicts. These types point

EMPIRICAL RESEARCH RESULTS 157

the solution towards their own lifeworld. This is particularly evident in the continuation of Ali's story after the initial stimulus. The solution-oriented children are primarily concerned with Ali and his school friends reconciling and continuing to act together, while the type of moral relationship is more concerned with the dichotomy of being good and being bad. The initial story has thus already been processed differently in this respect. The type of moral relationship is more concerned with Ali being innocent and justified. This can be seen in the following quotations:

Canan 41–43:

Description of the text passage: Opening passage – Continuation of Ali's story – Text type differentiation: Narration

> Canan: and then ... Esad and his friends got in trouble with the teachers and his parents and then they /uhm/ maybe /uhm/ were not allowed to watch TV or something ... and then (8) is the story

Eljan 41–44:

Description of the text passage: Opening passage – Continuation of Ali's story Text type differentiation: Narration

> Eljan: Then /uh/ /uh/ they see that Ali is there and then they are amazed and then they want to catch him that he is tattling on the teacher so they go and want to catch him but he runs to the teacher and ta tat /uh/ /uh/ tells him and then /uhm/ means that they will then get a reprimand /uh/.

On the other hand, the other two types are less concerned with this, and instead place reconciliation and friendship in the foreground. This can be seen in the following quotations:

Dilara 34–41:

Description of the text passage: Opening passage – Continuation of Ali's story – Text type differentiation: Narration

> Dilara: /uhm/ it can also be that the children get a bad feeling and say we'll go and get him out again and then /uh/ they discuss it and say ok /uh/ and then maybe they get him out and say /uhm/ can you give us tutoring so

that we are as good as you are sorry that we did it and then they don't do it anymore and then they all study together then they are also good ... yes and afterwards the teacher is also proud that they have done so well // so that they are such good friends and have studied well together

Mesut 62–70:

Description of the text passage: Opening passage – Continuation of Ali's story – Text type differentiation: Narration

Mesut: Esad was Esad went to Ali and said sorry for what I did and then Ali said ok and the others who did with Esad also said sorry then the teach // the teacher was happy and ... and then Ali asked the teacher could I sit next to Esad and then .. the teacher said ok and then they did seating arrangements and then Ali was with Esad they both sat down /uhm/ /uhm/ they both did /uhm/ the assignments and then they both did the homework they both studied /uhm/ then they ... they went to the park they played ... with Esad and friends and are with

The dimension of perspectivity shows that this type tends to interpret the world on different levels in dichotomizing, moralizing categories. In the following, it becomes clear that God is also assigned a dichotomizing role from this dichotomous horizon of perception. In this context, it is above all the purposive-rational preoccupation with the divine that becomes clear.

We will begin with Filiz, whose narrations show a basic accessibility to transcendence-related interpretations of the world and the self. When stimulated to talk about her and Allah, her narrative takes on an argumentative character. She describes God and the angels based on her propositional knowledge. In reproducing the tradition according to which the angels have the function of recording the good and bad deeds of humans, she connects her dichotomous worldview with the image of God (156–166):

Description of the text passage: Exmanent inquiry stimulus on a story with God – Text type differentiation: Description

I: Tell me about you and Allah

Filiz: Allah is just very nice but has no parents no family he was not born and he never dies .. and has created people .. and is also very nice and good

EMPIRICAL RESEARCH RESULTS

> .. and also always helps .. and /uh/ has commanded people that they should pray the Muslims also the others and /uh/ whenever someone does something bad /uhm/ so there is always an angel who writes down the bad things and there is an angel who writes down the good things because if you do something bad or sin then the left angel writes it down or if you say for example hm if you fly there then it hurts the angel then it was written down as a good deed.

Her idea of the angels shows anthropomorphic traits. She worries about a possible injury that the angel sitting on her shoulder might suffer if she falls down (167–175):

Description of the text passage: Inquiry stimulus on angels – Text type differentiation: Description

> I: When you /uh/ hurt the angel?
>
> Filiz: Make well like this (( )) because there are you know two angels
>
> I: Yes ... and then when you do like this (( )) then?
>
> Filiz: And then /hm/ when you then ask /uhm/ have I hurt the angel now then then it's written down as a good deed.
>
> I: Yes mhm so if you hurt the angel it is written down as a good deed?
>
> Filiz: So if I do this now and ask if I have hurt the angel then it will be written down as a good deed.

Here, a concrete-operational way of thinking is revealed in the processing of a transcendental concept. Her view of God becomes clear. In her statements, she assumes that in the case of a mistake, the awareness of fault has already been evaluated as a good deed by God.[26] She thus frames moral actions religiously in terms of her dichotomizing reward-punishment concept. This is condensed by the following passage (183–190):

Description of the text passage: Exmanent inquiry stimulus on thinking about God – Text type differentiation: Description

> Filiz: Uh when I help an older person for example then I also think of Allah
>
> I: What do you think about then?
>
> Filiz: Uh Allah helps every person also just like Christians and stuff .. and also forgives everyone ...
>
> I: And what do you always ask Allah for?
>
> Filiz: He should always help me a good life give me a good life and that I will go to paradise.

The topic of prayer is also thematized within the framework of the concept of reward-punishment and the dichotomizing perspective of God. Filiz interprets prayer in a purposive way as an advance performance for paradise and not in the context of a personal relationship to God. This illustrates the dependence of her construction of God on her dichotomizing view of values and the world (131–141):

Description of the text passage: Exmanent inquiry stimulus on prayer – Text type differentiation: Argumentation, evaluation

> I: /Mhm/ and why should Muslims pray?
>
> Filiz: /Uhm/ so that they go to paradise and are good people if you don't pray you go to hell or if you are bad ...
>
> I: And what does Allah think about Esad and /ah/ these other children?
>
> Filiz: They are just that they are very bad and have locked Ali up even though he hasn't done anything to them .. /uh/ then he says then he thought he might give them a punishment after death ...
>
> I: After death?
>
> Filiz: And they get a punishment but they get another chance if they do something like that again then they get a punishment after death maybe they even go to hell.

EMPIRICAL RESEARCH RESULTS

In the context of the contrastive comparison, Betül also shows purposeful thinking in relation to the divine. However, during the sequence she also recognizes the limits of this thinking and accepts the unavailability of the divine. This is one of the many passages in the material in which it appears that the children in the sample are actively engaged with questions relevant to theology and in doing so also make progress in their knowledge (295–310):

Description of the text passage: Exmanent inquiry stimulus on own wishes – Text type differentiation: Description

> I: And /uhm/ if Allah does not allow or fulfil something for you for example then how is that for you a wish not fulfilled or if he allows you – he does not allow you something
>
> Betül: Then I'm always sad I say hey what happened why didn't Allah allow my wish now then I sometimes I thought maybe he had something else to do ((laughing)) and so I thought why didn't Allah tell me for the first time then I thought did I wish for something wrong and so and then I said yes ok then I wish for (that)? not then I wish for something else then it also didn't come true then I said huuuh then I was sad .. then /uhm/ ... I was sad and because I didn't get it I sometimes cried ((laughing)) and then I tried again and then it still came true (so I got it)? then I sometimes thought I would get it if I (didn't)? just go when I got the wish that if I cried I would get it but sometimes that happened and sometimes it didn't but I wasn't angry with Allah.

The quasi-magical, instrumental use of religious elements, which will be explained in the following, also confirms the reading of the purposive-rational preoccupation with the divine:

In the following sequence, Betül specifically constructs the relation to God under an aspect that is relevant to her life, namely her school career and her wish to attend grammar school (Gymnasium). It becomes apparent that she is attached to magical thinking. It is not her grades or other criteria that decide her type of school, but God. In retrospect, she complies with God's decision to send her to secondary school (Hauptschule) (278–292):

Description of the text passage: Exmanent inquiry stimulus on own wishes – Text type differentiation: Narration, description

> Betül: I say inshaallah or I always say um in Turkish Allah izin verirse so /uhm/ I say /uhm/ I'll go to Gymnasium for example Allah izin verirse if Allah allows it
>
> I: Aha ok
>
> Betül: I always say no matter what and /uhm/ I say example to Allah /uhm/: may I please go to Gymnasium but if you allow it I will say
>
> I: Yes
>
> Betül: And I once said to him no I say it several times Allah, if you think that the Gymnasium or Haupt or Gymmi uh Gymnasium is the best for me put me where you want where I'm secured what I where it is best for me I said then I came to Haupt and then I wasn't angry at all I said Allah has Allah has decided it I said to him what is best for me and then Haupt is best for me and then I just went to Haupt I am going to Haupt now

Betül very concretely constructs a reference from God to an aspect that is relevant to her life. Here it becomes apparent on an explicit level that the boundary between Betül and God is fluid for situational-magical reasons. Betül speaks about God as an effective, omnipotent, present third party. Her interaction with God is therefore emotional and childlike egocentric. The material shows that her childlike-egocentric relationship with God is not abstract, but experiential and characterized by context, i.e., God plays a role for her in certain situations and is used temporarily, magically and situationally.

This quasi-magical and situational reference is also evident in Jurislav's narration. First, when answering the question of how he deals with his fears, he mentions the protection cures and boxing as two examples. When asked what happens if the protection cures don't work, Jurislav is initially irritated and pauses for nine seconds, as he probably doesn't expect such a question (376–390):

Description of the text passage: Exmanent inquiry stimulus on dealing with one's own fears – Text type differentiation: Argumentation, evaluation

> I: And if not (9)
>
> Jurislav: I didn't expect that at all

EMPIRICAL RESEARCH RESULTS 163

I: ((smiling)) hmhm ...

Jurislav: Yes if not (10) I did something wrong at prayer

I: Hmm (11) for example (12)

Jurislav: Yes that I said a verse wrong ... or even just one word (6) or the beginning of the prayer and the end or the .. whole prayer

I: Mhm ...

Jurislav: Maybe I just did namaz

I: Hm (5)

Jurislav: Next

I: And if you only do namaz (6)

Jurislav: Then it doesn't work

I: Mhm ... tell

Jurislav: Yes if I only do namaz then it doesn't work at all

In Jurislav's case, his mode of speech in the context of the minimal comparison with Betül shows that he also has a magical way of thinking. He did not expect the question of what would happen if his prayers did not work. The question astonishes him. He answers that he must have done something wrong when he prayed. He gives this explanation several times. If he does something wrong, then it does not "work". It becomes clear that the meaning of his statements lies in the fact that one has to pronounce the "spell" correctly for the "spell" to work. This corresponds to childlike-magical thinking. For him, praying and supplication are quasi-magical actions to solve problems, or a technique to achieve something. Here a minimal contrast to Eljan becomes clear, but for Eljan happiness is in the foreground. Eljan narrates the following sequence (269–208) in response to the stimulus to talk about himself in comparison to the protagonists in the opening stimulus:

Description of the text passage: Exmanent inquiry stimulus on one's own person – Text type differentiation: Narration, description

Eljan: Yes I'm **quite** good at maths ... I got a lot of B's in maths ((disappointed)) but I **never** got an A never I would have liked to get one now in // and now there are no more tests because I would have also liked to // because /uh/ we wrote another test and I would have// got an F but the reports were already done and there was still luck so I could have written an F there too

I: Mhm

Eljan: It wasn't too bad then I was still lucky

I: Yes

Eljan: Otherwise /uhm/ did I ((laughs))( )? Nothing but but no one locked me up but except the strangulation was luck ... that Allah still (had?) helped me

Eljan talks about his grades in mathematics. He uses the term "luck" to express his relief that he did not get the grade F or that this grade did not affect his report card. Then, in the interview, he tells us again about the strangulation scene he experienced. Here, too, he describes the happy outcome of the story with the term "luck".

These two situations, especially the strangulation scenario, which he has already discussed elsewhere in the interview, are clearly present in his consciousness. He connects these two situations with each other by evaluating them as "luck". For him it was luck that God helped him, and he connects relief, luck, and God with each other.

In Jurislav's case, on the other hand, it can be reconstructed from his mode of speech (see above 376–390) that he makes a differentiation in the fulfilment of his wishes. On the one hand, he makes the fulfilment of his wishes dependent on "correctly" performed prayers. On the other hand, he also ascribes to himself his own autonomous action since he mentions the boxing gloves as an alternative to prayer. The meaning of his statements in the religious sphere points to magical thinking, but outside the religious sphere he demonstrates a pragmatic and immanent approach. In certain situations, he falls back on the traditional to achieve something. In this way, he orients himself towards tradition, but gives no substantial reference to it.

With the described, quasi-magical use of religious elements, the purposive-rational relationship to God is also condensed.

EMPIRICAL RESEARCH RESULTS

The instrumentalization or purposeful rationality shows up in the material in two different forms. One is a purposeful rationality in the sense of do ut des. In the other form, there is an instrumentalization of rites related to God for the attainment of one's own ends. The transcendent is used as a means, so to speak, when needed. What connects the two forms is the belief that there is a claim to God's attention. This thinking of entitlement takes the form of a certain form of advance performance vis-à-vis God. In the 'do ut des' form, it is a matter of having a claim for God's attention based on a morally advanced performance in the form of a morally good life. The other form is about praying and praying "correctly". This instrumental or rather magical use of the rites (praying correctly) also makes a claim for God's attention in the sense of prior performance.

In maximum contrast to the purposive-rational preoccupation with the divine, Qamar also shows a desire to do good things, but she arranges them in a completely different way in her worldview, almost as a gift to God in gratitude for his gifts (808–827):

Description of the text passage: Exmanent inquiry stimulus on religious actions –
Text type differentiation: Description, argumentation

Qamar: so there is everyone who does good things and bad things // so we can't ... es- tafirullah be good like the Imams

I: mhm

Qamar: we can't be infallible . we also make many mistakes ... and a child that makes mistakes that is not ... that // so // that is for example many are annoyed or don't give anything for Allah although he has given us all these trees this fresh air ... and that he has created us in the first place so that we don't do anything for him . that I find somehow not good .. well I don't want to say woah I'm the best // I just want to say that it is like that that I try to do my best // I hope other children do too // but if you don't do it you might do other good things too for example you don't shout at your parents or .. you /uhm/ are always ready to help and . well it's also the case that some don't yet know any su // many suras like that for example we have some here at school // I don't want to say their names now but some of them are very big and they only know two suras that's a pity . of course but ... they will learn it and with this learning with all this speaking they have also made a gift for Allah ... at least I think ((smiles)). (5)

166   CHAPTER 4

5.2.1.1   *Summary*
In the dimension of perspectivity, this pattern shows that the religious under-standing of norms is oriented towards a 'do ut des' context, within the frame in which the children interpret ritual action in a purposive-rational way.

5.2.2   Moralizing Speaking of God as a Social Marker of Belonging
Another facet in the dimension of perspectivity is the 'moralizing of God as a social marker of belonging'. This facet is characterized by the fact that propositional knowledge, which is marked by social markers in language, is reproduced without reference to one's own biography. The social markers in the language indicate that religiosity among the children of this type is reduced to the motive of belonging to their own religious community.

Following the prompt to talk about Ali, Canan provides a description of his characteristics that is only a repetition of what the interviewer had already told her in the opening stimulus. When Canan is asked to think further, she says questioningly that he might also have been a Muslim (63–65):

Description of the text passage: Immanent inquiry stimulus on Ali – Text type differentiation: Description, evaluation

> Canan: /uhm/ (8) he was also maybe a .. Muslim and something like that (6) mm (7) and further I don't know
>
> I: a Muslim

During the interview, it becomes clear that Canan interprets the interviewer's reformulation in terms of social desirability and focuses her further statements on this level. The framework in which she narrates indicates that the aspect of belonging to Islam is relevant to her. In minimal contrast to Filiz, Mesut, Navid, and Qamar, a religious framing is introduced here in response to a question from the interviewer, which is accompanied by long pauses in which Canan waits for the interviewer's reaction. Since she frames Ali as a Muslim and feels confirmed by the interviewer's prompt, she continues to narrate in this framing. Canan asks if she should continue. The interviewer tells her to do so and Canan frames Ali and later his parents as Muslims. She then relays her propositional knowledge, which she talks about despite an intervention by the interviewer that leads in a different direction (68–79):

Description of the text passage: Immanent inquiry stimulus on Ali – Text type differentiation: Description

EMPIRICAL RESEARCH RESULTS

167

> Canan: And his parents were also Muslims and prayed every day AND (5) mm (6) his parents also liked Ali .... mm ... and further I have no idea
>
> I: Tell me about Ali's feelings in the hut.
>
> Canan: Well ... it was just dark inside and maybe he was a bit afraid and maybe he said the sura /uhm/ an-Nas inside and maybe also ashhadu (4) and (25) so he was afraid and said the sura an-Nas and ashhadu AND (11) AND (41) maybe he also cried a bit inside and so ((voice goes up)) because it is dark inside he also had a bit of FEAR ((voice goes up)). (10) and maybe he also knew /uhm/ ... that Allah is with him and protects (15) AND further I don't know (8)

From the moment Canan becomes convinced that the interviewer is aiming at reproducing religious elements, she begins to meet this expectation. Rituals play an important role in her narrative, and it becomes clear that she is using traditional elements in this situation.

After the interviewer has taken up the topic of Sura an-Nās[27] and asked Canan to talk about it, the further reproduction of propositional knowledge follows (80–105):

Description of the text passage: Exmanent inquirystimulus on a Sura from the Qur'an and on the creed – Text type differentiation: Description, evaluation, argumentation

> I: An-Nas
>
> Canan: ((nodding))
>
> I: Tell me about it
>
> Canan: /uhm/ Sura an-Nas .. So am I supposed to say it now and ..
>
> I: Whatever you want just tell me about it
>
> Canan: So when you are afraid you say the Suraan-Nas /uhm/ .. because there /uhm/ when you are afraid you also say that .. /uhm/ then you know that Allah protects you and ... IS with you (18) that is a protection suramm (20) further I don't know

> I: And ashhadu
>
> Canan: Ashhadu is what you say before you die AND .. /uhm/ if you are also afraid for example you have to say it every day at /uhm/ (12) /uhm/ ashhadu is the key FOR /uhm/ dschannat and stuff like that … and further I don't know
>
> I: Tell me more about the key to dschanna dschannat
>
> Canan: If you were a good person and /uhm/ did the five prayers of the day and /uhm/ … donated and like helped the poor people and stuff like that … /uhm/ you go to jannat and if you were a bad person didn't pray and /uhm/ … like for example you stole things /uhm/ then you come to the dschahannam (5)I: Dschahannam Tell me about it
>
> Canan: So THERE … /uhm/ … if you were a bad person uhmm … on .. well there's a fire there you burn if you've been a bad person … mm … and if you were a good person go into dschannat then you can get eight people from dschahannam or seven /uhm/ from there (9) and further I don't know (7)

The whole sequence is about serving the horizon of social references. Canan even offers to recite the Sura an-Nās and thus clearly places the interview in the context of interrogative situations she is familiar with. It tells of the protective verses that help with fear; of the confession of faith (the *šahāda*, which begins with the word *ašhadu*), which is the key to *ǧannat* (paradise); of *ǧannat* and *ǧahannam* (hell); of good and bad people; of punishment and protection. The linguistic markers that Canan reproduces show that she has taken up the rules of convention of her social frame of reference and reproduces them, but without reference to her own lifeworld.

The active use of Islamic conceptual inventory is also evident in Qamar's narrative. She reports of a good grade that God has given her. Following the stimulus of whether she has also given something to God, comes the following sequence (794–798):

Description of the text passage: Exmanent inquiry stimulus on own actionsText type differentiation: Description

EMPIRICAL RESEARCH RESULTS

169

> I: mhm (4) did you also give something
>
> Qamar: ... I hope so / uhm / . because I always try to keep my prayer ... well try pra to pray .. and yes I just try .. and .. / uhm / I would also like ... to learn many suras ... that are from in the Qur'an

She establishes a 'do ut des' connection between grade and prayer, but then realizes the limits of this concept in the next sequence. In response to the stimulus on what happens to the children who do not do this, she uses the religious formula *astaġfiru llāh*,[28] which is a request for forgiveness from God (808–809):

Description of the text passage: Exmanent inquirystimulus on own actions – Text type differentiation: Argumentation, evaluation

> Qamar: so there is everyone who does good things and bad things // so we can't be ... ast- ghfirullah as good as the Imams

Here an inner-Islamic differentiation between Sunnis and Shiites appears, since Qamar mentions the "Imams".[29] At this point her Shi'ite molding becomes clear. The connection between the expression *astaġfirullāh* and the Imams is meant as abstention from arrogance towards the Imams.

Betül herself thematizes religious elements by mentioning the reciting of prayers in response to the stimulus which wondered who Ali was thinking of when trapped in the hut (148–159):

Description of the text passage: Immanent inquirystimulus on Ali's thoughts in the hut – Text type differentiation: Narration, description

> Betül: To the children .. no no to maybe the mum and the children where the children like were and the mum if I don't get out of here as soon as possible that mum will miss me and then he just tried to think of his mum all the time **aaah** and if he thinks of his mum then he is no longer afraid like that or he could also ... or he could also think of Allah then he also wouldn't be afraid or if he is a Muslim then he could pray and then he wouldn't be afraid anymore then he could say Allah please protect me I'm afraid or call someone so that I can get out then /uhm/ he might have prayed all the time and think thought of Allah and then he wouldn't be afraid and then coincidentally the sheep // the man with the sheep came (5) ((smiling)) ((sighing)) (8)

Betül also constructs being Muslim as a space of belonging by having Ali pray in her story, as he belongs to the Muslim community.

The way Betül talks about praying is part of her staging of the story, which does not reveal any connection to experience. This way of reading the story is due to the fact that Betül performs scenes that are very foreign to the lifeworld in response to the stimulus on what the protective verses protect against (177–185):

Description of the text passage: Exmanent inquiry stimulus on the protective verses – Text type differentiation: Description

> Betül: /uhm/ from people or for animals from animals or if him that nothing can happen to him (ah)? For example if he is inside now and example a wolf comes then nothing can happen to him or a person urh wants to kill him then nothing can happen to him because this sura prote- urh because this sura protects him ... and ... or example /uhm/ he fell into a cave /uhm/ then nothing can happen to him that he dies or something (5) /uhm/ ... or he is protected by or the sura protects him from bad people and () things that want to harm him and (12) I can't think of anything either

This passage condenses the way of reading that the recitation of protective suras is not saturated with experience. It becomes clear that Betül is recounting a fantasy story in which praying is a dramatic element. It does not show that praying is anchored in the lifeworld, but rather that it is mentioned here as a reproduction of propositional knowledge and as a sign of belonging to the Muslim community.

In maximum contrast, the interview with Leyla shows how she thematizes the prayer in connection with her lifeworld (181–191):

Description of the text passage: Exmanent inquiry stimulus on own fears – Text type differentiation: Narration

> Leyla: ... so . my cousin was like 17 or 16 /uhm/ . she // well she wanted to cross the street it was green but she was run over by a coach . was very sad I cried . so I told Allah that nothing like that should ever happen not even to my parents or relatives or someone I like very much and that's why I usually find someone nice now before they die or something like that (15)
>
> I: ((asking)) you said this to Allah

EMPIRICAL RESEARCH RESULTS

171

> Leyla: yes I opened my hands said that nothing like this should ever happen did dua Also told my mother that she also // well should make dua that it maybe has an effect or something like that (5) and since then I've always prayed namaz I just doHere we see two different ways of telling the story of prayer. In Betül's case, praying becomes a set piece in a media production, while in Leyla's case it is clear that she takes up elements of her everyday world, which includes praying.

This contrast supports the facet of the pattern that although there is propositional knowledge about praying, the children do not classify it as relevant to their lives. In contrast to Leyla, Betül tells a sonorous story which she enriches with religious elements. She does this on her own initiative, and she knows the rituals of reciting protective suras that are spoken in certain situations. It becomes clear that the rituals represent more of a social marker for Betül here. These social markers symbolized by rituals possess a technical character and emphasize belonging to the Muslim community.

It is also clear in Gökmen's case that he observes a social horizon of expectations in the interview situation. He tells of the death of his grandmother (193–213). There are no transcendence-related elements. He remains on the immanent level. When asked about his thoughts and feelings in this situation, he describes his grandmother's death from a subjective perspective and relates her death to himself (216–225). Again, he does not bring in God or any transcendence-related thoughts. In the question-answer sequence that follows, he then describes what happens to dead people (229–241):

Description of the text passage: Exmanent inquiry stimulus on own experiences – Text type differentiation: Argumentation

> I: What happens then when you are dead?
>
> Gökmen: /Uh/ you go to the grave
>
> I: Mhm
>
> Gökmen: And then /uh/ Allah brings up (so brings up)? He and then .. where she goes .. and there she stays
>
> I: Mhm Allah?

> Gökmen: ((whispers)) Allah yes
>
> I: Tell me
>
> Gökmen: Huh how?

In the context of the contrastive analysis against the backdrop of the cases of Hagen, Paiman, and Qamar, which interpret death in terms of transcendence-relatedness, Gökmen introduces death of his own accord, but he does not show any inner-worldly or transcendent engagement with the topic. Rather, he observes the interviewer's horizon of expectations.

Not only the mention of individual religious elements, but also the mention of religion per se can represent a social marker that emphasizes belonging to the Muslim community. This is evident in Kaltrina's case, who is concerned about her cousin's position as Muslim or non-Muslim. She talks about her aunt who married a German man who is apparently not Muslim. They have daughter and Kaltrina is concerned about the child's religious affiliation (535–546):

Description of the text passage: Narrative about cousin without stimulus – Text type differentiation: Narration

> Kaltrina: But my uncle // but my aunt doesn't have one // so my aunt is Muslim and my aunt married a German and the woman said it always depends on the father what the child is but my aunt said but that doesn't work because the child wasn't you know baptized.
>
> I: Mhm
>
> Kaltrina: And that's why it's Islamic
>
> I: Mhm
>
> Kaltrina: And my uncle wanted to // he doesn't know what he wants to do // he still wants to be German or stay Islamic then I asked him he said so I would submit to Islam all right he said

Kaltrina places "being German" and "being Muslim" in contextual opposition and thus uses a widespread pattern in which nationality and religiosity are placed in one. This placement of nationality and religion is also found among

EMPIRICAL RESEARCH RESULTS

adults who could be assigned to this ideal type (Seufert, 1997). In Kaltrina's case, the use of religion as a social marker and the juxtaposition of "being German" and "being Muslim" make clear the manufacturing of a sense of "we" and a collective Muslim identity.

5.2.2.1 *Summary*

In the dimension of perspectivity the type of moral relationship is characterized by the fact that it reproduces propositional knowledge, which, however, is not regarded as lifeworldly relevant. The knowledge is represented in the form of social markers that indicate that religiosity is reduced to the motive of belonging to one's own religious community.

Kaltrina shows how these social markers gain another function, namely demarcation as a group. The markers then stand for a 'national-religious we'. Social markers can thus be used to emphasize the affiliation to a national-religious 'we' that is traditionally Muslim. Religious orientation thus becomes a part of culture and nationality.

In this context, the lack of relevance of religious knowledge to everyday life is addressed in the following.

5.2.3 Moralizing Speaking of God without Demonstrable Relevance to Action

The third facet, 'moralizing speaking of God without demonstrable relevance to action' in the dimension of perspectivity is characterized by the fact that speaking of God and religious elements is not reflected, and is ultimately a mirror of social desirability.

Filiz, like Canan, does not connect religion and God with Ali's story in any way. Only when asked does she bring up the subject of God. This reveals the mode of speaking in which her explicitly available knowledge of God is presented (96–102):

Description of the text passage: Explicit inquiry about God – Text type differentiation: Description

I: Can you imagine that hm Ali also thought of God of Allah?

Filiz: He prayed and then Allah just a boy just in his mind told him hm to go in to an old hut to an old hut then he went and he heard something and then he called the fire brigade and then he was freed ... hm (and then he went back)? to school ... and then he always prayed at home (26).

174 CHAPTER 4

After the interviewer asked whether Ali had also thought about God or Allah, Filiz speaks of an inspiration from God in the thoughts of a boy who goes to the hut, hears something there, and calls the fire brigade, which finally frees Ali. Filiz did not introduce this statement into her narrative on her own, but she incorporates God into the story as an actor afterwards. This shows that her narrations are oriented towards the religiously expected and the tradition. This is also made clear by the following passages (113–130):

Description of the text passage: Explicit inquiry about God – Text type differentiation: Description

> I: What do you think he said to Allah when he was locked up in the cabin?
>
> Filiz: Allah help me please I am locked up here by four children … and then he /uhm/ continued his prayers and then (when he was freed) he always thanked Allah and /hm/ maybe he was locked up in the hut he prayed again and again and then also always prayed (outside) even before he was locked up in the hut .. and in front of this old hut he always /uhm/ rode his bike .. and no longer played computer games or something (16) I can't think of anything else now
>
> I: Ok and /uhm/ what does Allah think about … Ali?
>
> Filiz: /Uhm/ he is a very nice helpful boy and he is very nice and good helps the ( )? always and everyone and also always prays five times a day and has always helped him too
>
> I: Why does he pray five times a day?
>
> Filiz: /hm/ because Allah said it to the /uhm/ Muslim people but before actually he said you should pray 50 times a day now he said our Prophet Muhammad /uhm/ Allah can you please make it less then he made five times a day

Filiz reproduces known traditional religious narratives, but a reference to imagery is evident because she tells the traditional stories simply as stories, such as Muhammad's dealings with God regarding the daily obligatory prayers. It becomes clear that Muhammad's dealings are not reflected. She reproduces these traditional narratives, such as the function of the scribal angels in the following quotation but there is no metaphorical treatment of the narratives, but rather a literal understanding. Filiz has propositional knowledge in relation to traditional narratives, whereby she has a passive and aestheticizing relationship

EMPIRICAL RESEARCH RESULTS

175

to them, as also becomes clear in the following passages. In the process, Islamic religious markers become visible in her mode of speech (157–166):

Description of the text passage: Explicit inquiry about God – Text type differentiation: Description

> Filiz: Allah is just very nice but has no parents no family he was not born and he never dies .. and has created people .. and is also very nice and good .. and also always helps .. and /uh/ has commanded the people that they should pray the Muslims also the others and /uh/ whenever someone does something bad /uhm/ so there is always an angel who writes down the bad things and there is an angel who writes down the good things because if you do something bad or sin then the left angel writes it down or if you say for example hm if you fly there then it hurts the angel then it was written down as a good deed.

In response to the stimulus to talk about herself and Allah, Filiz refers to textbook-like content. She does not make any relation to God, even on an explicit level. Instead, she talks about the scribal angels who, according to the Qur'an, write down people's deeds, thoughts, and secret conversations and who, according to a tradition of the Prophet Muhammad, are located on people's right and left shoulders. Here, too, her propositional knowledge of traditional narratives is evident. She finds pleasure in these narratives and reproduces them in an aestheticized form.

In Qamar's case, too, the lack of everyday relevance of her (propositional) knowledge about religion is evident in the way she includes God as an actor in her story when asked. When asked about her real fear, Qamar reveals how she was once locked in a toilet. God does not play a role in her story. She then brings him in when asked by the interviewer and incorporates him as an actor in her story (710–725):

Description of the text passage: Explicit inquiry about God – Text type differentiation: Description

> I: when you were in the toilet
>
> Qamar: mhm
>
> I: were locked up there ... thought of God

> Qamar: ((thoughtful)) kind of .. because .. /uhm/ you already think . umm . bismillahirrahmanir- Rahim . hopefully Allah will help me . by sending a teacher to me
>
> I: mhm
>
> Qamar: because it is so the thought of a teacher .. /uhm/ now you think hopefully Allah sends a signal ... to a teacher or to a child ... for example a signal that someone has to go to the toilet and can then save me // or a signal .. that the children have to go to the toilet and then the teachers /uhm/ also go with them . because mostly the small children can't crack open the door

Qamar does not address God on her own initiative, but she takes up the interviewer's im- pulse for Ali's story by constructing God into the story as an actor who sends a signal. She brings in the *basmala*[30] as a religious formula. In the context of the contrastive comparison, it becomes clear that Betül, Canan, Filiz, and Jurislav brought in the protection verses of the Qur'an in this situation and not primarily the *basmala*. Qamar does not mention the protective verses at all. These minimal contrasts consolidate the thesis that this statement is peripheral for Qamar. In the interview situation, she falls back on traditional knowledge without expecting anything substantial from this tradition. In addition, the use of the third person singular (she does not speak of God as a you) also shows the lack of everyday relevance of her (propositional) religious knowledge.

The lack of relevance of religious knowledge for action is also evident in Kaltrina's questioning about fear situations. Kaltrina reports fear in which she makes no connection to religion or God (474–483):

Description of the text passage: Exmanent inquiry stimulus on fears – Text type differentiation: Narration, description

> Kaltrina: YES once when I was picked up late from school it was eleven fifteen and I was still all alone outside I was standing there in front of the school and there were no cars driving around so much and I thought no one was picking me up they completely forgot about me and so and then I went to the school administration myself because I knew where it was you know then I said can you call home? then I waited for half an hour and then I went to the school administration again but then // I was so panicked and I almost wanted to cry that no one would pick me up but then the school administration // but then all of a sudden my mother called is she still there?

EMPIRICAL RESEARCH RESULTS

(493–498):

Description of the text passage: Exmanent inquiry stimulus on fears – Text type differentiation: Description

> Kaltrina: .. and once I was picked up late from the after-school care center there was no one there but a teacher and me and all the children were picked up but I wasn't so scared because the teacher said if your mum or someone doesn't pick you up then we have to call and if not then you just stay here but I wasn't so scared because the teacher was also really nice and stuff

In response to the stimulus about what helps her when she is afraid, she also refers to the protective verses, in minimal contrast to Betül, Filiz, Canan, Paiman, Jurislav, and Qamar. The children explicitly connect the topic of fear with the protection verses. It becomes clear, however, that Kaltrina does not connect these protective verses with the fear situations described above, but with the moment before going to bed (501–506):

Description of the text passage: Exmanent inquiry stimulus on fears – Text type differentiation: Description, argumentation

> Kaltrina: Yes ... I always say my suras then I believe but I also always believe in them and then I'm no longer afraid even at night I always say that after sleeping before sleeping (4) I'm not so afraid with Allah with me I'm not so afraid .. but when I don't believe in them then I'm afraid ( ) (14) that's a nice necklace

The style of Kaltrina's remarks is indicative of the lack of everyday relevance of her religious knowledge, which can be seen in the contradictory representations: "Then I believe, but I also always believe in it" as well as "I am then no longer afraid ... I am not so afraid with Allah". Her statements document that she does not really believe in the protective verses, but wants to convince herself to:

"But if I don't believe in it, then I'm afraid". The lack of everyday relevance of her knowledge is also made clear by the fact that after a 14 second break she shifts the topic to the interviewer's necklace. She has nothing more to contribute to this stimulus. Accordingly, there is no action-guiding reference to the protective verses in fearful situations. In a comparative analysis against the background

178 CHAPTER 4

of the cases of Betül, Filiz, Canan, Jurislav, and Qamar, Kaltrina also has propositional knowledge, but this has no substantive relevance to her everyday life.

Jurislav also shows that he addresses the protective verses in connection with his fears, but on the stimulus from situations in which he specifically uses the supplication, he introduces other aspects. On the stimulus concerning his fears, Jurislav expresses his propositional knowledge (335–350):

Description of the text passage: Exmanent inquiry stimulus on fears – Text type differentiation: Description

Jurislav: Yes when I am in dark rooms yes (5) mostly not when I see spiders and snakes

I: Mhm ...

Jurislav: Okay some spiders I'm afraid of

I: Mhm ...

Jurislav: They are not poisonous but they have long legs

I: Mhm (22) is there something that helps you when you are afraid ...

Jurislav: (first of all?) ... Prayer ... and then just do nothing (5) so as ... say el-Nas el-Felek

I: Mhm (5)

Jurislav: Nas supports you // protects you from creatures .. and al-felek .. protects you from ... /uhm/ spaces ...

I: Mhm ...

Jurislav: In front of such .. rooms .. something /uhm/ (7) and that's it // or just put on boxing gloves and ... anyone who gets in my way I box him ...

The contrasting comparison shows that the connection between fear and protective verses is established in Betül, Filiz, Canan, Paiman, Kaltrina, and Qamar, since many Muslim children learn these verses and recite them before bed as prayers against bad dreams and fear, or their parents often recite them

EMPIRICAL RESEARCH RESULTS

to them before bed. Jurislav also has an immanent solution to his fear: boxing. In response to the stimulus about the situations in which he has used prayer, as he himself says above, he thematizes a completely different situation, namely the prayers for his father, who works on a construction site (355–371):

Description of the text passage: Exmanent inquiry stimulus on praying – Text type differentiation: Description

I: Is there a situation where you used prayer ...

Jurislav: /Uhm/ (5) yes

I: Mhm

Jurislav: Yes when // because my father is // works on construction sites .. and .. he earns // he doesn't earn that much money .. and we always pray that he comes home without any wounds ... that he comes home clean that he comes home happy .. and gets a bit more pay

I: Mhm (6)

Jurislav: Yes ... it was (5)

I: Does that help ...

Jurislav: Hm yes .. so sometimes it just (8) sometimes it helps

I: Mhm ... and then ...

Jurislav: Yes then he comes home without wounds // he comes home clean

I: Mhm

Jurislav: And with a little more pay he comes home

Jurislav refers to his religious knowledge of the protective verses. The style of his explanations is characteristic of his orientation towards tradition. He reproduces his religious knowledge without it having any relevance to his life. Within the framework of the comparative analysis, in minimal contrast to Canan, Filiz, and Betül, it becomes clear that Jurislav also orients himself to

180　　　　　　　　　　　　　　　　　　　　　　　　　　　　CHAPTER 4

what is socially expected or to tradition, and that he passively receives religious patterns of interpretation about the protective verses. Accordingly, there is no action-guiding reference to these verses or prayers. In addition, he offers an immanent solution when he is afraid, namely boxing. The 'praying and boxing' is possibly a feature of the relationship between his religion and his life story.

The lack of everyday relevance of religious knowledge is also evident in Qamar's work in other places. Ali alone in the hut is a scenario that offers her a lot of narrative material. She tells a long and extensive variation of the story and adopts a wide variety of perspectives. She describes the feelings of the protagonists in detail. Finally, she decides that Ali has died, but she paraphrases what has happened. Inspired by this, she later begins to think about death and expresses her thoughts on it (268–291):

Description of the text passage: Immanent inquiry stimulus on Ali's death – Text type differentiation: Description, narration

> Qamar: but when you call it like that you can say // oh he's dead // then it's kind of a sad thing but also // it's also like you're happy for him that he's . now well // our life is you know a trial . so that we can go to heaven or hell for the rest of our life and .. it's nice but sometimes when you say // one of us has left this life and now you're without him // for example your friend dies and then of course you're sad too . but in reality you shouldn't be sad now because he can live a better life anyway so make
>
> I: mhm
>
> Qamar: ... and ... but death is also one of those things where some people say // well ... I think it's okay to talk about death but it's so ... you feel so strange for example when you say // oh I'll be dead soon // so what happens then ... yes // what happens when I'm up there or what happens when I die // and then you think // then I'm gone from the world and . and how does that work and ... that's one of those things you can't answer and then you think // death is something bad so don't talk about it
>
> I: mhm
>
> Qamar: and that's why it's somehow well ... a bit sad for others ... so then they think we shouldn't talk so much about it now and for others it's just ... uh // a good thing because it's also good for a person who has cancer for example that he doesn't have to suffer so much from it anymore

EMPIRICAL RESEARCH RESULTS

In this sequence, there is no narrative reference to the theme of life and death, but the presentation has a more argumentative character. Qamar often uses passive sentences and impersonal pronouns so as not to name an acting person, which makes her descriptive argument clear. The focus is on the question of the meaning of life and death.

She seeks a practical explanation for these questions and interprets the meaning of life as a test, which indicates a dichotomous worldview and is made so explicit by her (270–272):

Description of the text passage: Immanent inquiry stimulus on Ali's death – Text type differentiation: Description, narration

> Qamar: as if one would also be happy for him that he . now well // our life is you know a trial . so that we can go to heaven or to hell for the rest of our life and .. it is nice but

In the following, the fascination that this subject exerts on Qamar becomes clear. She speaks from the first-person perspective. Nevertheless, there is a descriptive preoccupation with the subject. Here, the emphasis on the positive side of death predominates. For her, death seems to be a fascinating, inexhaustible subject of conversation. In her explanations, death is something special, even enriching; in a certain way, the idea that it could be over after death and that one would be free of this pressure becomes the source of meaning in life (296–312):

Description of the text passage: Exmanent inquiry stimulus on dealing with the topic of death – Text type differentiation: Description, narration

> I: mhm . do you think about what would happen if
>
> Qamar: well /uhm/ I /uhm/ personally think about it .. because we don't know exactly // they say that it's like this when you're lying in the grave then something happens // but what happens there that you know that // or how does one feel then // sometimes I think to myself // death ok .. /uhm/ it's now a word where you can say .. it's sad at the same time and it's also something a great thing but when I think about it now .. then I say to myself what can happen then so .. what happens then // we are you know rich in this life .. so to speak ... we have everything .. but what happens when I'm dead

> // well I'm in the grave I know that but what happens then // that's exactly what I'd like to know // what happens then ... what happens when you're dead // this one thing is kind of .. I think to myself // ok there's a simple explanation you're in the grave and then /uhm / the angels come and write down what you did well and what you did badly ... but how does that make you feel // is that sad or // I can't say now // death when you talk about it // death is sad // I can't say .

It is clear from the narrative structure that Qamar has an inner distance towards the idea of life as a trial, as she can play with the thought of what it would be like to no longer be exposed to it. Her thoughts are free. She confesses that death is sad and a great thing at the same time because the dead person is then redeemed from the trial of life. In the contrastive case comparison, Betül, Filiz, Kaltrina, and Qamar converge in that they are imaginative and like to experience and act in a world of fantasy. They clothe their reflections in narrative forms, but there is no action-guiding reference to their religious knowledge.

5.2.3.1   *Summary*

In the dimension of perspectivity, this pattern shows that the children have propositional knowledge about religion. They are able to reproduce this knowledge on demand and to integrate it into the narratives in a coherent way. However, none of these children brings this knowledge into the narrative on their own initiative. This shows that although this knowledge is available and can be actualized in the conversation, it does not play a role in their individual relevance systems (Nestler, 2000). In maximum contrast to the other children of this type, Filiz, Qamar, and Kaltrina show that they enjoy telling these stories, i.e., the stories have an aesthetic value for them. Nevertheless, these two children also lack any indication of the relevance of their religious knowledge to everyday life.

5.2.4   Ethics: Convictional-ethical, Dichotomizing Moralization

In the following, the children's statements in the dimension of ethics will be shown in their convictional-ethical and dichotomizing moralization.

In response to the immanent inquiry stimulus on Ali's thoughts in the hut, Betül introduces thinking about God and praying to him in connection with warding off fear. She ascribes the role of a protector to God. Betül's dichotomizing way of thinking becomes visible in her construction of God. In connection with Ali, she discusses the confession of faith. First, she names the protective verses as prayers to God. In reaction to the inquiry stimulus, of what these verses protect against, her dichotomizing way of thinking is revealed, which she combines with religious elements (187–193):

EMPIRICAL RESEARCH RESULTS

Description of the text passage: Exmanent inquiry stimulus on the confession of faith – Text type differentiation: Description

> Betül: Then if example something happens to him after all or so then /uhm/ if he says the sura before he dies or so then it can be uh then he can go to paradise .. just
>
> I: Mhm (7)
>
> Betül: But if you don't say that then if you do too many things evil things then you go straight to hell but if you say ashhadu then you still have a chance

Betül's moralizing dichotomization is shaped by her propositional knowledge. Her statements about "evil things" point to her ethical convictions, which make distinctions according to good and evil. This rigid classification has an exclusionary function. From this perceptual horizon, Betül constructs God, to whom she also assigns a dichotomizing role. When asked about the "evil things", scenes are cited that are alien to life (195–204), which have a medial character. The nature and content of the narration shows that there is no personal experience behind the stories and no connection to biographical elements.

In Canan's case, the dimension of ethics shows that she divides people into "good" and "bad". She sees God's protection exclusively for the good people, whom she characterizes as adhering to religious practice as an external, formal framework of religion. Beyond that, however, these people in Canan's description also have more far-reaching ethical convictions, which she, however, again classifies in her dichotomous worldview (117–125):

Description of the text passage: Exmanent inquiry stimulus on the protection of God – Text type differentiation: Description, evaluation

> Canan: So when someone is in trouble /uhm/ Allah protects them AND ... punishes the other people IN hell and (29) well I think Allah is only there for good people and not for bad people (7) and further I don't know
>
> I: Good people
>
> Canan: Those who for example made five prayers a day AND /uhm/ ... just were hard-working like Ali and .. were good and polite and nice to everyone and not LIKE /uhm/ not like locked up AND /uhm/ .. like /uhm/ annoyed the teacher and stuff (5) AND (25) and further I don't know

Canan's dichotomous worldview is also extended to God. God is explicitly constructed not only as a protector, but also as a punisher. This establishes a correspondence between a dichotomous worldview and a dichotomous image of God.

This pattern is also evident in Filiz (131–133):

Description of the text passage: Explicit inquiry about prayer – Text type differentiation: Argumentation

> I: /Mhm/ and why should Muslims pray?
>
> Filiz: /Uhm/ so that they go to paradise and are good people if you don't pray you go to hell or if you are bad …

The dichotomous image of the world and God finds its continuation in this type in the assignment of people to hell and paradise.

This shows a maximum contrast to the children, such as Hagen, Paiman, Leyla, and Qamar, who also thematize hell and paradise, but in connection with their confrontation with the afterlife and death. These children deal with the subject matter, but not to divide people into good and evil. Qamar, for example, deals with death and the afterlife in a more philosophical way (278–285):

Description of the text passage: Exmanent inquiry stimulus on the topic of dying and death – Text type differentiation: Narration, description

> Qamar: … and … but death is also one of those things where some people say // well … I you know think it's okay to talk about death but it's like … you feel so strange for example when you say // oh I'll be dead soon // so what happens then … yeah // what happens when I'm up there or what happens when I've died // and then you think // then I'm gone from the world and . and how does that work and .. that's one of those things you can't answer and then you think // death is something bad so don't talk about it

Hagen thematizes in a comparable way the soul that is brought to God by the angels after death (370–383):

Description of the text passage: Exmanent inquiry stimulus on the topic of death – Text type differentiation: Description

EMPIRICAL RESEARCH RESULTS

> Hagen: Oh .. ok .. /uhm/ .. yes .. that you're not really dead yet just in the grave because you just wait until the world ends ... because /uhm/ . /uhm/ .. I don't know what this angel's name is / he blows then through like a horn ... and ... then people fall down because they have done a lot of good deeds ... and those who have done bad deeds ... they experience everything . and well the others too ... and ... then there are also tidal waves and so on .. yes ... and . in any case one . or two angels then come and then ask you like questions . who do you believe in and stuff like that (5) yes and then in any case there is a window to paradise or hell (10) /uhm/ ... death / there is also the angel of death he then . your / it is / I don't know any more I think pulls put the soul or something and then just TAKES it up to Allah ... yes well to the last day (4) myeah (5)

The convictional-ethical, dichotomizing moralization of the type of moral relationship acquires relevance to life in the dimension of ethics when the children translate it into the dualism of 'well behaved' versus 'naughty' behavior, as is clear from Canan's quotation above (117–125). For them, a good person is not only the religiously pious one, but also the kind and good one who receives God's protection and no place in hell.

This reading is condensed in the maximum contrast with the type of personal relationship and the type of God-distant relationship. Both types show a more complex understanding of ethics and a responsible-ethical attitude in the dimension of ethics. For example, Olivia shows that for her, being good consists of treating all living beings equally (423–433):

Description of the text passage: Exmanent inquiry stimulus on the meaning of God – Text type differentiation: Description

> Olivia: Yes (8) it has to be . every living being has to be treated equally . well so that for example . the dogs don't fare better than the cats or the other way round.
>
> I: mhm
>
> Olivia: but everyone has to be treated equally well .. that's actually also the case with people that they also have to be treated equally well .. not somehow the brown people are bad and the white people are good.
>
> I: mhm

> Olivia: well they are both equally good just because they look different doesn't mean they are different at heart

A similar attitude is also evident in Hagen. For him, being good means treating animals well (146–149 and 182–184):

Description of the text passage: Opening passage – Continuation of Ali's story – Text type differentiation: Narration

> Hagen: play and then . and then they discovered lots of new animal species and stuff like that ... and . and then they built something extra for the animals and /uhm/ then /uhm/ Ali ha had not paid attention and accidentally sat on a hedgehog (smiling) and then there was a

> Hagen: they always did so /uhm/ .. so the hunters were then allowed to shoot animals they had to do nothing more in the forest because that also hurts the animals . yes and then . the forest was like their home (5) and then the

In summary, it can be said that the type of moral relationship is characterized by dichotomizing, convictional-ethical morality, which the children of this type apply in their everyday lives broken down into to the categories 'well behaved' and 'naughty'. This is in maximum contrast to the other two types as they appear in the sample.

5.2.4.1 *Summary*

Within the framework of the reconstructive analysis, a convictional-ethical and moralizing dichotomization is documented regarding the construction of God of this type in the children's statements in the dimension of ethics. This means that black and white distinctions are made between good and evil, and these ideas are also extended to God. God is constructed as the protector of the good and the punisher of the bad. The convictional-ethical and moralizing dichotomization only gains real relevance for the children in the distinction between 'well behaved' and 'naughty' behavior. This is a distinction that represents an everyday category for them, but which they also construct in a convictional-ethical and dichotomous way. In maximum contrast to Olivia and Hagen, it can be seen that in this area, however, ethical constructions of responsibility can also be found in the type of personal relationship and God-distant relationship.

EMPIRICAL RESEARCH RESULTS

5.2.5   Temporality: God's Distance from Life without Biographical Reference

The facet 'God's distance from life without biographical reference' in the dimension of temporality is characterized by the fact that children who are ideally assigned to this type of moral relationship find it difficult to actualize biographical memories that they can interpret religiously.

Within the framework of the stimulus, the children of this type did not update any biographical history. However, it is evident that biographical experiences that lie further in the past are subsequently framed and interpreted in a religious way. Transcript excerpts from various interviews show that no connection to biographical elements can be reconstructed behind the stories that are told in connection with God. This shows that in the dimension of temporality, an arbitrary connection to God is established, whereby religious elements are used selectively and situationally.

Canan first reports that God protects 'good' people. When asked if she herself is a good person, she first denies it and then begins to talk about her good qualities (161–174):

Description of the text passage: Exmanent inquiry stimulus on good people – Text type differentiation: Description, evaluation

I: Are you a good person

Canan: ... no

I: Well what do you do

Canan: mm ... (24) well I'm so good at school too AND /uhm/ always do my homework ... AND if I don't UNDERSTAND something ((voice goes up)) then I ask and if I want to say something I raise MY HAND ((voice goes up)) and don't shout out ... AND /uhm/ ... for example if someone from our class is talking then I don't interrupt and maybe if it's /uhm/ wrong I don't shout out wrong ... /uhm/ or right ... otherwise I don't know any more ...

I: And at home

Canan: And at home I sometimes help my MOM ((voice goes up)) and do my homework at HOME ((voice goes up)) /uhm/ (20) there is nothing else (9)

188   CHAPTER 4

Following the prompt, as Canan realizes that Allah is with her, she remains in
the narrative context she introduced and explains how to behave as a proper,
good, and responsible girl. She uses the third person singular (175–183):

*Description of the text passage: Explicit inquiry about the presence of God – Text
type differentiation: Description*

> I: And how do you notice that Allah is with you
>
> Canan: EHM … for EXAMPLE … when you UHM … walk from one side of the
> street to the other /uhm/ for example when a car comes from there ((voice
> goes up)) /uhm/ … that I uh I don't know …
>
> I: Go ahead and tell
>
> Canan: and when uh and when there is a car coming I don't go over imme-
> diately but stand still and look left right and then left again … further I don't
> know.
>
> I: and Allah (27)
>
> Canan: I don't know (8)
>
> I: Is Allah with you then
>
> Canan: … mhhm ((affirmative))
>
> I: you notice that
>
> Canan: … mhhm ((affirmative))
>
> I: How
>
> Canan: (10) for example if something happens he protects ME ((voice goes
> up)) (9)

Canan gives a congruent answer to the stimulus "How do you know that Allah
is with you?" She does not discuss God but remains in the context of her life
and discusses her behavior when crossing the street. It becomes clear that God

EMPIRICAL RESEARCH RESULTS   189

plays no role in her story. It is she who takes care of herself when she crosses
the road. After a long pause, Canan answers the interviewer's question "and
Allah?" with the statement that she does not know. The long pause indicates
that Canan has no relation to God in this situation. Also, when asked if God is
with her then, she only answers with an affirmative "mhhm". This answer may
have arisen because she believes that she wants to be heard. It can be seen here
that Canan establishes or observes the social framework of expectations. This
is condensed by the following sequence, which shows the same pattern in relation to the stimulus on telling a story about where Allah protected her. In the
dimension of temporality, she reaches far back into her memory and reports
on a past dangerous situation (193–213):

Description of the text passage: Exmanent inquiry stimulus on God's protection –
Text type differentiation: Description

I: Is there a story where he protected you

Canan: (8) no idea (12)

I: I would be really interested in a story like that now (23).

Canan: There is one but I then I was very small I don't remember it so well

I: Then just tell me what you remember

Canan: So we were on like a picnic /uhm/ .. I was there with my fa// so I was
about three or four years old ... and I rode my bike into the STRET ((voice
goes up)) I think and then I got into like a bike /uhm/ like this and then the
bike stopped and /uhm/ they took me out ... there he could also maybe /
uhm/ continue riding and not stop (5)

I: and then

Canan: further I don't know

I: Did you hurt yourself

Canan: MM ((negating)) ... only my arm here hurt a bit I think (6)

> I: and Allah
>
> Canan: (6) So he protected me /uhm/ because bikes can keep on going and not stop and /uhm/ … and Allah has just protected me and (28)

When asked to tell a story about where God protected Canan, after a long pause she says, "no idea". This indicates that she cannot recall a story in which God protected her. After being asked again, the story about the bicycle, in which God does not play a role, is told in a rather confused way. On the interviewer's prompt "and Allah?", God is assigned the role of protector. This answer may also have arisen from the prompt. Within the framework of the contrastive analysis, the case-immanent comparison shows that Canan embeds her propositional knowledge of the protective verses in Ali's story. However, this does not play a role in her biographical narratives (72–79):

Description of the text passage: Immanent inquiry stimulus on Ali's feelings in the hut – Text type differentiation: Description

> Canan: Well … it was just dark inside and maybe he was a bit afraid and maybe he said the sura /uhm/ an-Nas inside and maybe also ashhadu (4) and (25) so he was afraid and said the sura an-Nas and ashhadu AND (11) AND (41) maybe he also cried a bit inside and so ((voice goes up)) because it is dark in there he was also a bit SCARED ((voice goes up)) (10) and maybe he also knew /uhm/ … that Allah is with him and protects (15) AND further I don't know (8)

Canan's statements reflect a break between the propositional, religious knowledge that is being referred to and her real lifeworld. Within the framework of the reconstructive analysis, it becomes apparent that in the dimension of temporality there is no relation between these two levels in the interview situation. This is also made clear by the following passage, in which she is in the third person and does not speak of herself (149–157):

Description of the text passage: Exmanent inquiry stimulus on stories with God – Text type differentiation: Argumentation, evaluation

> I: Do you know another story about you and Allah
>
> Canan: MM ((denying)) (8) MM ((negating)) (11)

EMPIRICAL RESEARCH RESULTS

191

I: Allah is with you

Canan: mhhm ((affirmative))

I: Tell me

Canan: WELL /uhm/ if you are a good HUMAN BEING ((voice goes up)) / uhm/ then Allah is always with you and with others too ....

I: Talk about yourself only you

Canan: How (12)

The nature of Canan's narrative suggests that she is unsure what is expected of her. She wants to present herself with her religious school knowledge, but the questions about her biography unsettle her. In the interview situation, the material shows that Canan establishes neither an explicit nor an implicit relation to God in the dimension of temporality and that her propositional knowledge does not play a guiding role for her own way of life. She only makes a reference to religion on the basis of the interviewer's prompts.

In summary, it can be reconstructed in the dimension of temporality that Canan reaches far back into her horizon of experience and interprets past experiences religiously in retrospect. Her statements document that these patterns of religious interpretation are oriented towards tradition. The material shows that the question about the role of God is a requirement of the horizon of social reference that she can serve situationally. By asking about God, the interviewer is possibly a persona of this social frame of reference.

Betül also tells stories about herself and God when asked (205–221):

Description of the text passage: Exmanent inquiry stimulus on own experiences – Text type differentiation: Description

I: Have you /uhm/ experienced a situation like that

Betül: (4) /uhm/ that someone locked me up or how

I: Yes or where you were afraid

Betül: Yes … /uhm/ … my friend at this school locked me in the toilet ((laughing)) she kept it shut all the time and I couldn't get out and you're not allowed to say anything in the toilet and then I was really scared and then /uhm/ there were two doors and there was one door where it went to the toilet and one where it was just a washbasin then I closed the door so that you couldn't see the toilets and then I said (ma)? I said sorry Allah I know that I will get a sin now but please help me out so that I can get out and then yes I was really scared then I said Allah please /uhm/ … help me just I know /uhm/ forgive me if I said something in the toilet (before)? in the toilet but you are my only chance please do something so that I can get out of here then I just said like that and then just well then my fri// then I pulled again then my friend was no longer there ((laughing)) and then I told my caretaker then she got in trouble

It becomes apparent that the way Betül tells the story and incorporates the religious elements into it is part of a non-experiential enactment. Betül's response may have arisen from her instinct to serve a horizon of social reference. This thesis is condensed by the following sequence (224–253):

Description of the text passage: Exmanent inquiry stimulus on stories with Allah – Text type differentiation: Description

I: Yes mhm (12) Can you tell me more stories about you and God and tell Allah about you and Allah

Betül: /uhm/ .. When I /uhm/ (7) right where I went ou// where I went out there I was alone and there a man was following me and I was always completely afraid and then I immediately /uhm/ always just said the suras everything I could do and so and I said the protective suras I said eschhadu and the man was always following me I was afraid I ran and then I said / uhm/ I am completely afraid because (I)? the man is stronger than me if something happens to me I said eschhadu again and then I just said the protective suras then I kept walking and then I got together with my girlfriend// no not girlfriend I was just alone then I just hid … well the man was there he was basically behind me then I quickly went to the corner then I ran and then I hid and there was /uhm/ I just said the man was gone and I was in front of this school and there was a man who was watching me all the time but my mum was still there and she () followed me all the way () so I quickly went to my mum and then when she left she just left again then (the man)? was coming after me I was afraid again then I prayed to Allah I said please

EMPIRICAL RESEARCH RESULTS

Allah help me please I am very afraid he can do something to me and then I said the protective suras again I said eschhadu again and then I said Allah please /uhm/ /uhm/ make the man leave I am afraid something will happen he should leave then I ran I looked from the window the man was also gone then ((sighs)) then I have my /uhm/ then before I always sleep I say Allah /uhm/ I thank you that whenever I say something you always fulfill it and then I have I always say Allah I know that in reality you there and so and I also thank you for everything I always say

What is striking is that Betül's plot is imagined in a very creative way, on a superficial level. In addition, the narrative is presented here in the form of a medial dramaturgy. The media character and the type of narrative indicate that there is no reference to experience. The excerpt shows that Betül's stories do not conceal any personal experience, i.e., there is no connection to biographical elements. In the dimension of temporality, therefore, no biographical memories are actualized.

On the other hand, it can also be concluded that the lack of experiential orientation gives the narrative a medial character, whereby the entire narrative sounds like a replay of a television series.

This clearly shows that Betül's ideas about what is a threat and what is serious diverge. It becomes clear that she does not take the narrated situation seriously. This also shows that this is a fictional, fabricated story that is not bound to experience.

Although Betül names and addresses emotions here, it is clear from the lack of experience and the nature of the narrative that there are no "real" emotions behind them.

Filiz also connects a biographical experience with God in retrospect, whereby it becomes clear that an arbitrary connection is made to serve the social reference horizon and give an answer that pleases the interviewer (146–155):

Description of the text passage: Exmanent inquiry stimulus on situations in which God was thought of – Text type differentiation: Description

I: And /uhm/ have you ever experienced a situation where you thought of Allah ... Tell me

Filiz: /Uh/ well my little sister had once ((laughs)) locked me in the toilet and I thought of Allah and my father ((laughs)) suddenly got up because my little brother woke him up and then he wanted to go to the toilet and the

194   CHAPTER 4

> door was locked and then he thought it was my little sister and then he took
> the key away from her and opened the door again.
>
> I: Mhm ... what happened when you thought of Allah
>
> Filiz: Hm I then got help and was no longer afraid then ...

Filiz reaches far back into her memory and tells of an incident in which she
was locked in the toilet by her little sister. She describes this as a situation of
fear and distress. She brings this up on the interviewer's prompting and, based
on the course of the interview, connects it with God. It becomes clear that
Filiz is familiar with religious matters and she deals with these questions and
establishes a situational relation to God on an explicit level, which, however,
has a referential form ("I then got help and was no longer afraid"), whereby no
connection to biographical elements can be reconstructed.

The material shows that this passage also contributes to the condensation of the pattern that a child of this type can fall back on the traditional in
the dimension of temporality in certain social situations, where there is no
biographical stability.

Jurislav also reaches far back into his memory and recounts two incidents that
embarrassed him and that still bother him. In response to the stimulus to tell a
story about himself, his account takes on an argumentative character (146–150):

*Description of the text passage: Exmanent inquiry stimulus on own experiences –
Text type differentiation: Description*

> Jurislav: I mean what I really did
>
> I: Ok ...
>
> Jurislav: /Uhm/ (9) that's really stupid now
>
> I: Why
>
> Jurislav: That is like really forbidden for us Muslims ...

He first says that what he has done is "like really forbidden for us Muslims". The
"us" possibly indicates that he sees the interviewer as a person from his own
experiential space and that a sufficient basis of trust has developed between

EMPIRICAL RESEARCH RESULTS

the interviewer and the child. Therefore, he may also have the self-confidence to talk about his actions (161–182):

Description of the text passage: Exmanent inquiry stimulus on own experiences – Text type differentiation: Narration

Jurislav: I once STOLE

I: Mhm ....

Jurislav: And then ... the police came ... but actually I didn't even know that ... // I was at like a shop

I: Mhm

Jurislav: There I looked at the shoes

I: Hm

Jurislav: I was there with my friend ... and .. I think he put shoes in my bag

I: Mhm ...

Jurislav: Because my bag opened (only)? quietly ... and .. there I was in the first grade then // my bag there opened quietly and he put it in // I then went through these alarm things

I: Mhm

Jurislav: Then the alarm went off and I didn't know what that was

I: Mhm

Jurislav: And then they searched my bag and there were shoes and then

I: Mhm ....

Jurislav: I didn't know myself that there were shoes inside // and then the police came and drove me home ... and then I got into real trouble ...

In this story, an entanglement of events is depicted that Jurislav has suffered, but a rupture also becomes clear. He says that he was in the department store with another boy and the latter put shoes in his bag, whereupon he was suspected of being a thief. In passing, he says that he freaked out and almost broke the owner's arm and beat up the friend. What bothers and torments him, however, is not that he stole and hurt the owner and the boy. What bothers and burdens him is that he was called a liar. He makes a point of not being called a liar. This event seems to preoccupy him, and he processes it theoretically afterwards in the interview situation. His own definition of the situation and that of the environment do not seem to coincide. He himself defines the situation in such a way that his friend put his shoes in his bag and the environment makes him out to be a liar (192–202):

Description of the text passage: Exmanent inquiry stimulus on his feelings – Text type differentiation: Narration

I: Mhm (5) when it happened with the … shoes … how did you feel then …

Yurislav: Well scared … and my legs were shaking

I: Mhm

Jurislav: That's how it is with me // when I get caught doing something or just haven't done something and then I get caught somehow and I don't know it then my legs always shake (14) and I also like felt as if now // so scared that … that // as if a plane would fall on me

I: Mhm …

Jurislav: So scared // and I freaked out too

(211–224):

Description of the text passage: Exmanent inquiry stimulus on his reaction – Text type differentiation: Narration

I: Mhm (11) you freaked out … tell me …

Jurislav: My friend he was like in the … fourth (grade) … and I freaked out and beat him up …

EMPIRICAL RESEARCH RESULTS

I: Mhm

Jurislav: Because it's ... all because of him

I: Mhm ...

Jurislav: I almost went to prison ...

I: Hmm (4)

Jurislav: I gave him a black eye

I: Mhm (7) and then ...

Jurislav: Well ... then he ran away when the police came ...

I: Hm ...

Jurislav: I was so freaked out that I almost the owner of the shop ... broke her arm

In Jurislav's story there is only a religious connotation at the beginning, when he points out that his deed is forbidden for "us Muslims". His statements and thoughts are worldly and worldly oriented (prison, police, running away). Elements related to transcendence do not appear. Like Canan and Gökmen, he remains on the immanent level. The interviewer then asks about his thoughts in the situation, which also have a worldly orientation (242–244):

Description of the text passage: Exmanent inquiry stimulus on own thoughts – Text type differentiation: Description

Jurislav: Then I also like felt now ... // not felt but // in my thoughts now ... // I talked myself into // thoughts // thinking .. that I should run away quickly ...

Jurislav's own theory of punishment also shows that the problem for him was not stealing, but that he was called a liar. It becomes clear that Jurislav cannot cope with the story. In the lines 253–257, it becomes apparent that he sees being called a liar as the punishment for his theft:

Description of the text passage: Exmanent inquiry stimulus on own theory – Text type differentiation: Description

> I: Mhm … the punishment (5) tell me about the punishment
>
> Jurislav: Yes I also stopped because the police were at the door and that was the punishment that the // that was the punishment that … that they didn't believe me … that they thought I had lied to them

In minimal contrast to Filiz, Betül, and Canan, Jurislav also reaches far back into his memory. However, he remains very much with himself, and it is not clear whether he can leave the first-person perspective and decenter. The presentation of biographical experiences takes on an argumentative character. He tries to process these experiences theoretically afterwards, to ward off the story of the theft and to defend himself, because his own definition of the situation does not match that of his environment. In his presentation, contradictions in his theoretical processing become visible. The question of guilt is in the foreground and Jurislav presents himself as a victim of local and situational conditions. He has not yet distanced himself from the time and the event and he sees his integrity called into question because he has been called a liar. He wants to ward off this attribution because it is a moral judgement of his own person. The characterization as a liar represents a substantial assertion about his person, to which he responds argumentatively. His argumentation, however, is marked by a contradiction, for first he tells us that he "stole", and in his narration he presents the theft as being pushed on him. This also gives rise to the argumentative structure of the account. A narrative reference to this incident may not be possible for him (Riemann, 1986).

5.2.5.1 *Summary*

When asked about events in which God has played a role in their lives, the children find it recognizably difficult in the dimension of temporality to update biographical memories that they can interpret as religious for themselves and possibly for the interviewer. The children search their biographies for experiences and events that they believe, based on their propositional religious knowledge, can be interpreted in a traditional religious way and establish such a reference. However, it becomes clear from the sequences that this reference is artificial and only caused by the inquiries.

EMPIRICAL RESEARCH RESULTS

6 Type C: Relating of the Self to Immanent Dimensions in the Mode of Distance from God

In the following, the ideal type 'Relating of the self in the mode of distance from God' is described, which has successively emerged through comparative analysis and theoretical condensation.

The respective central orientations of the children are reconstructed on the basis of selected passages from the interviews. These passages are characterized either by focal metaphors or by interactive sequences that serve the cognitive interest of the study.

The respective patterns of the type are described in detail in the subsections (first in brief and then in detail). The dimensions of the speech modes perspectivity, ethics, and temporality serve the representation of the respective patterns. We begin with the dimension of perspectivity, which does not document an active relation to God. Then the dimensions of ethics and temporality, which illustrate life in immanence, friendship, and family are followed.

6.1 Brief Description of Type C

6.1.1 Methodical Caveat

The following type is primarily defined by the absence of certain findings. Therefore, it is important to recall that when terms such as 'distance from God', 'blank space' and 'non-thematization' are used in the following, they do not refer to the children's lives, but to the children's statements about their lives as reflected in the interview material.

From the structure of the interviews, the distinction between the three ideal types can be characterized as follows:

– for the personal relationship type, statements about God can be found in the narrative as well as in the inquiry period;
– for the moral relationship type, statements about God can only be found in the inquiry period;
– for God-distant relationship type, statements about God are neither found in the narrative nor in the inquiry period.

6.1.2 Perspectivity: No active Relation to God

The pattern of the type 'God-distant relationship' neither shows an existential reference to religious practice nor to God during the context of the interview. The relationship to God has a blank space. God is not automatically the subject of discussion. The corresponding distance to God is characterized by the fact that the children's narrations do not reveal whether they have an active access to religious patterns of interpretation in close connection with biographically significant events during the interview. Religious patterns of interpretation are received purely passively and are only reproduced superficially and marginally when asked. They do not matter in the children's own narrations, ways of thinking, and explanations.

An individual responsiveness to religious questions or a general accessibility to transcendence-related self and world interpretations is not evident on an implicit or on an explicit level. Religious contents are therefore not action-guiding in the interview situation. Transcendence-related phenomena (such as death) are interpreted inner worldly or immanently. This means that people and their needs or one's own person is placed at the center and phenomena are related to one's own self. No connection is made between a situation associated with danger, fear, and distress and religious patterns of interpretation. Past dramatic events – if experienced – are also not contextualized with religious patterns of interpretation. The children's strategies for coping with fear show an immanence and, in maximum contrast to the moral relationship type, do not point to religious connection points (e.g., protective verses), whereby likewise for the moral relationship type, no action-guiding relation to God can be reconstructed.

Overall, this indicates that for the God-distant relationship type not only the relation to God, but also the reference to religion does not play any action-guiding role in biographical narratives.

Declarative knowledge about God is hardly presented by this type, which shows that the children of this type have learned something about God and religion, but talking about God, faith and religion is extremely limited. This means that this type does not or does only marginally address God, faith, and religion.

When asked, it becomes clear that God exists exclusively as an element of the children's social reality. This type accepts that the environment speaks about God and is also socially competent to adopt this way of speaking when necessary as it becomes apparent in the material. There is a clear separation between fantasy and reality. God is usually located in the fantasy realm. Accordingly, the relating of the self takes place in a God-distant mode.

In maximum contrast to the other two types, this pattern shows that the response strategies have no social, cultural or religious markers that are linguistically shaped by Islamic-religious phrases. Children of this pattern hardly present religious knowledge. All in all, thinking is exclusively at the level of anthropology.

EMPIRICAL RESEARCH RESULTS

6.1.3   Ethics and Temporality: Life within Immanence, Friendship, and Family

Since the dimensions of ethics and temporality coincide in this type, they are dealt with under one heading here.

It is typical for this pattern that the children interpret their lives and the phenomena occurring in it in a purely inner-worldly way.

This shows a focusing on interpersonal interactions and references, as well as a focusing on the present and on this world.

Furthermore, it is typical for this pattern that the external world is viewed exclusively in social terms. This is in maximum contrast to the personal relationship type in which a social orientation is also evident, though interwoven with God and religion. The framework in which a topic is dealt with in metaphorically dense passages of the interview is characterized by interpersonal interactions and social references located in the here and now.

It is also typical for this pattern that the mode of speech is not differentiated in the dimension of perspectivity and that the horizon of perception focuses on the anthropological level. However, the narrations in the dimension of ethics show a differentiation and decentration (abstraction of oneself) with regard to interactions and social relations.

Within the framework of contrastive comparison, the conflict resolution strategy of the children that is ideally assigned to this type is the avoidance of conflicts and the urge to resolve the situation well. Here, an ethic of responsibility becomes apparent in Weberian terms. The children's statements are socially embedded. There is no behavior that could be described as convictional-ethics according to Weber. Topics with normative potential are not framed religiously in maximum contrast to the other two types.

A comparison of the different cases reveals that the narrations of this type are close to reality and separate fantasy from reality. When God is thematized in the children's narrations, God is usually located in the realm of fantasy.

6.2   *Perspectivity: No Active Relation to God*

The inactive attention to the belief in God in the dimension of perspectivity is shown by three facets: firstly, by an immanent interpretation of biographical events, secondly, by establishing a reference to a peripheral God through inquiry, thirdly, by a distanced attitude towards religious practice.

The reconstruction should begin with the aspect that the children who are ideally assigned to this type do not establish a connection between religious patterns of interpretation and biographically significant events and interpret the latter immanently.

202   CHAPTER 4

6.2.1   Immanent Interpretation of Biographical Events
In this pattern, the relation to God as 'inactive' or as a 'blank space' is shown in its specific form by the fact that in the interview situation biographically significant events are not brought together with transcendence-related questions or interpretations. Events such as the death of a family member, the sinking in water or a car accident are interpreted immanently or inner-worldly.

Reacting to the stimulus of telling a story in which Gökmen is in a "bad" situation, he talks about his grandmother who died due to a heart attack in a hospital (193–213):

Description of the text passage: Own experiences – Text type differentiation: Narration, description

> I: Mhm and /uhm/ tell me a story about you where you like .. experienced a bad situation.
>
> Gökmen: /Uhm/ yes /uh/ I was with my dad I was like once away like city XXX or so I forgot well in a city far away and there /uh/ my grandma was sick but not in city XXX but in city XXX still she was sick and /uhm/ when we had come we were next day there ( )? And then /uh/ we had to go back so ( )? And to my grandma she was in the hospital ... and then well she had (heart attack)? And in the mor /uh/ morning we came and she had died ... AND then yes then I was allowed to go into the room so I was like a doctor looking at her like and ()? And then I went in I said // well I talked to my grandma and then /uhm/ there was a device and there was heart and there was always nine five always like up down and then all of a sudden when I went and then I went back and it was on the ( )? And there she was dead
>
> I: Mhm what did you think then?
>
> Gökmen: That she was dead
>
> I: And what happens then?
>
> Gökmen: Then /uh/ my mu /uh/ // my dad flew with her to Turkey and buried her there
>
> I: Mhm
>
> Gökmen: Yes and ((whispers)) ... done? (14) ((whispers)) done?

EMPIRICAL RESEARCH RESULTS   203

When he is asked what he thought then, he immanently describes the circumstance: "That she was dead". Gökmen wants to end the conversation about this topic by whispering "done?" twice. The inquiry and the 14-second pause do not encourage him to continue. However, the interviewer continues to ask (216–225):

Description of the text passage: Own experiences – Text type differentiation: Description

> Gökmen: /Uh/ I felt // well I thought when she was dead that I no longer had a grandma /uh/ and ... that I can no longer see her and only a picture where I still have her and such a picture I can still see her /uh/ ... I had a feeling where I came into the room again /uh/ // I came and then she was dead there I had a feeling that I could like well (12) ( )?
>
> I: Go ahead and think about it
>
> Gökmen: (25) forgotten

Gökmen cannot describe his feelings in this regard in the interview situation. He describes death from a subjective perspective and relates the death of his grandmother to himself by saying that he would no longer have a grandmother and would no longer be able to see her. He does not associate the death with God or with transcendence-related thoughts. Therefore, in the dimension of perspectivity, this sequence shows instead a childlike egocentric view, in the sense that the person himself is seen as the center and the death of the grandmother is related to the own ego. In a sense, death is interpreted in terms of the child himself rather than the dying person. This speechlessness is followed by a question-answer sequence (229–241):

Description of the text passage: Own experiences – Text type differentiation: Argumentation

> I: What happens when you are dead?
>
> Gökmen: /Uh/ you go to the grave
>
> I: Mhm

> Gökmen: And then /uh/ Allah does up (that is, bring up)? He and then ... where it goes ... and there it stays
>
> I: Mhm Allah?
>
> Gökmen: ((whispers)) Allah yes
>
> I: Tell me
>
> Gökmen: Huh how?
>
> I: Tell me about Allah
>
> Gökmen: /Uh/ Allah is the greatest /uh/ and Allah can decide what happens to this person
>
> /uh/ and ... mhm ... Allah has created us /uh/ ... /uh/ (12) Allah has servants (15)

In this sequence, Gökmen brings in God of his own accord in line 234, to whom he attributes bringing the deceased "up". Here it can be seen that he believes that God takes the person to himself after death. In the context of contrastive analysis, the fact that Gökmen refers to this statement without relation to God or to transcendence can be condensed against the counter-horizon of the cases of Hagen and Qamar, who interpret death in terms of transcendence. The crucial thing for him is that the grandmother is dead. Gökmen does bring in death by himself, but he does not show any inner-worldly or transcendent engagement with the subject matter. In the interviews with Hagen and Qamar, in which death is introduced as a topic by the children, it becomes apparent that they deal extensively with the phenomenon of dying and what happens after death. They show a basic accessibility to transcendence-related interpretations of self and world, but not in the case of Gökmen. The maximum contrast to Hagen and Qamar, who deal with death and events after death in a transcendence-related way, condenses the thesis that for Gökmen death is a non-existence in the perceivable world, which he does not want to talk about further. This is shown by the fact that he does bring in God in connection with death, but when the interviewer plays the word back to him, he does not take this up, but shows his astonishment in the form of "Huh how?" in response to

EMPIRICAL RESEARCH RESULTS

the stimulus "Tell me". The stimulus follows directly on his explanation that God brings "up" the person after death. Thereupon he refers to what he knows about God by describing him. Here it becomes apparent that he can explain death with God abstractly using "bringing up". Even on this explicit level, in the dimension of perspectivity, speaking about God, and describing him falls very short. The following 15-second pause does not generate any further narration or description. The meaning that tentatively suggests itself in Gökmen's utterances in the dimension of perspectivity is a materialistically oriented thinking and acting, in the sense that he explains the world and the processes taking place in it without spiritual or immaterial elements.

To condense this thesis, the following passage is added, which also contains a biographically significant event (283–305):

Description of the text passage: Own experiences – Text type differentiation: Narration, description

I: Swimming . tell me

Gökmen: /Uhm/ when I was in the second grade I was with Miss well in the // with the class we were swimming pool and then where we like with the bus we have to you know ride and when we arrived /uh/ we got out and walked in there was boys and there was girls we like inside got changed /uh/ and yes and there we have waited here until Miss comes we had shampoo with us yes and then we are over it and have (thought?) should we shower that you first shower and then go into the water and ... then I took soap I put on my hand and then I put there so there is a thing that you do thing then I'm there (flat?) and there was water and then I like everywhere and then I have water yes then I was wet then I'm like out in // well there we have first waited for our teacher Miss and then we are in the pool .. well yes and then we waited we were all together ha have opened this door and are like and then we walked a bit Miss told us do not run so fast or you will fall down or into the pool deep pool that was either way (height?) water I was still in like normal water beginners yes and then we swam first and I was almost suffocated yes I like dived like (?) and turned around and then I wanted to go back to normal and Miss was talking to someone else and didn't see me and then co // /uh/ and then I went like up again and did ((takes a deep breath)) and yes and then a teacher taught me he taught us how to swim

206 CHAPTER 4

In response to the exmanent stimulus on what he enjoys doing, Gökmen talks about swimming. He talks about an event that happened to him and that relates to fear and distress. He narrates at length and in detail, reaching far back into his memory. He begins the narration of the course of action well before the actual event. In doing so, he describes what movements he has performed and breathes deeply. The dense narrative structure and the manner of narration make it clear that the incident was formative for him and is still very present. In his entire narrative, no transcendence-related utterances occur. Therefore, the interviewer first asks who he was thinking about in this situation (306–329).

Description of the text passage: Own experiences – Text type differentiation: Argumentation

> I: And when you suffocated there // almost suffocated what did you think then
>
> Gökmen: That I am ... suffocating and dead ... mhm and that no one saw me and no one saved me
>
> I: Mhm and who were you thinking of when you were in that moment // in that terrible moment?
>
> Gökmen: How
>
> I: Who were you thinking of then
>
> Gökmen: No one
>
> I: Of no one .. And what feelings did you have
>
> Gökmen: Bad ones .. /uh/ well that I stay inside and that I don't come up / uh/ and that no one sees me and that I stay down yes
>
> I: What would have happened if no one had seen you and you had stayed down
>
> Gökmen: I would have suffocated and I would be dead
>
> I: Mhm and then what would have happened then

EMPIRICAL RESEARCH RESULTS   207

Gökmen: Then I would be dead

I: Is that bad

Gökmen: To be dead

I: Mhm

Gökmen: Yes

I: Well why

Gökmen: Uh because then you are not dead you are not in the world then you are up there

In this question-answer sequence, which is argumentative in character, Gökmen answers the question of what he was thinking about when he almost suffocated: "that I am ... suffocating and dead ...". To the question of whom he was thinking about, he answers "no one". Again, the question is asked what would have happened if no one had seen him and he had stayed down. He answers again: "I would have suffocated and I would be dead". He is asked again what would have happened then and answers: "Then I would be dead". In reference to the above sequence with the death of his grandmother, it becomes apparent here that he does not thematize the grave and God as he did with his grandmother but repeats his statement when asked what would have happened then. The dimension of perspectivity shows a homology in his way of thinking, in the sense that he remains attached to the immanent way of thinking and does not introduce the transcendent dimension.

This sequence represents a homology to the sequence above, for the implicit meaning underlying his utterances about death shows that for Gökmen death is a fact that he does not address further. He does not interpret the phenomenon religiously like Hagen or Qamar. Here, too, the thesis of his childishly materialistic argumentation is condensed, in the sense that he explains the world and the processes taking place in it without spiritual or immaterial elements. The idea that "you" are then "up there", which he offers about his grandmother without differentiating it further, is an explanation that he does not pursue further.

In summary, the comparative analysis shows that Gökmen addresses the death of his grandmother as a biographical fact but does not establish a subjective relationship to God. He also does not connect the dangerous situation

208 CHAPTER 4

in which he found himself with religiously interpretive content or God. In maximum contrast to the type of moral relationship, no dichotomous thinking is evident. Also, no thoughts about paradise and hell show up. No moral codes are visible in his speech either. In none of his narratives, descriptions or argumentations linguistic phrases are visible, i.e., he does not use any Islamic conceptual inventory, and this in maximum contrast to the type of moral relationship, in which the linguistic imprinting becomes visible through religious phrases such as astaġfiru llāh.

Overall, it becomes apparent that Gökmen does not deal with the death of his grandmother and his own experience in the swimming pool within the framework of transcendence-related questions. God is in fact formulated as an ontic fact in the world, but as an element of his social reality, Gökmen offers neither transcendental nor religious nor scientific or ethical patterns of interpretation for the topic of death. It becomes apparent that death is for him a non-existence in his lifeworld.

Mesut also recounts a biographically significant event: a car accident in which his entire family was endangered. He expresses his relief about the good outcome of the event with the phrase "Thank God". However, it is evident in the material that he does not connect his experience with this situation to the religious level of interpretation (283–297):

Description of the text passage: Own experiences – Text type differentiation: Narration

> Mesut: /Uhm/ we we went with car my father drove too fast then we almost we almost slid down but my father had still stopped
>
> I: Where slid down
>
> Mesut: From from the highway
>
> I: Oh and then
>
> Mesut: Then my father like braked an and and we stopped and then there were two cars that were also completely stopped and and then they called the hospital we were ... was there my father injured
>
> I: Mhm

EMPIRICAL RESEARCH RESULTS

> Mesut: He was injured here
>
> I: Mhm
>
> Mesut: And my .. /uh/ my little brother thank God nothing happened to him my mother and my father something happened ... they were two days in the hospital

Mesut tells a story about a car accident on the highway where he, his parents, and his two brothers were in the car. He says that his parents were injured and that nothing happened to his little brother. Looking at his little brother, he uses the expression "Thank God".

The interviewer plays back to him the expression "Thank God", which he does not take in. He repeats the events and concludes with "further nothing". He is not talking about God's protection or gratitude for God's protection in this dangerous situation, which is meant by the expression "Thank God". He uses this phrase as an expression of emphasis, expressing his relief (300–305).

Description of the text passage: Own experiences – Text type differentiation: Explanation

> I: ((asking)) Thank God (5) tell me why Thank God
>
> Mesut: Because nothing happened to my little brother he is still two years old he was sleeping and then he woke up and he was crying but nothing happened to him (9) and is ... my father had to my mother was fine but my father had to stay at home in bed for three days ... further nothing

In the contrastive minimal case comparison with Gökmen and Canan (see below), it becomes apparent that Mesut does not establish a connection between danger/fear/distress and religious interpretive content. These do not play a role for his actions in this situation.

The following passage is used to highlight this thesis (306–314):

Description of the text passage: Own experiences – Text type differentiation: Description

> I: Tell me about your fear
>
> Mesut: (9) /Uh/ (17) once when I'm scared then always my feet shake and my hands sweat and then I always have stomach ache
>
> I: Mhm is there something that helps you then
>
> Mesut: /Uh/ my friends always help me when something happens my father my brother ... and /uh/ my grandpa and so on
>
> I: Mhm
>
> Mesut: My my aunt ... they help me when something happens to me (12) ah and /uh/ ... and any they they ... and further nothing more

Mesut does not bring God or religious patterns of interpretation to bear on the stimulus on his fear and its overcoming, despite the previous thematization of God. He describes his fear authentically by describing its physical effects ("my feet shake"). This description of fear in which the "feet shake" is homologous to the continuation of Ali's story (188–191):

Description of the text passage: Immanent inquiry stimulus on Ali's feelings – Text type differentiation: Description

> I: Mhm tell me about Ali's feelings in the hut
>
> Mesut: He was scared he didn't know what to do ... and /uh/ he has /uhm/ his feet were shaking he couldn't he didn't know what to do and he was sweating ... further I don't know

It can be seen here that Mesut has experience with anxiety and can also describe its characteristics. Regarding his anxiety coping strategy, he mentions people like his friends, his father, his brother, his grandfather, and his aunt, who help him to cope with his anxiety. He assumes that it is important for him to have people or to be close to people who are there for him in order not to be afraid or to help him when something has happened. In maximum contrast to Paiman, it becomes clear here that Mesut prefers immanent, anthropological solution strategies in the context of fear and difficult life events and that

EMPIRICAL RESEARCH RESULTS

no connection to transcendence-related strategies is apparent. Paiman, on the other hand, combines both a transcendence-related strategy, namely the belief in the effect of the Qur'anic verses, and an immanent, anthropological strategy, namely the search for closeness to other people (cf. Chapter 4, Section 4.2).

Mesut describes the adults or the older brother as people who actively help in dangerous situations and himself as someone who has trust in these people. The reading shows that Mesut does not use the expression "Thank God" in the context of a relation to God, but as an expression of emphasis. A relation to God or religion cannot be reconstructed in the interview situation.

This trust in adults is also shown in minimal contrast to Canan, who constructs herself as well as Ali as extremely passive persons in dangerous situations, who have great trust in adults. God does not play a role for Canan either, neither for Ali nor for herself nor for the externally introduced persons (129–137):

Description of the text passage: Exmanent inquiry stimulus on own experiences with fear – Text type differentiation: Narration, description

> Canan: When I once went shopping with my mother /uhm/ ... like /uhm/ I once /uhm/ just got lost in the big market /uhm/ and I was /uhm/ afraid ((voice goes up)) and ... /uhm/ ... I went somewhere and they /uhm/ like said through the speakers /uhm/ well I had given my name and my age ((voice goes up)) and that I was lost and then they /uhm/ spoke into loud-speakers and /uhm/ then my mother found me ((voice goes up)) and I was afraid ((voice goes up)) (22) and further I don't know ...

Referring to a situation in which Canan was afraid, she tells of shopping with her mother at the market when she was younger. She got lost there. When asked about her feelings, she repeats three times that she was afraid (139–140). When asked about her thoughts in the situation, she reports that she assumed that her mother would find her "anyway" (144–146):

Description of the text passage: Exmanent inquiry stimulus on own experiences with fear – Text type differentiation: Description

> Canan: My THOUGHTS well I thought anyway that /uhm/ my mother would find me anyway AND we would (go) home again and nothing else (6)

This passage shows a homology to Ali's opening narration. In the case-internal comparison, a logical continuation or connectivity of this passage to the opening narrative becomes clear. In maximum contrast to Betül and Dilara, who place their own actions in the foreground, Canan constructs Ali as passive, just as she also portrays herself in the market story as a very passive person who has absolute trust in adults. In the continuation of Ali's story, Canan, in maximum contrast to Betül and Dilara, does not bring God or other religious content into play. There is no religious pattern of interpretation, even concerning the incident at the market.

6.2.1.1 *Summary*

The reading reinforces the idea that for the children who are assigned to the God-distant relationship type, religious interpretations do not play a dominant role in acting in dangerous situations. Existential biographical events are therefore not interpreted religiously by this type. Here, a gap between their practical experiences and the religious level is documented in their narratives. This reconstruction is significant, because the children of this sample move in a context that is permeated and saturated with God and religion. Although there is an access or connection to religion and God on the formal level, there is a blank space in the material. In the interview situation, the children of this type do not connect their own lifeworld with religious elements or God.

In the dimension of perspectivity, the interview situation shows that the children of this type do not explain transcendence-related phenomena in religious, spiritual, or immaterial terms. In relation to conditions of danger, fear, and distress in their lives, they construct adults as people of reference. Overall, it is evident that the relation to a God who exists ontically and peripherally for the children of the type of God-distant relationship represents a blank space.

6.2.2 Peripheral God through Inquiry

Another facet of inactive attention to the belief in God in the dimension of perspectivity is the establishment of a reference to a peripheral God through inquiry. This facet is characterized by the fact that God is introduced based on an exmanent inquiry, but it can be reconstructed that the topic of 'God' is peripheral for the children and is more located in the realm of fantasy.

Mesut tells of a life-threatening situation he experienced together with his family: an accident on the highway. Regarding this event, he shows his emphatic expression by saying "Thank God". In the reconstructive analysis in the mode of perspectivity, however, it becomes apparent that this emphatic phrase has no reference to transcendence (for a detailed description, cf. Chapter 4, Section 6.2). Following the description of the accident situation and the thematization of his fear, God is introduced as a stimulus (315–321):

EMPIRICAL RESEARCH RESULTS 213

Description of the text passage: Own experiences – Text type differentiation:
Description

I: And God

Mesut: ( )?

I: Mhm tell me

Mesut: I /uh/ had was I was a week in the room I was not allowed outside there I prayed whether I can I please go outside and then has and then has my mother with my father come and may you you may go outside again my father said and then there has Allah Allah has helped me

The contrastive case comparison shows a minimal contrast to Gökmen, Betül, and Canan, who also tell a story that they associate with God, because the interviewer directly asks about God. It is interesting that the car accident, which was mentioned shortly before, is not the topic here, and neither is God, in connection with fears because the previous stimulus refers to what helps him when he is afraid. This also consolidates the thesis that the phrase "Thank God" is an expression of emphasis. Mesut addresses his confinement to his room and retroactively establishes a relation to God. The confinement in the room might possibly have greater relevance for Mesut. In minimal contrast to Eljan, Jurislav, and Betül, he also shows a purposive-rational relationship to God when he says that God helped him because of his own turning towards him in the form of a prayer. In the dimension of perspectivity, the children establish the relationship to God by showing an activity themselves, based on which God then fulfills a wish. In response to the interviewer's inquiry, Mesut frames his confinement religiously and establishes the relation to God in a 'do ut des' context.

Mesut can contextualize the dramatic experience of the car accident, but it becomes apparent that in the dimension of perspectivity, God or religious patterns of interpretation do not play a role. In contrast to the cases of Canan, Filiz, Kaltrina, Jurislav, and Qamar, who argue in terms of tradition and reproduce their propositional knowledge, Mesut also shows no reference to tradition.

Olivia also shows the establishment of a relation to God in response to the interviewer's inquiry. Her view of God shows in the dimension of perspectivity that God exists peripherally for her and that the thematization of God takes place marginally.

214   CHAPTER 4

It is evident that Olivia constructs Ali in the story as a Muslim because of his name and triggers the dislike of his classmates in his religious affiliation (74–85):

Description of the text passage: Immanent inquiry stimulus on Ali – Text type differentiation: Description, explanation

> I: tell me about Ali
>
> Olivia: hm I don't know him but
>
> I: what do you imagine
>
> Olivia: I think he is Muslim
>
> I: mhm
>
> Olivia: and I think the children /uhm/ are just not Muslims and then they don't understand him so well either
>
> I: mhm …
>
> Olivia: and that // but I think maybe it's not the reason but (7)
>
> I: what makes you think that Ali could be Muslim
>
> Olivia: somehow the name sounds like that

Olivia constructs this location of Ali as a counter-horizon to her own situation as a Muslim (95–112):

Description of the text passage: Exmanent inquiry stimulus on own experiences – Text type differentiation: Explanation

> I: mhm (17) tell me a story about yourself …
>
> Olivia: hm I know rather badly so …
>
> I: what is important for you

EMPIRICAL RESEARCH RESULTS

Olivia: that my friends like me and ... well that they are not stupid to me

I: mhm

Olivia: yes but they're not either you know

I: mhm ...

Olivia: they also don't think somehow that I have a stupid religion // they don't say anything about my religion so

I: mhm

Olivia: we don't argue about it like that we . are just friends

I: mhm ... has a situation ever happened to you in which you were afraid of something

Olivia: m-m actually not as afraid as when I'm locked up and no one is there ... somehow not yet

I: mhm . and another situation where you were afraid

Olivia: hm . m-m ... not // I can't think of any right now somehow

The last two passages have explanatory and argumentative character. No narrations are produced here since the stimulus may not have any biographical meaning for Olivia. Possibly this horizon of experience does not exist for Olivia in the narrative framework of this story.

Olivia has no solution for Ali's hopeless situation. When asked how she would have reacted in Ali's place, she explains that there is not much you can do except scream because you're in shock. She describes reaching her limits, and this is the time when thinking about God or religious practice could have been activated. However, it turns out that Olivia does not give a transcendence-related explanation here (133–143):

Description of the text passage: Immanent inquiry stimulus on Ali – Text type differentiation: Explanation

> Olivia: maybe write something on a piece of paper or something if you have it with you or something
>
> I: mhm
>
> Olivia: then somehow that then . no idea
>
> I: mhm . yes keep on telling
>
> Olivia: hm maybe the wind carries it away or something
>
> I: mhm ...
>
> Olivia: uhm then maybe someone sees it and can tell it // it kind of says // you know I'm trapped in an .. old hut . my name is so and so and I live there . // and if they can inform the parents and so . yes

Olivia is looking for a solution that has no reference to transcendence. Her explanation of writing something on a piece of paper and hoping that the wind would carry it away and someone would find it, is expressed in the subjunctive. It becomes clear that she assumes that Ali's situation is hopeless. However, thinking about God is not activated. Therefore, the interviewer inquires further (149–157):

Description of the text passage: Immanent inquiry stimulus on Ali – Text type differentiation: Explanation

> I: would there be any other possibilities ...
>
> Olivia: I can't think of anything else you could do ...
>
> I: if no one comes by . what else could help
>
> Olivia: pray
>
> I: mhm
>
> Olivia: so that someone // or someone notices for example a call for help or something

EMPIRICAL RESEARCH RESULTS   217

> I: mhm
>
> Olivia: but that is now really in case of emergencies

Olivia addresses the issue of praying in response to the urgent questioning of the interviewer, which indicates that she would probably not have made any reference to it in the context of Ali's story on her own initiative.

Her statement "but that is now really in case of emergencies" condenses the thesis that she sees no relevance here for praying in the context of Ali's situation.

In the direct inquiry stimulus on God, her view of God becomes clear at the explicit level (176–183):

Description of the text passage: Exmanent inquiry stimulus on God – Text type differentiation: Explanation

> I: mhm (8) mhm (12) tell me about God . or about Allah
>
> Olivia: hm I don't know him that well you know
>
> I: mhm
>
> Olivia: that's why ... I can't imagine him either . you also shouldn't do that I think
>
> I: mhm
>
> Olivia: that's why . well I think of God when something nice has happened

Olivia actively shifts her gaze from imagining God to thinking about him. For her, God is not possible in her imagination because she does not know him. She explains that she thinks of him, and then describes situations in which she does. Her view of God on the explicit level does not correspond to the other children's conceptions. In maximum contrast to Gökmen and Betül, Olivia does not provide descriptions of God that she references from her propositional knowledge (185–196):

Description of the text passage: Exmanent inquiry stimulus on God – Text type differentiation: Description

> Olivia: yeah and I thank him then also often. for . that he . did that
>
> I: tell me more of it ..
>
> Olivia: well no idea . that's just always like that .. that I often think about it
>
> I: just tell me a story where you then think about it or something has happened
>
> Olivia: for example
>
> I: mhm
>
> Olivia: /uhm/ ... /uhm/ well I often think of it when . something almost would happen to me . and it just only didn't happen but . really . almost happened . so to say my . guardian angels protected me from it and also Allah . that it didn't happen to me ..

In the dimension of perspectivity, Olivia independently directs the topic from imagining God to thinking about God. However, in response to the stimulus on examples, she thematizes within the framework of her explicit knowledge rather than directly describing God. Instead, she first describes the guardian angels who protect her from dangerous situations, and then she adds God. The interviewer plays the subject of the guardian angels back to her again (224–239):

Description of the text passage: Exmanent inquiry stimulus on the guardian angels – Text type differentiation: Description

> I: and you talked about guardian angels . right
>
> Olivia: mhm
>
> I: tell me more about it
>
> Olivia: well I do think that they exist // some people don't believe it but ... I'm often protected by them somehow // I also don't know why // I also don't know if it's Allah or the guardian angels or both . that .. and then I often just thank them both that they have protected me

EMPIRICAL RESEARCH RESULTS

I: mhm

Olivia: from . yeah from things like that

I: yes ...

Olivia: because things like that often happen to me . but only almost

I: mhm

Olivia: and it doesn't really happen to me but // well for example I can already fall off a swing but I haven't hurt myself .. yes (7)

Here it can be seen that Olivia is aware that the belief in guardian angels is not necessarily shared by all Muslims. However, she consciously connects the theme of protection with the guardian angels. In minimal contrast to Olivia, it becomes clear that Dilara also addresses guardian angels in the context of protection and also assigns them a primary position in contrast to God in terms of protection (58–68):

Description of the text passage: Opening passage – Continuation of Ali's story – Text type differentiation: Narration

Dilara: /Uhm/ maybe /uhm/ something is /uh/ well like a lock door on the ground maybe he can open it and through that well go under there and find a way to get out or he just digs with his hand and /uhm/ Allah helps him and it can also be that Allah gives him a good feeling that he is not lonely because Allah is next to him and the guardian angel /uhm/ and the guardian angel can always stay with him then he gives a feeling that he is next to him and that he should not be afraid because surely /uh/ also something good will happen then /uh/ the guardian angel can say /uh/ well like give a feeling someone is coming or someone hears you they are coming soon or other things that should not make him so lonely should not make him sad and after that surely something good will happen.. yes..

Olivia and Dilara thematize guardian angels in the context of protection. This is striking, since the belief in angels, who take on various tasks and bear their names according to their tasks, such as the scripture angels or the angels of death, is essential in the Islamic context, but there are no angels in the Islamic tradition who explicitly assume the task of protection and bear this name.

In maximum contrast to Olivia and Dilara, Hagen also addresses angels in the interview, but in connection with the topic of God he addresses the angels of death, who in the Islamic tradition have the task of accompanying people's souls to God after their death. In maximum contrast to Olivia and Dilara, Filiz also addresses angels, namely the scripture angels, who in the Islamic tradition have the task of documenting people's deeds. Overall, in this respect and in maximum contrast to Olivia and Dilara, Hagen and Filiz orient themselves to what is handed down in religion.

Overall, the above passages (and other passages from Olivia's interview that are not listed here) are characterized by a strong question-answer form since she is not engaging herself for the narrative. Here, a minimal contrast to Canan becomes apparent, as the linguistic aspects and the long pauses indicate that the topic of the interview may have little biographical relevance for Olivia. It is possible that the topic does not concern her in the interview situation.

A similar reference is evident in Gökmen. In answer to the stimulus to talk about Allah, he reproduces some learned, propositional knowledge which is clichéd and formal. In answer to the stimulus to tell a story about himself and Allah, he recalls a dream. It is possible that he feels he has no story that he could tell. Thus, he talks of a dream in which God and religious patterns of interpretation play no role (242–263):

Description of the text passage: Own experiences – Text type differentiation: Narration, description

I: Tell me a story about you and Allah

Gökmen: /Uh/ ... so a dream

I: What you want

Gökmen: I don't have a story (me?) and Allah

I: Mhm think about it .. can you think of anything

Gökmen: A story

I: Mhm anything

EMPIRICAL RESEARCH RESULTS

> Gökmen: Mhm .. well in dream I saw that // in my dream I saw that I was in my yard // yard where I live /uh/ and ... **there** was then like swing six pieces and there I was my sister and my brother and there was also a man was hiding behind the ... bush with motorcycle and then we like that were six girls and I // were at the swing and they have already swinged for two hours and then we said can you go down we also want to swing you know and then they are down and then he /uh/ man so (?) My sister was here and I was there upfront and then the /uh/ engine like came /uh/ has /uh/ has shot something /uh/ and then he like went and came on my foot /uh/ and yes there I was awake
>
> I: Mhm:
>
> Gökmen: Done
>
> I: And that was ... a dream mhm
>
> Gökmen: A dream is a story

In the dimension of perspectivity, Gökmen clearly differentiates between phantasy and reality. He locates God in the realm of fantasy or dream. However, he does not tell a story about God from this fantasy or dream realm. Overall, the material shows that Gökmen presents little religious knowledge and does not deal with transcendence-related questions in the interview situation. Religious patterns of interpretation are only passively received and do not substantiate his actions.

Kaltrina, Filiz, Navid, and Olivia also show a separation between fantasy and reality, which will be described below:

Kaltrina tells a detailed and stringent story following the opening stimulus. In the process, it becomes apparent that she leaves her own narration in the meantime, reflects on it, and then re-enters it and continues telling the story (168–170):

Description of the text passage: Opening passage – Continuation of Ali's story – Text type differentiation: Narration with insertion of an explanation

> Kaltrina: best friends after a few weeks they didn't even fight anymore and Ali was so happy that he finally had a best friend ((laughs)) better than a boy and Jonathan still had nothing

In this passage, Kaltrina's differentiation between her imaginative story and reality becomes apparent. Kaltrina constructs a best friend for Ali, exits her narration with a laugh, reflects on her construction by inserting "better than a boy", and then re-enters the story. She listens to herself during her narration (320–322):

Description of the text passage: Immanent inquiry stimulus on Ali – Text type differentiation: Explanation

> Kaltrina: But that cave where You said they were locked up I wanted to do that again because then it would be a bit more exciting because I'm also writing an essay tomorrow

Kaltrina deliberately revisits the scene in the cave in her narration, giving it more tension to prepare for her essay the next day. These reflective passages occur more frequently in the interview. She makes a clear separation between fantasy and reality here. Kaltrina's view of God also shows a certain separation, namely between immanence and transcendence, which is expressed in the following passage:

In the only passage in the interview that deals with God, it is evident that Kaltrina is aware that faith in God and in the efficacy of the protective verses must be present for her not to be afraid (500–506):

Description of the text passage: Own experiences – Text type differentiation: Narration, description

> I: Is there something that helps you when you are afraid like that of something ..
>
> Kaltrina: Myeah ... I always say my suras then I believe but I also always believe in it and then I'm no longer afraid even at night I also always say that after sleeping before sleeping (4) I'm not so afraid with Allah with me I'm not so afraid ... but if I don't believe in it then I'm afraid ( ) (14) that's a nice necklace

If Kaltrina believes in God, then she is not afraid, and if she does not believe, then she is afraid. Here she makes a linguistic distinction between transcendence and immanence. It can be seen that faith is the prerequisite for Kaltrina

EMPIRICAL RESEARCH RESULTS

to locate God from transcendence in her lifeworld. In her description, however, an uncertainty becomes clear as to whether this faith is present in her.

Filiz, Olivia, and Navid stringently strive to offer an immanent and inner-worldly solution for Ali's liberation. In their continuation of his story, its solution takes on a reality because the events could have taken place as the children narrate. Their narrations are close to reality. The incidents they construct narratively correspond to reality until the end; they do not insert fictitious or media-charged narratives. In doing so, they bring in generalized knowledge from their childlike lifeworld, namely what is available to them in terms of solution strategies. However, this knowledge has no religious connection.

All in all, it becomes clear that the type of God-distant relationship clearly separates between fantasy and reality in the dimension of perspectivity and locates God in the realm of fantasy instead. Although God is recognized as an element of social reality, the material shows that he is of peripheral importance for this type.

6.2.2.1 *Summary*

In the context of the contrastive, reconstructive analysis, it becomes clear that the children of the type of God-distant relationship in the dimension of perspectivity do establish a relation to God by inquiry, but this reference is established on the basis of an exmanent inquiry and is not action-guiding. Overall, it can be seen that religious contents are not action-guiding for them in the interview situation. From the interpretation of the interviews, it can be concluded that neither an action-guiding reference to religion nor a relation to God can be reconstructed in the interview situation, as God and religion are not addressed as such. In the context of the contrastive comparison, the linguistic level indicates overall less pronounced narrative passages in relation to God and religion as well as a low connection to the everyday world. This reinforces the assumption on the content level that the topic 'God' is only of secondary importance for the children. It can be seen that they clearly differentiate between fantasy and reality and that God is located more in the realm of fantasy due to his peripheral position.

6.2.3 Distanced Attitude towards Religious Practice

The third facet of the inactive turning to faith in God in the dimension of perspectivity is the facet of the 'distanced attitude towards religious practice'. This is characterized by the fact that the children, who are ideally assigned to the type of God-distant relationship, address religious elements, which they bring in themselves, from a distanced perspective and establish worldly relations to them in the dimension of perspectivity.

224   CHAPTER 4

The aspect of the distanced attitude is evident in Navid, who addresses his coping strategies in the context of an unpleasant situation. He describes his outburst of anger in response to the exmanent question stimulus as to whether he has experienced a situation like Ali's in which he did not feel comfortable (277–287):

Description of the text passage: Own experiences – Text type differentiation: Description

> Navid: yes but I don't remember it so well (5) I think of it . seven students from my class against me.
>
> I: ((asking)) yes
>
> Navid: and once he he is my friend also in my class he accidentally threw a stone at me I had I had a tantrum . wanted to attack him and not even four students tried to hold me . but I slowly moved forward (5) otherwise I do not know .. oh . one more thing I know ... it's not a situation like Ali ... I have a girlfriend and I'm in love with her ... she's dark-skinned she's older than me and her name is [incomprehensible?] lives ?in a metropolitan city? // I visited her once

Navid addresses three situations that he compares to Ali's situation. He does not address Ali's fear in the hut, but rather that seven students from his class were against him, like Ali's four classmates, and that he was once held down by four classmates during an anger outburst. He describes this situation and reflects on the fact that he was able to move forward despite being held down. The third situation he relates to Ali's situation is his falling in love with his girlfriend. He expresses his feelings very openly, which indicates a familiarity towards the interviewer. This correlation is somewhat surprising. What is decisive here is that he does not connote Ali's situation with fear, but with anger at the people who have held him.

In response to the stimulus of what would calm him down in such situations, he enumerates his strategies (296–299):

Description of the text passage: Own experiences – Text type differentiation: Description

EMPIRICAL RESEARCH RESULTS

225

> Navid: calms down for example if I don't see the person for a while then it helps me . then I am calmed down (5) or sometimes when I am at home relaxing in the balcony ... that helps me (6) or sometimes drawing pictures . helps me too . yes ... otherwise . otherwise I don't know any more things

Navid has adopted some conflict resolution strategies that help him calm down in situations where he is angry, such as distance, relaxation, and drawing. These strategies do not contain religious elements. They are inner-worldly.

Therefore, the following exmanent stimulus relates to Navid's anxiety (305–315):

Description of the text passage: Own experiences – Text type differentiation: Narration, description

> Navid: mmh ... but I already think sometimes in nightmares . there come / once when I was little . there . // in a dream there was the world almost flooded . of of thing ... /uh/ of water with shampoo and then I was still afraid . and otherwise (5) /uh/ uh fear . Fear sometimes ... with nightmares ... sometimes when everyone is asleep I'm outside it's dark ...
>
> I: mhm
>
> Navid: and ... then thing . and once I was I think second or first grade there I was really really scared . then I ((disturbance from outside)) there I // on the way to school I // I immediately stopped there I thought there was a wolf there I immediately stopped . but it didn't attack me ...

Like most children, Navid mentions fear in connection with nightmares. When asked what helps him when he is afraid, he also brings up immanent or inner-worldly solution strategies (330–340):

Description of the text passage: Own experiences – Text type differentiation: Narration, description

> I: Is there something that helps you when you are afraid of anything?
>
> Navid: something something that helps me . in darkness I am alone outside there then the opposite I am inside it is bright ..

> I: mhm
>
> Navid: A bright day . that helps me then . or for example with nightmares . when I get up then it helps me again
>
> I: mhm
>
> Navid: or sometimes for example // sometimes there are monsters in my nightmares // they fizzle out all at once . that helps me then .. otherwise ... I know ... well . like otherwise for example when I lie down on the bed and relax .. and .. there's nothing else either.

In the contrastive case comparison against the counter-horizon of the cases of Betül, Canan, Filiz, Jurislav, and Paiman, who frame the dangerous situation in religious terms, it is evident in Navid's case that he does not frame situations associated with fear, danger, and distress in religious terms. Betül, Canan, Filiz, Jurislav, and Paiman bring in the protective verses and their propositional knowledge in relation to them. Navid, on the other hand, in minimal contrast to Mesut, also has strategies that are immanent and inner-worldly. The interpretation of the interview shows that he does not make any transcendence-related interpretations of the world and himself but deals rationally with the situations of fear and distress and has immanent and inner-worldly solution strategies for them.

The only thing that Navid addresses about religion on his own initiative is fasting. In response to the stimulus to talk about himself, Navid tells us in the context of his eating habits and his weight that he can also fast (227–237):

Description of the text passage: Own experiences – Text type differentiation: Narration

> Navid: at school .. and .. otherwise . he is my best friend sometimes I was allowed to spend the night at his place then I usually got up faster /uhm/ mostly I got up earlier and sometimes he was allowed to spend the night at my place then he usually got up faster .. and he had a PlayStation ... and and before I went to kindergarten / I also had a PlayStation with games and I could even play these games I didn't play them wrong ... and until now the PlayStation is still broken (5) my favorite drink is Sprite . I was born in 2003 .. then .. I weigh I think I weigh 29.9 or 29.6 kilos now .. and . thing .. I could eat very little when I was little and now I can eat very little I can even fast

EMPIRICAL RESEARCH RESULTS

It becomes apparent that Navid is eager to communicate and talks a lot about himself. In his narration he jumps from one event to the next and broadly recounts everything that seems relevant to him. The reflection of his own person shows up again and again in his narrations. He discusses his abilities as a small child and makes references to his current life.

When asked if he has ever fasted, Navid addresses fasting in the context of losing weight (238–249):

Description of the text passage: Own experiences – Text type differentiation: Narration

> I: ((asking)) yes . have you ever
>
> Navid: no . but I think I can . I can / and I can lose weight very quickly and once there I have I have where one well where you weigh yourself that I have put o on such a bath mat then I stood on it then I think I saw / 23.6 but that was not correct because the weight was changed because it was on the bath mat on the floor it was then correct again (9) well ... and ... I go onc I have also children's fireworks in the last New Year's Eve I bought a fireworks package there were 230 bangers or 320 ... there were a lot ... then I have I spent the night at my friend's he had like a / a firework lit that flew into the air and banged against a house and fell down again

Here it can be seen that even when the interviewer picks up the topic of fasting and plays it back to him, Navid goes on about losing weight. He talks about his weight, which he states quite accurately, mentioning that the bathmat might have changed the figure. He observes closely and has an interest in numbers. Although the interview takes place during the time of Islamic religious education and he is prompted to talk about fasting in a context that is visibly religious, it is evident here that he does not engage in religious framing but locates fasting in the secular context and addresses it immanently in the context of weight loss.

In summary, it is clear from the material that Navid does not establish a connection between a situation associated with danger, fear, and distress and religious patterns of interpretation. In general, comparative analysis shows that Navid's narrations reveal a distanced attitude towards religious practice. He does address fasting, but he does so in the context of losing weight rather than a religious act or God. God is not thematized in Ali, in his own person, or in the externally introduced characters. Navid can actualize biographical experience, but this is done in the context of interpersonal relationships and social-world phenomena. In the contrasting case comparison, Navid shows no reference to the type of moral relationship, which thematizes religious practice and establishes a relationship to it.

Kaltrina also addresses God once in her detailed and reflective interview, whereby her distanced attitude towards religious practice is evident in her statements. God is thematized regarding fear, and in connection with this, the recitation of the protective verses before sleeping. This shows a minimal contrast to Betül, Filiz, and Paiman, who also discuss the recitation of protective verses before going to bed (501–506):

Description of the text passage: Exmanent inquiry stimulus on anxiety coping strategies – Text type differentiation: Description

> Kaltrina: Myeah .. I always say my suras then I believe but I also always believe in it and then I'm no longer afraid even at night I also always say this after sleeping before sleeping (4) I'm not so afraid with Allah with me I'm not so afraid .. but if I don't believe in it then I'm afraid ( ) (14) that's a nice necklace

The style of Kaltrina's remarks characterizes her distanced attitude towards this religious practice, which can be seen in the contradictory representations: "Then I believe, but I also always believe in it" and "I am not afraid then ... I am not so afraid with Allah". A distance to the effect of the protective verses is documented in her statements: "But if I do not believe in it, then I am afraid".

Kaltrina's distance is also made clear by her shifting the topic to the interviewer's necklace after a 14-second pause. She has nothing more to contribute to this stimulus. No experience with the use of protective cues becomes clear. In comparative analysis against the counter-horizon of the cases of Betül, Paiman, and Filiz, Kaltrina does have a 'child courage belief' that many parents pass on to their children, but no substantial reference to it emerges.

6.2.3.1   *Summary*

In the mode of perspectivity, it becomes clear through the narrative structure and the narrative perspective that the children of the type of God-distant relationship establish neither an abstract nor a concrete reference between God or religious practice and their everyday world. Therefore, the level of abstraction cannot be assessed in this regard either. Religious elements, which they bring in of their own accord, thematize from a distanced perspective and establish

EMPIRICAL RESEARCH RESULTS   229

worldly references. Their mode of speech does not show any transcendence-related thinking in the dimension of perspectivity.

In the context of the contrastive, reconstructive analysis, neither a moralizing nor a religious framing of situations is evident in the children who are ideally assigned to this type. In maximum contrast to the type of moral relationship, their response strategies do not make visible any Islamic-religious markers characterized by linguistic phrases, although they are accustomed to the explication of religious semantics in the context of religious education and partly also in the context of religious schooling in mosques. From the interpretation of the interviews, it can be concluded that no reference to transcendence is evident in the interview situation. In their narrations, the children's distanced attitude documents a blank space in relation to God.

6.2.4   Ethics and Temporality: Life in Immanence, Friendship, and Family

The children who are ideally assigned to the type of relating in a distance from God show a close relationship to human beings and their possibilities of action in the sense of an ethics of responsibility in the dimensions of ethics and temporality. In the dimension of temporality, they focus on the present, in the dimension of ethics on interpersonal interactions and social relations. The outside is conceived socially. The facet 'Life in Immanence, Friendship, and Family' is characterized by the fact that friendship, family, and harmonization are at the center of their narrations.

In Olivia's case, it becomes clear that in view of the significance of God for herself, she begins to address his significance for all of creation. She moves away from her own person and speaks generalizing in the 'we' mode. As in the passages presented above in Chapter 4, Section 6.2, it is evident here that Olivia does not make an individual reference between God and herself in the interview situation. She focuses on the collective here (371–389):

Description of the text passage: Exmanent inquiry stimulus on the meaning of God – Text type differentiation: Description

I: does he have a meaning . in your life . apart from what you have already told

Olivia: yes he created the earth for me so to speak . for all of us and // yes that is something important so already and even that we don't have to starve and that . we are well off that we have a house and that we are not cold

> I: mhm
>
> Olivia: Allah does all that so to speak
>
> I: mhm ... so he provides . for us
>
> Olivia: yes
>
> I: and does he do anything else . besides
>
> Olivia: yes he protects us
>
> I: mhm
>
> Olivia: he does everything for us
>
> I: mhm ...
>
> Olivia: yes and because he gives us everything and stuff like that we just have to . just /uhm/ pray
>
> I: mhm
>
> Olivia: and make Fatiha and stuff like that

Olivia speaks on the explicit level in a purposive-rational relation to God. God creates, provides, and protects, whereas the human being prays. Prayer is synonymous with the *fātiḥa* (Arabic: the opening), the first chapter (sura) in the Qur'an, which is an integral part of the regular ritual prayer of Muslims.

In the further course of the interview, Olivia addresses her reflections in the context of moral considerations, moving away from the religious level. In response to the stimulus of what humans can do, she describes the responsibility of humans for animals, the environment, and the equal treatment of living creatures (423–433):

Description of the text passage: Exmanent inquiry stimulus on the meaning of God – Text type differentiation: Description

EMPIRICAL RESEARCH RESULTS

> Olivia: yes (8) that must just . treat every living being equally well . well that it is not now for example . the dogs better off than the cats or the other way around
>
> I: mhm
>
> Olivia: but they all have to be treated equally well … it's actually the same with people that they also have to be treated equally well . not somehow the browns are bad and the whites are good
>
> I: mhm
>
> Olivia: well they are both equally good just because they look different doesn't mean that they are different at heart

When asked about the possibilities for human action, Olivia addresses animal welfare and environmental protection, the excessive consumption of meat or the topic of eating in moderation, and the equal treatment of people of different skin colors. She uses the terms "white people" and "brown people". She separates external differences from internal differences on an emotional level by focusing on people's "hearts" and thereby establishing equality between people. The social actions she addresses lose their religious framing, and she begins to address social-worldly aspects and interpersonal relationships. The theme of the human right to equal treatment, leads over into her own lifeworld (435–451):

Description of the text passage: Exmanent inquiry stimulus on the meaning of God – Text type differentiation: Description

> Olivia: I also have a lot of friends who are brown. my best friend is also brown
>
> I: mhm
>
> Olivia: and we still get along well . and our parents don't mind either
>
> I: yes …
>
> Olivia: that's why . everyone has to be treated equally well

> I: mhm … do you do that // why do you that that you treat everyone equally well and also the animals and so on
>
> Olivia: because they . deserve it well . they can't help it that . they are brown // if the father are brown // well . it's not bad if they are brown or
>
> I: mhm
>
> Olivia: so that's why … I don't understand it . why some are brown and treated badly and only some whites are good
>
> I: mhm
>
> Olivia: yes. that's why I think everyone should be treated equally well

The topic of equal treatment of people of different skin color is an issue that Olivia deals with and confronts in the reality of her life. The question of people and their responsibility for them is in the foreground. The interviewer's question (442–443) aims to find out what motives underlie her decision to treat all people equally, i.e., whether there are immanent or transcendence-related reasons. In the dimension of ethics, Olivia's mode of speech reveals that she claims a universal rather than a religious validity for her statements about norms.

In her discussion of the differences in skin color, Olivia actualizes aspects of her life (435–436: "I also have a lot of friends who are brown . my best friend is also brown"). It becomes clear that this sequence, which is relevant to her life, does not contain any religious connotations. It deals with the topic of skin color differences in the context of interpersonal relationships and ethical perspectives.

In the dimension of ethics, Olivia's mode of speech in relation to social-worldly phenomena and interpersonal relationships shows a high degree of abstraction and thus a decentering in the sense of abandoning the egocentric and anthropocentric worldview in favor of a holistic or ecological worldview. For Olivia, the creation, and the interaction with it are in the foreground.

In the interview, it becomes apparent that interpersonal relationships have relevance for Olivia. This is also evident in the following passage, which is characterized by a focusing metaphor. In this passage, which is about what made Olivia sad the last time, she discusses the fight with her friend. Olivia was given a loft bed by her friend, which, during an argument, the friend demanded

EMPIRICAL RESEARCH RESULTS

from her to return. She says that she was surprised about the friend's behavior, because one cannot ask for a large object back. The sequence in which she discusses the argument with the friend and describes her own theories about her friend's behavior is very long, which is why only an excerpt is included here. This incident is of great concern to Olivia (304–319):

Description of the text passage: Own experiences – Text type differentiation: Narration

> Olivia: it was now like this there was . another friend of mine and /uh/ mine and my friend there . and then . and she was just somehow also on my side because she also thought that was a gift and then . she has somehow felt excluded and that has also been noticed . but . we actually did not want that // we just had other opinions and . she has probably thought that it is now here somehow // that here both are against her but that was not at all like that
>
> I: did you feel sorry for her .
>
> Olivia: yes a bit because . // I can understand her you know but . I just really thought it was a gift and . she probably did too and . yes
>
> I: mhm (11) and when you then sometime /uhm/ if you're ever in a situation where you're excluded from your friends ...
>
> Olivia: well for me that wouldn't be a real exclusion for me that would be a . discussion but then I would have just said // it doesn't matter now // and stuff like that . I wouldn't also demand it back either I would also say

Overall, this sequence is experientially close because there is a high metaphorical density here. Olivia updates aspects within her lifeworld reference. Here, too, her ability to adopt perspectives becomes clear, since she can also put herself in her friend's place. In the cross-case comparison, she does not reach far back into her horizon of experience when thematizing the incident, like the type of moral relationship but remains in the here and now. In doing so, she does not frame the story in religious terms, although God and religion had been thematized before (176–248), but she treats the topic within the framework of her ethical convictions (responsibility ethics), to which she tends to ascribe universal validity.

In summary, the reconstructive analysis shows that Olivia can actualize biographical experience in the context of interpersonal relationships, social world phenomena, and ethical values.

In this respect, the dimension of temporality can be reconstructed as being related to the present and locating the events in the worldly dimension. God, religion, and transcendence-related questions are not addressed by themselves.

Kaltrina's minimal contrast with Olivia also reveals that her practice is shaped by social references that run throughout the interview. She addresses Ali's story and her own biographical narratives within this framework. In doing so, she is reflective and puts herself in the shoes of others. A religious framing and a moral charge of her statements are not visible. Overall, it is evident that her expressions are socially anchored and that she has an urge to resolve conflicts well. The opening narrative Kaltrina offers is compelling and well thought out. Kaltrina sticks to a narrative thread and brings social processes into the action, revealing a strong capacity for abstraction and reflection.

She develops the story, adds new characters, invents a new name for Esad (Jonathan), removes Jonathan as Ali's best friend, and deliberately replaces him with a girl. However, she maintains the narrative thread (157–171):

Description of the text passage: Opening passage – Continuation of Ali's story – Text type differentiation: Narration

> Kaltrina: had nothing more to do with him then a girl came to him and said why are you crying Ali then Ali said how do you know me how do you know my name then the girl said oh I saw you once in class where the teacher called you once Ali and I think you're very great you're good at school // but I don't have a friend anymore he always holds up better than me ... then the girl said // oh come on let's play together just ignore him Ali pulled himself together again went to the playground with the girl played all day and then they wanted to study together they did and her mother of the // of the girl and Ali's father got to know each other and then they finally became best friends after a few weeks they didn't even fight anymore and Ali was so happy that he finally had a best friend ((laughs)) better than a boy and Jonathan still didn't have anything to do with /uhm/ with Ali but Jonathan was very angry that he was now

Kaltrina constructs a girl into the story and inserts a theoretical comment into her narration: "better than a boy". This own theoretical, argumentative insertion points to the relevance of gender. It turns out that Kaltrina wants

EMPIRICAL RESEARCH RESULTS   235

to change the fact that the story does not contain a girl. She introduces a girl
and inserts the explanation in a subordinate clause. She not only says that it
is nicer when there is a girl in the story, but distinctly that a girl is "better"
here. This is also made clear by the construction of Ali's father's acquaintance
with the girl's mother. Thus, it is not the fathers of the children who have met,
or the mothers, but the mother of the girl and the father of the boy. For Kaltrina,
the protagonists of her story and their relationships to each other are in the
foreground.

The girl Kaltrina weaves into the story takes over the direction and the lead
role in her story (184–188):

*Description of the text passage: Opening passage – Continuation of Ali's story –
Text type differentiation: Narration*

> Kaltrina: stuck in the cave ... the next day ... the girl had said oh he was really
> so mean if you had told me that then we would have gone somewhere else
> if only we hadn't gone into that cave Ali was crying again but the girl said
> oh just leave it we'll get out of here again Ali meant well alright but they still
> have the matches you know

The narrative line and the sequence of events are stringent and consistent.
Kaltrina listens to herself narrate and distances herself from her own narration
(320–322):

*Description of the text passage: Reflection on Ali's story without stimulus – Text
type differentiation: Description*

> Kaltrina: But that cave where You said they were like locked up then I wanted
> to do that again because then it would be a bit more exciting because I'm
> also writing an essay tomorrow.

She deliberately embellishes the cave sequence to prepare for an essay.

Kaltrina's statements on the ethical and her theoretical commentaries also
reveal a high level of reflection (281–297 and 412–417):

*Description of the text passage: Reflection on Ali's story without stimulus – Text
type differentiation: Description*

Kaltrina: And this Jonathan where I said he somehow doesn't sound like you can // well tell him everything and stuff like that because he sounds somehow so nice and not so nice at the same time ... I also have a girlfriend like that ... almost like him (4) but Ali in our school is also almost like him

I: Yes

Kaltrina: He's also good at school 's also nice has a lot of friends but he's also always got someone that's why I thought of that ((laughs)) hey ... and this girl also sounded kind of nice ... but I think Ali has to show a bad side as well because he can't always just be nice .. but somehow I couldn't express it like that in the story because that wouldn't have fit him at all and if he had a sister for example // he would have been jealous of her then it wouldn't have fit him at all somehow not like that

I: Mhm ...

Kaltrina: And Ali I find // I will rather not take him as a friend because he has good grades you can be jealous very quickly

Kaltrina: But I wonder how you can be so jealous of the others so quickly

I: Yes

Kaltrina: How does it happen so quickly ... because one in my class also has one // a boy who also always has A's and A's and I'm not jealous

Kaltrina's narrations show that she differentiates precisely between the story and reality, in maximum contrast to Betül, Mesut, and Hagen, where fantasy and reality merge. Kaltrina has a clear understanding of reality, as is also evident in Gökmen, Canan, Navid, and Olivia. She puts herself in Ali's shoes and those of his mother and switches perspectives. In doing so, she no longer enters the story, but speaks of herself. Inspired by this, her expressions on the ethical come to the surface. Here Kaltrina's capacity for abstraction and her ability to decenter become apparent. Her expressions tend to contain universal considerations (262–269):

Description of the text passage: Immanent inquiry stimulus on Ali's feelings – Text type differentiation: Description

EMPIRICAL RESEARCH RESULTS 237

> Kaltrina: ... but Ali I realize if he would be for example small right and thrown in a cave then I find it somehow fully sad if I locked myself in the cave I would have also totally cried if he would be for example my son for example I would have also completely cried .. if I would not sit in the cave ... but that would be really sad because some people are also in the hospital and because you can't see that because the woman also once had a sprain in her foot and she walked the whole way the woman told us

The sequence of events in this story suggests that for Kaltrina, social relationships and interpersonal references are paramount.

From Ali's story and his feelings, she leads independently without stimulus into her own life-historical frame of events and experiences (375–383):

Description of the text passage: Immanent inquiry stimulus on Ali's feelings – Text type differentiation: Description

> Kaltrina: And I think it's a real shame ... and whenever someone like // when someone is sick or something like that I feel very sorry for him
>
> I: Mhm
>
> Kaltrina: And And I think it is a real shame and very sad .. because my grandmother is also at the hospital
>
> I: Yes
>
> Kaltrina: And I have totally cried at home ...
>
> I: Mhm
>
> Kaltrina: Und she is still there she will remain another week ..

In these sequences, too, the thesis that Kaltrina deals with topics within the framework of social relationships is condensed, because the entire narrative or descriptive text types continuously depict social processes in which such relationships are at stake. What is striking here is the relevance of the theme of illness, which is a significant basis for relationships (527–528):

Description of the text passage: Exmanent inquiry stimulus on a biographical story – Text type differentiation: Description

> Kaltrina: But I // but I think it's a real shame when she's always sick like that or just so ... but the baby well the child that really makes the

Based on the case comparison, a common orientation framework emerges for Dilara, Filiz, Hagen, Kaltrina, Leyla, Mesut, and Olivia. They deal with the entire topic within the framework of interpersonal relationships. Their mode of speech in the dimension of ethics is differentiated with respect to social-world aspects.

The children who are ideally assigned to this type actualize the topic of friendship from their lifeworld concerning interpersonal references. The metaphorically dense passages show an orientation towards family and friends as well as their interactions and activities. For the children, the significance of Ali's story is shown in the fact that they quickly and harmonizingly resolve the situation in which Ali finds himself and transform the negative perspective into a positive one.

Gökmen updates the interaction between Ali and his friends in a metaphorically dense passage as a continuation of the opening narrative (72–85):

Description of the text passage: Opening passage – Continuation of Ali's story – Text type differentiation: Narration

> Gökmen: yes and then they went home Ali went to his mother and said may I go out with my friends other friends not the four boys /uh/ allowed his mother went to his other friends home and pick them up and then they went to the playground and played and then Ali his dad came half an hour ago said you have to go home and then Ali went home and saw the four boys and then /uh/ his dad said ask the boys what they told me and then he asked and then he said it and then Ali got in trouble and had /uhm/ had a day to no longer go out well ban and then .. one day was already and was allowed to go out and then Ali has /uh/ tattled on the four friends to his mother and then they were not allowed two days
>
> /uhm/ out and then Ali was happy and two days he was not allowed to see with them well they were only allowed to go to school and back ... on the way /uh/ and ... then had // well ... ((whispers)) finished?

EMPIRICAL RESEARCH RESULTS

Gökmen acts narratively here and can actualize the scenario from his lifeworld. He uses terms from his everyday life. In the context of current events, being locked up is not relevant for him; this situation is quickly resolved. The interaction between the children is in the foreground for him, as he relates this to his lifeworld. The thematization shows that the significance of Ali's story for Gökmen consists in the negotiation of social processes between friends or controversies.

The following passage is used to condense this thesis (177–192):

Description of the text passage: Own experiences – Text type differentiation: Narration

Gökmen: Yes /uh/ I am with my friend // he he had birthday and we are well with his mother and his dad stepdad are WE are Geiselwind

I: Mhm

Gökmen: And so we had celebrated because it was his birthday and then we did a lot of things there and the best thing was on the /uh/ way back where we went home and slept together well he sits there and I sit there and we lay down well in the middle like that that we could sleep and then /uhm/ ... and then we went home and we are still sleeping and his /uh/ /uh/ parents woke us up that ( )?

And we didn't wake up and then /uh/ they went home and left us in the car and then they /uh/ came ten minutes or so later we did like that we sleep /uh/ and then they came still sleeping they woke us up again and and we didn't get up you know and yes on the weekend I went with him garden to his garden and were in pool and and and we made water fight pistols /uhm/ and then we were in the pool .. yes

This passage makes it clear that Gökmen introduces the theme, which has biographic relevance for him, in the context of friendship and interpersonal relationships.

In the dimension of temporality, Gökmen's reference to the present can be reconstructed, for the framework in which he treats a theme in metaphorically dense passages is characterized by interpersonal interactions and references that are in the here and now. In this context, he does not deal with transcendence-related questions.

In Mesut's case, a connection to biographical elements is evident, as there is a similarity between the opening narrative and his biographical narratives

240 CHAPTER 4

(both text passages are presented below). In the opening narration to Ali's story, he includes activities with his brother and friends from his lifeworld (55–71):

Description of the text passage: Opening passage – Continuation of Ali's story – Text type differentiation: Narration

> Mesut: /uhm/ he went home did his homework studied … and then he went with his friend with his brother ((clears throat)) /uhm/ out and then … they went with friend swimming pool there was Esad and /uhm/ Ali then hid and then his brother said why are you hiding and then Ali said ((clears throat)) your Esad is there ( )? come he can't do anything to you /uhm/ they come and Esad didn't do anything /uhm/ then they had school did /uhm/ /uhm/ did Esad went to to Ali and said I'm sorry what I did and then Ali said ok and the others who did with Esad also said sorry then the teacher had // the teacher was happy and … and then Ali asked to the teacher may I sit next to Esad and then .. the teacher said ok and then have made seating arrangement and then was Ali with Esad both have sat down /uhm/ /uhm/ they have done both /uhm/ the tasks and then they have done both the homework both learned /uhm/ then they have .. have gone park have played .. with Esad and friends and have gone to eat ice cream with their mother / uhm/ and have destroyed the hut and …

In the continuation of Ali's story, Mesut describes his own brother and what he does together with his friends. When Mesut makes Esad and Ali best friends who study and do homework together, he is showing a strong need for harmonization. Mesut decides to destroy the place of fear, the hut. The place where the negative experience took place is destroyed. Here, a link between Filiz, Hagen, and Mesut emerges (257–272):

Description of the text passage: Own experiences – Text type differentiation: Narration, description

> I: Mhm tell me a story about you
>
> Mesut: /Uh/ /uh/ I I always go to to to the to the to the city with my brother ((coughs)) with my brother and … I always go out with my friends then I go to school … and then I learn I learn I go I go swimming pool few times I go i Turkey few times I go to a fun park

EMPIRICAL RESEARCH RESULTS   241

> I: mhm
>
> Mesut: Nothing more
>
> I: Mhm ... tell me something about your friends
>
> Mesut: /Uhm/ my friends are nice they help me when something happens they always call me out ... /uhm/ we always go city swimming pool ... /uh/ ... they are they ar qui quite nice .. they we go phone calling and say that you for example eat ice cream city or out or /uh/
>
> I: Mhm
>
> Mesut: Or to you to me and /uh/ and /uh/ that to swimming pool further I do not know

Mesut thematizes the interaction between the protagonists, which runs through the entire interview. For him, the interaction between the children is probably in the foreground, since he relates it to his own lifeworld, and not the dangerous situation Ali found himself in. He also quickly resolves this situation of danger. Filiz slips out of the structure of the stimulus whenever she can attach lifeworldly aspects to the story. This shows that the narrative becomes denser and thus the significance of the story becomes clear to her after she has brought it to a harmonious end and begins to construct the children as friends (37–48):

Description of the text passage: Opening passage – Continuation of Ali's story – Text type differentiation: Narration

> Filiz: .. and then all four of them had played with Ali at recess and were friends together ... and then all five of them had always played together and exchanged lunch snacks /uhm/ brought each other home and always laughed ... and always watched videos or movies at a house of their friends .. and always laughed there .. and they always went to the playground and played there ... and then they always went to this old hut and had picnics in there when it was very hot outside (19) and they still read something at the library and did their homework together ... and then they always went back to playing and watching movies in front of the computer ... have also made walks ( )? ... and then they were always friends

In minimal contrast to Dilara, Hagen, Mesut, Leyla, Navid, and Kaltrina, Filiz also resolves the situation in a harmonizing way. The conflict resolution strategy of these children consists of transforming the negative perspective given in the story into a positive one.

In Navid's case, Ali's story has meaning for him in the context of the interview situation and at the time of the interview in the context of his own family situation. The story has no meaning in the context of danger or a threatening situation. In response to the immanent inquiry stimulus to talk about Ali, Navid weaves aspects from his own lifeworld into the narrative, which concern his preferences for fireworks and his scientific, mathematical, and artistic abilities. The immanent case comparison shows that Navid reinvents Ali's family and thereby actualizes his own family, but constructs it the way he wants it to be (128–154):

Description of the text passage: Immanent inquiry stimulus on the story of Ali – Text type differentiation: Description

Navid: Well Ali had ha had a good family . who are not rich but also are not poor . so a very normal family . his father had the profession as a cab driver and he had and he had a brother and a sister . his brother was already in grammar school his sister was in the third grade . and his brother played with sometimes also with Ali . with Ali and also with his sister ... sometimes they also went into the forest and climb also on trees ... and sometimes they also played hide and seek in the forest ... and . Ali mostly volunteered to count and it was also a lot of fun for them ... when it starts to get evening then the mother brings in her / the three children to eat ... they mostly ate . they mostly ate .. chicken . a baked chicken it also tasted good to the family . and it was also enough . each had their own room .. and at eight o'clock all three went to sleep all three went to sleep ... Ali's favorite food is . Ali's favorite food is baked chicken and his favorite drink is apple spritzer .... Ali got mostly A's in his tests ... in math he got only A's ... not even a B ... in German he got a few B's ... in HSU too ... in music he was very good ... in art he could draw very creative pictures ... ((thinking)) (5) in HSU he was good at experiments ... Ali was 1.55 m tall ... his sister was one meter one meter 1.49 m tall ... his brother was ... 1.70 m tall ... ((thinking)) (10) Ali and his siblings like fireworks very much they loved it and watched the exploding rockets every New Year's Eve ... it looked beautiful to them ... the best time was / the best firework was in 2005 ... there was a huge fireworks display that tha that all three found very beautiful ... Ali is 10 years old . he is blond . has blue eyes . and went to the fourth grade (5)

EMPIRICAL RESEARCH RESULTS

Navid leaves the given narrative context and reinvents Ali's family. This meta-phorically dense passage suggests that he is updating events and experiences from his lifeworld. He begins with the expression "Ali had a very normal family" and then begins to paint this picture of the "normal family" in detail. He describes meticulously everything Ali likes. He invents a brother and a sister for Ali, just as he himself has an older brother and a younger sister. He brings up the subject of his older brother, who is autistic, even before the interview begins.

He may therefore be constructing a "normal" family for Ali. The school performance, which he discusses, is also very important to him. In addition, he talks about Ali's love of fireworks, which also applies to him, as the following passages show (183–195 and 244–257):

Description of the text passage: Immanent inquiry stimulus on the story of Ali – Text type differentiation: Description

I: What did you like most

Navid: thing that Ali writes good grades . but I also very good grades and never wrote a B in math . in the fourth grade . only A's . and my teacher Mrs. Schmidt said I will be her substitute teacher in math

I: Great

Navid: I think in math I am the best student in the class ... and it has never happened in the fourth grade that I have ever written a C ... only A's and B's but mostly A's

I: Great

Navid: and half year report card there was music there / in P.E. I got a B in WTG I got a B and I think also art . and otherwise I have everywhere A's

Navid: well ... and ... I go ma I have also children's fireworks in the last New Year's Eve there I bought a fireworks package there were 230 firecrackers or 320 ... there were very many . there I stayed with my there I stayed with my friend he had like / lit a firework that flew into the air and banged against a house and fell down again

I: ((laughing)) aha

> Navid: and I was even allowed to light rockets alone
>
> I: ah yes
>
> Navid: mhm nothing went wrong .. and once there . I lit a firecracker that fell into my jacket pocket but luckily nothing happened . nothing broke . and it didn't hurt at all ... and children's fireworks I also like (8) well .. do not know what I can still say ...

It turns out that the stimulus aimed at activating thinking about and praying to God in a threatening situation has no biographical significance for Navid. He quickly resolves the situation and actualizes his own relevances to Ali's story. His mode of speech exhibits anthropocentric thinking regarding reflexivity or perspective-taking.

In the dimension of ethics, Navid's narrations document, in minimal contrast to Dilara, Filiz, Hagen, Leyla, and Kaltrina, the need to resolve conflicts quickly (need for harmonization). However, in maximum contrast to Dilara, Hagen, and Leyla, this does not show any highly moral behavior that is actualized. No topics within the framework of normative beliefs or moral requirements are addressed.

6.2.4.1 *Summary*

In summary, the comparative analysis shows that for the children who are assigned to the type of relating in a distance from God, thoughts of God play no role in the continuation of Ali's story. These children can actualize biographical experience, but only within the framework of friendship, family, and harmony. They do not connect their practical experiences with difficult life events at the religious level.

In the dimension of perspectivity, children who are assigned to the type of God-distant relationship show a reference distant from God, which is referential, weak, schematic, and standardized. They offer immanent and inner-worldly possibilities for the resolution of difficult life events. It turns out that they can differentiate clearly between fantasy and reality.

In the dimension of perspectivity, the children's narratives document an anthropocentric position, in the sense that people and their needs are placed in the center, together with a materialistic argumentation, in the sense that they explain the world and the processes taking place in it without spiritual or immaterial elements. From the interpretation of the interview, it can be concluded that in the interview situation an individual responsiveness for

EMPIRICAL RESEARCH RESULTS   245

religious questions or a principal accessibility for transcendent self- and world-interpretations is neither shown on an explicit nor on an implicit level.

In the dimension of ethics, a strong need for harmonization is documented in the statements of these children. Their expressions on the ethical are not framed in religious terms. At the same time, they show decentered thinking regarding interpersonal interactions and relationships. In the dimension of temporality, a relation to the present can be reconstructed, because the framework in which these children deal with a topic in metaphorically dense passages is characterized by interpersonal interactions that are in the here and now. In doing so, they do not deal with transcendence-related questions.

7   Summary: Types of Relations to God among Muslim Children

The children's way of relating to God and to religion shows a broad spectrum, ranging from a strong relation to God (type A), a strong relation to tradition (type B), to a lack of any relation to both variables (type C).

The material shows that in the type of personalizing as well as of moral relationship, a relation to God becomes visible. The type of God-distant relationship, despite its formal religious socialization, shows no relation to God.

The different forms of self-relating and the relations to God and to tradition as well as distance to God have different consequences for the construction of God, for world- and self-interpretations, for ethical dimensions, for religious practice, and for anthropological aspects. The specifics of the individual types are now presented and summarized.

7.1   *God as Responsive Reality and/or Social Reality*

The personal relationship type and the moral relationship type show a religious connotation and framing in the context of the interview situation and the introductory narrative. Religion is addressed in the context of rituals such as prayer, supplication, and fasting. This reveals a practice of action that can be traced back to a conjunctive experiential space. The corresponding conjunctive, atheoretical knowledge is "closely linked to the specific practice of people in their biographies and milieus" (Nohl, 2012, p. 5). Here it is confirmed that the relation to God or to religious practice is not to be understood as the product of an isolated human being but develops in fundamental social practice. For the children who are ideally assigned to these types, it becomes particularly clear that they possess "these contents in the way of the existential community, a way which is wholly concrete and perspectivistic and which can only be shared conjunctivlely" (Mannheim, 1997, p. 265).

For the personal relationship type, God is a reality in person like other persons, i.e., a responsive reality. This relating is based on everyday life experiences. For this type, God is a 'you' whose existence is not doubted. It can be seen that this type addresses social-worldly and interpersonal phenomena with a high degree of abstraction and thereby establishes relations to God. Here, turning to God from a positive perspective, or out of need, is a transcendence-related contingency coping strategy.

On the other hand, the God-distant relationship type regards God as a social construction. For this type, God exists only as an element of social reality. This type accepts that the environment speaks about God and can adopt this way of speaking when necessary. For this type, God may even be an imaginary construct, i.e., God belongs to the realm of stories, fairy tales, and dreams, that is, to the realm of fantasy.

This type of God-distant relationship only becomes visible when there is no direct question about God. If directly asked about God, the great majority of the children of this type could be expected to speak of God in a way that would presumably assign them to the moral relationship type. This type not only is empirically invisible when directly asked about God, but also theoretically invisible if a stage model is applied. If it is implicitly assumed in such schemes that every human being is religious and an areligious person is empirically asked about God on the basis of such an assumption, s/he become the very Other who is methodically and theoretically invisible (cf. Chapter 2, Section 1.4).

The moral relationship type fluctuates back and forth between a self-relating to God as a responsive reality and a self-relating to God as a social reality. Here, God is the creator of a reward-penalty system. The material demonstrates that this type concentrates on the system, rather than on the creator. God as a 'you' disappears, so to speak, into tradition which, in turn, shows itself as a strongly moralizing system.

7.2   *Transcendence-Related and Immanence-Related World- and Self-Interpretations*

Depending on the construction of God as a responsive reality or a social reality, different world- and self-interpretations appear in the types that can either be described as immanent, intra-worldly, anthropological, or as transcendent, extra-worldly, quasi-magical.

The personal relationship type shows a fundamental accessibility to both immanent and transcendent self- and world-interpretations that are based on experience. They play an action-guiding role in certain situations. At the same time, an individual responsiveness to religious questions becomes apparent in which religious patterns of interpretation are actively received. The moral

EMPIRICAL RESEARCH RESULTS

relationship type shows a fundamental accessibility to transcendent self- and world-interpretations, but this accessibility is presented by the children due to their orientation towards the socially expected, i.e., there is no independent, action-guiding reference to transcendence.

The God-distant relationship type does not display transcendence-related, but rather immanent, rational, and worldly self-interpretations. There is neither an active nor a passive reception of religious patterns of interpretation. This type is characterized by the absence of a reference to transcendence as well as by a reference to the present and a focus on interpersonal interactions and relations.

7.3 Ethics of Conviction and Ethics of Responsibility

The narrations document that the children justified ethical decisions by referring to a convictional-ethical or responsible-ethical maxim in a Weberian sense (Weber, 2008).

Both forms of ethics are based on responsibility. This responsibility must meet two criteria: objectivity and compatibility with one's own conviction and attitude (Honecker, 1990, p. 16). The personal relationship type addresses responsibility from both perspectives. Thus, this type takes responsibility for other lives, on the one hand out of religious conscience, on the other hand with regard to the morally justifiable success of the action.

The tendency shows that the moral relationship type deals with responsibility more from a convictional-ethical perspective that is linked to the orientation towards tradition and the socially expected. From this point of view, rules are followed based on the assumption that the right action is taken per se, regardless of the outcome. This is one of the most important findings of this study, because it shows that a religious convictional-pedagogy does not necessarily lead to establishing a relation to God. Practicing rituals and propositional knowledge do not result in the children actively relating to God. Religious knowledge, therefore, does not necessarily result in children also acting religiously. It is difficult for this type to build a relation to God that goes beyond a formulaic and moral religiosity.

The type of God-distant relationship, on the other hand, shows no convictional-ethics. For this type, the point of reference of a social action is its intended morally justifying success. Here, it becomes manifest that responsibility is not based on religious attitude.

7.4 The Question of Relation Orientation (Anthropological Level)

With regard to the actions under the ethical maxims of conviction and/ or responsibility, the reference to the social level also becomes evident. The reference to the level of the social does not represent an antithesis to the relation to God. The God-distant relationship type lacks a relation to God. A clear reference to the level of the social can be noticed. In this type, the transcendence orientation is replaced by a social relation orientation. The material shows a strong emphasis on the topics of friendship, harmony, play, and fun. The children's engagement is located on the relationship level. This type is characterized by an orientation towards this world as well as an immanent interpretation of the world.

The personal relationship type also articulates social-worldly and interpersonal phenomena with a high degree of abstraction but establishes relations to God while doing so. Thus, the social level is religiously framed. It can be seen that the character of the relation orientation is different. The material clearly shows that the children's relation orientation and their orientation towards God play an important role in dealing with the topic of fear.

7.5   *The Question of Practice, which Becomes Visible*

The material demonstrates that religious practice is an independent variable. The difference between a reference to religious practice and a relation to God is evident.

The personal relationship type shows an action-guiding reference to both levels. An emotional closeness to God and to religious practice, but also to immanent world and self-interpretations can be seen.

The moral relationship type is interested in practice, has propositional knowledge, and can reproduce traditional knowledge. The type is characterized by knowing verses from the Qur'an by heart as well as by theoretically understanding when and where to use them. Religious reference tends to emerge from an instrumental intention. This means that often a quasi-magical approach to religion becomes apparent in order to achieve something through religious practice, i.e., the fulfillment of wishes or protection against fear and nightmares. In this type, the relevance that is assigned to God is very strongly fed by this intention. Here, religion is strongly connected with religious practice such as prayer. An active reference to practice and tradition could be reconstructed, but no action-guiding relation to God beyond practice or even further.

The God-distant relationship type can also reflect a minimum of religious knowledge about God and religious practice. However, no action-guiding relation to God or to religion exists, neither autonomously nor through religious tradition. All in all, there is an intellectual distance to both levels, but no emotional closeness.

EMPIRICAL RESEARCH RESULTS

7.6 Occupation with Theology-Relevant Questions

The material shows that the children actively deal with theology-relevant questions. Some, for example, consider the question of what may happen if God does not fulfill their wishes. From their initially purposively rational thinking in relation to God, it emerges that they become aware of the limits of this type of thinking so that they finally conclude God's unavailability. They come to the conclusion that purposively rational thinking towards God does not lead anywhere.

In summary, the material demonstrates that children use different ways of dealing with reality. This empirical research has made it possible to reconstruct the children's constructions of reality as well as their attributions of meaning. It becomes clear that a complete picture can only be drawn by assessing the two dimensions of faith in God, i.e., the cognitive as well as the emotional dimensions. The God-distant relationship type only becomes visible if one starts from the children's systems of reference and does not directly ask about God.

Notes

1   The dimension of perspectivity describes the way in which children present God, their relationship to him as well as, where appropriate, their speaking to him, and about him in the interviews.
2   The dimension of ethics describes the way in which morality, divine commandments, and everyday ethics are presented by the children in the interviews.
3   The dimension of temporality describes the way in which the children portray questions of temporality, of this world and the hereafter – i.e., 'time' and 'eternity' – in the interviews.
4   Here, a difference exists in relation to the connection between deeds and consequences in which the cause of the misfortune suffered is sought in one's own religious or moral misconduct.
5   The term 'egocentric' is not associated with any assessment, since 'childlike egocentrism' is a psychological technical term. The word combination 'childlike-egocentric' means that, according to developmental psychological findings, this perspective is not surprising at this age.
6   The type illustration is based on the type illustration in the work of Julia Franz (2016).
7   The definition of the ethical modes of conviction and responsibility (*Gesinnungsethik/ Verantwortungsethik*) which are used in the following are presented in Max Weber's essay "Politics as a Vocation" (Weber, 2008).
8   During the narrative prompt, which was provided by the Kamishibai narrative theater, the four children who locked Ali in the hut were represented as a mixed-gender group by small wooden puppets. There were two boys and two girls visually identifiable. It is possible that Hagen and Kaltrina picked up on this visual prompt and thereby incorporated girls into their story.
9   *āḏān*: Call to prayer. Hereby, the caller to prayer in the mosque calls for communal prayer five times a day.

10 *du'ā'*: supplication.

11 *namaz*: Ritual obligatory prayer.

12 From a theological point of view, aspects of faith practice become clear here, divided into the areas of acts of worship (*'ibādāt*) and interpersonal acts (*mu'āmalāt*). These realms serve different purposes in the theological context and represent a path to God. In Leyla's case, it can be seen that she implicitly assumes that through acts of worship she can ensure that such events will no longer happen. In the area of interpersonal actions, it is also evident that she feels activated to meet people positively in order to positively face such catastrophes through her own actions and to influence or ward them off.

13 This reflects an element of Muslim faith, that faith practice and faith are closely related.

14 It is part of Islamic-influenced cultures to know the so-called protective verses 113 and 114 by heart and to recite them as protection. Children are often recited the protective verses before going to bed or they recite them there themselves. These verses are about taking refuge in God from all evil.

15 Hadith refers to the reports of sayings, orders and actions of the Prophet Muhammad, the transmission of which is traced back to his companions.

16 In the Qur'an, this is called *ḥalīfa* (deputy, successor).

17 In the 'do ut des' context ('I give so you may give'), the cause of the misfortune suffered is sought in one's own religious or moral misconduct. Here there is a difference to the 'do ut des' context, which is about acting with God and the claim to be able to influence him through religious performance.

18 Defamation is strongly condemned in the Islamic sources Qur'an and Hadith as it portrays a violation of human dignity. In these sources, reference is made to the consequences of this act. Points of reference are the immorality of the act as well as its moral consequences. Ethical responsibility in this area is thus based on two criteria: on the one hand, the criterion of the compatibility of the defamatory act with one's own convictions of conscience and on the other hand, the criterion of being morally responsible for the consequences of one's own actions.

19 *Ṯawāb* is the Arabic term for 'reward'. From an Islamic theological perspective, *ṯawāb* refers to a reward that results from good deeds and piety.

20 *Günah* is an original Persian term for 'sin' that is common in Turkish religious language usage. In contemporary Islamic theology, sin is often understood as a crisis. It should be dealt with either by changing the person's behavior or by changing his situation.

21 A narrative perspective in which the narrator reports in an overviewing but not participatory manner.

22 This corresponds to a central message of the Qur'an, which 'Alī Ibn Abī Ṭālib (Cousin and son-in-law of the Prophet Mohammed who became the fourth caliph after his death) summarized in one sentence: "People sleep, and when they die, they awaken". In the Qur'an, the focus is often on the aspect that man is temporarily released by God into the world with the promise of returning to him.

23 In the Qur'an, the angel of death, who is called 'Azrā'īl in the Islamic tradition, is discussed in 32:11. He has the task of receiving the soul of the human being at the moment of death.

24 This understanding of God is also stated in an *ḥadīṯ qudsī* (a tradition of the Prophet, which, however, at the same time contains a word of God), which says: "On the authority of Abū Hurayrah (may Allah be pleased with him), who said that the Prophet said: 'Allah the Almighty said: I am as My servant thinks I am. I am with him when he makes mention of Me. If he makes mention of Me to himself, I make mention of him to Myself; and if he makes mention of Me in an assembly, I make mention of him in an assembly better than it. And if he draws near to Me an arm's length, I draw near to him a cubit, and if he draws near to Me

EMPIRICAL RESEARCH RESULTS

251

a cubit, I draw near to him a fathom. And if he comes to Me walking, I go to him at speed'. It was related by al-Buhkari (also by Muslim, at-Tirmidhi and Ibn-Majah)" (Ibrahim & Johnson-Davies, 1997, p. 78). The notion of a God who subjectivizes himself to the human counterpart tends to appear in mystical thought, although this hadith is theologically significant.

25 This determination of the relationship between man and God is referred to in the Qur'an as the relationship between *rabb* and *ʿabd*. Here, *ʿabd* is the one who receives God's care.

26 The consciousness of fault as a good deed can be traced back theologically to a well-known saying of Muhammad: "Actions are [measured] only according to intentions, and each person is entitled only to that which corresponds to his intention" (Schöller, 2007, p. 13).

27 Sura *an-Nās* (The People) is one of the two frequently recited verses of refuge in the Qur'an that ask for God's protection.

28 This formula is considered an essential part of worship. Muslims often use this expression in conversation with others when they want to refrain from envy, jealousy, pride, and haughtiness.

29 According to Mannheim (1980, 1997), every social frame of reference is shaped by a bundle of social, cultural, and linguistic patterns that make up a conjunctive experiential space (cf. Chapter 2, Section 2.3). In Qamar's case, this experiential space is shaped by Shi'ism. The relevant marker is the mention of the Imams. The Imams have a special position in the Shi'ite tradition.

30 The *basmala* (*bismi llāhi r-raḥmāni r-raḥīm* = In the name of God, the All-beneficent, the All-merciful) is pronounced by Muslims before many activities, e.g., before eating or travelling, to remind themselves of the constant presence of God. All chapters in the Qur'an, except for the 9th chapter, begin with these words.

CHAPTER 5

Discussion of the Research Results

1 Discussion of the Research Results in the Educational Context

The discussion of the results from an educational science perspective focuses on the fields of development, socialization, and education that are central topics of educational science.

In the following, five central results of the present study are outlined which show the contribution of this study to the scientific discussion with reference to classical and current developmental psychology and religious sociology studies.

1.1 *There Is No Homogeneous Relation to God – Children Believe in Different Ways*

The results of this study clearly demonstrate that the children in the sample show a strong heterogeneity regarding their relations to God. This heterogeneity is considerably greater than current developmental psychological stage theories as well as studies such as the Shell Youth Study[1] suggest; both assuming a relatively high degree of homogeneity among Muslim children and adolescents. The World Vision Children's Studies (World Vision Deutschland e.V., 2010), also present Muslim children as particularly religious, especially with regard to the importance of religion, belief in God, and prayer (references in: Pirner, 2012a, pp. 241–242). The sample in this study, however, shows a differentiation of various religious attitudes among children at the age of about ten years. The children's relations to God and to religion show a broad spectrum, ranging from a strong relation to God (personal relationship, Chapter 4, Section 4) to a strong relation to tradition (moral relationship, Chapter 4, Section 5) to a substantial lack of any relation to both variables (God-distant relationship, Chapter 4, Section 6).

The personal relationship type is characterized by turning to God as a 'you' whose existence is not questioned (cf. Chapter 4, Section 4.2). The moral relationship type is dominated by a religious socialization focused on tradition which makes it visibly difficult for the children of this type to establish an independent relationship to God (cf. Chapter 4, Section 5.2). God-distant relationship is shaped by the fact that one's own lifeworld is neither related to any religious level nor to God (cf. Chapter 4, Section 6.2). Although religious education in family and school is recognizably similar, the children in the sample

© FAHIMAH ULFAT, 2023 | DOI:10.1163/9789004533219_005

DISCUSSION OF THE RESEARCH RESULTS

already show different approaches to religious belief at their age and developmental stage, depending on their life experiences and individual decisions.

The data material demonstrates that the children in the sample, who are at about the same stage of development in terms of developmental psychology and age, show three distinctly different religious attitudes which clearly cannot be attributed to their stage of development. With regard to the religious education studies work with young Muslims, it can be deduced from these findings that it makes more sense and corresponds more closely to the inner reality of the children's lives not to work exclusively with diachronic stage models; likewise, models should be used that start from the synchronous differentiation of different stable forms of acquisition of religious knowledge (cf. Chapter 2, Section 1).

Muslim children are thus able to think independently about various topics that lead to autonomous theological and philosophical views. They can therefore feel and think in a highly individual way.

In summary, the present study shows that a homogeneous relation to God does not exist, but rather that even within religious traditions a strong heterogeneity of relations to God does prevail. These results, in turn, shed an interesting light on a number of classical stage models of developmental psychology which are discussed below.

1.2 Relation to God as a Process of Active Co-Construction instead of Passive Development

The core idea of Fowler's stage scheme, which he developed in 1974, is based on the assumption that people's beliefs depend on their cognitive development (for Fowler's theory cf. Chapter 2, Section 1.3). In the reconstructed ideal types we simultaneously find facets of Fowler's stages of "mythical-literal faith", "synthetic-conventional faith", and "individuative-reflective faith". For example, a consciousness of one's own self-determination – albeit unreflected – which corresponds to the level of Fowler's "individuative-reflective faith" (Fowler, 2000, pp. 200–202; cf. also Chapter 4, Section 4.2 and 6.3) becomes apparent in the personal relationship type as well as in the type of God-distant relationship. The moral relationship type reveals facets of "mythical-literal faith" as well as of "synthetic-conventional faith" (Fowler, 2000, pp. 191–193; cf. also Chapter 4, Section 5.2).

In summary, the comparison demonstrates that Fowler's characterization of development as a sequence of stages presents itself as a *relatively stable*, simultaneous differentiation in this research study. *Relatively stable* does not mean that the children will have this mindset for the rest of their lives, but that different forms of relations to God and religion evidently do exist at the same time that cannot be represented as stages of a development model. Fowler's stage model is based on the assumption that over the course of a development process, one stage inevitably leads to the next. The present research, however, shows that different stages can emerge at the same age (cf. Groms' criticism of Fowler in Chapter 2, Section 1.3); they are manifestations that are partly similar to Fowler's stages, but are more transverse to them.

As far as the stage model of the development of religious judgement according to Oser and Gmünder is concerned, the present study highlights that the ideal types also show different facets of different stages of development although the children of the sample are of the same age (for Oser's and Gmünder's theory cf. Chapter 2, Section 1.4). The moral relationship type reveals facets of stage 2, in which God is seen as omnipotent but can be influenced by religious efforts (cf. Chapter 4, Section 5.2). The personal relationship type shows facets of stage 3, in which God represents his own greatness but the individual action of the human being and their autonomy have their own status. Here there is an interactive connection between the ultimate being and the human being (cf. Chapter 4, Section 4.2).

However, the God-distant relationship type has no equivalent neither in Fowler's nor in Osers' or Gmünders' stage model. This is not surprising given the methodological reasons. In this study, children were not directly asked about God. Rather it was left to the children themselves to express religious subjects according to their own personal relevance. Thus, the God-distant relationship type focuses exclusively on interpersonal interactions and references and offers only inner-worldly interpretations and understandings of transcendent phenomena (cf. Chapter 4, Section 6.2 and 6.3).

In accordance with the results of the studies by Szagun (2014), Ritter et al. (2006), Eckerle (2008), Orth and Hanisch (1998), Klein (2000), Flöter (2006) and Zimmermann (2012) (cf. Chapter 2, Section 1.5 and 1.6), the results of the present study show that the development of individual beliefs and religious viewpoints is certainly based on the cognitive and emotional maturation processes of childhood and adolescence, as described by Fowler and Oser and Gmünder. However, it does not merge into these stages which are rather stages of the development of the theological ability to reflect. Instead, the children's individual beliefs and religious viewpoints develop – so to speak – transversely to them, driven by the active searching of the individual who seeks answers to their biographical and social as well as theological challenges. In this process, individual concepts of God are developed which are interwoven with the social and biographical contexts of the individual. Thus, a kind of pluralism of relations to God develops that is transverse to the stage models.

It is of course problematic to compare a cross-sectional study such as the present one with longitudinal studies and structural genetic stage models. However, the opposite horizon of studies such as those by Tressat (2011),

DISCUSSION OF THE RESEARCH RESULTS   255

Karakaşoğlu-Aydın (2000), Klinkhammer (2000), Tietze (2001), Gerlach (2006) and many more can be useful. Similarly, the ideal-typical reconstructions from the available data material prove that even at the age mentioned, differentiated and relatively stable attitudes and viewpoints can be found. Thus, the results of the present study correspond to religious-sociological studies on adolescent and young adult Muslims (cf. Chapter 1, Section 1.2).

The results show that the previous discourse on religious education, both on the Christian side as well as in Islamic religious education studies, can no longer only be based on models of maturity. It should at least be additionally assumed that there are processes of subject-oriented co-constructions that lead to different, simultaneous, relatively stable attitudes. For religious education it means that one group of students can be strongly heterogeneous, if their relation to God is strongly heterogeneous as well.

1.3   Children with an Individual and Mature Relation to God that Allows for a Reflexive Relation to Religious and Non-Religious Worlds

The present study highlights the fact that children of the personal relationship type already develop elements of a relation to God at the age of about ten that is based on but not determined by tradition (in contrast to the moral relationship type). Here, an individual engagement with the interpretation of the world and the human from an Islamic perspective becomes evident (cf. Chapter 4, Section 4.2). Following religious-sociological studies with adolescent and young adult Muslims (cf. Nökel, 2007, Gerlach, 2006; Tressat, 2011; Karakaşoğlu-Aydın, 2000; Klinkhammer, 2000; Tietze, 2001), it becomes clear that this type is capable of autonomously framing religiosity in a highly individualized and pluralistic society (cf. also Szagun's argument that children are "theologically and philosophically competent and productive subjects" in Chapter 2, Section 1.5; Szagun & Fiedler, 2008, pp. 458–459).

For example, Gerlach could demonstrate that many Muslim youths do not see any contradiction in being pious believers and active co-creators of a democratic state simultaneously (cf. Chapter 1, Section 1.2; Gerlach, 2006, p. 210). This tendency is also described by other scientists such as Ammann (2004), Grillo and Soares (2005) and Nökel (2007).

In the context of the present study, it is particularly relevant that the young Muslims interviewed by Gerlach live according to Muslim orthopraxy out of inner conviction, but not because they are integrated into authoritarian structures. The rules young people face in Muslim autocratic societies do not matter to them; they weigh up, assess, and choose for themselves. They make their *own* decisions in reflective distance to their upbringing and socialization. This reveals similarities to the attitudes of the children in the sample of the present study, albeit with age-related differences. Particularly the children of the types of personal relationship and God-distant relationship show that they already shape themselves – even if unreflected – as autonomous, acting subjects at an early age (cf. Chapter 4, Section 4.2 and 6.3).

This finding has also been confirmed by other researchers. Michael Tressat, who reconstructed the biographical significance of Muslim religiosity from the perspective of Muslim youth, emphasizes "that these patterns must be understood as an expression of an individualized and individuated Islam which in each case produces its own forms of Muslim religiosity" (Tressat, 2011, p. 16).[2]

Nikola Tietze who has researched forms of Muslim religiosity among young men in difficult social, economic, and political situations in Germany and France gives a similar description and characterizes Muslim religiosity in modernity as a religiosity in "the mode of subjectivation". Tietze explains that subjectivation is to be understood as a process "in which a person on the one hand distances themselves from their own social experiences and on the other hand chooses between different principles of action or combines them" (Tietze, 2001, pp. 7–8). Similar to the present study, Tietze's research also shows that although an identification with Islamic tradition takes place, tradition nevertheless is reconstructed in order to provide meaning in the biographical and social situation of the individual (cf. Chapter 4, Section 4.2). This results in an individualized identification with Islam that is compatible with modernity.[3]

The personal relationship type reinforces the thesis which Tietze also advocates (Tietze, 2001, pp. 7–8): religiosity or the relationship to religion and to God depends on the subjective relationship of the individual to her/his biographical and social situation (cf. Chapter 4, Section 4.2).

Similar to the present work, the above studies also show that the reconstruction and subjectivation achievements by which young Muslims acquire Islam and Islamic tradition can be understood as an expression of the challenges of modernity or late modernity, but also as an answer to them.

It is the personal relationship type that, at its core, allows for flexibility in religious thought and action. This finding is supported and confirmed by the above-mentioned studies.

How this flexibility develops biographically cannot be evaluated due to the methodological approach of the present study. Other studies, such as Bochinger et al. (2009), provide evidence that the practice of this flexibility in religious socialization is also a special resource in adulthood. The authors, like Tietze, describe a "subjectivation" of religiosity in "late modern" times. Here, a detachment of "religiosity" from the "objective side"[4] of religion occurs so that a "subjective side" emerges. According to Bochinger et al., the late modern general framework of secularization and individualization make this process possible. Secularization is a necessary prerequisite here for the freedom of subjective

DISCUSSION OF THE RESEARCH RESULTS

adaption of spiritual contents. Individualization is the necessary precondition for the idea of "self-empowerment of the religious subject" (Bochinger et al., 2009; cf. also Chapter 1, Section 1.2).

In summary, the present study demonstrates that there are children whose relation to God enables them to connect to religious worlds as well as to secular worlds and modernity. This finding is particularly important for Islamic religious education studies in view of the widespread prejudices in public discourses that Islam as a whole has no connection to modernity.

This raises the question as to which events and characteristics arise that enable the children from the present study as well as the young people from the studies of Gerlach, Tietze, Tressat, and others to make their faith compatible with the secular world.

Furthermore, didactics of religious education face the task of supporting the autonomy of the religious subject and enabling children to make their religiosity compatible with the secular world and modernity.

1.4   Children with a Tradition-Dominated Relation to God that does not Allow for a Reflexive Relation to Non-Religious Worlds

The results of the present study highlight the fact that a moralizing, dichotomizing perspective of God prevails among children of the moral relationship type. This type shows no inner relation to God as a 'you' which constitutes the core of the personal relationship type. Thus, relation to God in the moral relationship type manifests itself as a moral shell (cf. Chapter 4, Section 5.2). This difference shows a clear proximity to Gordon Allport's (1967) difference between "intrinsic" (convinced) and "extrinsic" (benefit-oriented) religiosity (Allport & Ross, 1967). Allport assumes that there is an intrinsic religious motivation when religion determines a person's experience and behavior: "Having embraced a creed the individual endeavors to internalize it and follow it fully. It is in this sense that he lives his religion" (Allport & Ross, 1967, p. 434). Otherwise, Allport postulates an extrinsic religious motivation, meaning that the motives are instead non-religious, such as security, sociality, self-justification, etc. (Allport & Ross, 1967, p. 434). The moral relationship type shows clear parallels to this extrinsic form.

An individual interaction with religious-traditional socialization is atypical here. This type displays a high degree of propositional knowledge about Islam and knows traditional religious narratives. However, the response strategies show that the connection made to religion often mirrors social aspirations (cf. Chapter 4, Section 5.2). It could be reconstructed that this type interprets life situations from a religious point of view based on the knowledge drawn from the cultural system, but that these interpretations do not determine their own actions. This means that in certain social situations this type can refer back to what has been handed down, but it does reproduce the heard and learned for the sake of social expectation and not because it uses tradition as something substantial in itself. This type has difficulties in establishing a relation to God that goes beyond a purely formulaic and moral religiosity. The research results show a religious socialization in tradition, but no interaction with it (cf. Chapter 4, Section 5.2).

The present results thus illustrate that this tradition-dominated relation to God does not offer any resource for connecting to non-religious worlds.

For methodological reasons, the emergence of a reference to tradition and the causes of the lack of subject autonomy cannot be researched any further here. More details are provided by other studies, such as those by Tressat (2011) who described comparable attitudes.

The "pragmatic-functional pattern" that Tressat (2011, p. 125) describes shows parallels to the moral relationship type. According to him, this type originates from an unmodified continuation of parental religiosity. Here, tradition is not questioned, but simply adopted as is also the case for the moral relationship type. Tressat describes how the religious identity of the family is individualized only in the course of adolescent conflicts and thus adapted to individual ideas of religiosity in one's life plan (Tressat, 2011, pp. 128–131).

For this type, social perception as a Muslim is the main concern, but not an internalized religious practice (Tressat, 2011, pp. 128–131). The aspect of affiliation plays an essential role. In contrast to the aspect of subject autonomy, a non-individualized religiosity is typical here. This leads to a lack of subjective adaption of religious tradition and thus, according to Tressat, to an inability to connect to the secular world. The answers given from the perspective of social desirability of the type of moral relationship indicate that for him religiosity is reduced to the motive of affiliation to one's own religious community (cf. Chapter 4, Section 5.2). This is also presented in detail by Tressat whose "statically ambivalent pattern" is characterized by an unproductive usage of religiosity as a resource for biographical development tasks which has not been individualized during adolescence. But religiosity creates a feeling of essential affiliation to the Muslim community. According to Tressat this form of religiosity thus has an "ambivalent meaning" and a "passive effectiveness" (Tressat, 2011, pp. 131–132).

Similar to the present study, Tietze (2001) was also able to show that her second type "Islam as a community of remembrance and affiliation to a group" emphasizes affiliation to Islam and that "religious practice has a rather mechanical character" (Tietze, 2001, p. 158). Furthermore, her fourth type "Islam as part of social identity" displays facets of moral relationship, since religiosity is "culturalized". It becomes a part of culture, and affiliation to this culture is subsequently also determined by religion (cf. Chapter 4, Section 5.2).

DISCUSSION OF THE RESEARCH RESULTS

Religious practice promotes "integration into a certain milieu" (Tietze, 2001, p. 159) which is often a 'national religion'.

The present study, like those of Tietze and Tressat, documents that the moral relationship type satisfies a social reference horizon. For this type, rituals predominantly represent a social marker that underlines the affiliation to the Muslim community (cf. Chapter 4, Section 5.2).

The aspect of affiliation is also important regarding protection and prevention against forms of radicalization. The moral relationship type demonstrates the importance of being part of and having a place within a religious system that is represented by the horizon of social reference. If this space is denied and religious didactics does not offer any possibility of constructing this space of affiliation, there is a danger that others will fill this vacuum. Didactics is faced with the difficult challenge of making students aware of these connections in order to offer them protection against radicalization.

1.5   *Children with an Absent Relation to God and a Distance to Tradition*
The present study illustrates that children of the God-distant relationship type regard God as having no or only minimal relevance in contingency situations. In this research, the areligious human being represents a worldview decision that is an integral part of the inner Muslim plurality. The inner-Islamic plurality in Germany is evident in the existence of various orientations such as those of liberal, secular, or culturally-oriented Muslims. These orientations are documented e.g., in studies examining Muslims' lifeworld's and their attitudes towards values and life (Gerlach, 2006; Tressat, 2011; Karakaşoğlu-Aydın, 2000; Klinkhammer, 2000; Nökel, 2007; Tietze, 2001; and many others).

The God-distant relationship type shows no relation to God. Religious patterns of interpretation are irrelevant in biographical narrations. They are only reproduced marginally and superficially when asked (cf. Chapter 4, Section 6.2). Transcendence-related phenomena such as death are interpreted inner-worldly or immanently. This type does not relate one's own lifeworld to the religious realm. God is rather assigned to the dimension of phantasy (cf. Chapter 4, Section 6.2). Since the children in the sample took part in religious education at school, it can be assumed that this type also learned about God and religion. However, the propositional knowledge about God and religion is hardly presented which is in maximum contrast to the moral relationship type. Both the knowledge and its reference are missing here.

This result is also supported by current empirical studies on young Muslims. A quantitative study by Boos-Nünning and Karakaşoğlu on the religiosity of young Muslim women shows that young Muslim women are significantly more religiously oriented than girls and young women of other religious groups, but the sample also contains young female Muslims with lower or no religious orientation (Boos-Nünning, 2007, p. 122). The quantitative results of the study of the Religion Monitor on "Religiosity and Solidarity in Germany" (Religionsmonitor, 2013) also mention a larger number of barely religious to non-religious Muslims.

Didactics of religious education must answer the question of how to give children of the God-distant relationship type the opportunity to build up a personal relationship to God while at the same time autonomously determining their proximity and distance to God.

1.6 *Summary*

The present study presents the following results:

1. The empirically based attitudes of adolescents and young adults are already apparent at the age of approximately ten. Crucial for this result was the methodical strategy of *not directly addressing religious topics* in the interviews. The children were allowed to speak for themselves and articulate what was relevant to them. It was this alone which made the type of God-distant relationship visible in the first place.
2. Even at the age of about ten, Muslim children show synchronous, relatively stable differentiated types of religiosity, which arise in the context of their subjective adaptation of tradition. In this age group, relations to God are already distinctly heterogeneous.
3. The relation to God represents a process of active co-construction of the subject. Religious attitudes do not evolve in a one-dimensional developmental process and cannot be classified into a stage scheme. Various relatively stable attitudes diverge simultaneously.
4. There are also Muslim children whose reference to tradition does not enable them to connect to the secular world. The relation to God does not exceed a purely formulaic and moral religiosity. The reduction of religious socialization to being part of a particular Muslim community can lead to moral rigidity.
5. There are Muslim children who had a religious education, but do not make any relation to God or to tradition.
6. Religiosity among Muslims is by far not as homogeneous as many quantitative studies suggest. Furthermore, among Muslim children we find the whole range of plurality of religious attitudes.

Thus, this study offers an important contribution to the theoretical foundations of religious education studies. It cannot be assumed that one type merges into one of the other types due to an inevitable maturity process. Rather it

DISCUSSION OF THE RESEARCH RESULTS 261

can be assumed that this is not a question of maturity, but of processes of co-construction[5] that require intensive pedagogical support.

Hence there is no inevitability for the development of a 'mature' image of God at a certain age. The children in the sample deal with religious topics very individually, independently, and actively. Despite all existing similarities, each child takes an individual path in dealing with contingency. This is particularly interesting because all the children in the sample come from a Muslim parental home that they claim to be religious and have participated in religious education in school and/or religious schooling in mosques. The type of God-distant relationship, however, exclusively shows inner-worldly strategies of interpretation and solution during the interviews but no religious strategies.

A modification through external influences in the form of religious pedagogy is possible. However, if the types are to be transferred into one another, this must be done actively.

From the religious pedagogical perspective, the attitudes that are manifest in the three types are not equally capable of connecting to life in a differentiated plural society. Islamic educational teaching states that the teacher is tasked with guiding adolescents to "increase in religious autonomy and personal responsibility" (Behr, 1998, p. 201). From these two points of view, it is desirable to offer options to both the moral relationship type as well as the God-distant relationship type to broaden their respective attitudes and further develop them to a subjective personal relation to God that can be connected to the secular, modern world. In both the God-distant relationship type as well as the type of moral relationship, the aim is to create the necessary conditions to *bring* their faith in God *to life*.

2 Discussion of the Results in the Theological Context

2.1 *Preliminary Considerations*

The empirical findings of this study suggest that they should also be reflected upon in light of Islamic theology. They represent a challenge for Islamic Theology and religious education studies and thus have a number of important challenges in store. These subjects should address these results in order to question certain prevailing views or to reformulate them with recourse to scripture and tradition. To be able to connect with secular worlds does not mean in any way to abandon or disempower the religious worlds, quite the contrary. Rather, it is about using the potential of the religious worlds (Behr, 2014b, pp. 162–164). The sentiment of religious education studies that it is important to offer children of the types of moral relationship and of God-distant relationship options for enlivening the relation to God, must also be considered at the theological level. Thus, it is also about a revitalization of theology by reviving countless elements of tradition neglected by the current mainstream, triggered and guided by the challenges of empiricism (Sahin, 2015, pp. 237–239).

In the framework of the empirical surveys the action-oriented relevance of the relation to God was investigated. Of course, no theological norms can be derived from empirical results. However, they can show that the formulations of the children in the sample reveal orientations that will be questioned and discussed in the following section as to how theological discourses are reflected in them and how theologically we can respond to the empirically visible expressions of faith by young Muslims. In this way it becomes clear that children develop theological interpretations as a reflection of their own faith against the background of their lifeworld. They should be taken seriously in this process, and Islamic religious education should be oriented toward this. Hence, it meets the challenge, which, according to Harry Harun Behr (2008), consists in "stimulating and cultivating a theologically based way of thinking about education and upbringing in Islam which, in philosophical freedom, penetrates and integrates the various areas between education as a challenge to society as a whole, right down to the I-Thou relationship" (Behr, 2008, p. 33). This call will be addressed with the following explanations.

2.1.1 On the Theological Positioning of the Present Work

In the early period of Islam (8th–10th centuries), four central issues were discussed, among others: the image of God, the image of man, the nature of the Qur'an, and the question of the relationship between faith and reason. This gave rise to trends in thought such as the *Ğabrīya*, the *Qadarīya*, the *Murği'a*, the *Ḥāriğīya*, and the *Ğahmīya*, as well as various theological movements such as those of the *Mu'tazila*, the Aš'arīya, and the *Māturīdīya*. From the early discourses, especially that of the *Mu'tazila*, arose the science of the *kalām*, a discipline that sought to justify faith by rational methods.

Over time, this discourse was closed, especially in the Sunni-Arab world, in favor of a consensus limited to the schools of the *Aš'arīya* and the *Māturīdīya*. This closure does not lead anywhere today. Therefore, Muslim theologians such as Asma Barlas, Harry Harun Behr, Soheib Bencheikh, Shirin Ebadi, Ömer Özsoy, Mehmet Paçacı, Mohammed Shabestari, Abdolkarim Sorush, Amina Wadood, and many more plead for the restoration of openness (Amirpur & Ammann, 2006). This is possible via what Behr (2016) calls "mental agility in aesthetic, spiritual, and analytical terms". With this agility in thinking, he postulates a "turning point for Islam" (Behr, 2016). Only in this way will a reformulation of tradition in terms of revitalization become possible. At present, we

DISCUSSION OF THE RESEARCH RESULTS

are faced with the challenge of formulating a theological concept of religious education in the sense of philosophical and thoughtful descriptions of competencies, oriented towards the lifeworld of children and authentic with regard to the Islamic tradition.

In the following, an overview of the image of God and man in Islamic theology will be given in order to enable the reader to better classify the various areas of tension that can be seen in the types in the area of the construction of the image of the world and of God. These areas of tension move between 'freedom and bondage', 'faith and reason', 'thinking and speaking', 'reference to this world and the hereafter' as well as 'religion and religiosity'. Subsequently, what is documented in the children's narrations as Islamic-theological discourses is reconstructed within the mentioned fields of tension (cf. Chapter 5, Section 2.3). In doing so, cultural codings become clear that are not necessarily based on theological tradition but on cultural-national consensus. Finally, the findings are reflected on in relation to the meaning of religious education (cf. Chapter 5, Section 3).

2.2 *Image of God and Man in Islamic Theology*

In the following, narratives of God are presented that have emerged through theological discourses of different schools of thought in the course of the history of theology, and in Chapter 5, Section 2.3 they are brought into discussion with the results of empiricism. Empiricism can illustrate that certain attitudes correspond better to educational-scientific and theological criteria than others.

2.2.1 The Construction of God in Islamic Theological History

In Islam, it is more theologically coherent and meaningful to refer to constructions of God not as images of God, but as narratives of God. The variety of narratives that have emerged through theological discourses of different schools of thought in the course of history decisively shapes the constructions of God in Islam.

According to Thomas Hildebrandt (2007), in connection with the question of rightful rule after the assassination of the third caliph 'Uṯmān ibn 'Affān (d. 656), various problems arose that led to different tendencies. These fields concerned questions about "man's capacity to act" (*qudra*), "God's counsel" (*qadar*), the nature of the Qur'an, the nature of God, predestination, dealing with an unrighteous ruler and thus "sinner", and many more, which were discussed in connection with the questions of rulership and the ruler (Hildebrandt, 2007, pp. 120–121).

A tendency known as *Qadarīya* took the position that assumed man's absolute power of will, decision, action, and effect (*qudra*) and rejected determinism (Hildebrandt, 2007, p. 121).

264   CHAPTER 5

Another tendency, called *Ǧabrīya*, assumed that man, in principle, has no power of will, decision, action or effect. They postulated an absolute determinism of all things by the "divine counsel" (*qadar*) (Hildebrandt, 2007, p. 121).

Various schools or movements have emerged from these and other tendencies. One of these movements is the *Muʿtazila*, which began in the *Qadarite* circle of Basra (Hildebrandt, 2007, p. 123).

2.2.1.1   The God Narrative of the Muʿtazila

The *Muʿtazila* emerged around the beginning of the 8th century CE. Among its founding fathers were the students of al-Ḥasan al-Baṣrī (d. 728) Wāṣil ibn ʿAṭāʾ (d. 748) and ʿAmr ibn ʿUbayd (d. 761). The school is described in the literature as critically rational. The questions which the *Muʿtazila* dealt are among the central issues of Islam. The school established five principles: 1) the unity of God (*tauḥīd*), 2) the justice of God (*ʿadl*), 3) "promise and threat" (*al-waʿd wa-l-waʿīd*), 4) the "intermediate position" of the sinner (*al-manzila bayna l-manzilatayn*) and 5) the "commanding that which is befitting and preventing that which is reprehensible" (*al-amr bi-l-maʿrūf wa-n-nahy ʿan al-munkar*) (Hildebrandt, 2007, pp. 134–143).

Reason (*ʿaql*) was considered the "link between the principles" (Hildebrandt, 2007, p. 135). The tension between revelation and reason was resolved through the allegorical interpretation (*tāwīl*) (Hildebrandt, 2007, p. 135) of certain Qurʾanic verses. This interpretation also served to reinterpret any form of anthropomorphism in relation to God and to construct an abstract image of God. In addition, the *Muʿtazila* was critical of the traditional statements and deeds of the prophet's companions (Hildebrandt, 2007, p. 143).

The first principle of the *Muʿtazila* assumes that there are no other gods besides God and that no parts can be distinguished in him. For this reason, the school divided the attributes with which God can be described into "attributes of essence" (*ṣifāt aḏ-ḏāt*) and "attributes of action" (*ṣifāt al-fiʿl*) (Hildebrandt, 2007, p. 137). This division was made with the aim of avoiding polytheism (*širk*), for in this way "entities" such as his knowing-being, etc., which could be independent of God and thus stand quasi beside him, could be integrated into his being or seen as identical with his being (Hildebrandt, 2007, p. 136). The attributes of action, on the other hand, were seen as separate from his essence, because these would only have a meaning after the creation of the world, since this was about God's dealings with it. This also affected the location of the "speech of God" (*kalām Allāh*). This was placed in the realm of the attributes of deeds, with which the Qurʾan was seen as created (*maḫlūq*) and not as eternal (Hildebrandt, 2007, p. 137).

DISCUSSION OF THE RESEARCH RESULTS

The principle of God's justice (*'adl*), which assumes that God is obligated to adhere to an "objectively existing value system" (Hildebrandt, 2007, p. 138), had the effect of rejecting any form of predetermination by God. This had an impact on the Qur'anic obligation of man to live a moral and godly life. Thus, reward and punishment in the hereafter only made sense if man fulfilled his obligation of his own free will. Therefore, the *Mu'tazila* postulated that man is endowed with the "capacity to act" (*qudra*) in order to determine his decisions and deeds on his own responsibility (Hildebrandt, 2007, p. 138).

This is connected with the third principle, according to which God is obliged to reward the believer in the hereafter and to punish the sinner (as announced in the Qur'an). Belonging to Islam alone does not guarantee a place in paradise, but the actions and consequences of these actions are the responsibility of the individual and thus play an important role (Hildebrandt, 2007, p. 139).

The fourth principle is related to the third. Here it is postulated that the person who commits grave sins is neither a believer nor an unbeliever, but that they stand between these two states. This does not exclude the sinner from the community, nor does it negate the Qur'an's moral teaching that the latter will be punished in the hereafter (Hildebrandt, 2007, p. 124). However, the *Mu'tazilites* postulated that a sinner should not hope for the prophet's intercession in the hereafter.

The fifth principle, which corresponds to a Qur'anic principle, calls for a "moral and godly way of life" (Hildebrandt, 2007, p. 140).[6]

2.2.1.2   *The God Narrative of the Aš'arīya*

The school of the *Aš'arites* dates back to the jurist Abū l-Ḥasan al-Aš'arī (d. 935). The beginning of the *Aš'arites* goes hand in hand with the time of the *miḥna*. This period[7] is characterized by the fact that in 827 the Abbasid Kalif al-Māmūn proclaimed the "creation of the Qur'an", and every judge and *ḥadīt* scholar was scrutinized for his stance in this regard (Hildebrandt, 2007, p. 128). The Sunni jurist Aḥmad ibn Ḥanbal positioned himself against the doctrine of creation of the Qur'an and was placed under house arrest. The end of the miḥna was marked by a "political turn", which is also known as the "Sunni turnaround" (Hildebrandt, 2007, p. 146). Hadith scholars[8] (*muḥadditūn*) and ḥanbalite jurists in particular positioned themselves against the doctrine of creation (Hildebrandt, 2007, p. 144). Al-Aš'arī sought a middle ground between these two positions (Hildebrandt, 2007, p. 147):

In *Aš'arite* thought, the role of reason is limited. God is seen as omnipotent and omniscient, and he is said to be neither subject to nor comprehensible by reason. The anthropomorphic statements about God in the Qur'an are no longer seen allegorically, but literally; and the image of God became more vivid.

However, it was defined that the human being could not determine what it means concretely when e.g., the hand of God is spoken of. As a result, one must believe in it without asking how it is to be understood (*bi-lā kayf*) (Hildebrandt, 2007, p. 148). The handed-down statements and deeds of the prophets' comrades now took up more space.

According to the *Ašʿarīya*, God's attributes are considered identical with his essence. With regard to God's speech, i.e., the Qur'an, the school assumed that it is an attribute of God's essence, i.e., eternal like God, but "created in time as a recitation (*kalām lafẓī*), but eternal and uncreated in its capacity as a content of consciousness (*kalām nafsī*)" (Hildebrandt, 2007, p. 148).

With regard to God's justice, the *Ašʿarīya* assumes that God is not bound by human principles of good and evil in moral terms. God himself establishes morality and values, which need not be rationally comprehensible. The school thus emphasizes the omnipotence and freedom of God. Accordingly, humans are unable to rationally determine what is good and bad and are therefore relegated to revelation (Rudolph, 1996, p. 331). Therefore, the *Ašʿarites* assume that God does not necessarily have to reward the good and punish the bad, whereby no one can be sure, not even the pious, that salvation will be granted in the hereafter. In this context, a sinner may hope for the prophet's intercession in the hereafter.

With regard to man's freedom of will, the *Ašʿarīya* develops the theory of "acquisition" (*kasb*), which states that man makes his actions, which are created by God, his own, by consciously performing them (van Ess, 1991, p. 503).

2.2.1.3 The God Narrative of the Māturīdīya

This school goes back to Abū Manṣūr al-Māturīdī (d. 944) and is a recognized theological direction in Sunni Islam. The school chooses a middle course in the central theological question of determining the relationship between faith and reason. It postulates a rational human being and places the wisdom of God in the foreground (Berger, 2010, p. 84).

According to Ulrich Rudolph, the *Māturīdīya* rejects any form of anthropomorphism and refers to God as something "being" (*šay'*) (Rudolph, 1996, p. 309). With regard to the attributes of God, al-Māturīdī stated that these could neither be compared to human attributes, nor are "time-bound" but "all eternal" and "real" (Rudolph, 1996, p. 319). God is neither localizable nor in need of a place (Rudolph, 1996, p. 328). However, one can believe the Qur'an that God sits on a throne, only the concrete way is here withdrawn from the human imagination (Rudolph, 1996, p. 329).

With regard to the question of whether God is bound to an objective norm or to standards of value that humans can rationally comprehend, al-Māturīdī

DISCUSSION OF THE RESEARCH RESULTS

developed the concept of God's "wisdom" (*ḥikma*), which expresses itself through "goodness" (*faḍl*) and "justice" (*'adl*) (Rudolph, 1996, p. 333). Al-Māturīdī attempted to consider the very opposing positions of the *Mu'tazila* and the *Aš'arīya*. He emphasized divine omnipotence and freedom, with God's commandments determining what was good and what was bad, which then resulted in "a stable and intelligible system of norms" (Rudolph, 1996 p. 332). That is, God communicates his "counsels" to humans through the "rationality of ethical norms" (Rudolph, 1996, p. 332) (and at other levels as well). Thus, al-Māturīdī also integrated the view of the *Mu'tazila*, for whom humans can rationally discern the good and the bad. Divine wisdom manifests itself through immeasurable goodness and through justice, which is characterized by his "treating each thing as is appropriate for it" (Rudolph, 1996, p. 333). Thus, man's "rational faculty" has a central role in al-Māturīdī's concept (Rudolph, 1996, p. 335).

Al-Māturīdī's theory of action lies between the extremes of the *Qadarīya* and the *Ğabrīya*. It assumes an interplay between creator and creature, in the sense that God creates the actions and man performs them, whereby man "always possesses the capacity for two opposite actions" (Rudolph, 1996, p. 340). Here he enshrines the "free choice of man" (*iḫtiyār*) (Rudolph, 1996, p. 340). A believer was considered to be one who agreed to the creed with his heart and confessed to it with his tongue. Thus, deeds did not count toward faith (Rudolph, 1996, p. 345).

Regarding the question of the sinner's fate, al-Māturīdī assumes that even if a believer commits a grave sin, he is still considered a believer, he does not have to expect eternal punishment in hell, and he can hope for the intercession of the Prophet in the hereafter (Rudolph, 1996, pp. 344–345).

For further discussion of the various narratives of God, see Josef van Ess, who presents the various narratives of God of this period as part of his account of the history of religious thought in the second and third centuries after the hijra (*hiǧra*)[9] (van Ess, 1991).

2.2.1.4 Transcendence and Immanence of God

The difference between the transcendence and immanence of God also plays a role in the different narratives of God.[10]

The Qur'an itself describes God as the unapproachable one, "the first and the last, the Manifest and the Hidden" (57:3), and as the one who is "nearer to him [man] than his jugular vein" (50:16) (Schimmel, 1995, p. 41). God's nearness is also expressed in verse 2:186, which says: "When My servants ask you about Me, [tell them that] I am indeed near most. I answer the supplicant's call when he calls Me. So let them respond to Me, and let them have faith in Me, so that they may fare rightly".

268   CHAPTER 5

God's transcendence and remoteness find their core in chapter/sura 112 (*al-Iḫlāṣ* = "faith without reservation", translation according to Paret, 2007, p. 439), an early Meccan sura that states, "Say, 'He is Allah, the One. Allah is the All-embracing. He neither begat, nor was begotten. Nor has He any equal'".

The Qur'an emphasizes this strictly monotheistic idea in numerous passages, referring to the association with God (*širk*) as the only fault that God does not forgive.

The dichotomy between God's transcendence and immanence has led to various positions and concepts on the nature of God in the Islamic tradition, such as *tašbīh* (comparison of God with man, anthropomorphism), *taʿṭīl* (emptying God of all attributes), *tafwīḍ* (affirmation of Qur'anic statements about God's human-like form, but abstention about its nature), *tåwīl* (metaphorical understanding of said statements about God), and the like (Dziri, 2013, pp. 12–13; Ragab, 2012, pp. 148–149).

Milad Karimi (2013) presents a theological approach to bridging this dichotomy involving Western philosophy. This approach is briefly presented here.

The Qur'an as revelation opens up the possibility of "transgressing the uncatchable boundary that is necessarily inherent in God" (Karimi, 2013, p. 97), but without violating God's absolute oneness. Karimi suggests that God's absolute transcendence consists in the fact that he is the epitome of immanent transcendence, that is, the epitome of transgression. This in the sense that "through his comprehensive infinity he has always already transcended the 'boundary' to the immanent world" (Karimi, 2012, p. 104). Accordingly, Qur'an 4:126 also states, "To Allah belongs whatever is in the heavens and whatever is on the earth, and Allah comprehends all things".

Karimi describes revelation as the possibility to experience the presence of God in the world, which he explains with the revelation event of the prophet Muhammad, explaining that Muhammad went to a mountain cave in search of the One, but would not have found him if the One had not turned to him. Of particular interest in the encounter is that it is not Muhammad's mind that receives the revelation but his heart, for he reports that it was as if the words were written in his heart (Karimi, 2013, p. 105). Karimi summarizes that it was not Muhammad who "unveiled" God and crossed the border, but God himself who "conquered" the heart of his messenger. He "get under his skin" in the sense that he "made his immanent presence felt in the act of revelation, in the event of the Qur'an" (Karimi, 2012, p. 107). This transgression of boundaries through revelation is expressed in verse 39:23:

> Allah has sent down the best of discourses, a scripture [composed] of similar motifs, whereat quiver the skins of those who fear their Lord, then

DISCUSSION OF THE RESEARCH RESULTS

their skins and hearts soften to Allah's remembrance. That is Allah's guidance, by which He guides whomever He wishes; and whomever Allah leads astray, has no guide.

In the above, it can be seen that the emotional dimension of faith in God, which is the focus of this paper, makes one aware of God's immanence.

Karimi is not the only one to conclude that the human heart plays an essential role in the perception of God. Medieval writers like al-Ġazālī have also addressed this question of the heart.[11]

The heart is a metaphysical concept and is taken up in the Qur'an with four different terms: the breast ($ṣadr$),[12] the heart ($qalb$),[13] the "innermost heart" ($fu'ād$)[14] and the innermost ($lubb$).[15] The concept of the heart is unfolded in some mystical traditions of Islam in the form of different levels and stages (Pavlis, 2001).

In summary, it can be stated that the different narratives of God are reflected in certain interview sequences among the children of the sample. Because the interviews did not directly ask about God, but rather focused on the children's emotions and what is meaningful to them, this study makes the meaning of God in certain life situations of children empirically accessible in a special way. Of course, the diversity of God narratives is not completely reflected in the interview sequences. Nevertheless, the different ways of relating to God that are shown by the children can be linked back to the heritage of the God narratives of the different schools of thought. This is addressed in Chapter 5, Section 2.3.

2.2.2   The Construction of the Human Being in Islamic Theological History

As a central topic of Islamic theology, the question of human being's natural disposition (*fiṭra*) toward religion must be addressed. The concept of the *fiṭra* is controversially discussed in Islamic religious education studies literature. In this context, the question is pursued as to what influence nature or culture[16] can be attributed to a person's religiosity.

This work is not designed to investigate this question empirically in any way. It maintains the constructivist position, because a hasty reference to such an anthropological concept would just complicate the perception of the type of God-distant relationship.

Nevertheless, from a theological perspective, the construction of man is strongly connected with the construction of God, and therefore it is discussed here in connection with the construction of God. At the same time, it has relevance for the meaning of an Islamic religious education. Thus, it will be shown in the following that a widespread understanding of the relationship between nature and culture from an Islamic perspective is that human beings are born into the world with a natural disposition toward God and religion, but that this disposition requires socialization and enculturation for its development. This interpretation of *fiṭra* will be discussed in its relevance for religious education at the end of this chapter.

Ideas and concepts of anthropology are discussed from an Islamic perspective below. There are different accounts in this field that have a common denominator.

According to the Qur'an, the heart is considered the place of spirituality and understanding. Thus, verse 2:10[17] speaks of "sickness in their hearts". Verses 7:179[18] and 22:46[19] address the fact that man sees and understands only with his heart. The Qur'an also exposes its "prophetic protagonists to darkness so that the inner images shine all the brighter – usually in the context of a fundamental transformation: Abraham under the vast night sky, Joseph at the very bottom of the cistern, Jonah deep inside the belly of the fish, or Muhammad in the niche in the rock at the top of the mountain" (Behr, 2012b, p. 3).

From an Islamic anthropological perspective, this ability of man to understand with his heart points to man's natural ability to relate to God, which is also evident in his openness, even neediness, for meaning in verse 39:22: "Is someone whose breast Allah has opened to Islam so that he follows a light from His Lord? So woe to those whose hearts have been hardened to the remembrance of Allah. They are in manifest error". Man's ability to relate to God is also based on the capacity for speech, communication (2:31–37),[20] perception, reflection, and insight (4:82).[21] Behr (2005) concludes from the above considerations that humans are "capable of religion" (Behr, 2005, p. 77). Overall, this illustrates, as Schuon notes, that the human being is "not regarded as a fallen creature in need of a redemptive miracle, but as a theomorphic creature gifted with an intelligence capable of discerning the absolute and a will capable of choosing what leads there" (Schuon, 2002, p. 11).

Thus, man is capable of religion and capable of fulfilling his mission as a deputy (*ḫalīfa*) (6:165)[22] in the sense of being God's representative on earth and preserving "order" (*iṣlāḥ*) (7:56).[23]

The prerequisite for man's ability to relate and to be religious is the ability to recognize God. To this end, "man is endowed with the 'natural, inner structure' (30:30) necessary for this" (Behr, 2005, p. 77). Verse 30:30 reads:

> So set your heart on the religion (*dīn*) as a people of pure faith, the origination of Allah (*fiṭratallāh*) according to which He originated mankind. There is no altering Allah's creation; that is the upright religion (*dīn*), but most people do not know.

DISCUSSION OF THE RESEARCH RESULTS 271

In this verse the Arabic word *dīn* is used, which means "religion, view, way of life". Islam, in this sense, is a way of life focused on meeting God on the day when he owes a response to him as God's governor on earth. *Dīn* is thus more than religion; it is a way of life of turning to God and an attitude of devotion to God. The word *fiṭra*, which is the subject here, is used in combination with the word Allah and translated as "origination of Allah". This verse is discussed in classical literature in connection with the following *ḥadīt*:

> Abu Huraira, Allah's pleasure be upon him, reported that the Prophet, Allah's blessings and peace be upon him, said: 'Every child is born with the fiṭra, and his parents then make him either a Jew, a Christian, or a Sabaean. Just like the animal that gives birth to an animal: do you see any discrepancy in this?'[24] (Abu-r-Rida' & Rassoul, 1989)

The concept of the "nature-given, inner disposition" (*fiṭra*) was already intensively discussed by scholars in the eighth century in connection with the question of the extent to which man and his behavior are free or predetermined. According to Yasien Mohamed, three different classical positions can be identified: the "predestinatory", the "neutral", and the "positive" interpretation of this concept (Mohamed, 1996, pp. 3–4). The predestinatory interpretation, espoused by scholars such as Ibn Mubārak (d. 797) and 'Abd al-Qādir al-Ǧīlānī (d. 1106) before the mid-eighth century, assumes that all of man's deeds are created by God. Accordingly, every individual is either inherently good or bad by divine decree from birth. The immutability of nature postulated in verse 30:30 pertains to man's destiny to go either to paradise or to hell. Thus, regardless of external influences of guidance or misguidance, the individual is bound by God's will to live his life that was designed for him in his pre-existence (Mohamed, 1996, pp. 4–5).

This position of innate good or evil *fiṭra* is problematic because it contradicts human free will and responsibility. In response to this view, the neutral view of the concept of *fiṭra* postulated by Ibn 'Abd al-Barr (d. 1071) emerged, stating that it is neither inherently good nor evil. Good or evil character was a result of environmental influences, that is, behavior was exclusively by environmental stimuli, whereby Ibn 'Abd al-Barr also emphasized man's free will. He concluded that man is born in a state of ignorance and innocence and acquires knowledge of good and evil from his environment. Because of man's free will, which the Qur'an postulates, he can consciously decide which environmental stimuli to accept and which to reject in order to achieve God's pleasure (Mohamed, 1996, pp. 5–7).[25]

Mohamed further states that the positive interpretation of the concept of *fiṭra* is held by most classical scholars such as Ibn Taymīya (d. 1328), Sahl at-Tustarī

(d. 896), ar-Rāġib al-Iṣfahānī (d. 1108), and also by the majority of modern scholars. This position states that every child is born in the state of *fiṭra*, the nature-given, inner disposition. Islam corresponds with human nature so that man naturally adapts to Islam, which provides the ideal conditions for the preservation and satisfaction of man's nature-given, inner qualities. This resulted from verse 30:30, in which the proper *dīn* is described as God's *fiṭra* and this *fiṭra* is thus linked to Islam as a way of life of turning to God, so that it is assumed that the condition of a newborn child harmonizes with Islam as an attitude. The *fiṭra*, according to Ibn Taymīya,[26] is not just a dormant potential that must be awakened from the outside, but the source of awakening from within oneself. Only a damaged social environment could cause the individual to deviate from this state. A correct monotheist is guided inwardly but has to practice divine guidance consciously. Ibn Taymīya relates the *ḥadīṯ* to the social environment that can bring about change, thus placing a high value on religious socialization. He believes that through positive Islamic religious socialization, the individual is led to faith (*īmān*) and good behavior, as he or she is naturally receptive to divine guidance. Furthermore, he assumes that the good already forms the natural, inner state of the human being before birth, but the evil only occurs after the birth of the human being, which means that deviations emerge after birth due to the influences of the social environment (Mohamed, 1996, pp. 7–9).

Jon Hoover (2007) states that Ibn Taymīya connects the natural, inner disposition to the covenant God made with humanity in primordial time:

> When your Lord took from the Children of Adam, from their loins, their descendants and made them bear witness over themselves, [He said to them,] 'Am I not your Lord?' They said, 'Yes indeed! We bear witness'. [This,] lest you should say on the Day of Resurrection, 'Indeed we were unaware of this'. (7:172)

However, Ibn Taymīya assumes that children do not have any concrete knowledge from birth, but they have an immanent receptive capacity towards this knowledge that grows with time, as long as there are no negative influences (in the sense of education). Ibn Taymīya connects the *fiṭra* with the human faculty of understanding (*ʿaql*). According to Ibn Taymīya, the nature-given, inner disposition to believe in God is even stronger than the nature-given infantile instinct to drink milk from the mother. According to him, the *fiṭra* also guides man to want what is good and profitable for him and to reject what is harmful for him. Thus, he argues, man is constituted by nature to find satisfaction in good, and if man existed outside corrupting influences, he would necessarily soon recognize, praise, extol, and worship his Lord (Hoover, 2007, pp. 41–42).[27]

DISCUSSION OF THE RESEARCH RESULTS 273

According to Ibn Qayyim al-Ǧawzīya (d. 1350), a disciple of Ibn Taymīya, *fiṭra* is not the mere cognitive recognition of good and evil, but an active, innate love for the good and a recognition of God as the Creator. That is, the *fiṭra* is not the mere passive capacity to receive Islam, but a nature-given disposition to recognize God, his uniqueness or indivisibility (*tauḥīd*). Overall, it becomes clear that *fiṭra* is seen as an active, nature-given disposition to believe in God and to act according to his will (Mohamed, 1996, pp. 7–9).

This shows that the Islamic conception of the human being assumes a natural disposition of man to God and *dīn*, but that faith and good behavior are seen above all as imparted through socialization and also require an active devotion and attitude on the part of man. Religious education is therefore an integral part of Islam.

The author of this study is aware that both the *ḥadīṯ* presented above and verse 30:30 allow for different readings. For example, they can be read in such a way that only Islam as a religious system corresponds to the nature of man. That is, those who are Muslim have taken the right path and the others have not. Another reading, according to Behr, is that the term *dīn* used in verse 30:30 is not to be understood in the sense of a practiced religion as a doctrine, nor in the sense of a religious affiliation, but alludes to 'Islam' as a turning toward in the sense of an attitude of the subject (Behr, 2014c, p. 496), i.e., the devotion or turning toward God out of one's own inwardness and not out of belonging to a certain religion. Because of the pedagogical value, the continuation of the educational idea in Islam, and the consequences for the didactics of religious education, the latter reading is preferred here.

Behr goes on to say that the relationship between man and God is characterized by a reciprocal relationship, in the sense that God as *rabb* (Lord) holds and provides for man and man as *'abd* is the one who is there for God. The term *'abd* is usually translated as 'servant', meaning man as God's servant. "To 'serve' God in Islam means to be there for him *alone* (3:18)[28] – aware that he is also there (2:256).[29] The Qur'an urges man to seek, find, and walk his own path here, at his own responsibility (109:6)"[30] (Behr, 2014c, p. 497).

This reciprocal relationship is also found in the creation story, in which God tells the angels about his plan to install a deputy on earth. The angels doubt a deputy who acts in the sense of God on earth and trust him with "the potential of destroying all order" (Behr, 2014c, p. 494). In this regard, verse 2:30:

> When your Lord said to the angels, 'Indeed I am going to set a viceroy on the earth', they said, 'Will You set in it someone who will cause corruption in it, and shed blood, while we celebrate Your praise and proclaim Your sanctity?' He said, 'Indeed I know what you do not know'.

274   CHAPTER 5

The verse shows that the angels seem to refer to what is known and thus express their concerns, but God trusts Adam. "In contrast, human 'confidence' in God (*tawakkul*; 3:159[31]) is grounded in the experiential 'certainty' (*yaqīn*; 6:75[32]) that he has not been mandated with a hopeless endeavor and left alone, but experiences in it 'guidance' (*hidāya*), 'support' (*dīn*), and 'indication of destination' (*ṣirāṭ*) from God (1:6, 6:161[33]). He is just not only able to believe in God, but also to believe him" (Behr, 2014c, p. 494).

According to Behr, the relationship between man and God is also characterized by encounter. The encounter with God takes place through the encounter with fellow human beings, as will be told in the following *ḥadīṯ qudsī*:[34]

> On the authority of Abū Hurayrah (may Allah be pleased with him), who said that the Messenger of Allah said: 'Allah (mighty and sublime be He) will say on the Day of Resurrection: O son of Adam, I fell ill and you visited Me not. He will say: O Lord, and how should I visit You when You are the Lord of the worlds? He will say: Did you not know that My servant So-and-so had fallen ill and you visited him not? Did you not know that had you visited him you would have found Me with him? O son of Adam, I asked you for food and you fed Me not. He will say: O Lord, and how should I feed You when You are the Lord of the worlds? He will say: Did you not know that My servant So-and-so asked you for food and you fed him not? Did you not know that had you fed him you would surely have found that (the reward for doing so) with Me? O son of Adam, I asked you to give Me to drink and you gave Me not to drink. He will say: O Lord, how should I give You to drink when You are the Lord of the worlds? He will say: My servant So-and-so asked you to give him to drink and you gave him not to drink. Had you given him to drink you would have surely found that with Me'. It was related by Muslim. (Ibrahim & Johnson-Davies, 1997, pp. 88–89)[35]

In this *ḥadīṯ*, as well as in many Qur'anic verses, it can be seen that the relationship between man and God is reflected in his relationship and in his coexistence with his fellow human beings. This relationship is illustrated in the Qur'an with the symbol of a rope: *ḥablun min Allāh* and *ḥablun min an-nās* (3:103[36], 3:112[37]) (Behr, 2014c, p. 498).

Humans are also endowed with language:

> And He taught Adam the Names, all of them; then presented them to the angels and said, 'Tell me the names of these, if you are truthful'. They said, 'Immaculate are You! We have no knowledge except what You

DISCUSSION OF THE RESEARCH RESULTS

have taught us. Indeed You are the All-knowing, the All-wise'. He said, 'O Adam, inform them of their names', and when he had informed them of their names, He said, 'Did I not tell you that I indeed know the Unseen in the heavens and the earth, and that I know whatever you disclose and whatever you were concealing?' (2:31–33)

The ideas of this verse are taken further by Reinhard Leuze (1994) and Amina Boumaaiz et al. (2013): "The act of naming is always of fundamental importance for the ancient understanding, because naming means at the same time exercising dominion" (Leuze, 1994, p. 240). Here God teaches the names of all things to Adam, who can then name them in contrast to the angels. Adam's teaching makes "the human being the bearer of divine knowledge and gives him such honor that the angels have to bow down before him on God's command" (Boumaaiz et al., 2013, p. 111).

Here the dignity of man plays a special role, because in the Qur'anic narrative there is one who does not prostrate himself before Adam. It is about Satan,[38] who in this context bears the name Iblīs[39] in Qur'an 38:73–76,[40] among others. Iblīs is derived by some philologists from the root *b-l-s* and means "a state of shock, to be overwhelmed with grief, to fall into utter despair; to be cut off; to be confused and bewildered" (Badawi & Abdel Haleem, 2008, p. 111). He justifies his opposition by accusing God of having given man more dignity (*karāma*) than he has given him (17:62[41]). Dignity, however, is not scalable but absolute. Iblīs begins to relativize man's dignity on the basis of external characteristics ("'I am better than him', he said. 'You created me from fire and You created him from clay'" (38:76)). He evaluates man and assigns him a place under himself. In doing so, he elevates himself next to God by "making himself greater" (cf. the verb *istakbara* in 2:34[42]). This is a mode of behavior that can be found again today. People are given a place in society according to characteristics such as language, gender, skin color, migrant background, etc.

In summary, a widespread and historically developed interpretation of the *fiṭra* is that every human being is born into the world with a natural predisposition to God. This natural predisposition exhibits a positive, intact turn to God. It is ultimately socialization and religious education that lead a child to or away from faith.

From an Islamic perspective, the relationship between nature and culture consists in the fact that, on the one hand, human beings have natural dispositions given to them by God, but on the other hand, they need guidance, stimulation, education, and upbringing from their social environment in order to develop them. This means: "Only along the foil of a religious doctrine, according to the general Muslim view, are children able to develop their own religious identity in the sense of conscious positionality, completely independent of their spiritual disposition" (Behr, 2014c, p. 506).

The children in the study's sample are all of the Muslim faith.[43] However, they differ in their religious socialization, mother tongue, culture, and gender. The conjunctive experiential space they share is their religious tradition. Most of the children in the sample participate in Islamic religious education at the state school and receive additional religious schooling in mosques. It is precisely on this basis that it becomes clear in the material that the children who are assigned to the type of God-distant relationship, despite the above-mentioned same prerequisites (participation in religious education at school and in most cases also in religious schooling in mosques), do not establish an existential relationship to religious practice or to God in comparison with the children of the other types. Here it becomes clear that although guidance, stimulation, education, and upbringing from the social environment are present, the type of God-distant relationship is characterized by the absence of a relationship with God and by distance from tradition (cf. Chapter 4, Section 6.2). In the case of the type of moral relationship, it is noticeable that these children find it difficult to establish a relationship to God that goes beyond a purely formulaic and moral religiosity (cf. Chapter 4, Section 5.2).

On the basis of the material, it is possible to formulate an understanding of *fiṭra* that can be operationalized in pedagogical terms: In this sense, the core understanding of *fiṭra* would be man's ability and willingness to try out religion and to seek a path in the process. By verse 30:30, it can at least be assumed that man is open to all sides with respect to God. He is, so to speak, capable of religion, that is of an active construction, as described in Chapter 5, Section 1.2. Thus, the fluidity of this concept and also of the construction of God becomes clear.

2.3 *Theological Tensions*

In the material, the children show orientations that can be ideally condensed into types. It becomes clear that areas of tension become visible, such as between freedom and bondedness, faith and reason, thinking and speaking, reference to this world and the hereafter, as well as religion and religiosity. These will be discussed theologically in the following. The list is not exclusive but other topics will not be treated here for reasons of priority.

2.3.1 Freedom and Boundedness – Determining the Relationship between God's Omnipotence and Man's Freedom of Will

We will begin with the question of how the tension between freedom and boundedness emerges in the different types. The material shows that the children activate different or no perspectives of action in relation to the narrations

DISCUSSION OF THE RESEARCH RESULTS

they have about God. This becomes clear from the fact that the relationship between God's omnipotence and human freedom of will is weighted differently. Transcendence-related and immanence-related interpretations of self and world make this weighting clear:

In the personal relationship type, children are not passive recipients. They construct their own concept of God individually, depending on their experiences in their lifeworld. God is constructed in the interview situation as a You, to whom a power of influence is assigned. The human being is also assigned power of influence, with the freedom to make decisions. The children distinguish between an area in which God is effective and an area in which they are effective as humans, although these areas can also overlap (cf. Chapter 4, Section 4.2). The type of personal relationship basically relates man's freedom of will to all areas of life except death. This type is aware that one's existence is dependent on the existence of God. His ethical action is autonomous but is also placed in a God perspective.

The type of moral relationship, on the other hand, constructs God as an omnipotent being whom man can influence through religious performance. Here, prayers are assigned a quasi-magical function through which a purpose is to be achieved. Man is assigned the role of performing prayers 'correctly' to obtain what he desires or to be protected. Thereby, a purposive-rational relationship to God becomes evident, in which he is seen in the role of the more powerful (cf. Chapter 4, Section 5.2 and 6.2). Submission to God's will is especially evident in the thematics of wish fulfillment and fears. However, the children of this type are aware that the 'effect' of their prayers does not necessarily come to pass, and their wishes are not necessarily fulfilled. If wishes are not fulfilled, the fault is first sought in oneself (cf. Chapter 4, Section 5.2). Aspirations and hopes are then placed in a God perspective when it is certain that one cannot do anything oneself. But even if the children have influence on events, but fail in doing so, there is a tendency to attribute what has happened to God, not least for one's own relief (cf. Chapter 4, Section 5.2).

In the type of God-distant relationship, the freedom of will of man is without counterpart. God tends to be located in the realm of fantasy and, if asked, is sometimes associated with death. However, the effects of God's will on their lives do not play a role in the interviews of the children of this type (cf. Chapter 4, Section 6.2).

In the following these findings are discussed theologically.

According to William Montgomery Watt (1972), the discussion about the attributes of God developed from the discussion about the creation or noncreation of the Qur'an as the word of God (Watt, 1972, p. 64). The three major schools of thought[44] that developed in the course of Islamic theological history treated the doctrine of the uniqueness or indivisibility of God (*tauḥīd*)[45] from this point of view and arrived at different narratives of God. They also dealt with the question of whether God or man produces man's deeds. This question significantly affects the question of man's freedom and bondedness. The type of personal relationship tends to reflect the God constructions of the *mu'tazilite* school of thought, while that of moral relationship tends to reflect the *aš'arite* school of thought, although there is also some overlap. This means that fundamental theological questions are indeed reflected in the interviews.

In the type of personal relationship, the construction of a human being with free will and an omnipresent God shows traits of a *mu'tazilite* image of God. In addressing the question of God's justice (*'adl*), the *Mu'tazila* argued that humans have free will without restriction. The narrations of the personal relationship type also show that the children assume that humans have free will. However, they also place their actions in a God perspective and thus frame precisely moral questions in a religious way (cf. Chapter 4, Section 4.3). On the other hand, they do not refer to a punishing God who rewards the pious and punishes sinners, as is typical of *mu'tazilite* doctrine. They believe or want to believe that God is good.

On the other hand, the omnipotence of God, which is not a problem for the moral relationship, plays an essential role and is a specific feature of the *aš'arite* school of thought. In the narrations of the type of moral relationship, it is documented that the will of man ultimately depends on the will of God and that things that happen in life are due to God and not to the decisions of man. In this sense, God creates people's deeds (cf. Chapter 4, Section 5.2).

This type, on the other hand, also shows *mu'tazilite* traits, for it assumes that God will reward the good and punish the bad, so that the pious person can be sure that he will be granted salvation in the hereafter. Man can thus obtain a place in paradise through prayer and behavior agreeable to God (cf. Chapter 4, Section 5.3).

Beyond the theological schools of thought, it can be summarized that God in the Qur'an is the one "who measures and establishes" (2:21–22[46]), who has "permanent dominion over things" (1:4, 6:75[47]), who is the "sustainer of the heavens and the earth" (1:2[48]) and who empowers man in partial areas to break through limitations and cross horizons (55:33[49]) (Behr, 2014c, p. 495). On the one hand, the human being's potential to break through in an area promised to him by God is set forth; on the other hand, it is open to him "to position himself for or against God's offer as a point of reference or not to respond to God's address at all or to negate any reality that cannot be experienced in reality" (Behr, 2014c, p. 501).

The subject autonomy and self-determination of the human being, for example, are discussed in some verses such as 6:111,[50] 7:35–37,[51] 36:62,[52] 61:5[53]

DISCUSSION OF THE RESEARCH RESULTS

and 99:7–8.[54] The autonomy of the subject in the sense of a self-determined positioning in relation to God is also supported by a famous tradition that belongs to the *ḥadīṯ qudsī* text type:

> On the authority of Abū Hurayrah (may Allah be pleased with him), who said that the Prophet said: 'Allah the Almighty said: I am as My servant thinks I am.[55] I am with him when he makes mention of Me. If he makes mention of Me to himself, I make mention of him to Myself; and if he makes mention of Me in an assembly, I make mention of him in an assembly better than it. And if he draws near to Me an arm's length, I draw near to him a cubit, and if he draws near to Me a cubit, I draw near to him a fathom. And if he comes to Me walking, I go to him at speed'. It was related by al-Buhkari (also by Muslim, at-Tirmidhi and Ibn-Majah). (Ibrahim & Johnson-Davies, 1997)

This understanding of God, who subjectivizes himself for the human counterpart, emerges more in mystical thought, although this *ḥadīṯ* has a high theological value.

This narrative of God is most likely to be reflected in the statements of the children of the type of personal relationship. The children talk about God as a good being whom they meet with sympathy and warmth. For them, this goodness of God is at the center of their religiosity (cf. Chapter 4, Section 4.2).

On the other hand, the predestination of man by God is addressed in verses such as 7:89,[56] 12:76,[57] 18:23–24,[58] 74:56[59] and 81:29.[60] God is described as the one who has power of disposal over the world and man.

For the children of the type of moral relationship, this aspect of power of disposal is at the center of their relationship with God. It is not a matter of liking God, just as one does not have to like a policeman or a teacher, but it is a matter of keeping his rules and winning him over through the channels he provides (prayer, good conduct) (cf. Chapter 4, Section 5.2 and 6.2).

In the Qur'an, therefore, both God's unrestricted power of disposal and man's freedom of will and responsibility are thematized. These statements seem to express a contrast or to offer two poles for religious self-location.

In summary, it can be stated that recognizing, interpreting, and discussing the diversity of God narratives lead to agility in thinking and to changes in perspective. Especially with the type of moral relationship, it becomes clear that this diversity is not given. This means that narration must occupy a much larger place in religious education. This will be taken up in Chapter 5, Section 3 and Chapter 6, Section 2.

2.3.2 Faith and Reason

In the following, we will show how the tension between faith and reason is revealed through the different types. In the material it becomes clear that the types take up a clear position between wanting to believe and being able to believe, the cognitive and the emotional dimensions of belief in God as well as immanence- and transcendence-related strategies of interpretation. Types could be reconstructed whose relation to God is positioned in a different weighting between wanting to believe and being able to believe. The tension between faith and reason can be linked back to the different God narratives (cf. Chapter 4, Section 3).

This question touches the core discourses of theology. The determination of the relationship between faith or revelation and reason is complex in the Islamic scientific system. Thus, the meaning of reason in *kalām*[61] is different from that in *fiqh*.[62] Reason in the sense of *'aql*[63] has different definitions in the various disciplines. In general, *kalām* assumes that the premises and foundations of religion can be explained rationally, that is without reference to the Qur'an or Sunna.[64] In *fiqh*, on the other hand, reason plays no normative role. That means mere reason is not normative; it is always so only in combination with the text or with other foundations derived from the texts. Reason here has the role of understanding, not of proving. In *kalām*, the problem of proving whether the Qur'an is true, and if so why, arises. To answer this question, the Qur'an is not consulted since that would be circular reasoning. In this question, reason stands above the Qur'an because it wants to prove its correctness. In *fiqh*, the question of what the Qur'an (or the Sunna) wants to say is discussed. Reason is subordinate to the Qur'an.

From an Islamic anthropological perspective, man is endowed with a "natural, inner disposition" (*fiṭra*), which determines his religious ability (cf. Chapter 5, Section 2.2.2). However, in being so, he requires guidance (*hidāya*) from the Qur'an as a guide to truth and a straight path (46:30[65]), prudence (72:1–2[66]), and remembrance of God (39:23[67]). On the other hand, man is also endowed with understanding, i.e., with the ability to deal with creation and thus to recognize God (3:190[68]) (Behr, 2014c).

In the type of personal relationship, it becomes apparent that the role assigned to God in the interview situation is that of a you who is part of the reality of life. However, this type clearly separates between transcendence- and immanence-related interpretations of the world and the self. God and belief in him have their place in the lifeworld, but man's efficacy and reason have their own place too (cf. Chapter 4, Section 4.2).

In the case of the type of moral relationship, it becomes apparent that the children of this type refer to the effect of protective verses and other forms of ritual as a quasi-magical action in order to solve problems. They do not assign

DISCUSSION OF THE RESEARCH RESULTS

any power of action to humans in this respect. If the protective verses do not unfold their hoped-for effect, for example, they look for the fault within themselves. This interpretation is reflexively used as evidence for the belief in the effect of the protection verses (cf. Chapter 4, Section 5.2). "Reality as reflexive activity" is one of the five features of reality described by Hugh Mehan and Houston Wood (1976). They show that a premise that holds for someone functions like an "uncorrectable proposition". Empirical experiences that thus deny this belief in the effect of protective verses are explained away by children of this type. Thus, belief in the effect of the protective verses is part of reality in the world of children with these type characteristics. Referring to Mehan and Wood, it can be assumed that the children formulate "auxiliary constructions" that save their belief in the reality of the effect of protective verses. In doing so, Mehan and Wood point out that this "self-perpetuating reflexive process […] is common to oracular, scientific, and everyday thinking" (Mehan & Wood, 1976, p. 35). According to Mehan and Wood, the reflexive character of reality is not only a feature of thought, but also "a recurrent fact of everyday social life" (Mehan & Wood, 1976, p. 35), and this reflexivity "provides the grounds for absolute belief in the validity of knowledge. […] The absolute belief in the uncorrectability of one's own knowledge enables the believer to reject mutual evidence" (Mehan & Wood, 1976, p. 37). This is also very clear in this type (cf. Chapter 4, Section 5.2). Here, the aspect of faith predominates.

The type of God-distant relationship uses exclusively immanent or anthropological interpretations of the world and the self. Religious interpretations play no role in his reality. This type is more focused on sociality and interaction (cf. Chapter 4, Section 6.3). Metaphysical phenomena are rather explained rationally. Here, the aspect of reason is predominant.

In summary, it can be said that both reason and faith are constitutive components of an engagement with religion that are interrelated. For educational theory, this means that this interrelationship represents an important productive category in which the children can place themselves. The material shows that the children in the sample find themselves in a coordinate system between certainties of faith and doubts, between reason and faith, and between secular and religious claims to truth. The related philosophical questions must be practiced so that the children do not get lost in this system of coordinates.

2.3.3 Thinking and Speaking

In the following, it will be shown how the tension between thinking and speaking appears in the types. In the material it becomes clear that the verbalization of religious experience is a difficulty for the type of God-distant relationship.

It is possible that the remoteness from God is also connected with a "religious unmusicality"[69], which then leads to non-verbalization.

As explained in detail in Chapter 5, Section 2.2.1, from a theological perspective, people are basically free to position themselves against God's offer or not to respond to his address at all. The remoteness from God is therefore not demonized from a theological perspective. Thus, the exercise of religious duties is also a private matter, which is not subject to any state or other control.

Following on from this theme, Behr (2014c) postulates that "children's actions, cognition, and experience correspond with their articulation ability, and that the linguization of religious experience is a component of self-discovery" (Behr, 2014c, p. 505). Accordingly, bridging this distance is possible through language. This aspect is specifically expressed in the Qur'anic creation story. Here, the sudden experience of being separated from God is described in terms of an awakening of Adam. Satan lures Adam and his wife into the trap with the prospect of immortality. After their transgression they immediately feel remorse. To express this inner emotion, they need words to turn back to God. God teaches them the words of forgiveness. Thus, language plays an important role because it is a means of negotiating, representing and managing closeness and distance.

The linguistic ability of the children in the sample is evident in their use of narrations. In the material it becomes clear that the children of the type of God-distant relationship have learned something about God and religion, but it is noticeable that the speaking about God, faith, and religion is low. Here, an independence from school performance becomes clear (cf. Chapter 4, Section 6.2). In the narrations of the type of moral relationship, an assumption of the external perspective and a passivity in the narrative are evident. The adoption of the external perspective could also be a kind of protective reflex, since the stringent retelling of an episode relieves the children of the temptation to reveal something about their own feelings or thoughts. In the response strategies of the children with the type characteristics of moral relationship, it becomes apparent that the connection they make to religion is in many aspects a mirror of social desirability (cf. Chapter 4, Section 5.2).

On the other hand, in the case of personal relationship, concrete references are made between the religious patterns of interpretation and one's own life. This reveals a personal approach to religion in which children can view events in their lives and their environment from a religious perspective and interpret them in terms of transcendence (cf. Chapter 4, Section 4).

Conversely, in the case of the type of God-distant relationship, on the other hand, it is noticeable that a non-thematization and a blank space characterize the self-relating (cf. Chapter 4, Section 6.2).

DISCUSSION OF THE RESEARCH RESULTS

The fact that individual children do or do not engage with God is also evident in the discourses within Islam and the diverse opinions about God expressed there. The narrative power of the Qur'an can help to stimulate a process of cognition and enable a discovery of God (Ulfat, 2020).

The variety of God narratives and the narrative power of the Qur'an can contribute to being able to position oneself in a self-responsible way with regard to Islam and God (Behr et al., 2011). Through the experience of the Qur'an as language or speech, the immediacy of God's proximity can be experienced, namely through the linguistic experience in prayer as a ritual act. Overall, the area of communication plays an essential role, because from an Islamic anthropological perspective, the "ability to relate" to God is characterized by "verbal communication" (Behr, 2014c, p. 495). Suggestions for practice can be found in Chapter 5, Section 3 and Chapter 6, Section 2.

2.3.4   Reference to This World (Relationship Orientation) and Reference to the Hereafter

In the following, we will show how the tension between the reference to this world and the hereafter is reflected in the types. The type of personal relationship addresses the dimension of the invisible, that is, the question of life after death, and the design of afterlife. Phenomena related to the hereafter are mentioned with a high degree of abstraction, and relations to God are made. Here it becomes apparent that religious or transcendence-related interpretations of self and world play a role in certain situations for the actions of this type. The type of personal relationship deals emotionally and cognitively with the nature of what happens after death (cf. Chapter 4, Section 4.4).

From a theological point of view, the construction of Abraham in the Qur'an makes clear the distinction between the dimensions of the visible and the non-visible world that Behr elaborates (Behr, 2009, p. 170): The Qur'an presents Abraham as a wanderer and seeker. His search refers to the realm that lies beyond the visible, triggered by a conflict with his father, who accepts figures as gods (6:74).[70]

During his emigration and search, Abraham deals with the natural phenomena of the visible world:

> When night darkened over him, he saw a star and said, 'This is my Lord!' But when it set, he said, 'I do not like those who set'. Then, when he saw the moon rising, he said, 'This is my Lord!' But when it set, he said, 'Had my Lord not guided me, I would surely have been among the astray lot'. Then, when he saw the sun rising, he said, 'This is my Lord! This is bigger!' But when it set, he said, 'O my people, indeed I disown what you take as [His] partners'. (6:76–78)

Abraham comes to the conclusion to turn to the one who created the heavens and the earth (6:79). But he needs visible proof to calm his heart, and he asks God to show him how the latter brings the dead back to life:

> And when Abraham said, 'My Lord! Show me how You revive the dead', He said, 'Do you not believe?' He said, 'Yes indeed, but in order that my heart may be at rest'. He said, 'Take four of the birds. Then cut them into pieces, and place a part of them on every mountain, then call them; they will come to you hastening. And know that Allah is all-mighty and all-wise'. (2:260)

God uses the term *īmān* in his question to Abraham. The areas concerning the non-visible world are described in the Qur'an with terms such as "faith" (*īmān*), "certainty" (*yaqīn*) and "trust" (*tawakkul*), and they refer to subjective constitutions of faith. This is about much more than "believing *in* God" It is about "*believing* God" (Behr, 2009, p. 170). Especially in the type of personal relationship, it becomes apparent that trust, certainty, and faith are subjectively constructed as well as emotionally and cognitively processed.

The type of moral relationship thematizes the afterlife dimension in connection with dichotomizing morality. This means that the afterlife is thematized in connection with paradise and hell. According to this conception, those who have a tradition compliant, Islamic way of life receive their place in paradise and the others in hell (cf. Chapter 4, Section 5.2).

It is typical for the type of God-distant relationship that the children interpret their life and the phenomena occurring in it in an inner-worldly way. This shows a focus on interpersonal interactions and references. These are located in the here and now. This shows that this type is present-oriented and oriented towards this world (cf. Chapter 4, Section 6.3). The type of personal relationship also shows a social and relational orientation, but this is interwoven with the themes of God and religion (cf. Chapter 4, Section 4.3).

The relationship aspect is addressed in the Qur'an in verses such as 2:177,[71] 17:23–24[72] and 31:12–19.[73] In 2:177, it is about giving money "out of love" to the relatives, the orphans, the needy, the traveler and the beggars. There are three possible interpretations for the phrase "out of love". Either 'for the love towards God' or 'for the love towards the needy' or 'despite the love towards wealth'. Classical Qur'anic commentators such as aṭ-Ṭabarī and az-Zamaḫšarī allow all three interpretations but prefer the third variant with reference to other verses. The verse revolves around the theme of *ḥubb* (love). Such a theme can be addressed on the relational level between people as well as between God and man. Verses 17:23–24 are about respect and kindness toward the parents,

DISCUSSION OF THE RESEARCH RESULTS   285

and 31:12–19 is about a pedagogical conversation between the Prophet Luqmān
and his son, from which operationalizable behaviors can be derived.

2.3.5 Religion and Religiosity

In the following, we will show how the tension between religion and religiosity
is reflected in the types. It becomes clear in the material that religious practice
is an independent variable and that the reference to this practice does not necessarily include a relation to God.

This tension is also addressed in the Qur'an. It distinguishes between a formal (religion) and a subject-related (religiosity) level and does not juxtapose
them, but sees the potential in their union:

> Secure hold (*birr*) is not in turning your faces eastward or westward, but
> in believing in God, in the resurrection on the Last Day, in the angels, in
> the Scriptures, and in the messengers, and in giving out of love, to the
> kinsman, the orphan, to the needy, to the travelers, to those by the way-
> side, and for the deliverance of the downtrodden and the captives, and
> in the performing of prayer and giving, and in the fulfillment of com-
> mitments made, and in patience in times of hardship and suffering and
> violence. Those who do these things are those who are truthful inwardly
> and who respect God. (Behr, 2014a, p. 21, verse 2:177[74])

Behr refers to the semantic field of the term *birr* and, with reference to the
word *barr* (mainland), renders this term as "hold".[75] Seen in this way, the verse
means that a firm standpoint in religion is not expressed solely in performing
a formal rite, but also in ethical maxims and orientation toward the encounter with God. Here, the Qur'an thematizes the formal level (religion) and the
subject-related level (religiosity). It becomes clear that the Qur'an appreciates
and integrates both levels. Faith without formal framing and ritual without religious experience are not the ideal. Form and function are mutually dependent.

In the case of the type of moral relationship in particular, it becomes clear
that rituals are practiced and knowledge about them is present, but that this
does not lead to an inner attitude. The children who are ideally assigned to this
type have a tradition-compliant perspective of God, based on the fact that they
locate themselves and others in their morally dichotomizing worldview on the
side of the good, if and as long as they have a tradition-compliant attitude and
way of life (cf. Chapter 4, Section 5.3). This way of life refers to the practice of
ritual acts such as prayer, fasting, etc. The themes of good and evil are always
discussed in connection with the idea of hell and paradise (reward and punishment). This results in a quasi-purposive-rational relationship to God, which

does not go beyond a formulaic and moral relationship to God. The religious performances are in the foreground here, not the inner attitude. This is also made clear by convictional-ethical positions. The material shows that the connection to religion is in many aspects a mirror of social desirability and is based on convictional-ethical maxims (cf. Chapter 4, Section 5.2).

In summary, the empirical results show that Muslim religiosity can go hand in hand with an autonomous, modern self-image. As explained in detail above, such an attitude can be theologically legitimized through recourse to the sources of Islam.

3 Reflection on the Results Regarding the Importance of Religious Education

After theologically discussing the fields of tension visible in the different types in Chapter 5, Section 2.3, the results are now reflected regarding the significance of religious education. For this purpose, the tasks and challenges of Islamic religious education are outlined based on the results of this study. They consist of the following points:

- In order to open up restrictive narrations to enable flexibility, a broadening of horizons of perception, and changes in perspectives, it is necessary to introduce a diversity of narratives about God (cf. Chapter 5, Section 3.2).
- In order to supplement an unreflected faith due to enculturation, a kind of 'religious narrativity' must be promoted (cf. Chapter 5, Section 3.3).
- In order to address both religious-traditional bounded as well as secular students, „religious communication in contrast to the difference between immanence and transcendence" must be made possible (Treml, 2000, p. 249; cf. Chapter 5, Section 3.4).

These tasks are explained in detail below, after the preliminary considerations.

3.1 *Preliminary Considerations*
Faith in God cannot be explained without the influences of socialization. Socialization theories focus on the relationship between the individual and the environment. Klaus Hurrelmann describes socialization as the "process of the emergence and development of a personality within the mutual interaction of a societally mediated social and material environment" (Hurrelmann, 2002, p. 15). Socialization must therefore be seen in the broader context of enculturation.[76]

DISCUSSION OF THE RESEARCH RESULTS

In this context, sociologists of knowledge describe human thinking as conditioned by collective modes of thought, and everyday life as a place of subjective appropriation of these collective modes of thought. Karl Mannheim (1985) described such collective modes of thought as necessarily perspectivistic and thus as "existentially bound" (Mannheim, 1985, pp. 229–231). Individual knowledge and thinking are necessarily anchored in both the social space and the space of collective modes of thought. Mannheim uses the term "conjunctive experiential space" in this context. Human beings develop their knowledge and thinking in these conjunctive, socially shaped and shared experiential spaces.

The relatively high stability of the three types is also substantiated by the findings of Mannheim. There is not a single child in the sample who was brought up atheistically. According to the children's own statements they were all brought up religiously, i.e., even those children who were assigned to the type of God-distant relationship. Children of this type can mentally distance themselves from God at an early age. God is located in the imaginary realm. The results of recent studies suggest that at the end of every form of religious upbringing there is a certain proportion of primarily tradition-bound persons, a certain proportion of primarily God-related persons, and a certain proportion of primarily far from faith persons. The relating to God and religion is determined by life experience and by individual decisions about how to deal with this experience. The children in the sample take a broad spectrum of decisions. In Mannheim's sense, they come from similarly shaped religious and cultural "experiential spaces" (apart from Olivia and Hagen, who underwent different socialization as they have no migration background). Nevertheless, they do come to different theological conclusions. Worldviews thus depend on both the circumstances of one's life as well as the person's individual decisions. In terms of religious education studies, this is also a sign of the maturity of the children in the sample.

An example: for children of the personal relationship type, a subjective relation to God characterized by trust and positive emotionality is at the heart of the attitude (quote from the interview with Hagen, line 446–449):

> Hagen: I think you definitely feel safe or … because he has created us … you have to imagine him to be quite nice . because if you imagine him like this then he is also nice . but if you imagine him evil then well he is also evil

On the other hand, the moral relationship type shows a relation to God that is more purposively rational oriented and has a formulaic, moralizing, and dichotomous perspective. The following example is a quote from the interview with Canan (line 117–125):

> Canan: So if someone is in trouble /uhm/ Allah protects them AND ... punishes the other people IN hell and (29) well I think Allah is only there with good people and not with bad ones (7) and further I don't know
>
> I: Good people
>
> Canan: For example those who prayed five prayers a day AND /uhm/ ... just were busy like Ali and ... were good and polite to everyone and nice and did not LIKE /uhm/ not lock up AND /uhm/ ... so /um/ DID annoy the teacher and stuff like that (5) AND (25) and further I don't know.

The results present a thematization of God within the dimensions and categories of learned tradition, but no engagement with it. Here the tension between individuation and enculturation or tradition becomes manifest which is unilaterally dissolved in favor of tradition. The responsibilities of Islamic religious education start at this point.

For the type of God-distant relationship, God exists peripherally as an element of social reality. A personal relation to God does not become evident. Instead, God is located in the realm of fantasy. One example is given by Gökmen (quote from the interview with Gökmen, line 242–245):

> I: Tell me a story about you and Allah
>
> Gökmen: /Uh/ ... So a dream?
>
> I: Whatever you want
>
> Gökmen: I have no story (me?) and Allah

Although this type has also participated in Islamic religious education and is familiar with the explication of religious semantics, it becomes evident – in maximum contrast to the moralizing and tradition-compliant type – that propositional knowledge about God is hardly presented. This shows a discrepancy between intentional learning and its practice. With this type, the starting point and challenge for Islamic religious education is located exactly here.

The above-mentioned three quotations once again exemplify the core results of this study. They illustrate the function and the task as well as the challenge of Islamic religious education in an exemplary way.

DISCUSSION OF THE RESEARCH RESULTS

In the following, three theses are formulated and explained in detail from the perspective of Islamic religious education.

3.2   'Narrative' "Constitutive Rationality" vs. Other Forms of Rationality

Thesis 1: Islamic religious education has the specific task of familiarizing students with the diversity of religious narrations and thus enables flexibility in thinking, a multidimensional broadening of the horizon of perception, the ability to change perspectives, and a 'feeling of belonging', also in religious terms.

Educational researcher Jürgen Baumert highlighted universal aspects regarding the structure of educational content in modern societies: "School is the only institution in modern societies that ensures the generalization of universal communication prerequisites in the next generation by systematically dealing with different modes of encountering the world" (Baumert, 2002, p. 106). Baumert refers to Wilhelm von Humboldt and presents four different forms of rationality, each opening up its own "horizons of understanding the world":

1.   "cognitive-instrumental modelling of the world" (mathematics, natural sciences)
2.   "aesthetic-expressive encounter and design" (language/literature, music/painting/visual arts, physical expression)
3.   "normative-evaluative examination of economy and society" (history, economy, politics/society, law)
4.   "problems of constitutive rationality" (religion, philosophy)

Each of these modes of encountering the world follows its own logic, is fundamental to education and is not replaceable. According to Baumert, they form the basis of modern general education. It is particularly important in this context that schools in modern societies institutionalize "the reflexive encounter with *each* of these different forms of human rationality" (Baumert, 2002, p. 107).[77]

From this educational science perspective, religious education represents an independent approach to the world and makes its own contribution to general school education. In Germany, Article 3, paragraph 7 of the Basic Constitutional Law grants religious education a place in the secular school system. Religion is the only subject that is regulated in the Basic Constitutional Law, namely as a *res mixta*. Both freedom of religious confession and students' freedom from religious paternalism are respected; the students are autonomous subjects in this respect.

The priority of reflexive access to questions of religion is just as important here as it is with all other forms of rationality.[78] The subject of Islamic religious education is based on the guiding principles of the educational mission of public schools in general.

Education in general thus opens up different approaches to the world, i.e., students should acquire the ability to understand that one can "read" the world in different ways ("literacy" concept; Dressler, 2007, p. 130). Each "reading" of the world results in one's own "modelling" of the world (Dressler, 2007, p. 130). According to Bernhard Dressler, this is to be attributed to the fact that education today must provide an answer to the loss of the world's unity due to functional differentiations in modern societies and the associated pluralization of forms of rationality. Education can therefore no longer be thought of as an integrative overall concept and cannot refer to a "unified scientific world view" (Dressler, 2007, p. 133). Dressler emphasizes that education is aimed at "uncertainty tolerance" (Dressler, 2007, p. 134) since it has to prepare young people for an uncertain future and for an experience of diversity as a result of the differentiation process described above. "Differentiation competence" (Dressler, 2007, p. 134) is a capacity for differentiation, meaning that educational processes take place via the ability to change perspective since different life situations require different perspectives of world perceptions and therefore every perspective has a blind spot. Religion is also a phenomenon of differentiation as it offers its own mode of world access and interpretation (Dressler, 2007, p. 135). In system-theoretical terms, religion is a code that makes the world accessible in an interpretive way. The religious system is thus a "cultural subsystem" in a functionally differentiated society that interprets the world by means of a "code" (Treml, 2007, p. 35).

With reference to the above-mentioned diversity of narratives about God (cf. Chapter 5, Section 2.2.1), for Islamic religious education studies, the claim arises, to outline something like a 'narrative' "constitutive rationality". In this context, there is also the demand to establish dealing appropriately with narrative rationality as an educational mandate. The aim is to interpret the world religiously with the help of a narrative understanding of God. The diversity of narratives is of particular importance to broaden the horizon of perception and bring a change in perspective because the religious "reading" of the world can happen in many different ways. There is no such thing as only one religious reading.

Furthermore, the challenge of religious education lies in its "paradoxical didactics" which is – according to Annette Scheunpflug – characterized by "uncertainties" with regard to the "social and factual dimension". Scheunpflug points out that within the social dimension, the "freedom of the subject" represents an element of uncertainty. Thus, the cooperation of the students as "self-dynamic, non-transparent, and non-linear operating individuals" becomes essential (Scheunpflug, 2011, p. 108). Moreover, this uncertainty is reinforced by the factual dimension. This is because religious education, like any other school subject, should above all lead to a secure pool of knowledge

DISCUSSION OF THE RESEARCH RESULTS

and defined competences in its field. But the bond to "ultimate concerns" is also fundamental for religious education. This, however, is unavailable and may therefore trigger the factual dimension's unsettling effect in religious education (Scheunpflug, 2011, p. 109).

Another paradox of religious education lies in the fact that what already exists, namely a bond to religion, should be made connectable to language, society, and reflection. The bond to religion cannot of course be assumed for all children. Since it is not possible to make connectable what is not yet there, the paradox arises that what is fundamental for religious education must be simultaneously developed in it. Religious education can only escape this paradox by offering the possibility of establishing a bond with religion through forms of experience. Especially with the concept of *'religious narrativity'* (cf. detailed explanation following in Chapter 5, Section 3.3), the forms of experience can be defined more precisely because they are a staged form of experience. *'Religious narrativity'* also provides the concept of space. In this sense religion can thus be made accessible to experience. The experiential nature of religion also includes the habitualizing approach: "The shared development of rules and rites creates an atmosphere and makes religion directly perceptible through the explorative spaces of action" (Behr, 2014c, p. 508). These different approaches enable and facilitate greater flexibility in the development of individual religiosity.

In this sense, Behr describes education – including religious education – from an educational philosophical perspective with the terms *tazkiya*, *tādīb* and *ta'līm*. *Ta'līm* refers to informing and points to the *head*; *tādīb* denotes the development of good and God-pleasing behavior and points to the *hand*; *tazkiya* originates from the verb *zakiya* (to be good inside, to grow, to purify) and describes the ability of the human being to guide her/himself and thus points to the *heart*. Behr therefore postulates that education is understood as *"Bildung"* and that human beings are regarded as learning with all their senses. In addition, *Bildung* is not only limited to the reality of this world, but – from an Islamic perspective – also points to the hereafter. The interpretation of the world thus takes place from both perspectives, whereby the human being depends on God's guidance when it comes to interpreting the hereafter (Behr, 2014c, p. 508).

The results of the present study illustrate that although the children of the sample took part in (denominational) Islamic religious education or religious schooling in mosques, this by no means inevitably led to their developing a relation to God and religion. But that is exactly what religious education, with its curricula, is based on. Consequently, religious education must take place in a form that is on the one hand open to plurality in order to reach the types of personalizing and God-distant relationship, but on the other hand also offers a connection to tradition in order to integrate the moral relationship type. In addition, religious education must offer opportunities in order to not only understand religion in its various dimensions, but also to make it experienceable.

In particular, the moral relationship type constructs the world and God from a dichotomous perspective. Good and evil are always discussed in connection with the idea of hell and paradise (reward and punishment). This indicates that the members of this type regard those elements of tradition they know as the truth which is not further interpreted narratively. The connection that is made to religion is a mirror of social desirability in many aspects. Hence, this type uses the religious information given by the cultural reference system in order to deal with certain situations and occasions in a religious way, but knowledge has no action-guiding reference here.

With reference to the dichotomous, moralizing perspective of God, the question of how to deal with a punishing God in religious education arises from the didactic perspective. Are the numinous experiential worlds of children de-demonized? Is it acceptable to thematize evil spirits and hell? And if so, then how?[79] For example, the curriculum for Islamic religious education at the Bavarian elementary school stipulates that hell is not a topic, although it is assumed that children have a natural interest in existential questions and ask for criteria of good and evil. Nevertheless, the topic of evil is more or less ignored in the curriculum. Faith and an honest life are thematized as ways to paradise. If, however, it is assumed that Muslim children also develop their very own accesses to spiritual and religious worlds as well as their very own ways in experiencing the numinous, one would have to ask here how their ideas can be taken up in order to expand their perceptual horizon in a multidimensional way.

Hans Mendl (2015, p. 97) specifies that it is just as problematic to instill fear by a punishing God as it is to only speak about a loving God, since such faith is not sustainable and therefore might collapse if individual strokes of fate happen in life.

Petra Freudenberger-Lötz (2013) offers an approach to a solution by emphasizing that "the challenge of constructing a multi-faceted image of God can build a positive, hopeful basis that forms a supporting foundation for religious development". Therefore, neither a pure "Buddy God" nor a pure "Boss God" produces substantial faith that gives hope. Due to the children's individual understandings of God which they construct depending on suggestions and experiences from their lifeworld and their school environment, she sees the task of religious-pedagogical assistance in "supporting the children in order to develop a multi-faceted understanding of God and thus to develop a multi-dimensional perception of reality and a multi-dimensional understanding of tradition and the world in which they live" (Freudenberger-Lötz, 2013, p. 263). This means that only a multifaceted narrative about God enables children "to

DISCUSSION OF THE RESEARCH RESULTS   293

contour their personal image of God and to give direction to their faith. They find approaches for addressing God, for being addressed by God, and for experiencing that God is always at their side protecting them equally, but also confronting them with challenges" (Fachlehrplan [Curriculum for Islamic religious education], 2004, p. 2).

Consequently, there is a possibility for promoting an individual reflection of faith in God and a conscious managing of the question of God. Freudenberger-Lötz emphasizes that "offers for interpretation must be linked to existing structures of knowledge, opinions, and attitudes" (Freudenberger-Lötz, 2013, p. 264). With reference to Islamic religious education, this means that with the help of Qur'anic or religious narratives the relevance of faith in God in existential situations can be demonstrated and a reference to the students' lifeworlds can be established. Hence, the children can connect the interpretations that religion offers to their own experiences. Doubts and criticism also play an important role in a conscious approach to faith in God.

Regarding the moralizing perspective on God, it is didactically appropriate to thematize responsible-ethical maxims. This is because the material shows particularly for the moral relationship type that highly moral behavior is actualized which in Weber's sense can be described as convictional ethics. This means that the intrinsic value of ethical action alone suffices to justify it, regardless of the consequences of the action.

Regarding the responsible-ethical perspective, the Qur'an offers a variety of narratives. The Qur'an establishes a "canon of operationalizable behavioral goals" (Behr, 2014c, p. 501) as expressed in verses 25:63–77[80] and 31:12–19.[81] Verses 25:63–77 talk about behavioral characteristics like modesty, peace ableness, piety, generosity, attentiveness, penitence, trust in God, love of truth, respectability, serenity, attention, thirst for knowledge, success orientation, patience, and hope for the hereafter. Verses 31:12–19 provide concrete instructions for good behavior such as: enjoining what is right, forbidding what is reprehensible, patiently enduring what befalls oneself (in the sense of strength, determination, and a firm mind), not cold-shouldering others, not being haughty, arrogant, conceited and boastful, being humble and lowering one's voice. These and other verses such as 6:66[82] point to self-responsibility and responsibility towards others. In the classroom, it is important to reflect on the consequences of such behavior. If the emphasis is placed on the responsible-ethical perspective, then awareness for as well as a distance from oneself must be developed in order to refrain from an egocentric world view.

Developing a distance from oneself also plays a role in the unfolding of the self. "The unfolding of 'I' and 'You' as schemata of the human differentiation between the self and the world is the fulcrum in the determination of the relationship between proximity and distance as a didactic challenge" (Behr, 2009,

p. 167). From the didactic perspective, this represents an educational goal: the ability to autonomously determine by something like 'religious narrativity' (cf. Chapter 5, Section 3.3) the level of closeness and distance and thus of commitment and freedom – including to God.

3.3 Enculturation vs. Verbalization and Narrative Access to Faith

Thesis 2: The task of Islamic religious education is to supplement unreflected faith due to enculturation on the individual level with a narrative and rational approach to faith and to offer forms of verbalization. The point is therefore to promote some sort of 'religious narrativity'.

The term 'religious narrativity' describes the ability and skill

1. to recognize, to interpret, and to discuss the religious narratives that have developed in the course of Islamic theological history with regard to their diversity of interpretations. This refers – particularly in relation to the question about God – to the diversity of Muslim narratives of God as described in detail in Chapter 5, Section 3.2. The material clearly shows that the recognition, interpretation, and discussion of this diversity is the prerequisite for flexibility in the children's thinking that allows for a change of perspective and thus creates spaces for the religious pedagogue to stimulate and promote education.

2. to be able to switch between observation of the 1st order and observation of the 2nd order according to Luhmann. This describes the change of perspective between, on the one hand, religious speaking, i.e., participating in religious practice, and, on the other hand, observing and discussing this practice i.e. to critically reflect on the role of religion in one's own life and in society. This dialectic of participation and reflection which is the basis of religious education goes back to Bernhard Dressler (2007, p. 135; cf. in detail in this section below).

3. to distinguish between "religious truth" and "historical reality" in religious narratives and to recognize, interpret, and analyze these two levels regarding their respective potential. Behr talks about a "reality" that can be experienced and a "theological truth of faith" in this context (Behr, 2008, p. 34). The ability to distinguish between these two levels constitutes the core of a 'religious narrativity' (cf. in detail in this section below).

Point 1 has already been explained in Chapter 5, Section 3.2. Now, point 2 will be explained:

According to Alfred Treml (2007), education can be understood as a social stimulus as the realization of thoughts and their integration into existing knowledge must be carried out by the learner her/himself. "Education then

DISCUSSION OF THE RESEARCH RESULTS

is – if it is successful – the social stimulation of a self-transformation of mental systems" (Treml, 2007, p. 37). Hence, education happens through change. If this change happens unreflectedly, education is called "functional education" ("everyday education"). If this change is reflected, it is referred to as "intentional education" ("pedagogy"). The latter aims to enable learners to change themselves (Treml, 2007, p. 38). If intentional education is the impetus for self-transformation for the learner, thought must be given to how this impetus and this change will take place. This happens through reflection. A differentiation made by Dressler (2007) is useful here. According to him, religious communication can take place in two forms: as "religious speech" and as "reflection on religion" (Dressler, 2007, p. 135). Religious speech means communicating in a religious way as well as looking at the world through religion. This takes place from an "internal perspective". Reflection on religion means communicating about religion and observing how religion sees the world. This takes place from an "external perspective". Both perspectives require the possibility of a "change of perspective" (Dressler, 2007, p. 135).

However, religious education as a reflection on religion cannot take on the task of conveying faith, as faith is unavailable and religious interpretation of the world is closely linked to socialization, i.e., to functional education which usually takes place in the family and community. In their lifeworld, students can experience in their lifeworlds how religion copes with contingency and thus develop faith in God. "Faith evades an intentional and at the same time formal teaching situation, e.g. in school" (Scheunpflug & Mette, 2007, p. 50).

Religious education cannot therefore produce the spiritual foundations on which it is built. Basically, religious education in school is "only possible where it is not needed [...], and it is impossible where it is necessary" (Treml, 2000, p. 248). This means that intentional education is easier if a bond to religion already exists.

Thus, in religious education an encounter between an internal perspective (religious speech) and an external perspective (reflection on religion) must take place. Religious communication must therefore also be possible from an "observer's position" as a second order communication (Dressler, 2007, p. 136). The point is not what other people (whether they are religious or not) say about Islam, rather we talk about two different perspectives that Muslims themselves can take: the religious internal perspective and the reflective external perspective. In the communication of these two perspectives, authentic Muslim religion-theoretical statements are possible that are neither under the pressure of a defense to the outside nor under the relativizing pull of a religiously pluralistic perspective.[83] Consequently, it becomes possible to use the potentials of the various narratives about God that have developed in the course of Islamic theological history and to revive the relation to God by reactivating the religious narratives.

Haci-Halil Uslucan (2008) describes the predominant Islamic style of upbringing in his study on religious value education in Muslim families. He notes that religious upbringing is more about establishing a positive, affective, and spiritual basis for faith than about rational understanding. As an example, he lists the recitation of Qur'an verses that are often not understood by non-Arab Muslims, especially not by children.

> Non-Arab Muslim children learn to read the Qur'an in their religious socialization, but this competence is limited to reading and does not include understanding or interpretation skills. The ability of literal reproduction is practiced; Qur'anic verses are learned by heart; the phonetically correct reproduction of the word order is the criterion. From the perspective of learning theory or pedagogical psychology, this form of learning is a very superficial, failure-prone method hardly suitable for tackling practical everyday problem situations since there is no absorption, no independent cognitive elaboration and semantic penetration of the content. However, this instruction (presentation – memorization) is more about the constitution of a positive, benevolent 'habitus' towards religion; it is about the implementation of an affective anchor to which certain contents can be attached in the course of socialization. Similar forms of introduction to religion can also be found in other religions. Perhaps this early establishment of an affective basis – and not so much a rational understanding – is responsible for a firm grounding of the internal religious system of the person. To learn by heart or to know the Qur'anic verses literally is a prerequisite of religious practice; it is not primarily a question of 'intellectual penetration'. (Uslucan, 2008, pp. 32–33)

Uslucan describes here the practice in the families and/or in the mosques.

In the sample all except two children went through an Islamic religious education at school. The propositional knowledge they reproduce as well as the narrations of the type of moral relationship in particular lead to the assumption that Uslucan's descriptions also apply, at least occasionally, to the situation in Islamic religious education at school. This means that Islamic religious education, despite its curricula, does not transcend the boundaries of a non-reflective transmission of tradition and therefore reflection on religion does not take place. If one of the two approaches (religious speech and speaking about religion) fails to develop, there will be an increase in the probability that forms of piety similar to those in the types of moral relationship as well

DISCUSSION OF THE RESEARCH RESULTS

as of God-distant relationship will emerge, instead of imbuing the connection to God with life. The double approach can help the moral relationship type to open rigid traditional hulls and let a reflective faith come to life. Here, we face a decisive challenge for Islamic religious education studies. It is not about acquiring further knowledge as the interviews show that religious socialization already exists. The didactic problem lies in how teachers can enable students to get to know the diversity of narratives of God, to make this knowledge relevant for action and to apply it critically and constructively.

The results of the present study show that in a highly individualized society such as the German or European one, religion must be addressed in its diverse narrativity in order to imbue faith with life. However, if the religious knowledge of children is determined by tradition and social desirabilities and the children are not in a position to apply it to the challenges of their biographies and everyday lives in a reflective way, the fostering of 'religious individuation' is considerably more difficult (cf. Chapter 5, Section 3.4).

In this context, the topic of affiliation plays an important role. If religious affiliation is read in the Qur'an as a universal category that is not superficially attached to questions of confession, this can – theologically speaking – be understood as the subject's self-positioning to God which is not culturally or nationally determined. That means the subject's attitude replaces the question of affiliation with the concept of devotion and turning to God (cf. Chapter 5, Section 2.3).

To take children and their own interpretations seriously is a prerequisite for their developing a substantiated position on theological issues and topics of faith. Here it is useful to let children express their own perceptions and interpretations in the form of theological conversations that could be taken up and used to start a theological dialogue. Such an approach basically leads to philosophical competence, which plays a significant role for good Islamic religious education. This is not about a positioning of theology versus philosophy, since theological conversations are a certain kind of philosophizing but with a metaphysical reference. In these conversations, the children can be offered theological interpretations, which can also be oriented towards tradition, but the children themselves are free to take up and continue them and to deal with them in an individualized and in-depth way. This starts a dialogue between the interpretations of the children and those of tradition; at the same time, the teacher has the task of offering the children opportunities for reflection in order to develop their own, self-determined view of tradition (cf. theoretical foundation of a children's theology in Islamic religious education in Ulfat, 2017).

Overall, however, it is indispensable for the classroom to negotiate "between *discursive* and *normative* approaches, between *inductive* and *deductive* learning pathways, between *experiential* and *theology-based*" methods, depending on the particular situation (Behr, 2008, p. 36).

Bible didactics is specific to Protestant and Catholic religious education studies. It addresses principles such as giving the biblical traditions a 'place in life', taking up the experiences and the life context of the students, encouraging them to identify with the persons mentioned in the texts, etc. Islamic religious education studies faces the task of developing some kind of *'narrative Qur'an didactics'* which is to be understood as an Islamic counterpart to Bible didactics that can lead to a *'religious narrativity'* in the sense outlined above (Ulfat, 2020).

Understanding the Qur'anic narrations with their own conceptual world is essential in this context. Klaus von Stosch, who examines the relation between revelation and reason in Islam and Christianity, writes: "But understanding, as Gadamer has shown in his classical analyses, only takes place when my conceptual world and the world of the text come together and a fusion of horizons takes place, but not when I take the foreign world of the text as an unquestioned starting point of my thoughts" (von Stosch, 2011, p. 107). This shows another challenge in working with the Qur'an: What is needed is a language-sensitive work with the text (Ulfat, 2019) that is also able to use the potential of encountering the text in an aesthetically mediated way (Kermani, 2007).

In the following, point 3 is explained:
From the perspective of system-theoretical educational science, the question of the purpose and function of religious education is not "to practice faith, but to keep it enabled to speak and reflect on it in a world that is characterized by science" (Scheunpflug & Mette, 2007, p. 50). Faith is therefore not transmittable, but it can be represented and communicated. From an Islamic-theological perspective, faith is an unavailable gift and thus depends on the freedom of the subject (cf. Verse 2:256: "There is no compulsion in religion").

In this respect, the challenge for the didactics of Islamic religious education is to reflect on the tension between 'theological truth' and 'empirical reality'. 'Reality' is meant in the sense of the present experiential world which is limited to perception. 'Truth' refers to the narratable theological truth of faith (Behr, 2008, p. 34).

In concrete terms this means that the distinction between 'theological truth' and 'historical reality' shows itself in the tension between tradition and the present situation. On the one hand there are the religious sources and on the other hand there is the situation of the students with their experiences. Reality unfolds a tangible effect as it can be experienced by the senses. Theological truth, on the other hand, cannot be proven. For example, the statement "God created everything out of nothing" is a theological truth, but it does not

DISCUSSION OF THE RESEARCH RESULTS

represent reality because it cannot be verified. Further, the *šahāda* (creed) is a truth sentence and not a reality because it cannot be proven. It then becomes an effective motive if it leads the person who pronounces it to use it purposefully or intentionally in her/his actions.

To make the students aware of this tension between truth and reality is the challenge for religious education. The question about the nature of truth in relation to reality can be addressed in the field of prophetic narratives. In this respect, the narration of Noah and the Ark, for example, is of interest depending on the competence orientation. The point here is to interpret this narration on the basis of religious information as well as on the basis of one's own lifeworld. The ability to interpret things is one of the horizons of religious education that Behr (2011) has developed from the classical philosophy of Islamic education. Here, allegoresis would be an interpretation technique. In Noah's narration the question about the symbols of the ark, Noah, the sea, and the new horizon can be explored. One possibility for an allegorical reading would be to interpret the ship as a symbol for religion, the sea as a symbol for the world, and the new horizon as a symbol for the hereafter. This gives a completely new meaning to the one who enters the ark or fails to do so. Here there is great potential for religious learning in religious education. Through such an interpretative opening, the significance of these narratives can be worked out in relation to the present and the lifeworld. In this sense, the students have the opportunity to reflect on the fact that they at some point in their lives are faced with the decision of whether they want to embark on the journey and enter 'their' ark and which course they will take.

It becomes clear that the importance of narratives and their 'religious truth'" are in the foreground, not their historical reality. Religious truth is thus not necessarily identical with historical reality. Reality is limited to perception; truth goes beyond that. In particular, the tension between wording (text) and meaning (spirit), that is between what is written in the Qur'an and its interpretation, reveals the potential that exists here for religious contemplation. The Qur'an offers various approaches to this. One approach is understanding the world through observation and measuring (empiricism) as in verse 4:82: "Do they not contemplate the Qur'an?" or in the figurative sense: "Do you not want to deconstruct the Qur'an?" A second approach is an anamnestic one through the narration as shown above in the narration about Noah.

3.3.1   Conclusion
Religious narrativity' and empirical understanding of the world thus allow for a multidimensional perception of reality and are a key to theological competence. Jacob formulates this competence towards his son Joseph at the beginning of Sura 12. When Joseph talks about his dream, Jacob says that God teaches

him to understand things in their meaning and to interpret them in the sense of an allegorical interpretation (*tāwīl*).

Being able to assess the consequences of one's behavior is a prerequisite for the behavioral change mentioned in Chapter 5, Section 3.2 and represents a prognostic, anticipatory competence. In this difficult learning task in adolescence, religion has an essential educational significance: it offers various approaches to understanding empiricism, anamnesis, and theory in order to ultimately understand what God actually *enables* man to do (not what God wants) as here begins man's own responsibility. These reflections show that a religious normativity can be reformulated from pedagogical considerations. Fundamental reflections emerge from the research material regarding the relationship between predetermination and free choice. There is, after all, a difference between whether I want to know what God wants from me or whether I try to discover what God makes possible for me. A shift of emphasis regarding the idea of man becomes visible here. Religious education should give students the opportunity to discover what God enables them to do; ultimately, it should give students theological competence. In addition, religious learning is strongly linked back to the subject and 'individuation' is promoted. This 'individuation' is a maxim of religious-pedagogically reflected action (Schröder, 2012, pp. 232–249). In this context Boschki is also worth reading (Boschki, 2008, pp. 107–109) as parallels to the subjectivation processes described in various sociological studies on religion can be found in his work (cf. Chapter 5, Section 1.3).

3.4 *Religion and Secularity*

The question of the relation between religion and secularity is one of the essential points that will determine the future of Islamic religious education and its further development. Until now the discourse around this education has been institutional, not substantive. It is only through the discourse on its content that Islamic religious education studies will be able to occupy this field and establish Islamic religious education. It is precisely the moral relationship type as well as the God-distant relationship type that make the question of this relation particularly interesting.

Thesis 3: The task of Islamic religious education is to enable "religious communication in contrast of the difference between immanence and transcendence" (Treml, 2000, p. 249).

According to Treml, religion can be studied at the level of a second-order observation. That is, religion itself is not observed but people's communication about it. From this perspective, religion is therefore a communicative

DISCUSSION OF THE RESEARCH RESULTS

event. Systems theory states that religion exists as a system because it fulfils a "function". Treml clarifies, with reference to the systems theorist Bronisław Malinowski, that "function" in this context means satisfying a need. In relation to religion this signifies that religion has the function of satisfying a longing for meaning and offering a solution for a problem of reference, namely to update meaning (Treml, 2007, p. 32). According to Treml, the function of religion therefore consists of coping with contingency, i.e., religion answers the deficits of meaning that arise from tensions and discontinuities in modern societies.

According to Luhmann (2002), "communication always becomes religious [...] when the immanent is examined from the perspective of transcendence" (p. 77, cited in Treml, 2007, p. 34).[84] This means that the immanently percepti- ble world can be related to transcendence and thus be reformulated. Luhmann describes this distinction between immanence and transcendence as a "binary code" which is characteristic for religion (Treml, 2007, p. 34). Thus, religious communication can only be seen systems-theoretically in the "contrast of the difference between immanence and transcendence" (Treml, 2000, p. 249).

In this context, the difference between internal and external perspectives also plays an important role. Dressler emphasizes that "the decisive criterion for religious education as an indispensable aspect of general education is [...] the ability to relate the internal perspective of practicing a religion to the exter- nal perspective of a distanced reflection on religion without one determining the other" (Dressler, 2007, p. 136). The difference between "religious speech" and "speaking about religion" must be made consciously and kept conscious in religious education (change of perspective). Following the modes of encoun- tering the world (Baumert, 2002), which also include religion, Dressler thus draws attention to the difference that religious-educational processes also carry *within themselves*. This means that reality can be viewed multidimen- sionally through the alternation between religious speech and speaking *about* religion (Dressler, 2007).

It becomes evident that for religious education the external perspective is necessary instead of being destructive. The types of moral relationship as well as of God-distant relationship show deficits from the religious-pedagogical point of view. With the help of the double perspective of an internal and exter- nal view, religious education can offer options to overcome these deficient attitudes.

As already pointed out, the task and function of religious education from an educational science perspective is to offer a language to individual faith, to establish a relation between faith and intellect, and not to missionize.

According to Baumert, the reflection on religion from an outside perspec- tive is particularly important as school "opens up a primarily reflexive access to different areas of life. Reflexivity and the primacy of the cognitive are probably schools' inherent protection against indoctrination" (Baumert, 2002, p. 105).

The God-distant relationship type can also be reached by speaking *about* religion. Faith does not need to be already present in order to initiate the reflection on faith.

The data material of this study shows that the moral relationship type among the children know the rituals and can also practice them. This type possesses a high proportion of propositional knowledge but have no action-guiding reference to it. Children of this type seem to primarily learn about rules, rituals, and traditions in the classroom or in the context of their religious socialization. They have no access to the reflexive level. In their statements it becomes clear that despite their practice in rituals and despite their propositional knowledge, they do not develop an independent inner attitude that goes beyond the fulfilment of social desirability within their social environment.

Behr (2014d) points out that the medieval discussions about the determination of the relation between faith and reason as well as between reality and truth "drew their vehemence from the growing recognition of the necessity to relate text and spirit in a rational way for the good of mankind" (Behr, 2014d, p. 2). The aim of religious education, among other things, is to accompany students in establishing this very relation between text and spirit in a well-founded way. It should aim to foster the development of their own reasoned perspective on questions of worldview and faith, as well as the determination of their own independent view, to be able to speak, communicate, and provide information within social discourse.

4 Summary

Since there is no single world view capable of consensus in late modernity, the pedagogical challenge lies in empowering children to find their own way in a world of multiple, contradictory world interpretations. Especially when preparing young believers for living in a religiously plural society, a personal relation to God and the reflexivity of one's own religion are decisive prerequisites for preventing radicalization and moral rigidity.

Developments such as the emergence of the so-called "Islamic State" confront both theology and religious education with the challenge to counteract spiritually and mentally the destruction of the own tradition and to provide orientation. As the material shows, the children of this study stand between two poles: being Muslim as a sign of cultural-spatial and collective affiliation; and being Muslim as a sign of an active and subjective religious construction.

DISCUSSION OF THE RESEARCH RESULTS   303

The educational idea of Islam that is based on the idea of a subject capable of learning and of conducting her/himself gives children and young people access to Islam as a resource. The challenge of Islamic religious education therefore lies in an "anthropological turn" (Behr, 2016) in which the autonomy of the subject is placed in the foreground and the function of spirituality is highlighted as a resource for solving problems in a modern, individualized, and pluralistic society.

The results of the present study are of particular importance for the further development of modern Islamic religious education as they emphasize how young believers can be prepared for life in a religiously plural society regarding their relation to God.

Notes

1 The 18th Shell Youth Study from 2019, entitled "A generation speaks up", also examines young people's religiosity and states that Muslim young people are more religious than Catholic and Protestant young people and put more emphasis on faith in God (Albert et al., 2019).

2 For example, the "creative-reflexive pattern" shows parallels to the type of personal relationship. According to Tressat, this pattern characterizes a type of religiosity that represents a multifunctional resource in migration. Here, religiosity serves to develop one's own life plan and to deal with biographical and worldly issues in a creative-productive way. Trust in God and self-confidence are the two dimensions in which this type operates. In addition, a conscious and individual decision to believe is apparent here (Tressat, 2011, pp. 126–128).

3 In Tietze's first type, religiosity is "ethicized" so that autonomy is acquired and faith becomes a "manual of action" (Tietze, 2001, p. 157). Here, parallels to the type of personal relationship are evident.

4 Components of the religious symbol system.

5 Cf. the article by Schweitzer and Dubiski (2012) for processes of construction and co-construction in childhood.

6 The mu'tazilite world of thought found its way into the theology of Zaidites and Imamites, but also into Arab Judaism. Worthy of mention here is the rabbinic theologian Sa'adyā Gaon (882–942), whose work "Emunot we-Deot" deals with the philosophical justification of Jewish dogmas Stroumsa (2003). On the Greek influences on Mu'tazila thought and the reasons for its discrediting and decline (Hildebrandt, 2007, pp. 143–145)

7 Today, the *miḥna* is attributed to political rather than religious aspects (Hildebrandt, 2007, pp. 129–130).

8 The *ḥadīṯ* scholars saw themselves as "collectors and systematizers of the tradition of the Prophet and his contemporaries. They called themselves the "representatives of tradition and community" (*ahl as-sunna wa-l-ǧamāʿa*) and claimed to speak for the majority of Muslims (Hildebrandt, 2007, p. 144).

9 The word *hiǧra* refers to the emigration of Muhammad from Mecca to Medina on 12 *Rabīʿ al-awwal* (September 24, 622). It marks the beginning of the Islamic time measurement.

10 Both classical and contemporary discourses are primarily concerned with the focal theme of God's transcendence and immanence. This discourse is closely linked to the doctrine of the

304 CHAPTER 5

uniqueness or indivisibility of God (*tauḥīd*) and his adversarial attributes. In this regard, too, there are different approaches among the various schools of theological thought, which are explained in detail by Hajatpour (2013, pp. 81–95).

11 For al-Ġazālī (1940), too, the heart is the place of transcendent spiritual perception.

12 The term *ṣadr* often occurs in the Qur'an in the phrase *ḏāt aṣ-ṣudūr*, in the sense of the 'essence of the breasts'. In the Qur'anic context, this phrase is associated with God's knowledge of what man cherishes in his innermost being, even if he wishes to keep it secret (examples: 3:119, 31:23, 35:38, 57:6). The breast is named in the Qur'an as the place into which fear, strife, and forgetfulness can be whispered (114:5). However, it is also the place where expansion, unfolding, or constriction can take place. God is described in this regard as the one who opens the breast and leads to faith or makes the breast tremulous and oppressed and leads away from faith (6:125) (Pavlis, 2001, pp. 27–29).

13 The term *qalb* and its plural *qulūb* occur frequently in the Qur'an and refer to recognition. The heart is a place of communication between man and God. It is the place of comprehending, seeing, and hearing the divine signs. These perceptions of the heart can be veiled, hardened, sick, and closed, but also open, soft, and pliable (Pavlis, 2001, pp. 35–37).

14 The term *fuʾād* and its plural *afʾida* are used in the Qur'an, similarly to qalb, for the place of sensory perception such as hearing and seeing. The Qur'an speaks of strengthening the hearts in 11:120 and 25:32. Although the two terms are often used in the same way in the Qur'an, they are not interchangeable (Pavlis, 2001, pp. 35–37).

15 In the Qur'an, only the plural of the term *lubb* is used: *albāb*. It is used in addressing people who are insightful and allow themselves to be admonished (14:52, 2:269). Remembering God is also associated with this term in the Qur'an (38:29). In this regard, the Book is sent down full of blessings to the insightful who consider its verses rightly and are admonished. Thus, what is at issue here is insight, pondering, and cognition, which in the mystical tradition are referred to as the innermost sphere of the heart as well as the recipient of God's grace and mercy (Pavlis, 2001, pp. 35–37).

16 Culture is understood here in the sense of Erich Weber (2003) as a transformed nature that is useful to human life and enriches existence.

17 "There is a sickness in their hearts; then Allah increased their sickness, and there is a painful punishment for them because of the lies they used to tell".

18 "Certainly We have created for hell many of the jinn and humans: they have hearts with which they do not understand, they have eyes with which they do not see, they have ears with which they do not hear. They are like cattle; rather they are more astray. It is they who are the heedless".

19 "Have they not traveled over the land so that they may have hearts by which they may apply reason, or ears by which they may hear? Indeed it is not the eyes that turn blind, but the hearts turn blind – those that are in the breasts".

20 "And He taught Adam the Names, all of them; then presented them to the angels and said, 'Tell me the names of these, if you are truthful'. They said, 'Immaculate are You! We have no knowledge except what You have taught us. Indeed You are the All-knowing, the All-wise'. He said, 'O Adam, inform them of their names', and when he had informed them of their names, He said, 'Did I not tell you that I indeed know the Unseen in the heavens and the earth, and that I know whatever you disclose and whatever you were concealing?' [...]".

21 "Do they not contemplate the Qur'an? Had it been from [someone] other than Allah, they would have surely found much discrepancy in it".

22 "It is He who has made you successors on the earth, and raised some of you in rank above others so that He may test you in respect to what He has given you. Indeed your Lord is swift in retribution, and indeed He is all-forgiving, all-merciful".

DISCUSSION OF THE RESEARCH RESULTS

23 "And do not cause corruption on the earth after its restoration, and supplicate Him with fear and hope: indeed Allah's mercy is close to the virtuous".

24 What is meant here is that young animals are not born with markings, that is with slit ears that their parents have received to mark them as sacrificial animals for certain cults.

25 The extent to which the Qur'an postulates human free will is an open question. The Qur'an also postulates the opposite, for example in verse 76:30, which states, "but you do not wish unless it is wished by Allah".

26 To justify the reception of Ibn Taymīya and Ibn Qayyim al-Ǧawzīya, to whom representatives of very conservative Islam also refer, we should refer to the remarks of Birgit Krawietz, who deals with the question of whether Ibn Taymīya can be seen as the father of Islamic fundamentalism Krawietz (2003).

27 In this context, reference should be made to Ibn Ṭufayl's (d. 1185) philosophical island novel *Ḥayy Ibn Yaqẓān*, Daniel Defoe's *Robinson Crusoe* and William Golding's *Lord of the Flies*.

28 "Allah bears witness that there is no god except Him – and [so do] the angels and those who possess knowledge – maintainer of justice, there is no god but Him, the Almighty, the All-wise".

29 "There is no compulsion in religion: rectitude has become distinct from error. So one who disavows the Rebels and has faith in Allah has held fast to the firmest handle for which there is no breaking; and Allah is all-hearing, all-knowing".

30 "To you your religion, and to me my religion".

31 "It is by Allah's mercy that you are gentle to them; and had you been harsh and hardhearted, surely they would have scattered from around you. So excuse them, and plead for forgiveness for them, and consult them in the affairs, and once you are resolved, put your trust in Allah. Indeed Allah loves those who trust in Him".

32 "It is He who created the heavens and the earth with reason, and the day He says [to something], 'Be!' it is. His word is the truth, and to Him belongs all sovereignty on the day when the Trumpet will be blown. Knower of the sensible and the Unseen, He is the All-wise, the All-aware".

33 "Say, 'Indeed my Lord has guided me to a straight path, the upright religion, the creed of Abraham, a true believer, and he was not one of the polytheists'".

34 A *ḥadīṯ qudsī* is a special form of the prophet's utterance that is attributed to an immediate inspiration from God.

35 Comparable to this *ḥadīṯ* is the statement of Jesus in Mt 25, 34–46. For a better understanding here from 31–46: "31 When the Son of Man comes in his glory, and all the angels with him, then he will sit on his glorious throne. 32 Before him will be gathered all the nations, and he will separate people one from another as a shepherd separates the sheep from the goats. 33 And he will place the sheep on his right, but the goats on the left. 34 Then the King will say to those on his right, 'Come, you who are blessed by my Father, inherit the kingdom prepared for you from the foundation of the world. 35 For I was hungry and you gave me food, I was thirsty and you gave me drink, I was a stranger and you welcomed me, 36 I was naked and you clothed me, I was sick and you visited me, I was in prison and you came to me'. 37 Then the righteous will answer him, saying, 'Lord, when did we see you hungry and feed you, or thirsty and give you drink? 38 And when did we see you a stranger and welcome you, or naked and clothe you? 39 And when did we see you sick or in prison and visit you?' 40 And the King will answer them, '"Truly, I say to you, as you did it to one of the least of these my brothers, 6 you did it to me'. 41 Then he will say to those on his left, 'Depart from me, you cursed, into the eternal fire prepared for the devil and his angels. 42 For I was hungry and you gave me no food, I was thirsty and you gave me no drink, 43 I was a stranger and you did not welcome me, naked and you did not clothe me, sick and in prison and you did not visit me'. 44 Then they

also will answer, saying, 'Lord, when did we see you hungry or thirsty or a stranger or naked or sick or in prison, and did not minister to you?' 45 Then he will answer them, saying, 'Truly, I say to you, as you did not do it to one of the least of these, you did not do it to me'. 46 And these will go away into eternal punishment, but the righteous into eternal life" (Engelbrecht, 2009).

36 "Hold fast, all together, to Allah's cord, and do not be divided [into sects]. And remember Allah's blessing upon you when you were enemies, then He brought your hearts together, so you became brothers with His blessing. And you were on the brink of a pit of Fire, whereat He saved you from it. Thus does Allah clarify His signs for you so that you may be guided".

37 "Abasement has been stamped upon them wherever they are confronted, except for an asylum from Allah and an asylum from the people; and they earned the wrath of Allah, and poverty was stamped upon them [...]".

38 The mystic al-Ḥallāǧ (executed in 922) refers to Satan as a true monotheist. He is referred to as *kāfir* in the Qur'an in verse 2:34. Thus, it is not that he does not recognize the uniqueness of God or does not have knowledge, but that he makes himself the reference and puts himself in the center (*istakbara*).

39 In other places, Satan is also referred to as *šayṭān*, which is derived from the word *šayṭana* and means "the distant one".

40 "There at the angels prostrated, all of them. but not Iblis; he acted arrogantly and he was one of the faithless. He said, 'O Iblis! What keeps you from prostrating before that which I have created with My [own] two hands? Are you arrogant, or are you [one] of the exalted ones?' 'I am better than him', he said. 'You created me from fire and You created him from clay'".

41 "Said he, 'Do You see this one whom You have honoured above me? If You respite me until the Day of Resurrection, I will surely destroy his progeny, [all] except a few'".

42 "And when We said to the angels, 'Prostrate before Adam', they prostrated, but not Iblis: he refused (*istakbara*) and acted arrogantly, and he was one of the faithless".

43 The question arises as to what actually lies behind this assignment to the Muslim faith: Cultural practice? Islamic lifestyle? Belonging to an ethnic group? Own spiritual experiences? (Behr, 2011).

44 Here we are referring to the muʿtazilite, the ašʿarite, and the māturīdite schools, which emerged in the period between the 8th and 10th centuries.

45 The meaning of *tauḥīd* becomes clear in verse 3:18, in which God testifies that there is no God but him.

46 "O mankind! Worship your Lord, who created you and those who were before you, so that you may be Godwary. He who made the earth a place of repose for you, and the sky a canopy, and He sends down water from the sky, and with it He brings forth crops for your sustenance. So do not set up equals to Allah, while you know!"

47 "It is He who created the heavens and the earth with reason, and the day He says [to something], 'Be!' it is. His word is the truth, and to Him belongs all sovereignty on the day when the Trumpet will be blown. Knower of the sensible and the Unseen, He is the All-wise, the All-aware".

48 "All praise belongs to Allah, Lord of all the worlds".

49 "O company of jinn and humans! If you can pass through the confines of the heavens and the earth, then do pass through. But you will not pass through except by an authority [from Allah]".

50 "Even if We had sent down angels to them, and the dead had spoken to them, and We had gathered before them all things manifestly, they would [still] not believe unless Allah wished. But most of them are ignorant".

DISCUSSION OF THE RESEARCH RESULTS

51 "O Children of Adam! If there come to you apostles from among yourselves, recounting to you My signs, then those who are Godwary and righteous will have no fear, nor will they grieve. But those who deny Our signs and are disdainful of them, they shall be the inmates of the Fire and they shall remain in it [forever]. So who is a greater wrongdoer than him who fabricates a lie against Allah, or denies His signs? Their share, as decreed in the Book, shall reach them. When Our messengers come to take them away, they will say, 'Where is that which you used to invoke besides Allah?' They will say, 'They have forsaken us', and they will testify against themselves that they were faithless".

52 "Certainly he has led astray many of your generations. Did you not use to apply reason?"

53 "When Moses said to his people, 'O my people! Why do you torment me, when you certainly know that I am Allah's apostle to you?' So when they swerved [from the right path] Allah made their hearts swerve, and Allah does not guide the transgressing lot".

54 "So whoever does an atom's weight of good will see it and whoever does an atom's weight of evil will see it".

55 "Another possible rendering of the Arabic is: 'I am as My servant expects Me to be'. The meaning is that forgiveness and acceptance of repentance by the Almighty is subject to His servant truly believing that He is forgiving and merciful. However, not to accompany such belief with right action would be to mock the Almighty" (Ibrahim & Johnson-Davies, 1997, p. 78).

56 "We would be fabricating a lie against Allah should we revert to your creed after Allah had delivered us from it. It does not behoove us to return to it, unless Allah, our Lord, should wish so. Our Lord embraces all things in [His] knowledge. In Allah we have put our trust'. 'Our Lord! Judge justly between us and our people, and You are the best of judges!'"

57 "Then he began with their sacks, before [opening] his brother's sack. Then he took it out from his brother's sack. Thus did We devise for Joseph's sake. He could not have held his brother under the king's law unless Allah willed [otherwise]. We raise in rank whomever We please, and above every man of knowledge is One who knows best".

58 "Do not say about anything, 'I will indeed do it tomorrow', without [adding], 'if Allah wishes'. And when you forget, remember your Lord, and say, 'Maybe my Lord will guide me to [something] more akin to rectitude than this'".

59 "And they will not remember unless Allah wishes. He is worthy of [your] being wary [of Him] and He is worthy to forgive".

60 "But you do not wish unless it is wished by Allah, the Lord of all the worlds".

61 In the Islamic scientific system, the term *kalām* refers to the discipline that relies on rational arguments to establish religious beliefs.

62 In the Islamic scientific system, the term *fiqh* refers to the discipline that deals with religious norms.

63 Literally: insight, mind, reason, ratio, spirit, intellect, intelligence.

64 "The Sunna includes everything that the Prophet said, did or condoned. Depending on the school of law, the scope of the term is expanded" (Ghandour, 2014, p. 60).

65 "They said, 'O our people! Indeed we have heard a Book which has been sent down after Moses, confirming what was before it. It guides to the truth and to a straight path'".

66 "Say, 'It has been revealed to me that a team of the jinn listened [to the Qur'an], and they said, "Indeed we heard a wonderful Qur'an which guides to rectitude. Hence we have believed in it and we will never ascribe any partner to our Lord"'".

67 "Allah has sent down the best of discourses, a scripture [composed] of similar motifs, whereat quiver the skins of those who fear their Lord, then their skins and hearts soften to Allah's remembrance. That is Allah's guidance, by which He guides whomever He wishes; and whomever Allah leads astray, has no guide".

68 "Indeed in the creation of the heavens and the earth and the alternation of night and day, there are signs for those who possess intellects".

69 The phrase "religiously unmusical" goes back to Max Weber, who described himself in this way (Weber, 1994, p. 65).

70 "When Abraham said to Azar, his father, 'Do you take idols for gods? Indeed I see you and your people in manifest error'".

71 "Secure hold (*birr*) is not in turning your faces eastward or westward, but in believing in God, in the resurrection on the Last Day, in the angels, in the Scriptures, and in the messengers, and in giving out of love, to the kinsman, the orphan, to the needy, to the travelers, to those by the wayside, and for the deliverance of the downtrodden and the captives, and in the performing of prayer and giving, and in the fulfillment of commitments made, and in patience in times of hardship and suffering and violence. Those who do these things are those who are truthful inwardly and who respect God" (verse 2:177 in Behr, 2014a, p. 21).

72 "Your Lord has decreed that you shall not worship anyone except Him, and [He has enjoined] kindness to parents. Should they reach old age at your side – one of them or both – do not say to them, 'Fie!' And do not chide them, but speak to them noble words. Lower the wing of humility to them, out of mercy, and say, 'My Lord! Have mercy on them, just as they reared me when I was [a] small [child]!'"

73 "Certainly We gave Luqman wisdom, saying, 'Give thanks to Allah; and whoever gives thanks, gives thanks only for his own sake. And whoever is ungrateful, [let him know that] Allah is indeed all-sufficient, all-laudable'. When Luqman said to his son, as he advised him: 'O my son! Do not ascribe any partners to Allah. Polytheism is indeed a great injustice'. We have enjoined man concerning his parents: His mother carried him through weakness upon weakness, and his weaning takes two years. Give thanks to Me and to your parents. To Me is the return. But if they urge you to ascribe to Me as partner that of which you have no knowledge, then do not obey them. Keep their company honourably in this world and follow the way of him who turns to Me penitently. Then to Me will be your return, whereat I will inform you concerning what you used to do. 'O my son! Even if it should be the weight of a mustard seed, and [even though] it should be in a rock, or in the heavens, or in the earth, Allah will produce it. Indeed Allah is all-attentive, all-aware. O my son! Maintain the prayer and bid what is right and forbid what is wrong, and be patient through whatever may visit you. That is indeed the steadiest of courses. Do not turn your cheek disdainfully from the people, and do not walk exultantly on the earth. Indeed Allah does not like any swaggering braggart. Be modest in your bearing, and lower your voice. Indeed the ungainliest of voices is the donkey's voice'".

74 Here, as an exception, Behr's rendering is used, since it underlines well the unification between the formal level (religion) and the subject-related level (religiosity) emphasized here.

75 Others translate the term as piety, righteousness (in the sense of good character) or being kind. For didactic work with the verse, Behr's translation is helpful.

76 Enculturation as a comprehensive object of pedagogy includes socialization as "becoming social", upbringing as "making social" and individuation as "forming and controlling oneself by means of learning and educational processes through which a person unfolds their personality in responding to society and culture" (Raithel, 2009, p. 60).

77 As a prerequisite for the reflexive and communicative access to all modes of encountering the world, Baumert formulates basic competences which he calls basal cultural tools that open up access to the symbolic objects of culture: Mastery of the lingua franca, mathematization competence, foreign language competence, IT competence, self-regulation of knowledge acquisition (Baumert, 2002).

DISCUSSION OF THE RESEARCH RESULTS

78 Dressler (2007) points out that by "constitutive rationality" Baumert does not mean religious education according to Article 7.3 in German Basic Constitutional Law, but the negotiation of transcendental questions as in the field of metaphysics.

79 This complex question is related to the children's numinous and emotional worldview construction. The philosophical complexity arises from the tension between the numinous relation to God and situations in which one must behave as if God does not exist. Children also have to learn how to deal with this tension, especially since the sample illustrates the children's quasi magical approach and their own ways of dealing with it.

80 "The servants of the All-beneficent are those who walk humbly on the earth, and when the ignorant address them, say, 'Peace!' Those who spend the night for their Lord, prostrating and standing [in worship]. [...] Those who, when spending, are neither wasteful nor tight-fisted, and moderation lies between these [extremes]. Those who do not invoke another god besides Allah, and do not kill a soul [whose life] Allah has made inviolable, except with due cause, and do not commit fornication. Whoever does that shall encounter its retribution the punishment being doubled for him on the Day of Resurrection. [...] Those who do not give false testimony, and when they come upon vain talk, pass by nobly. Those who, when reminded of the signs of their Lord, do not turn a deaf ear and a blind eye to them. And those who say, 'Our Lord! Grant us comfort in our spouses and descendants, and make us imams of the Godwary'".

81 "Certainly We gave Luqman wisdom, saying, 'Give thanks to Allah; and whoever gives thanks, gives thanks only for his own sake. And whoever is ungrateful, [let him know that] Allah is indeed all-sufficient, all-laudable'. When Luqman said to his son, as he advised him: 'O my son! Do not ascribe any partners to Allah. Polytheism is indeed a great injustice'. We have enjoined man concerning his parents: His mother carried him through weakness upon weakness, and his weaning takes two years. Give thanks to Me and to your parents. To Me is the return. But if they urge you to ascribe to Me as partner that of which you have no knowledge, then do not obey them. Keep their company honourably in this world and follow the way of him who turns to Me penitently. Then to Me will be your return, whereat I will inform you concerning what you used to do. 'O my son! Even if it should be the weight of a mustard seed, and [even though] it should be in a rock, or in the heavens, or in the earth, Allah will produce it. Indeed Allah is all-attentive, all-aware. O my son! Maintain the prayer and bid what is right and forbid what is wrong, and be patient through whatever may visit you. That is indeed the steadiest of courses. Do not turn your cheek disdainfully from the people, and do not walk exultantly on the earth. Indeed Allah does not like any swaggering braggart. Be modest in your bearing, and lower your voice. Indeed the ungainliest of voices is the donkey's voice'".

82 "Your people have denied it, though it is the truth. Say, 'It is not my business to watch over you'".

83 Treml refers to the external observation of religious faith by (scientific) reason. "'Reason' and "God" are seen as "difference" and religious education studies that does not understand itself as religious socialization should train communicative approaches to it (Treml, 2000, p. 249). From an Islamic perspective, this "distinction" between "reason" and "God" is different which is briefly explained here: Thomas Bauer gives some vivid examples of how the relationship between religion and the world was different in the classical Islamic world from the European pre-modern age: "The Near Eastern societies in Islamic history present not only a high degree of division of labor, but also a differentiation of societal subsystems, which can be found in comparable measure in Europe only in the modern period. This differentiation does not necessarily follow the same lines as in modern-day Europe. Most importantly, in the Near East, the religious/secular dichotomy plays a smaller role – not because religion is

so omnipresent there, but because religion is not managed and defined by an ecclesiastical hierarchy; rather, in every partial system it assumes its own distinct function and therefore does not exist as a socially all-embracing system of 'religion'. It is true that the Islamic world was always aware of the difference between *dīn* (religion) and *dunyā* (world), but situations of conflict are different from those in Europe. Here, law, politics, medicine, literature, etc. can differentiate themselves as independent subsystems of society only after they have emancipated themselves from the supremacy of the churches and religiosity organized by them. The dichotomy between religion and the world is fundamental here. The Islamic world, in contrast, does not have churches that command the right to define the field of religion. Therefore, the development follows the opposite direction. The urban cultures of the Orient retain ancient standards to a high degree, and develop them, after less than a century of Arabic transformation, toward ever-higher levels of complexity. This leads to an ever-increasing division of labor and social differentiation" (Bauer, 2021, p. 134). Bauer thus points out that the European experiences with the difference between "religion" and "world", "God" and "reason" or "faith" and "science" cannot be transferred to the cultures of Islam. Regardless of the differences, the two perspectives are nevertheless also essential for Islam.

84 In religious studies and theology, a distinction is made between immanence (the entire reality/ world) and transcendence (non-world, non-being), that is everything happening in the world can be related to a 'background' and thus be communicated. Although the terms 'transcendence' and 'immanence' originate from Christian theology, they are used by Niklas Luhmann in systems theory without their Christian connotations. Luhmann refers immanence and transcendence to the difference between a marked and an unmarked side of a meaningful (here religious) communication. The unmarked side is called 'transcendence' which is embedded in an indeterminable horizon. Everything that can be described, i.e., 'immanence', would then be rooted in an indeterminable realm and would require the determinability of the indeterminable by considering the immanent from the viewpoint of transcendence. The indeterminable horizon is thus made communicable. Religious communication provides a contingency regulation as described above (Treml, 2007). Thus, religious communication can only be seen systems-theoretically in the contrast of the difference between immanence and transcendence. Therefore, the terms transcendence and immanence in Luhmann's sense can also be used here. What is special about different religions is the many differences in their content which Luhmann describes as "programs" that are historically contingent. With these programs, the historical not contingent formal code is filled in. From the viewpoint of systems theory, the Jewish, the Christian, and the Islamic religion "are each specific programs that allow observing and transcending the world in different ways on the basis of a common code" (Treml, 2007, p. 35).

CHAPTER 6

Conclusion

1 Introduction

This study brings the results of empirical research into conversation with some fundamental topics of theology in order to reflect on empirical evidence theologically. This approach is based on the orientational function that religious education should provide for everyday life. If Muslim teachers want to take children and young people seriously in religious education and accompany them as best as possible, religious education has to be designed in a way that is linked to the students' lifeworlds. This study therefore reconstructs children's own views of God and thus appreciates a theological dimension that is accessible to them.

Based on the empirical results presented here, which have been reflected from an educational science and theological perspective as well as in relation to the importance of a religious education, the last chapter of this study first provides praxeological suggestions (cf. Section 2) and then offers directions for further research (cf. Section 3).

2 Praxeological Suggestions

In the following, the potential of the present study for the practice of Islamic religious education is outlined.

On the basis of the reconstruction of the children's relationship to God, their childlike construction of the world and of reality as well as on the basis of theological reflections on empiricism, a religious education can be conceptualized that gives children opportunities for interpretation and further directions that they can take up and work on. Processes of appropriation and understanding of the basic beliefs of children and young people manifest more visibility. Accordingly, teaching contents can also be conceptualized in a student-oriented way with the aim of providing didactically reflected assistance in processes of orientation. In this way, students can acquire the competence, to make theological interpretations and to understand reality in a multidimensional way. These competences enable them to develop their own, reason-based positions on basic theological issues and questions of faith, allowing them to participate in

© FAHIMAH ULFAT, 2023 | DOI:10.1163/9789004533219_006

the social discourse on questions of worldview and faith which is one of the educational goals of Islamic religious education (Behr, 2008).

On the basis of the results of this study, the following potential for recommendation can be identified at various levels:

1. *Developing a culture of 'religious narrativity'*
   - Islamic religious education should be inspired to develop an explicit 'culture of narrativity' and a 'didactics of narratives in plurality', i.e., a didactics of the diversity and differences of narratives.
   - Islamic religious education should be encouraged to offer narrative and performative forms of learning to promote religious expressiveness and the ability to speak about oneself.
   - Islamic religious education should promote multidimensional perceptions of reality and foster the ability to change perspectives by introducing the diversity of narratives so that switching between religious speech and speaking about religion can take place.
   - Islamic religious education should endeavor to help students to a more complex understanding of the relationship between God's will and human freedom.
   - Islamic religious education should attempt to show students ways to deal with the interplay of commitment and freedom by means of a theologically grounded support. The teachings should not determine these aspects, but allow and show fluidity.
2. *Differentiate learning paths and forms of experience*
   - Islamic religious education should alternate between discursive and normative approaches, inductive and deductive learning paths as well as between experiential and theology-based methods (Behr, 2008).
   - Islamic religious education should offer habitualizing, reflexive, and lifeworld related forms of experience to make religion tangible.
   - Islamic religious education should be based on understanding and comprehension. The dimension of understanding is necessarily based on information, but the quality of information takes precedence over quantity.
   - Islamic religious education needs neither convictional pedagogy nor a pure transfer didactics.
3. *Finding a home in secularism*
   - Islamic religious education should be stimulated to develop a theory of atheism and secularity so that secular students can be approached from a religious perspective, for instance through offers of narrations rather than in a moralizing way.

CONCLUSION

- Islamic religious education should be inspired to constitute a didactics of a narrative change of perspective in order to be able to correspond with the unambiguity of today's scientific world.
- Islamic religious education should be encouraged to promote a practice of belonging beyond a national religion, i.e., to constitute an individual, not a national dimension of religion.
- Islamic religious education should be stimulated to offer concepts for finding a home in secularism. These concepts must be cognitive as well as emotional to provide knowledge, behavior and experience.

4. *Paradigm shift*
- Islamic religious education should make a "paradigm shift" (Behr, 2012a) by shifting from the text to the spirit, from the utopian to the pragmatic, from the collective to the subject, from the communal to the social, and from the traditional to the situational.
- Islamic religious education should take an "anthropological turn" (Behr, 2016) by placing the autonomy of the subject in the foreground.

These implications aim to offer children options for establishing a living relation with God.

From this perspective, Islamic religious education is indispensable in schools in order to enable young Muslims to find their personal 'pace' in religion (Behr, 2014a, p. 29), to be strengthened in their identity, to become plurality-conscious, and thus to feel at home as Muslims in a globalized world.

3 Suggestions for Further Research

The present study is to be assigned to empirical educational research in general and to empirical religious education studies in particular. Empirical religious education studies responds to challenges of the actual teaching situations that result, for instance, from the changing religious situation in Germany, but also from the scientific findings of empirical educational research in general.

Empirical research in the field of education provides important paths for development, socialization, and learning processes. It is characterized by "problem orientation", "interdisciplinarity", and the use of "empirical research methods" (Gräsel, 2015, p. 16). Empirical research has also played an important role in Protestant and Catholic religious education studies since the "empirical turning point" in the 1960s (Porzelt & Güth, 2000, pp. 11–13).

Islamic religious education studies, on the other hand, is a recent discipline in Germany, even though it is better established than Islamic theology.

However, it does not see itself as an "educational science in the service of an established theology" as it "operates its own form of theological expertise". It is also not a "variation of Christian religious education studies" (Behr, 2010, p. 2).

Islamic religious education studies faces great challenges in the conception and development of Islamic religious education: The curricula and textbooks for teaching are oriented towards the normative requirements of theology, taking into account pedagogical insights and findings from learning psychology. Islamic anthropology also finds its expression in curricula, textbooks, and didactics – for example with the concept of *fiṭra*, i.e., man's natural, inner disposition for turning towards the numinous. Furthermore, Islamic religious education should support positive integration, and strengthen and sensitize Muslim students against ideologically motivated manipulation, initiating a new discourse culture (due to today's multireligious society), and much more.

The Muslim children for whom these lessons, curricula, and textbooks are developed live in Germany and thus find themselves in a special social, cultural, legal, and religious context. Secularization and pluralization trends that also affect religion are shaping this context. This is shown by scientific studies in the field of sociology of religion (Bochinger et al., 2009; Woodhead & Heelas, 2000). However, Muslims' individual lifestyles and lived religiosity that have developed in Germany hardly play a role in the concepts of curricula and textbooks. This has an impact on the concepts of faith among the children and young people concerned, and up to now this has not been empirically recorded.

Muslim religious educationalists such as Bülent Ucar, Mouhanad Khorchide, and Harry Harun Behr emphasize: "the so-called lifeworld reference of religious education is just as much a part of the didactically based paradigm as is its reconnection to the normative system of the interpretation of the world and the human being" (Behr, 2010, p. 4). Likewise, in Islamic religious education studies, student orientation should have priority over "object orientation" (Behr, 2010, p. 9; also Khorchide, 2010; Ucar, 2010).

In other words, we are dealing here with moderating between religion as a human experience and the superordinate speech of God. The religious interpretation of the world by man is accessible to empirical research. It can be described, explained, and theologically interpreted with the help of empirical-analytical approaches. In this way, theology or tradition can be put into relation with today's situation and the questions that children and young people face in their everyday lives.

Since experience and the connection to the lifeworld play an essential role in religious education, and since empirical research is "closely related to the experiential nature of today's religious education 'landscape'" (Schnider, 2000, p. 47), it is particularly important to put the empirical-analytical paradigm in

CONCLUSION

the foreground in Islamic religious education studies as well. Thus, the practice of religious education can be supported and developed in order to adapt it to the conditions and processes of understanding of children and young people.

In this way, the lifeworld of children and young people, which became visible through the findings of the empirical research, can be brought into conversation with basic theological topics and reflected upon. In doing so, the lifeworld orientation function of religious education is taken into account, as processes of religious education and appropriation in childhood and adolescence can be initiated and accompanied by reflected didactics.

Empirical research, as mentioned previously, has the task of mediating between tradition and the lifeworld. The aim is not to contrast practice and theory (theology). Nor is it about establishing a dichotomy between tradition and situation and measuring the distance between today's life designs and traditional religion, but about mediation processes between tradition and the current situation (Ziebertz, 2000, p. 31). From an Islamic perspective, such mediation processes take place in two ways: as an interpretation of the present situation from the perspective of tradition, i.e., from the Qur'an and the Sunna as well as vice versa as an interpretation of tradition from the perspective of the present situation.

The potential of such empirical work which establishes mediation processes between present situations and tradition becomes clear in the present study:

– It is important to recognize that more attention should be paid to pluralization processes among adolescents which only empirical religious education studies can achieve.
– It is crucial that Islamic religious education studies, as a relatively recent subject, faces the task of permanently validating curricula and textbooks to ensure that they make a contribution to education (German: *Bildung*) and do justice to the living situation of young Muslims in Germany. This too can only be achieved by empirical religious education studies.
– The specific situation of migration makes it necessary in Islamic religious education to mediate between different cultures and religious peculiarities of the countries of origin and the lifeworlds of children and young people. This is a very dynamic situation in which the next generation of students often faces different challenges than the current one. Only empirical religious education studies can continuously observe this process and collect the relevant data.

In summary, Islamic religious education studies needs an empirical element in the sense of quality assurance despite the high standard of textbooks and curricula.

Islamic religious education studies have privileged access to young Muslims, which is made possible in particular by the religious education teacher as a person of trust. This access, however, is only fruitful if research closely reflects the reality of life of this group. Teachers themselves can only do this to a limited extent since they are dependent on professional sensitivity. Empirical religious education studies can offer teachers systematic and sound knowledge about the students' changing horizons of meaning so that their privileged position of trust in this group can be used constructively. Empirical religious education studies can therefore also be a service provider for teachers, helping them to keep in touch with the reality of their students' lives. Likewise, the results of empirical religious education studies are also indispensable through the course of academic study in order to train undergraduates for the students' understanding of God and religion.

The present study is followed by further research desiderata.

Due to the understanding that religious education studies cannot only be based on models of maturity but also has to be based on a subject-oriented co-construction, further research on this topic should be conducted. Here the question is, what are the exact conditions of such co-construction. Religious education should be a crucial factor in this context. Empirical research has to be done to verify this assumption.

Following the insight that there are children with an individual and mature relation to God that is equally compatible with the secular world as it is with tradition, the question about the reasons or events that lead to their acquiring this fluidity arises.

Following the realization that children show different preferences with regard to the determination of the relation between willing to believe and being able to believe, there is a need for further research in order to clarify where the different preferences of children originate from sociogenetically: Are they artifacts of the study or cultural patterns that overlay religion?

With regard to sociogenetic considerations, the question can be asked to what extent these types are artefacts of a particular situation such as the lessons the children attend or whether they are basic types of coping with the world, or both. If the types are artifacts of the school situation, this points to a problem in teacher education. This question must be investigated in future studies.

Following the present work, the relations of Muslim youth to God should also be examined in a comparative way. These concepts may differ from those of children in terms of influences from parental upbringing as well as peer groups, mosques, and the media.

In the field of interreligious learning, the concepts of God among Christian and Muslim children and young people should be researched, including the

CONCLUSION

question of whether there are connections between the concepts of God and the perception of other religions. In this way, dialogue-based teaching modules can be developed.

The current situation of people fleeing and migrating represents a major challenge for the German education system which requires in-depth research in the field of migration and education. Two areas of tension become apparent here: On the one hand between the culture of origin and the culture of immigration, on the other hand between the different cultures of origin themselves. Due to refuge and migration, shifts will probably occur here in the future. This results in further multifaceted research needs for religious education studies such as research on the interreligious competence of students and teachers. A further task would be to empirically document the effects of the differences between the various Sunni and Shiite groups that already exist in the countries of origin. In this way, suggestions can be developed for dealing with the challenges of religious heterogeneity.

Questions about the interaction of students' acquisition of knowledge and competence and the actual practice of Islamic religious education are still unanswered. In this field, the numerous approaches in Protestant and Catholic religious education studies could be useful for further research.

Children's conceptions of angels represent one aspect of their image of God, as the empirical material shows. A qualitative study which provides a theologically reflected approach to this topic in religious education could be carried out.

Furthermore, the present study should be followed by an empirical study on the connection between the image of God and the concept of gender, as religion and gender are historically considered to be two closely intertwined categories. This would be beneficial not only with regard to children, but especially to young people since the topic of 'gender' is a central challenge in religious education studies more broadly. In the Christian context it has already been found that girls and boys have different images of God. Interrelations between the perception of parents, lived gender role assignments, role models in culture and society, and the self-image of the children as well as religious tradition become apparent here. Therefore, a study on Muslim children as well as an interreligious comparison is of particular interest.

Another area that is opening up refers to research in the field of professional competence of teachers. In the field of research on the professionalism of RE teachers, the so-called 'competence theory approach' has become widespread in German-speaking countries (Burrichter et al., 2012; Simojoki & Henningsen, 2021). In the competence-theoretical approach, questions are asked about the competencies that teachers need for teaching. According to this approach, "professional competence" includes the competence aspects "professional knowledge", "beliefs/values/goals", "motivational orientations", and "self-regulation" (Baumert & Kunter, 2011, p. 32). Here, it could be of interest to investigate on the one hand the teachers' professional knowledge with regard to the topic of God, but also their own religious beliefs, because one of the characteristics and competencies that are specifically significant for religious education teachers, is their "own, reflexively enlightened religiosity" (Pirner, 2012b, p. 29).

The scientific evidence that pluralization processes are also present among Muslim students at an early age is a central output of the present study. It is likely that these processes become more diverse, complex, and multifaceted with increasing age. Accompanying these developments empirically is essential for the organization of religious education.

These suggestions for further research contribute to current scientific debates that are still lacking in the recent discipline of Islamic religious education studies. Research makes it possible to examine the above-mentioned points from an empirical perspective, to reflect on them theologically, and make teaching and learning processes at different levels more visible and fruitful.

Sample Table

Pseudonym	Sex (m/f)	Age	Grade	Migration background of the parents	Religious education at school	Religious schooling in mosques	Linguistic competence in the German language	Religious tend
Betül	F	10	4	Turkish	Since grade 1	No	Satisfactory	Sunni
Canan	F	10	4	Turkish	Unknown	No	Satisfactory	Sunni
Dilara	F	10	4	Turkish	Since grade 2	Since 4 years	Good	Sunni
Eljan	M	9	3	Serbian	Since grade 1	No	Satisfactory	Sunni
Filiz	F	9	4	Turkish	Since grade 1	Sometimes	very good	Sunni
Gökmen	M	10	4	Turkish	Since grade 1	Every Friday	Satisfactory	Sunni
Hagen	M	10	4	German	Since grade 4	Sometimes	very good	Sunni Family converted to Islam together about a year ago. Children have consciously witnessed the conversion.
Jurislav	M	9	4	Yugoslavian	Since grade 1	No	Satisfactory	Sunni

(*cont.*)

Pseudonym	Sex (m/f)	Age	Grade	Migration background of the parents	Religious education at school	Religious schooling in mosques	Linguistic competence in the German language	Religious tend
Kaltrina	F	9	4	Albanian	Since grade 1	No	Good	Sunni
Leyla	F	9	4	Turkish	Since grade 1	Since 2–3 years	Very good	Sunni
Mesut	M	10	4	Turkish	Since grade 1	Since 1 year	Satisfactory	Sunni
Navid	M	10	4	Iraqi	Since grade 1	No	Very good	Shiite Has an autistic older brother
Olivia	F	10	4	German	Ethics classes only	Irregular classes at home and in the Sufi order	Very good	Sufi
Paiman	M	10	5	Iraqi	Since grade 1	Since 1 year in a Shiite community	Good	Shiite
Qamar	F	10	4	Afghan	Ethics classes only	Since 4 years in a Shiite community	Very good	Shiite

SAMPLE TABLE

Transcription Rules

Sign	Meaning
..	Short break
...	Medium break
(seconds)	Long break
/eh/ /ehm/	Planning pauses
((action))	Non-linguistic actions, e.g. ((silence)) ((pointing at something))
((laughing)) ((excited)) ((annoyed))	Accompaniments of speech (the characterization precedes the relevant passages)
secure	Conspicuous emphasis, also volume
SMALL CAPS	Stretched speech
( )	Incomprehensible, no longer exactly understandable
(so terrible?)	Presumed wording
italics	Religious term
//	Sentence break

References

Abu-r-Rida', & Rassoul, M. (1989). *Auszüge aus Ṣaḥīḥ Al-Buḫāryy. Aus dem Arabischen übertragen und kommentiert von Abū-r-Riḍāʾ und Muḥammad Ibn Aḥmad Ibn Rassoul*. Islamische Bibliothek.

Albert, M., Hurrelmann, K., & Quenzel, G. (2015). *Jugend 2015–17. Shell Jugendstudie: Eine pragmatische Generation im Aufbruch*. Fischer Taschenbuch.

Albert, M., Hurrelmann, K., & Quenzel, G. (2019). *Jugend 2019–18. Shell Jugendstudie: Eine Generation meldet sich zu Wort*. Beltz.

Al-Ġazzālī, A. Ḥ. M. I. M. (1940). *Al-Ġazzālī's Buch vom Gottvertrauen*. Niemeyer.

Allolio-Näcke, L. (2021). *Anthropologie und Kulturpsychologie der religiösen Entwicklung: Eine Religionspsychologie*. Kohlhammer.

Allport, G. W., & Ross, M. J. (1967). Personal religious orientation and prejudice. *Journal of Personality and Social Psychology, 5*(4), 432–443.

Amirpur, K., & Ammann, L. (Eds.). (2006). *Der Islam am Wendepunkt. Liberale und konservative Reformer einer Weltreligion* (2nd ed.). Herder.

Ammann, L. (2004). *Cola und Koran. Herder-Spektrum: Vol. 5432*. Herder.

Arnold, U., Hanisch, H., & Orth, G. (Eds.). (1997). *Was Kinder glauben*. Calwer Verl.

Aygün, A. (2013). *Religiöse Sozialisation und Entwicklung bei islamischen Jugendlichen in Deutschland und in der Türkei: Empirische Analysen und religionspädagogische Herausforderungen*. Waxmann.

Badawi, E.-S. M., & Abdel Haleem, M. A. (2008). *Arabic-English dictionary of Qur'anic usage*. Brill.

Bamler, V., Werner, J., & Wustmann, C. (2010). *Lehrbuch Kindheitsforschung: Grundlagen, Zugänge und Methoden*. Beltz Juventa.

Bauer, T. (2021). *A culture of ambiguity: An alternative history of Islam* (H. H. Biesterfeldt & T. Tunstall, Trans.). Columbia University Press.

Baumert, J. (2002). Deutschland im internationalen Bildungsvergleich. In N. Killius, J. Kluge, & L. Reisch (Eds.), *Die Zukunft der Bildung* (pp. 100–151). Suhrkamp.

Baumert, J., & Kunter, M. (2011). Das Kompetenzmodell von COACTIV. In M. Kunter, J. Baumert, W. Blum, U. Klusmann, S. Krauss, & M. Neubrand (Eds.), *Professionelle Kompetenz von Lehrkräften. Ergebnisse des Forschungsprogramms COACTIV* (pp. 29–53). Waxmann.

Behr, H. H. (1998). *Islamische Bildungslehre*. Dâr-us-Salâm.

Behr, H. H. (2005). Zur pädagogischen Anthropologie des Islam. In M. Klöcker (Ed.), *Ethik der Weltreligionen. Ein Handbuch* (pp. 76–78). Wissenschaftliche Buchgesellschaft.

Behr, H. H. (2008). Welche Bildungsziele sind aus der Sicht des Islams vordringlich? In F. Schweitzer, A. Biesinger, & A. Edelbrock (Eds.), *Mein Gott – Dein Gott: Interkulturelle und interreligiöse Bildung in Kindertagesstätten* (pp. 31–47). Beltz.

REFERENCES

Behr, H. H. (2009). Ursprung und Wandel des Lehrerbildes im Islam mit besonderem Blick auf die deutsche Situation. In B. Schröder, H. H. Behr, & D. Krochmalnik (Eds.), *Was ist ein guter Religionslehrer? Antworten von Juden, Christen und Muslimen* (Vol. 1, pp. 149–190). Frank & Timme.

Behr, H. H. (2010). Worin liegt die Zukunft der islamischen Religionspädagogik in Deutschland? *Zeitschrift für die Religionslehre des Islam (ZRLI)*, 4(7), 22–32.

Behr, H. H. (2011). Muslimische Identitäten und Islamischer Religionsunterricht. In H. H. Behr, C. Bochinger, M. Rohe, & H. Schmidt (Eds.), *Islam und Bildung: Vol. 2. Was soll ich hier? Lebensweltorientierung muslimischer Schülerinnen und Schüler als Herausforderung für den Islamischen Religionsunterricht* (pp. 57–101). LIT-Verl.

Behr, H. H. (2012a). Islamische Theologie und der Paradigmenwechsel im muslimischen Denken. *Zeitschrift für die Religionslehre des Islam (ZRLI)*, 6(12), 32–34.

Behr, H. H. (2012b). Der Wechsel der Gebetsrichtung (Qibla) und die Konstruktion des psychologischen Raums im Islam. *Zeitschrift für die Religionslehre des Islam (ZRLI)*, 6(11), 2–13.

Behr, H. H. (2014a). Du und Ich. Zur anthropologischen Signatur des Korans. In H. H. Behr & F. Ulfat (Eds.), *Zwischen Himmel und Erde: Bildungsphilosophische Verhältnisbestimmungen von Heiligem Text und Geist* (pp. 11–31). Waxmann.

Behr, H. H. (2014b). Das islamische Gebet aus religionspädagogischer Perspektive. In D. Krochmalnik, K. Boehme, H. H. Behr, & B. Schröder (Eds.), *Das Gebet im Religionsunterricht in interreligiöser Perspektive* (pp. 145–168). Frank & Timme.

Behr, H. H. (2014c). Menschenbilder im Islam. In M. Rohe, H. Engin, M. Khorchide, Ö. Özsoy, & H. Schmid (Eds.), *Handbuch Christentum und Islam in Deutschland: Erfahrungen, Grundlagen und Perspektven im Zusammenleben* (pp. 489–529). Herder.

Behr, H. H. (2014d). *Tinte wiegt schwerer als Blut. Anmerkungen zum Anschlag auf die Redaktion des französischen Satiremagazins Charlie Hebdo vom 7. Januar 2014.* https://www.uni-frankfurt.de/53652810/Kommentar-Harun-Behr-zu-Paris.pdf

Behr, H. H. (2016, January 28). Gastkommentar: Wendezeit für den Islam [Guest commentary: Turning point for Islam]. *Süddeutsche Zeitung*. https://www.sueddeutsche.de/politik/gastkommentar-wendezeit-fuer-den-islam-1.2840328

Behr, H. H., Haußmann, W., & van der Velden, F. (2011). Yusuf oder Josef? Eine Probe dialogischer Didaktik in der Lehrerbildung. In F. van der Velden (Ed.), *Die Heiligen Schriften des anderen im Unterricht: Bibel und Koran im christlichen und islamischen Religionsunterricht einsetzen* (pp. 221–243). Vandenhoeck & Ruprecht.

Berger, L. (2010). *Islamische Theologie*. facultas.wuv.

Berger, P. L., & Luckmann, T. (2013). *Die gesellschaftliche Konstruktion der Wirklichkeit* (25th ed.). Fischer-Taschenbuch-Verl.

Bertenrath, Z. (2011). *Muslimische und christliche Gottesvorstellungen im Klassenraum: Eine qualitative Studie mit Schülerinnen und Schülern im islamischen und christlichen Religionsunterricht*. Verlag Dr. Kovač.

Bochinger, C. (2011). Religiöse Identität bei Migrantengruppen. In H. H. Behr, C. Bochinger, M. Rohe, & H. Schmidt (Eds.), *Islam und Bildung: Vol. 2. Was soll ich hier? Lebensweltorientierung muslimischer Schülerinnen und Schüler als Herausforderung für den Islamischen Religionsunterricht* (pp. 106–111). LIT-Verl.

Bochinger, C. (2014). Zur Funktion der Gemeinschaft in Religionen. Eine religionswissenschaftliche Außensicht. In H. Schmid, A. Dziri, M. Gharaibeh, & A. Middelbeck-Varwick (Eds.), *Theologisches Forum Christentum – Islam. Kirche und Umma* (pp. 23–42). Pustet.

Bochinger, C., Engelbrecht, M., & Gebhardt, W. (2009). *Die unsichtbare Religion in der sichtbaren Religion*. Kohlhammer.

Bochinger, C., & Frank, K. (2013). Religion, Spiritualität und Säkularität in der Schweiz. In A. M. Riedi, M. Zwilling, M. Meier Kressig, P. Benz Bartoletta, & D. Aebi Zindel (Eds.), *Handbuch Sozialwesen Schweiz* (pp. 201–213). Haupt.

Bohnsack, R. (1993). Dokumentsinn, intendierter Ausdruckssinn und Objektsinn. *Ethik und Sozialwissenschaften, 4*(4), pp. 518–521.

Bohnsack, R. (2003). *Rekonstruktive Sozialforschung. Einführung in Methodologie und Praxis qualitativer Forschung. Lehrtexte*. Leske + Budrich.

Bohnsack, R. (2005). Standards nicht-standardisierter Forschung in den Erziehungs- und Sozialwissenschaften. *Zeitschrift Für Erziehungswissenschaft, 8*(4), 63–81.

Bohnsack, R. (2009). Dokumentarische Methode. In R. Buber & H. H. Holzmüller (Eds.), *Lehrbuch. Qualitative Marktforschung. Konzepte – Methoden – Analysen* (2nd ed., pp. 319–331). Gabler.

Bohnsack, R. (2010a). Dokumentarische Methode und Typenbildung – Bezüge zur Systemtheorie. In R. John, A. Henkel, & J. Rückert-John (Eds.), *Die Methodologien des Systems*. VS Verlag für Sozialwissenschaften.

Bohnsack, R. (2010b). *Rekonstruktive Sozialforschung. Einführung in qualitative Methoden* (8th rev. ed.). Budrich.

Bohnsack, R., & Nohl, A.-M. (2013). Exemplarische Textinterpretation: Die Sequenzanalyse der dokumentarischen Methode. In R. Bohnsack, I. Nentwig-Gesemann, & A.-M. Nohl (Eds.), *Die dokumentarische Methode und ihre Forschungspraxis* (pp. 325–329). VS Verlag für Sozialwissenschaften. https://doi.org/10.1007/978-3-531-19895-8_14

Boos-Nünning, U. (2007). Religiosität junger Musliminnen im Einwandererkontext. In H.-J. von Wensierski & C. Lübcke (Eds.), *Junge Muslime in Deutschland. Lebenslagen, Aufwachsprozesse und Jugendkulturen* (pp. 117–135). Barbara Budrich.

Boos-Nünning, U., & Karakaşoğlu-Aydın, Y. (2005). *Viele Welten leben: Zur Lebenssituation von Mädchen und jungen Frauen mit Migrationshintergrund*. Waxmann.

REFERENCES

Boschki, R. (2008). *Einführung in die Religionspädagogik. Einführung Theologie*. WBG Wiss. Buchges.

Boumaaiz, A., Feininger, B., & Schröter, I. (2013). «Bin ich nicht Euer Herr?» (Sure 7, 172): Aspekte zum Menschenbild im Islam. In K. Boehme (Ed.), *Religionspädagogische Gespräche zwischen Juden, Christen und Muslimen. «Wer ist der Mensch?»: Anthropologie im interreligiösen Lernen und Lehren* (Vol. 4, pp. 101–143). Frank & Timme.

Bowlby, J. (1940). The influence of early environment in the development of neurosis and neurotic character. *International Journal of Psycho-Analysis, XXI*, 154–178.

Bucher, A. A. (1989). "Wenn wir immer tiefer graben, kommt vielleicht die Hölle ...": Plädoyer für die erste Naivität. *Katechetische Blätter, 9*(114), 654–662.

Bucher, A. A. (1994). Alter Gott zu neuen Kindern? Neuer Gott von altern Kindern? In V. Merz (Ed.), *Alter Gott für neue Kinder?* (pp. 79–100). Paulusverlag.

Bucher, A. A. (2000). Geschichte der empirischen Religionspädagogik. In B. Porzelt & R. Güth (Eds.), *Empirische Religionspädagogik: Grundlagen – Zugänge – Aktuelle Projekte* (Vol. 7, pp. 11–21). LIT.

Bucher, A. A. (2008). Kindertheologie: Provokation? Romantizismus? Neues Paradigma? In A. A. Bucher, G. Büttner, P. Freudenberger-Lötz, & M. Schreiner (Eds.), *Jahrbuch für Kindertheologie; "Mittendrin ist Gott". Kinder denken über Gott, Leben und Tod* (Vol. 1, pp. 9–27). Calwer Verlag.

Burrichter, R., Grümme, B., Mendl, H., Rothgangel, M., Schlag, T., & Pirner, M. L. (2012). *Professionell Religion unterrichten: Ein Arbeitsbuch*. Kohlhammer.

Büttner, G. (2010). Wie lernen Kinder Religion? Abschied von Piaget? *Katechetische Blätter, 135*(3), 208–212.

Büttner, G., & Dieterich, V.-J. (2013). *Entwicklungspsychologie in der Religionspädagogik*. UTB.

Coles, R. (1992). *Wird Gott naß, wenn es regnet?* Hoffmann und Campe.

de Roos, S. A. (2006). Young children's God concepts: Influences of attachment and religious socialization in a family and school context. *Religious Education, 101*(1), 84–103.

Dressler, B. (2007). Religiöse Bildung und funktionale Ausdifferenzierung. In G. Büttner, A. Scheunpflug, & V. Elsenbast (Eds.), *Schriften aus dem Comenius-Institut; 18. Zwischen Erziehung und Religion* (pp. 130–141). LIT.

Dziri, A. (Ed.). (2013). *Gottesvorstellungen im Islam: Zur Dialektik von Transzendenz und Immanenz*. Kalām.

Eckerle, S. (2001). Gott der Kinder: Eine Untersuchung zur religiösen Sozialisation von Kindern. In W. Schwendemann, S. Eckerle, R. Gleiß, & M. Otterbach (Eds.), *Schriftenreihe der Evangelischen Fachhochschule Freiburg: Vol. 12. Gott der Kinder – Ein Forschungsprojekt zu Bildern und Gottesvorstellungen von Kindern* (pp. 1–102). LIT.

Eckerle, S. (2008). Gottesbild und religiöse Sozialisation im Vorschulalter. Eine empirische Untersuchung zur religiösen Sozialisation von Kindern. In A. A. Bucher,

G. Büttner, P. Freudenberger-Lötz, & M. Schreiner (Eds.), *Jahrbuch für Kindertheologie; Mittendrin ist Gott* (Vol. 1, pp. 57–69). Calwer Verlag.

Engelbrecht, E. A. (Ed.). (2009). *Lutheran study bible: English standard version.* Concordia Pub House.

Engelbrecht, M. (2011). Islamische Identitätskonstruktion zwischen individueller Biographie und kollektiver Ideenpolitik. In H. H. Behr, C. Bochinger, M. Rohe, & H. Schmidt (Eds.), *Islam und Bildung: Vol. 2. Was soll ich hier? Lebensweltorientierung muslimischer Schülerinnen und Schüler als Herausforderung für den Islamischen Religionsunterricht* (pp. 117–131). LIT-Verl.

Erikson, E. H. (1976). *Kindheit und Gesellschaft* (6th ed.). Klett.

Fachlehrplan. (2004). *Fachlehrplan für den Schulversuch Islamunterricht an der bayerischen Grundschule.* https://edumedia-depot.gei.de/bitstream/handle/11163/163/688589367_2004_A.pdf?sequence=1

Fetz, R. L., Reich, K. H., & Valentin, P. (1992). Weltbildentwicklung und Gottesvorstellung: Eine strukturgenetische Untersuchung bei Kindern und Jugendlichen. In E. Schmitz & A. Dörr (Eds.), *Religionspsychologie. Eine Bestandsaufnahme des gegenwärtigen Forschungsstandes* (pp. 101–130). Hogrefe, Verl. für Psychologie.

Fikenscher, K. (1995). Die Herausforderungen der Kinder ernst nehmen. In U. Becker, & C. T. Scheilke (Eds.), *Aneignung und Vermittlung. Beiträge zu Theorie und Praxis einer religionspädagogischen Hermeneutik; für Klaus Goßmann zum 65. Geburtstag* (pp. 105–111). Gütersloher Verlagshaus.

Flick, U. (2011). *Qualitative Sozialforschung. Eine Einführung* (4th rev. and expanded ed.). Rowohlt-Taschenbuch-Verl.

Flick, U., von Kardorff, E., & Steinke, I. (2005). *Qualitative Forschung: Ein Handbuch* (11th ed.). Rowohlt.

Flöter, I. (2006). *Gott in Kinderköpfen und Kinderherzen.* LIT.

Fowler, J. W. (2000). *Stufen des Glaubens.* Kaiser.

Franz, J. (2016). *Kulturen des Lehrens eine Studie zu kollektiven Lehrorientierungen in Organisationen allgemeiner Erwachsenenbildung.* wbv.

Freudenberger-Lötz, P. (2013). Schüler/in: theologisch. In M. Rothgangel, G. Adam, & R. Lachmann (Eds.), *Religionspädagogisches Kompendium* (pp. 252–264). Vandenhoeck & Ruprecht.

Fuhs, B. (2012). Kinder im qualitativen Interview – Zur Erforschung subjektiver kindlicher Lebenswelten. In F. Heinzel (Ed.), *Methoden der Kindheitsforschung* (2nd ed., pp. 80–103). Beltz Juventa.

Geertz, C. (1987). *Dichte Beschreibung: Beiträge zum Verstehen kultureller Systeme* (B. Luchesi & R. Bindemann, Trans.) (14th ed.). Suhrkamp.

Gerlach, J. (2006). *Zwischen Pop und Dschihad: Muslimische Jugendliche in Deutschland.* Ch. Links Verlag.

Ghandour, A. (2014). *Fiqh: Einführung in die islamische Normenlehre.* Kalām.

REFERENCES

Glaser, B. G., & Strauss, A. (1967). *Discovery of grounded theory: Strategies for qualitative research*. Aldine Publishing Company.

Glaser, B. G., & Strauss, A. (2010). *Grounded theory* (3rd ed.). Huber.

Glock, C. Y. (1962). On the study of religious commitment. *Religious Education, 57*(4, Res. Suppl.), 98–110.

Goldman, R. (1968). *Religious thinking from childhood to adolescence*. Routledge & Kegan Paul.

Gräsel, C. (2015). Was ist Empirische Bildungsforschung? In H. Reinders (Ed.), *Empirische Bildungsforschung: Strukturen und Methoden* (2nd ed., pp. 15–30). Springer VS.

Grillo, R., & Soares, B. F. (2005). Transnational Islam in Western Europe. *ISIM Review, 15*(1), 11.

Grom, B. (2000). *Religionspädagogische Psychologie des Kleinkind-, Schul- und Jugendalters* (5th rev. ed.). Patmos-Verl.

Hajatpour, R. (2013). Die Einheit Gottes – Die Transzendenz Gottes. In A. Dziri (Ed.), *Gottesvorstellungen im Islam: Zur Dialektik von Transzendenz und Immanenz* (pp. 81–95). Kalām.

Hanisch, H. (1996). *Die zeichnerische Entwicklung des Gottesbildes bei Kindern und Jugendlichen: Eine empirische Vergleichsuntersuchung mit religiös und nicht-religiös Erzogenen im Alter von 7–16 Jahren*. Calwer Verlag.

Harms, E. (1944). The development of religious experience in children. *American Journal of Sociology, 50*(2), 112–122. https://www.jstor.org/stable/2770961

Heinzel, F. (2012). Qualitative Methoden in der Kindheitsforschung. Ein Überblick. In F. Heinzel (Ed.), *Methoden der Kindheitsforschung* (2nd ed., pp. 22–35). Beltz Juventa.

Helfferich, C. (2011). *Die Qualität qualitativer Daten: Das Manual zur qualitativen Sozialforschung* (4th ed.). VS Verlag für Sozialwissenschaften.

Hildebrandt, T. (2007). *Neo-Mu'tazilismus? Intention und Kontext im modernen arabischen Umgang mit dem rationalistischen Erbe des Islam*. Brill.

Hoffmann-Riem, C. (1984). *Das adoptierte Kind. Familienleben mit doppelter Elternschaft*. Fink.

Honecker, M. (1990). *Einführung in die theologische Ethik*. De Gruyter.

Hoover, J. (2007). *Ibn Taymiyya's theodicy of perpetual optimism*. Brill.

Huber, S. (2004). Zentralität und multidimensionale Struktur der Religiosität: Eine Synthese der theoretischen Ansätze von Allport und Glock zur Messung der Religiosität. In C. Zwingmann & H. Moosbrugger (Eds.), *Religiosität: Messverfahren und Studien zu Gesundheit und Lebensbewältigung*. Waxmann.

Hull, J. M. (1997). *Wie Kinder über Gott reden*. Gütersloher Verl.-Haus.

Hülst, D. (2012). Das wissenschaftliche Verstehen von Kindern. In F. Heinzel (Ed.), *Methoden der Kindheitsforschung* (2nd ed., pp. 52–77). Beltz Juventa.

Hurrelmann, K. (2002). *Einführung in die Sozialisationstheorie* (8th rev. ed.). Beltz.

Hurrelmann, K., & Bauer, U. (2015). *Einführung in die Sozialisationstheorie: Das Modell der produktiven Realitätsverarbeitung* (11th rev. ed.). Beltz.

Ibrahim, E., & Johnson-Davies, D. (Eds.). (1997). *Forty Hadith Qudsi* (bilingual ed.). The Islamic Texts Society.

Jung, C. G. (1940). *Psychologie und Religion: die Terry lectures 1937, gehalten an der Yale University*. Rascher.

Karakaşoğlu-Aydın, Y. (2000). *Muslimische Religiosität und Erziehungsvorstellungen*. IKO, Verl. für Interkulturelle Kommunikation.

Karimi, A. M. (2013). Von der Immanenz Gottes. In A. Dziri (Ed.), *Gottesvorstellungen im Islam: Zur Dialektik von Transzendenz und Immanenz* (pp. 95–109). Kalām.

Kerbs, D. (1998). *Handbuch der deutschen Reformbewegungen 1880–1933*. Hammer.

Kermani, N. (2007). *Gott ist schön: Das ästhetische Erleben des Koran* (3rd ed.). Beck.

Keupp, H. (2008). *Identitätskonstruktionen. Das Patchwork der Identitäten in der Spätmoderne* (2nd ed.). Rowohlt-Taschenbuch-Verl.

Khorchide, M. (2010). Die Beziehung zwischen islamischer Lehre und einer modernen Islamischen Religionspädagogik: Zur Notwendigkeit der Ausarbeitung humanistischer Ansätze in der islamischen Ideengeschichte. In M. Polat & C. Tosun (Eds.), *Islamische Theologie und Religionspädagogik* (pp. 145–158). Lang.

Klein, S. (2000). *Gottesbilder von Mädchen: Bilder und Gespräche als Zugänge zur kindlichen religiösen Vorstellungswelt*. Kohlhammer.

Klinkhammer, G. (2000). *Moderne Formen islamischer Lebensführung: Eine qualitatiiv-empirische Untersuchung zur Religiosität sunnitisch geprägter Türkinnen der zweiten Generation in Deutschland*. Diagonal-Verl.

Knoblauch, H. (1999). *Religionssoziologie*. De Gruyter.

Krawietz, B. (2003). Ibn Taymiyya, Vater des islamischen Fundamentalismus? Zur westlichen Rezeption eines mittelalterlichen Schariatsgelehrten. In M. Atienza, E. Pattaro, M. Schulte, B. Topornin, & D. Wyduckel (Eds.), *Theorie des Rechts und der Gesellschaft. Festschrift für Werner Krawietz zum 70. Geburtstag* (pp. 39–62). Duncker & Humblot.

Kuld, L. (2001). *Das Entscheidende ist unsichtbar: Wie Kinder und Jugendliche Religion verstehen*. Kösel.

Leuze, R. (1994). *Christentum und Islam*. Mohr.

Leyh, G. (1994). *Mit der Jugend von Gott sprechen: Gottesbilder kirchlich orientierter Jugendlicher im Horizont korrelativer Theologie*. Kohlhammer.

Luckmann, T. (1991). *Die unsichtbare Religion*. Suhrkamp.

Luhmann, N. (2002). *Die Religion der Gesellschaft*. Wiss. Buchges.

Mähler, C. (1995). *Weiß die Sonne, daß sie scheint? Eine experimentelle Studie zur Deutung des animistischen Denkens bei Kindern*. Waxmann.

Mannheim, K. (1980). *Strukturen des Denkens*. Suhrkamp.

Mannheim, K. (1985). *Ideologie und Utopie* (7th ed.). Klostermann.

REFERENCES

Mannheim, K. (1997). *Structures of thinking. Collected works of Karl Mannheim* (D. Kettler, V. Meja, & N. Stehr, Eds.). Routledge.

Mayring, P. (1983). *Qualitative Inhaltsanalyse: Grundlagen und Techniken.* Beltz.

Mehan, H., & Wood, H. (1976). Fünf Merkmale der Realität. In E. Weingarten, F. Sack, & J. Schenkein (Eds.), *Ethnomethodologie. Beiträge zu einer Soziologie des Alltagshandelns* (pp. 29–63). Suhrkamp.

Mendl, H. (2015). *Religionsdidaktik kompakt* (4th ed.). Kösel.

Merkens, H. (1997). Stichproben bei qualitativen Studien. In B. Friebertshäuser & A. Prengel (Eds.), *Handbuch Qualitative Forschungsmethoden in der Erziehungswissenschaft* (pp. 97–106). Juventa.

Mohamed, Y. (1996). *Fitrah: Islamic Concept of Human Nature.* Ta-Ha Publishers Ltd.

Naurath, E. (2014). Entwicklung der Religiosität und des Gottesbildes. In G. Lämmermann & B. Platow (Eds.), *Evangelische Religion – Didaktik für die Grundschule* (pp. 19–29). Cornelsen Scriptor.

Nentwig-Gesemann, I. (2007). Die Typenbildung der dokumentarischen Methode. In R. Bohnsack, I. Nentwig-Gesemann, & A.-M. Nohl (Eds.), *Die dokumentarische Methode und ihre Forschungspraxis* (pp. 277–302). VS Verlag für Sozialwissenschaften. https://doi.org/10.1007/978-3-531-90741-3_13

Nestler, E. (2000). Denkfähigkeiten und Denkweisen. Ein bereichs- und biographietheoretischer Rahmen zur Rekonstruktion der Entwicklung religiöser Kognition. In C. Henning & E. Nestler (Eds.), *Religionspsychologie heute* (pp. 123–159). Peter Lang.

Nipkow, K. E. (1988). Stufentheorien der Glaubensentwicklung als eine Herausforderung für Religionspädagogik und Praktische Theologie. In K. E. Nipkow, F. Schweitzer, & J. W. Fowler (Eds.). *Glaubensentwicklung und Erziehung* (pp. 270–289). Gütersloher Verl.-Haus Mohn.

Nohl, A.-M. (2005). Dokumentarische Interpretation narrativer Interviews. *Bildungsforschung, 2*(2).

Nohl, A.-M. (2012). *Interview und dokumentarische Methode. Anleitungen für die Forschungspraxis* (4th rev. ed.). Springer VS.

Nökel, S. (2007). 'Neo-Muslimas' – Alltags- und Geschlechterpolitiken junger muslimischer Frauen zwischen Religion, Tradition und Moderne. In H.-J. von Wensierski & C. Lübcke (Eds.), *Junge Muslime in Deutschland. Lebenslagen, Aufwachsprozesse und Jugendkulturen* (pp. 135–154). Barbara Budrich.

Nucci, L., & Turiel, E. (1993). God's word, religious rules, and their relation to Christian and Jewish children's concepts of morality. *Child Development, 64*(5), 1475–1491. https://doi.org/10.1111/j.1467-8624.1993.tb02965.x

Nye, W. C., & Carlson, J. S. (1984). The development of the concept of God in children. *The Journal of Genetic Psychology, 145*(1), 137–142. https://doi.org/10.1080/00221325.1984.10532259

Oerter, R. (1996). Was ist Religiosität, und warum entwickelt sie sich. In F. Oser & H. Reich (Eds.), *Eingebettet ins Menschsein: Beispiel Religion. Aktuelle psychologische Studien zur Entwicklung von Religiosität* (pp. 23–40). Pabst Verlag.

Oerter, R., & Montada, L. (2008). *Entwicklungspsychologie* (6th rev. ed.). *Lehrbuch.* Beltz PVU.

Orth, G., & Hanisch, H. (1998). *Glauben entdecken – Religion lernen.* Calwer Verl.

Oser, F. (1993). *Die emotionale Dimension der Entstehung Gottes im Kinde. Neuer Gott für neue Kinder.* Pädagogisches Institut.

Oser, F., & Gmünder, P. (1984). *Der Mensch – Stufen seiner religiösen Entwicklung: Ein strukturgenetischer Ansatz.* Benziger.

Oser, F., & Gmünder, P. (1992). *Der Mensch – Stufen seiner religiösen Entwicklung* (3rd ed.). Gütersloher Verl.-Haus Mohn.

Oser, F., & Reich, H. (1990). Nicht zurück zum alten Mann mit Bart, sondern vorwärts zum eigenständigen Kind. *Katechetische Blätter, 115*(3), 170–176.

Ovwigho, P. C., & Cole, A. (2010). Scriptural engagement, communication with God, and moral behavior among children. *International Journal of Children's Spirituality, 15*(2), 101–113.

Paret, R. (2007). *Der Koran* (10th ed.). Kohlhammer.

Pavlis, N. A. (2001). *An early Sufi concept of qalb: Hakim al-Tirmidhi's map of the heart* [Master thesis]. Institute of Islamic Studies, McGill University.

Petermann, F., & Windmann, S. (1993). Sozialwissenschaftliche Erhebungstechniken bei Kindern. In M. Markefka (Ed.), *Handbuch der Kindheitsforschung* (pp. 125–143). Luchterhand.

Piaget, J. (2003). *Meine Theorie der geistigen Entwicklung.* Beltz.

Pirner, M. L. (2012a). Schüler/in – soziologisch. In M. Rothgangel, G. Adam, & R. Lachmann (Eds.), *Religionspädagogisches Kompendium* (8th ed., pp. 237–251). Vandenhoeck & Ruprecht.

Pirner, M. L. (2012b). Wer ist ein guter Lehrer / eine gute Lehrerin? Ergebnisse der Lehrerprofessionsforschung. In H. Lenhard, R. Burrichter, B. Grümme, H. Mendl, M. L. Pirner, M. Rothgangel, & T. Schlag (Eds.), *Professionell Religion unterrichten: Ein Arbeitsbuch* (pp. 13–32). Kohlhammer.

Pitts, V. P. (1977). Drawing pictures of God. The religion in childhood and youth. A research report. *Learning for Living, 16*(3), 123–129.

Porzelt, B., & Güth, R. (Eds.). (2000). *Empirische Religionspädagogik: Grundlagen – Zugänge – Aktuelle Projekte.* LIT.

Power, C. (1988). Harte oder weiche Stufen der Entwicklung des Glaubens und des religiösen Urteils? Eine Piagetsche Kritik. In K. E. Nipkow, F. Schweitzer, & J. W. Fowler (Eds.), *Glaubensentwicklung und Erziehung* (pp. 108–123). Gütersloher Verl.-Haus Mohn.

REFERENCES

Przyborski, A., & Wohlrab-Sahr, M. (2014). *Qualitative Sozialforschung. Ein Arbeitsbuch* (4th ext. ed.). Oldenbourg Verlag.

Qara'i, A. Q. (2005). *The Qur'an. With a phrase-by-phrase English translation* (2nd rev. ed.). Islamic Pubns Intl.

Ragab, A.-H. (2012). Gott zwischen Transzendenz und Immanenz. Zum Gottesbild aus islamischer Perspektive. In A. Renz, M. Gharaibeh, A. Middelbeck-Varwick, & B. Ucar (Eds.), *«Der stets größere Gott»: Gottesvorstellungen im Christentum und Islam* (pp. 140–150). Friedrich Pustet.

Raithel, J. (2009). *Einführung Pädagogik* (3rd ed.). VS Verlag für Sozialwissenschaften.

Religionsmonitor. (2013). *Verstehen was verbindet. Religiosität und Zusammenhalt in Deutschland.* Bertelsmann Stiftung.

Riemann, G. (1986). Einige Anmerkungen dazu, wie und unter welchen Bedingungen das Argumentationsschema in biographisch-narrativen Interviews dominant werden kann. In H.-G. Soeffner (Ed.), *Sozialstruktur und soziale Typik* (pp. 112–157). Campus-Verl.

Ritter, W. H., Hanisch, H., Nestler, E., & Gramzow, C. (2006). *Leid und Gott: Aus der Perspektive von Kindern und Jugendlichen.* Vandenhoeck & Ruprecht.

Rizzuto, A.-M. (1979). *The birth of the living God: A psychoanalytic study.* University of Chicago Press.

Rudolph, U. (1996). *Al-Maturidi und die sunnitische Theologie in Samarkand.* Brill.

Rycroft, C. (1968). *Imagination and reality.* Hogarth Press.

Sahin, A. (2015). *New directions in Islamic education: Pedagogy and identity formation.* Kube Publishing Ltd.

Sandt, F.-O. (1996). *Religiosität von Jugendlichen in der multikulturellen Gesellschaft.* Waxmann.

Scheunpflug, A. (2011). Die Religionspädagogik als erziehungswissenschaftliche Disziplin – der Blick aus der Perspektive Allgemeiner Pädagogik. *Zeitschrift für Theologie und Pädagogik, 63*(2), 107–116.

Scheunpflug, A., & Mette, N. (2007). Anregungen aus Sicht einer systemtheoretischen Erziehungswissenschaft für das Verständnis eines Religionsunterrichts. In G. Büttner, A. Scheunpflug, & V. Elsenbast (Eds.), *Zwischen Erziehung und Religion. Religionspädagogische Perspektiven nach Niklas Luhmann* (pp. 41–55). LIT.

Schimmel, A. (1995). Meine Barmherzigkeit ist größer als mein Zorn. Gedanken zum islamischen Gottesbild. *Beiträge zum Gespräch zwischen Christen und Muslimen, 9*(2), 41–44.

Schlange, C. (2011). *Die Entwicklung von Gottesbildern bei Kindern unter Berücksichtigung ihrer religiösen Sozialisation: Eine Untersuchung im Blick auf Schülerinnen und Schüler der dritten und vierten Jahrgangsstufe.* Verlagshaus Monsenstein und Vannerdat OHG Münster.

Schnider, A. (2000). Kurzeinführung in quantitative Methoden der empirischen Sozialforschung. In B. Porzelt & R. Güth (Eds.), *Empirische Religionspädagogik: Grundlagen – Zugänge – Aktuelle Projekte* (pp. 47–62). LIT.

Schöller, M. (Ed.). (2007). *al-Nawawī. Das Buch der Vierzig Hadithe. Kitāb al-Arbaʿīn: mit dem Kommentar von Ibn Daqīq al-ʿĪd.* Verlag der Weltreligionen.

Schori, K. (2004). Gottesbild und Gotteserfahrung: Zur Praxis der empirischen Gottesbildforschung bei kleineren Kindern. *Zeitschrift für Pädagogik und Theologie, 56*(2), 164–174.

Schröder, B. (2012). *Religionspädagogik. Neue theologische Grundrisse.* Mohr Siebeck.

Schuon, F. (2002). *Den Islam verstehen: Eine Einführung in die innere Lehre einer Weltreligion.* Barth.

Schütz, A. (1971). *Das Problem der sozialen Wirklichkeit.* Nijhoff.

Schütz, A., & Luckmann, T. (2003). *Strukturen der Lebenswelt.* UVK Verlagsgesellschaft.

Schütze, F. (1976). Zur Hervorlockung und Analyse von Erzählungen thematisch relevanter Geschichten im Rahmen soziologischer Feldforschung: dargestellt an einem Projekt zur Erforschung von kommunalen Machtstrukturen. In A. Weymann (Ed.), *Kommunikative Sozialforschung: Alltagswissen und Alltagshandeln, Gemeindemachtforschung, Polizei, politische Erwachsenenbildung* (pp. 159–260). Fink.

Schweitzer, F. (1994). Elternbilder – Gottesbilder: Wandel der Elternrollen und die Entwicklung des Gottesbildes im Kindesalter. *Katechetische Blätter, 119,* 91–95.

Schweitzer, F. (2003). Was ist und wozu Kindertheologie? In A. A. Bucher, G. Büttner, P. Freudenberger-Lötz, & M. Schreiner (Eds.), *«Im Himmelreich ist keiner sauer»: Kinder als Exegeten. Jahrbuch für Kindertheologie* (Vol. 2, pp. 9–18). Calwer.

Schweitzer, F. (2010). *Lebensgeschichte und Religion: Religiöse Entwicklung und Erziehung im Kindes- und Jugendalter* (7th ed.). Gütersloher Verlagshaus. (Original work published 1987)

Schweitzer, F., & Dubiski, K. (2012). Wie Kinder mit religiöser Differenz umgehen. Prozesse von Konstruktion und Ko-Konstruktion in der religiösen Fremdwahrnehmung. In I. Noth & R. Kunz (Eds.), *Arbeiten zur Pastoraltheologie, Liturgik und Hymnologie. Nachdenkliche Seelsorge – seelsorgliches Nachdenken* (pp. 296–310). Vandenhoeck & Ruprecht.

Seufert, G. (1997). *Café Istanbul.* Beck.

Siegler, R. S., DeLoache, J., & Eisenberg, N. (2011). *Entwicklungspsychologie im Kindes- und Jugendalter* (3rd ed.). Spektrum Akad. Verlag.

Simojoki, H., & Henningsen, J. (2021). Theologisch-religionspädagogische Professionalisierung in der Religionslehrerbildung: Historische und systematische Perspektiven. *RpB, 44*(1), 7–14. https://rpb-journal.de/index.php/rpb/article/view/83

Stroumsa, S. (2003). Saadya and Jewish kalam. In D. H. Frank & O. Leaman (Eds.), *The Cambridge companion to medieval Jewish philosophy* (pp. 81–82). Cambridge Univ. Press.

REFERENCES

Szagun, A.-K. (2014). *Dem Sprachlosen Sprache verleihen*. Rostocker Langzeitstudie zu Gottesverständnis und Gottesbeziehung von Kindern, die in mehrheitlich konfessionslosem Kontext aufwachsen. IKS Garamond, Ed. Paideia.

Szagun, A.-K., & Fiedler, M. (2008). *Religiöse Heimaten: Rostocker Langzeitstudie zu Gottesverständnis und Gottesbeziehung von Kindern, die in mehrheitlich konfessionslosem Kontext aufwachsen*. IKS Garamond.

Tamm, M. E. (1996). The meaning of God for children and adolescents: A phenomenographic study of drawings. *British Journal of Religious Education, 19*(1), 33–44.

Tamminen, K. (1993). *Religiöse Entwicklung in Kindheit und Jugend*. Peter Lang.

ter Avest, I. (2009). Dutch children and their 'God': The development of the 'God' concept among indigenous and immigrant children in the Netherlands. *British Journal of Religious Education, 31*(3), pp. 251–262.

Thierfelder, C. (1998). *Gottes-Repräsentanz. Kritische Interpretation des religionspsychologischen Ansatzes von Ana-Maria Rizzuto*. Kohlhammer.

Thonak, S. (2003). *Religion in der Jugendforschung: eine kritische Analyse der Shell Jugendstudien in religionspädagogischer Absicht*. LIT.

Tietze, N. (2001). *Islamische Identitäten: Formen muslimischer Religiosität junger Männer in Deutschland und Frankreich*. Hamburger Edition.

Torstenson-Ed, T. (2006). Children and God in the multicultural society. *British Journal of Religious Education, 28*(1), 33–49.

Touraine, A. (1995). *Critique of modernity*. Blackwell.

Trautmann, T. (2010). *Interviews mit Kindern: Grundlagen, Techniken, Besonderheiten, Beispiele*. VS Verlag für Sozialwissenschaften.

Treml, A. K. (2000). *Allgemeine Pädagogik. Grundlagen, Handlungsfelder und Perspektiven der Erziehung*. Kohlhammer.

Treml, A. K. (2007). Religion und Erziehung aus systemtheoretischer Sicht. In G. Büttner, A. Scheunpflug, & V. Elsenbast (Eds.), *Zwischen Erziehung und Religion. Religionspädagogische Perspektiven nach Niklas Luhmann* (pp. 29–41). LIT.

Tressat, M. (2011). *Muslimische Adoleszenz? Zur Bedeutung muslimischer Religiosität bei jungen Migranten. Biografieanalytische Fallstudien*. Peter Lang.

Ucar, B. (2010). Islamische Religionspädagogik im deutschen Kontext: Die Neukonstituierung eines alten Fachs unter veränderten Rahmenbedingungen. In B. Ucar, M. Blasberg-Kuhnke, & A. von Scheliha (Eds.), *Religionen in der Schule und die Bedeutung des Islamischen Religionsunterrichts* (pp. 33–53). Vandenhoeck & Ruprecht Unipress.

Ulfat, F. (2017). Qualitative Untersuchungsergebnisse zur Gottesbeziehung von muslimischen Kindern als Basis für die theoretische Grundlegung einer Kindertheologie im Islamischen Religionsunterricht. *Hikma. Journal of Islamic Theology and Religious Education, 8*(2), 98–111.

Ulfat, F. (2019). Sprachsensibler Islamischer Religionsunterricht? – Mit Begriffsarbeit zu fachspezifischer Sprachreflexion. In C. Peuschel & A. Burkard (Eds.), *Studienbuch Sprachliche Bildung und Deutsch als Zweitsprache in den geistes- und gesellschaftswissenschaftlichen Fächern* (pp. 187–196). Narr Francke Attempto Verlag.

Ulfat, F. (2020). Mit der Kraft der Narrationen in den Islamischen Religionsunterricht – Auf dem Weg zu einer narrativen Kompetenz. In F. Ulfat & A. Ghandour (Eds.), *Islamische Bildungsarbeit in der Schule. Theologische und didaktische Überlegungen zum Umgang mit verschiedenen Themen im Islamischen Religionsunterricht* (pp. 49–64). Springer VS. https://doi.org/10.1007/978-3-658-26720-9_1

Ulrich, D. (1991). *Emotionale Entwicklung als Aufbau emotionaler Schemata: Positionsreferat auf der 10. Tagung Entwicklungspsychologie in Köln.* Augsburger Berichte zur Entwicklungspsychologie und Pädagogischen Psychologie Nr. 54. Universität Augsburg.

Uslucan, H.-H. (2008). *Religiöse Werteerziehung in islamischen Familien.* Commissioned by the Federal Ministry for Family Affairs, Senior Citizens, Women and Youth. https://www.bmfsfj.de/resource/blob/76348/87ca4069e35c50778880146191295373/expertise-religioese-werteerziehung-data.pdf

van Ess, J. (1991). *Theologie und Gesellschaft im 2. und 3. Jahrhundert Hidschra* (Vol. 3). De Gruyter.

Vogd, W. (2010). Methodologie und Verfahrensweise der dokumentarischen Methode und ihre Kompatibilität zur Systemtheorie. In R. John, A. Henkel, & J. Rückert-John (Eds.), *Die Methodologien des Systems* (pp. 121–141). VS Verlag für Sozialwissenschaften.

von Stosch, K. (2011). Offenbarung und Vernunft in Islam und Christentum. In A. Bettenworth (Ed.), *Herausforderung Islam* (pp. 100–130). Schöningh.

Watt, W. M. (1972). *Islamic philosophy and theology.* Edinburgh University Press.

Weber, E. (2003). *Pädagogik – Eine Einführung – Grundfragen und Grundbegriffe* (9th rev. and expanded ed.). Auer Verlag.

Weber, M. (1988). *Gesammelte Aufsätze zur Wissenschaftslehre.* J. C. B. Mohr.

Weber, M. (1994). *Max Weber-Gesamtausgabe:* Band II/6: Briefe 1909–1910 (M. R. Lepsius, & W. J. Mommsen, Eds.) Mohr Siebeck.

Weber, M. (2008). *Politik als Beruf.* Reclam.

Wegenast, K. (1968). Die empirische Wendung in der Religionspädagogik. *Zeitschrift für Pädagogik und Theologie – Der Evangelische Erzieher, 3*(20), 111–125.

Winnicott, D. W. (1973). *Vom Spiel zur Kreativität.* Klett-Cotta.

Woodhead, L., & Heelas, P. (2000). *Religion in modern times. An interpretative anthology.* John Wiley & Sons.

Woolley, J. D., & Phelps, K. E. (2001). The development of children's beliefs about prayer. *Journal of Cognition and Culture, 1*(2), 139–166.

World Vision Deutschland e.V. (Ed.). (2010). *Kinder in Deutschland 2010.* Fischer.

REFERENCES

Yıldız, M., & Arık, R. S. (2011). The image of God in children's compositions. *Journal of Islamic Research, 4*, 254–278.

Zengin, H. K. (2010). Almanya'daki Müslüman Çocuklarda Allah Kavramının Gelişimi: Âdem ve Havva Kıssası – Yaratılışı, Cennetten Çıkarılışları – Bağlamında 1–4, 6. Sınıf Çocukları Üzerine Bir Araştırma. *Ankara Üniversitesi İlahiyat Fakültesi Dergisi, 51*(1), 213–248.

Ziebertz, H.-G. (2000). Methodologische Multiperspektivität angesichts religiöser Umbrüche. In B. Porzelt & R. Güth (Eds.), *Empirische Religionspädagogik: Grundlagen – Zugänge – Aktuelle Projekte* (pp. 29–44). LIT.

Zimmermann, M. (2012). *Kindertheologie als theologische Kompetenz von Kindern. Grundlagen, Methodik und Ziel kindertheologischer Forschung am Beispiel der Deutung des Todes Jesu.* (2nd ed.). Neukirchener.

Zuberi, A. K. (1988). A qualitative study of Muslim children's concepts of God. *Pakistan Journal of Psychological Research, 3*(1–2), 1–22.

Index

action-guided orientations   12
action-guiding knowledge   26, 28, 36, 42, 59, 64, 65, 95, 111
atheoretical knowledge   11, 12, 59, 63, 64, 245
autonomy   5, 8, 22, 118, 254, 257, 258, 261, 278, 279, 303, 313

co-construction   253, 255, 260, 316
cognitive   2, 3, 9–12, 15–18, 20–22, 24–26, 28, 29, 31, 36–39, 43, 54, 93, 99, 128, 147, 199, 249, 253, 254, 273, 280, 283, 284, 289, 296, 302, 313
conjunctive experiential space   37, 40–42, 44–46, 49, 56, 245, 251, 276, 287
conjunctive knowledge   37, 41, 42, 92

didactics   13, 15, 257, 259, 260, 273, 290, 298, 312–315
documentary method   12, 24, 42, 63, 64, 66, 92, 94

emotion/emotional   2, 3, 9–12, 14, 19, 22, 24–26, 28, 32, 33, 37, 38, 43–45, 54, 96, 98, 99, 104, 108, 116, 119, 126–128, 144, 147, 148, 151, 152, 162, 193, 231, 248, 249, 254, 269, 280, 282–284, 309, 313
empirical study/research   15, 16, 19, 23, 28–30, 95, 37, 71, 249, 311, 313–316

faith in God   2, 3, 9, 11, 12, 26, 32–34, 36, 50, 95, 98, 100, 116, 130, 222, 223, 249, 261, 269, 286, 293, 295, 303

God-distant relationship   97, 129, 131, 156, 185, 186, 199, 200, 212, 223, 228, 244–249, 252–254, 256, 259–262, 269, 276, 277, 281, 282, 284, 288, 291, 297, 300–302

implicit knowledge   10–12, 16, 24, 29, 37, 40, 45, 48, 63, 64, 92
individual   3–9, 11, 12, 14, 17, 19, 20, 21, 23, 24, 26–29, 33, 37–39, 41–45, 47–49, 51, 54, 56, 60, 63, 64, 66, 67, 72, 73, 75, 76, 80, 90, 93, 96, 97, 99, 110, 152, 172, 182, 200, 229, 244–246, 253–258, 261, 265, 271, 272, 283, 286, 287, 290–294, 301, 303, 313, 314, 316
individualization of religion   5, 7
Islamic religious education   2, 3, 12, 13, 45, 57, 68, 69, 71, 73–75, 77–80, 82, 83, 85–88, 90, 227, 255, 257, 262, 269, 276, 286, 288–298, 300, 303, 311–318
Islamic theology   13, 250, 261, 263, 269, 313

Kamishibai   55, 58–61, 249
knowledge   3, 4, 10–12, 14, 16, 18, 21, 24–26, 28, 29, 31, 33, 35–37, 40–42, 44–46, 48–51, 53, 54, 59, 62–65, 67, 68, 70, 72–74, 77–79, 81, 91–93, 95–97, 99, 111, 113, 133, 135, 145, 146, 149, 152, 153, 155, 158, 161, 166, 167, 170, 171, 173–180, 182, 183, 190, 191, 198, 200, 213, 217, 218, 220, 221, 223, 226, 245, 247, 248, 253, 257, 259, 271, 272, 274, 275, 281, 285, 287, 288, 290, 292–294, 296, 297, 302, 304, 305–309, 313, 316–318

lifeworld   4, 7, 9, 23, 26, 30, 42, 45, 47, 48, 52, 56, 71, 73, 75, 76, 79, 81, 85, 93, 99, 103, 111, 114, 130, 134, 138, 141, 146, 151, 157, 168, 170, 173, 190, 208, 212, 223, 231, 233, 238–243, 252, 259, 262, 263, 277, 280, 292, 293, 295, 299, 311, 312, 314, 315

moral relationship   97–99, 130, 135, 150, 151, 153, 157, 173, 185–187, 199, 200, 208, 228, 229, 233, 245–248, 252–255, 257–259, 261, 262, 276–280, 282, 284–287, 291–293, 296, 297, 300–302

narration   36, 39, 42, 43, 45, 51, 58, 61, 62, 66, 72, 73, 75–91, 94, 96, 99–123, 131–136, 138–146, 150, 153–155, 157, 158, 161–163, 169, 170, 172, 174, 176, 180, 181, 183, 184, 186, 195, 196, 198–202, 205, 206, 208, 211, 212, 215, 219–223, 225–227, 229, 233–236, 238–241, 244, 247, 259, 263, 276, 278, 279, 282, 286, 289, 296, 298, 299, 312

INDEX

narrative interview   12, 20, 36, 43, 44, 49, 51, 52, 54, 61–63, 68, 69

personal relationship   25, 26, 33, 34, 72, 97, 130, 131, 145, 151, 160, 185, 186, 199, 201, 245–248, 252–257, 260, 277–280, 282–284, 287, 303
privatization of religion   5, 7
propositional knowledge   12, 25, 26, 31, 33, 36, 45, 50, 59, 72, 74, 78, 91, 92, 146, 158, 166, 167, 170, 171, 173–175, 178, 182, 183, 190, 191, 213, 217, 220, 226, 247, 248, 257, 288, 296, 302

qualitative research   48, 54, 69
Qur'an   13, 14, 89, 104, 167, 169, 175, 176, 211, 230, 248, 250, 251, 262–271, 273–275, 277–280, 282–285, 293, 296–299, 304–307, 315

rationality   29, 72, 165, 267, 289, 290, 309
reflexive relation   255, 257
relating of the self   36, 73–75, 77, 78, 80, 82, 88, 89, 91, 92, 94–98, 150, 199, 200
relation to God   9, 10, 19, 72, 73, 75, 80, 84, 86, 89, 92, 94, 96–98, 100, 103, 106, 116, 119, 120, 130, 150–153, 161, 175, 189, 191, 194, 199–202, 204, 211, 213, 223, 229, 230, 245, 247–249, 252, 253, 255, 257–262, 264, 279, 280, 285, 287, 288, 291, 296, 302, 303, 309, 316
relationship to God   2, 10–12, 14, 16, 20, 23–26, 28, 29, 31–33, 36–38, 40, 44, 49, 64, 92, 93, 96, 97, 119, 128, 130, 151, 153, 160, 164, 199, 207, 213, 252, 260, 276, 277, 285, 286, 311

religion   2–5, 7–11, 13, 14, 19, 22, 30–32, 34, 39, 42, 43, 55, 75–79, 81–86, 89, 91, 96, 97, 115, 121, 131, 141, 142, 149–153, 172, 173, 175, 176, 180, 182, 183, 191, 200, 201, 211, 212, 215, 220, 223, 226, 233, 234, 245, 252, 253, 256–260, 263, 269–271, 273, 276, 280–282, 284–287, 289–302, 305, 309–317
religiosity   1, 3–10, 12, 14, 16, 19, 28, 31, 34, 42, 45, 80, 116, 166, 172, 173, 247, 255–260, 263, 276, 279, 285, 286, 291, 303, 310, 314, 318
religious education   1–3, 9, 12, 13, 15, 18, 19, 21–25, 28, 30–33, 44, 45, 55, 57, 68, 69, 71, 73–75, 77–80, 82, 83, 85–88, 90, 227, 229, 252, 253, 255, 257, 259–263, 269, 270, 273, 275, 276, 279, 286–303, 309, 311–320
religious education studies   2, 15, 19, 21, 22, 24, 28, 44, 253, 255, 257, 260, 261, 269, 287, 290, 297, 298, 300, 309, 313–318
religious experiences   26, 31, 37–39, 45, 281, 282, 285, 291
religious narrativity   286, 291, 294, 298, 299, 312
religious socialization   11, 12, 24, 25, 28, 30, 33, 68, 69, 71, 73, 74, 76, 78, 80–83, 85–87, 89, 90, 136, 245, 252, 256, 258, 260, 272, 276, 296, 297, 302

sample   13, 30, 35, 49, 68, 69, 71, 94, 147, 161, 186, 212, 252–255, 259–262, 269, 276, 281, 282, 287, 291, 296, 309, 319
secular world   257, 258, 260, 261, 316
self-relating   36, 71, 95, 96, 245, 246, 282
system of relevance   37, 42–45, 48–50, 52, 60